# Excel Programming

*Your visual blueprint™ for creating interactive spreadsheets*

*2nd Edition*

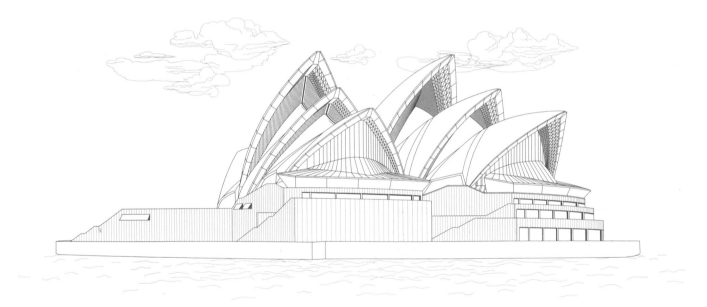

*by Jinjer Simon*

WILEY

Wiley Publishing, Inc.

## Excel Programming: Your visual blueprint™ for creating interactive spreadsheets, 2nd Edition

Published by
**Wiley Publishing, Inc.**
111 River Street
Hoboken, NJ 07030-5774

Published simultaneously in Canada

*Library of Congress Control Number: 2005923208*

ISBN-13: 978-0-7645-9781-7

ISBN-10: 0-7645-9781-7

Manufactured in the United States of America

10 9 8 7 6 5 4 3

2K/RS/QY/QV/IN

## Contact Us

For general information on our other products and services please contact our Customer Care Department within the U.S. at 800-762-2974, outside the U.S. at 317-572-3993 or fax 317-572-4002.

For technical support please visit www.wiley.com/techsupport.

## Permissions

**Microsoft**

Microsoft Excel screen shots reprinted with permission from Microsoft Corporation.

Sydney Opera House

A masterpiece of twentieth century architecture, Australia's Sydney Opera House is among the most recognizable structures in the world. It appears like a stately vessel sailing into Sydney Harbor, where its freestanding, sculptural tripartite form bears tribute to the vision of architect Jorn Utzon, who withdrew from the project amid political scandal in its eleventh year. Five years later, in 1973, the Opera House was completed under the direction of Peter Hall and opened to worldwide acclaim. Learn more about Australia's wonders, both constructed and natural, in *Frommer's Australia*, available wherever books are sold or at

**U.S. Sales**

Contact Wiley
at (800) 762-2974
or (317) 572-4002.

WILEY

# PRAISE FOR VISUAL BOOKS...

"This is absolutely the best computer-related book I have ever bought. Thank you so much for this fantastic text. Simply the best computer book series I have ever seen. I will look for, recommend, and purchase more of the same."

—David E. Prince (NeoNome.com)

"I have several of your Visual books and they are the best I have ever used."

—Stanley Clark (Crawfordville, FL)

"I just want to let you know that I really enjoy all your books. I'm a strong visual learner. You really know how to get people addicted to learning! I'm a very satisfied Visual customer. Keep up the excellent work!"

—Helen Lee (Calgary, Alberta, Canada)

"I have several books from the Visual series and have always found them to be valuable resources."

—Stephen P. Miller (Ballston Spa, NY)

"This book is PERFECT for me — it's highly visual and gets right to the point. What I like most about it is that each page presents a new task that you can try verbatim or, alternatively, take the ideas and build your own examples. Also, this book isn't bogged down with trying to 'tell all' — it gets right to the point. This is an EXCELLENT, EXCELLENT, EXCELLENT book and I look forward to purchasing other books in the series."

—Tom Dierickx (Malta, IL)

"I have quite a few of your Visual books and have been very pleased with all of them. I love the way the lessons are presented!"

—Mary Jane Newman (Yorba Linda, CA)

"I am an avid fan of your Visual books. If I need to learn anything, I just buy one of your books and learn the topic in no time. Wonders! I have even trained my friends to give me Visual books as gifts."

—Illona Bergstrom (Aventura, FL)

"I just had to let you and your company know how great I think your books are. I just purchased my third Visual book (my first two are dog-eared now!) and, once again, your product has surpassed my expectations. The expertise, thought, and effort that go into each book are obvious, and I sincerely appreciate your efforts."

—Tracey Moore (Memphis, TN)

"Compliments to the chef!! Your books are extraordinary! Or, simply put, extra-ordinary, meaning way above the rest! THANK YOU THANK YOU THANK YOU! I buy them for friends, family, and colleagues."

—Christine J. Manfrin (Castle Rock, CO)

"I write to extend my thanks and appreciation for your books. They are clear, easy to follow, and straight to the point. Keep up the good work! I bought several of your books and they are just right! No regrets! I will always buy your books because they are the best."

—Seward Kollie (Dakar, Senegal)

"I am an avid purchaser and reader of the Visual series, and they are the greatest computer books I've seen. Thank you very much for the hard work, effort, and dedication that you put into this series."

—Alex Diaz (Las Vegas, NV)

## Credits

**Project Editor**
Maureen Spears

**Acquisitions Editor**
Jody Lefevere

**Product Development Manager**
Lindsay Sandman

**Copy Editors**
Timothy Borek
Jill Mazurczyk

**Technical Editor**
Allen Wyatt

**Editorial Manager**
Robyn Siesky

**Permissions Editor**
Laura Moss

**Media Development Specialist**
Laura Moss

**Manufacturing**
Allan Conley
Linda Cook
Paul Gilchrist
Jennifer Guynn

**Book Design**
Kathryn S. Rickard

**Production Coordinator**
Maridee Ennis

**Layout**
Sean Decker
Jennifer Heleine
Amanda Spagnuolo

**Screen Artists**
Elizabeth Cardenas-Nelson
Jill A. Proll

**Cover Illustration**
Joni Burns

**Proofreader**
Vicki Broyles

**Quality Control**
Amanda Briggs

**Indexer**
TechBooks

**Special Help**
Cara Buitron

**Vice President and Executive
Group Publisher**
Richard Swadley

**Vice President and Publisher**
Barry Pruett

**Composition Director**
Debbie Stailey

## About the Author

**Jinjer Simon** has been actively involved in the computer industry for the past 18 years. Her involvement includes programming, providing software technical support, training end-users, developing written and online user documentation, creating software tutorials, and developing Web sites. She is the author of several computer books, including *Excel Programming: Your visual blueprint for creating interactive spreadsheets*, and *Windows CE 2 For Dummies*.

Jinjer and her husband live in Voppel, Texas with their two children. She currently works as a consultant for MillenniSoft, Inc., providing Web site development and online documentation development.

## Author's Acknowledgments

As an author, it is always exciting to finish the last chapter and send it to the publisher. At that point my work ends and many other individuals take on the responsibility of making sure the book actually makes it to the shelf. Because there are so many individuals involved, I am always concerned about overlooking someone. Therefore, before I thank specific individuals, I would like to acknowledge the efforts of everyone at Wiley who had a hand in completing the production of this book.

I really enjoyed working with the Wiley team. Jody Lefevere, my acquisitions editor, did a great job getting this project up and going, and dealing with all the little issues along the way. My project editor, Maureen Spears, was great to deal with. She was very patient as I learned how to develop using the visual blueprint style. Working along with her copy editing were Tim Borek and Jill Mazurczyk, who both did a great job making sure I said everything correctly. Along with them, Leslie Kersey and Amanda Foxworth helped make the process run smoothly. My technical editor, Allen Wyatt, did a fantastic job of making sure the content is technically accurate.

I also want to acknowledge the efforts of the graphics and production staff who tied everything together.

I want to acknowledge my agents, Neil Salkind and David Rogelberg at Studio B, for helping me get this project. Finally, I want to thank my husband, Richard, and children, Alex and Ashley, for their patience while I completed this project.

# TABLE OF CONTENTS

# TABLE OF CONTENTS

# TABLE OF CONTENTS

# HOW TO USE THIS BOOK

**Excel Programming: Your visual blueprint for creating interactive spreadsheets, 2nd Edition** uses simple, straightforward examples to teach you how to create powerful and dynamic programs.

To get the most out of this book, you should read each chapter in order, from beginning to end. Each chapter introduces new ideas and builds on the knowledge learned in previous chapters. When you become familiar with *Excel Programming: Your visual blueprint for creating interactive spreadsheets, 2nd Edition* you can use this book as an informative desktop reference.

## Who Needs This Book

This book is for the experienced computer user who wants to find out more about Excel programming. It is also for more experienced users who want to expand their knowledge of the different features that Excel has to offer.

## Book Organization

*Excel Programming: Your visual blueprint for creating interactive spreadsheets, 2nd Edition* has 15 chapters and two appendixes.

Chapter 1, "Getting Started with Excel Macros," shows you how to work with macros in Excel, how to record a simple macro, how to assign macros to a menu or toolbar button, how to launch a macro, and how to remove a macro from a workbook.

Chapter 2, "Using the Visual Basic Editor," shows you how to navigate and work with the Visual Basic Editor that comes with Microsoft Office applications. This chapter shows you how to set up your Visual Basic Editor window to quickly create and modify code modules.

Chapter 3, "VBA Programming Basics," introduces you to the essentials of Visual Basic for Applications (VBA). This chapter also covers some VBA programming fundamentals that enable you to use the material in the following chapters to create your own Excel macros.

Chapter 4, "Working with the Excel Object Model," shows you how to work with the Excel Object Model to access the various elements that make up the Excel application. This chapter provides a basis for the information covered in the remainder of the book, specifically Chapters 9 through 12.

Chapters 5 through 7 build on the VBA programming language by showing you how to work with variables and create arrays. You also learn how to use the various control statements to determine which code is executed within your macros. You create pop-up dialog boxes using the MsgBox and InputBox functions.

Chapter 8, "Debugging Macros," shows you how to use the various features of the Visual Basic Editor to find programming and logical errors within your VBA code.

Chapters 9 through 12 illustrate how you can use the Workbook, Worksheet, and Range objects to create custom macros. You also learn how to use the corresponding properties and methods associated with these objects.

Chapter 13, "Customizing Dialog Boxes, Menus, and Toolbars," shows you how to create a graphical interface for your macros by creating custom dialog boxes, adding new toolbars, and creating new menus and menu items.

Chapter 14, "Working with Charts," shows you how to create and modify charts from within your macro.

Chapter 15, "Automating Procedures with Excel Events," shows you how to capture both user- and system-created events and use those events to trigger various procedures. You also learn how to execute a procedure at a specific time, or how to determine when a specific key sequence is pressed.

Appendix A contains a reference section. After you become familiar with the contents of this book, you can use the references to obtain at-a-glance information for the VBA statements, functions, and constants used by VBA functions and Excel Object Model properties and methods.

## What You Need to Use This Book

To perform the tasks in this book, you need a computer with Microsoft Windows 98, ME, NT 4.0, 1000, or XP installed, as well as Microsoft Excel 2000 or 2002. You do not require any special development tools, because all the tools are part of Excel.

## The Conventions in This Book

A number of styles have been used throughout *Excel Programming: Your visual blueprint for creating interactive spreadsheets, 2nd Edition* to distinguish different types of information.

### Courier Font

Indicates the use of Visual Basic for Applications (VBA) code such as tags or attributes, scripting language code such as statements, operators, or functions, and code such as objects, methods, or properties.

### Bold

Indicates information that you must type.

### *Italics*

Indicates a new term.

An Apply It section takes the code from the preceding task one step further. Apply It sections allow you to take full advantage of the code.

An Extra section provides additional information about the preceding task. Extra sections contain the inside information to make working with Excel and VBA code easier and more efficient.

## What's on the CD-ROM

The CD-ROM included in this book contains the sample macro code from each of the two-page lessons in Chapters 5 through 15. This saves you from having to type the code and helps you quickly get started creating VBA code. The CD-ROM also contains several shareware and evaluation versions of the programs that you can use to work *with Excel Programming: Your visual blueprint for creating interactive spreadsheets, 2nd Edition.* An e-version of the book and all the URLs mentioned in the book are also available on the disc.

# An Introduction to Macros

**U**sing macros enables you to repeat tasks much more efficiently than tediously performing each step over and over. A *macro* is a set of instructions that you use to automate a task. For example, if you want to take each column of numbers, convert them to currency, and then add them together, you can create a simple macro to perform this task. The typical Excel user has a series of tasks that they perform frequently. By creating a macro to perform those tasks, you only require a simple keystroke to repeat the tasks.

You can create macros to perform a task as simple as adding two numbers, or as complex as creating a whole user interface within Excel. To do so, you can employ one, or a combination, of two different methods: You can use the Macro Recorder, or you can manually write a macro using the Visual Basic Editor. Although many macro users rarely venture past the Macro Recorder, this book shows you how to harness the power of *Visual Basic for Applications,* or VBA, to create more complex macros. No matter how simple or complex a macro, you write them all using VBA.

Macros are a term common to the spreadsheet world. All spreadsheet packages on the market provide the ability to create macros to automate tasks, and Excel is no exception. Although all Microsoft Office products provide the ability to create macros, they are best suited for Microsoft Excel.

As an Excel user, you may have a series of tasks that you perform frequently. By creating a macro to perform complex or repetitive tasks, you can save time by pressing a simple keystroke each time you want to perform the tasks.

## Macro History

### Macro and Lotus 1-2-3

Macros originated with Lotus 1-2-3 in a fashion similar to the Macro Recorder you find in Excel today. The Lotus macros recorded the keystrokes and enabled you to play them later.

### XLM Macro Sheets

Microsoft first entered the macro world with *XLM macro sheets.* XLM macro sheets are just sheets of functions that Excel evaluates in the sequence they exist within the selected macro. Although this macro language was powerful, it was difficult to use. Although Excel still supports XLM macro sheets for compatibility with early versions of Excel, it does not provide the ability to record an XLM macro.

### VBA Macros

The addition of Visual Basic for Applications (VBA) macros increased the popularity of Excel within the spreadsheet world. Essentially a subset of the popular Visual Basic language, VBA is familiar to many developers.

Also, VBA brings a much more powerful macro development platform to Excel than the macro development environment in other spreadsheet packages.

### Excel Macros

Although Microsoft did not originate the concept of macros and spreadsheets, they have definitely built upon it. The combination of the Macro Recorder and VBA makes macro creation a powerful feature of Excel.

## Macro Recorder

The *Macro Recorder* provides a great method for creating a macro without writing VBA code directly. The Macro Recorder holds true to its name. Just like a tape recorder, when you turn it on, it records all the events that occur within Excel. Excel takes the recorded events and creates the VBA code necessary to re-create the events. You can modify all macros you create with the Macro Recorder in the Visual Basic Editor. The Macro Recorder works well for creating simple macros, such as a macro that adds a column of numbers, or changes the layout of the page. But due to the fact that the Macro Recorder creates a macro by recording your actions, it cannot create a complex macro such as one that repeats a process until meeting a specific condition or displays a custom dialog box. More complex Excel macros require the use of VBA.

The Macro Recorder does work well in conjunction with the Visual Basic Editor. For example, if you want to create a macro that sums each column of data in your worksheet, you record the macro that sums a column. You then edit the macro in the Visual Basic Editor to run the macro until Excel process all columns. Combining the use of the Macro Recoder and the Visual Basic Editor simplifies the macro creation by allowing Excel to code part of it for you. See the section "Record a Macro" for more information on recording a macro in Excel.

## Macro Storage

The Store macro in option on the Macro dialog box instructs Excel where to store the macros you record. Excel provides three different storage locations for your macros: the current workbook, a new workbook, or the Personal Macro Workbook.

You can store a recorded macro to your current workbook, commonly referred to as the active workbook, by selecting the *This Workbook* option. Use this option if you plan to share the workbook with other users. Storing the macros in the active workbook makes macros available to any user who opens the workbook.

You can record a macro to a *New Workbook*. Excel creates the workbook automatically and adds the new macro to it. If you store a macro in another workbook, you need to open that workbook whenever you want to use that macro. You store macros in separate workbooks when you want to store specific types of macros in different workbooks. For example, you may want to place all macros that perform budget calculations in one workbook.

You can record a global macro by selecting *Personal Macro Workbook,* which serves as a common storage location for macros that you expect to use with other workbooks. Excel stores your Personal Macro Workbook as Personal.xls in the XlStart folder. This workbook does not exist until you store a macro in it. After you create the workbook, it loads whenever you run Excel as a hidden workbook. Excel hides the Personal Macro workbook so that you are unaware of its being open.

The storage location you select for a macro depends on where you want access to the macro. If you create the macro with the Macro Recorder, you can select the storage location of the macro when you create it on the Record Macro dialog box.

See the section "Record a Macro" for more information about storing macros.

# Record a Macro

You can use macros to automate a series of steps. The easiest method for creating a macro involves using the Macro Recorder option, which captures everything you do and saves it in a macro module with the name you specify. After you create the macro, you can run the macro again, modify it, or delete it.

Because the Macro Recorder records every action you perform when you use it, consider planning your steps before creating the macro. Because each macro action takes time to record, when you plan out the macro steps, the macro runs faster and more effectively. When you name a macro, use a name that starts with a letter and has no spaces in it; you can, however, use the underscore character to separate words.

Excel creates the macro with either relative or absolute reference to the cell where you apply it. You can specify the cell reference by selecting the Relative Reference button on the Stop Recording toolbar. If you select Relative Reference, the macro uses *relative* references, meaning that it performs the macro based upon the location of the cell. For example, you can have a macro add the values in the first four cells of a worksheet and place the total sum in a cell you select. With *absolute* positioning, however, the macro records in absolute mode and remembers the specific cells you use to record the macro. For example, the macro remembers always to add the same cells, such as A1 through A5, and place the total sum in cell A6. You can toggle between relative and absolute referencing while recording your macro via the Reference button.

## Record a Macro

① Click select the worksheet cell to contain the results of the macro.

If you intend to use other worksheet cells in your macro, make sure the cells contain the desired values.

② Click Tools→Macro→Record New Macro.

The Record Macro dialog box displays.

③ Type a unique name for the macro.

You can also create a keyboard shortcut for your macro by typing the desired shortcut key in the Shortcut Key field.

④ Click here to select a location where you want to store the macro.

**Note:** See the section "An Introduction to Macros" for more on the three areas to store a macro.

⑤ Click OK.

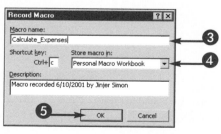

The Stop Recording toolbar appears.

● The status bar reminds you that a macro is recording.

**6** Press the appropriate key strokes to record the macro.

**7** When complete, click the Stop Recording button (■).

● Excel records the macro and the Stop Recording toolbar no longer displays on the screen.

---

### Extra

When you create a new macro, you have the option of assigning it to a keyboard shortcut by typing the shortcut in the Keyboard Shortcut box on the Record Macro dialog box. When you do this, the macro runs when you press the Ctrl key and the specified lowercase key simultaneously. If you specify an uppercase letter for the key, you can run the macro by pressing Ctrl+Shift+the specified key. Unfortunately, Excel does not stop you from creating shortcuts that override other predefined Excel shortcut keys. If you specify a shortcut key combination that matches a Microsoft Excel shortcut, your new shortcut overwrites it; each time you press the shortcut keys, your macro — not the Microsoft key combination — runs. For example, the Save command shortcut is Ctrl+s. If you create a macro with a shortcut key of s, your macro runs instead of the Save command when you press Ctrl+s. Excel does use many of the available shortcut keys, so you are bound to overwrite one. Keep in mind that if you use an Excel shortcut, you do not want to create a macro shortcut that overwrites it.

# Run a Macro

**E**xcel allows you to run macros in a worksheet that exists either in the current workbook or in any other Excel workbook. However, you can only run a macro from any other workbook as long as the corresponding workbook is open within Excel. When you run a macro, Excel re-creates the recorded steps that you performed to create it, or it runs the VBA code that you created in the Visual Basic Editor. See the section, "Record a Macro" to learn how to record a macro and Chapter 3 for more information on the Visual Basic Editor.

You select macros to run from the Macro dialog box, which lists all currently available macros. Available simply means that Excel can locate the macro in an open workbook. Because Excel only knows about macros in open workbooks, you must open the workbook containing the macro you want to run.

When you create a macro, Excel stores it in one of three locations, the current workbook, a new workbook, or the Personal Macro Workbook. Excel opens the Personal Macro Workbook as a hidden file each time you run Excel, and makes all macros you store there available to run with any workbook. If you store a macro in a separate workbook, you must open the workbook containing the macro in Excel. You can learn more about creating a macro in the section "Record a Macro."

To run a macro from another workbook, you must have a macro from a signed source, or you must set your macro security to either Medium or Low. The default macro security level, High, requires that all macros from other sources be signed. Setting your macro security to Medium or Low lets you run unsigned macros. See section "Set Macro Security" for more information about macro security.

## Run a Macro

**1** Click File→Open.

The Open dialog box displays.

**2** Click the workbook containing the macro you want to run.

The selected workbook opens.

③ Click the cell where you want the macro to execute.

④ Click Tools→Macro→ Macros.

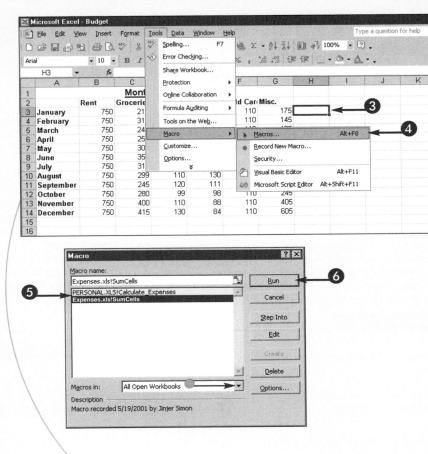

The Macro dialog box displays a list of available macros.

● If the macro is not listed, you can click here and click the location of the macro.

⑤ Click the macro you want to run.

⑥ Click Run.

The selected macro executes and makes the appropriate changes to the worksheet.

To run the macro again, repeat steps 3 to 6.

## Extra

You can use the Macros In field to limit the number of macros that display on the Macro dialog box. To see the macros in any open workbook, including the Personal Macro Workbook, you can click the ▼ and click the All Open Workbooks option. If you only want to see macros from a specific workbook, select the name of the desired workbook in the Macros In drop-down list. For the global macros stored in the Personal Macro Workbook, you need to select the PERSONAL.XLS option.

Excel differentiates between macros listed in the Macro dialog box by placing the name of the workbook that contains the macro in front of the macro name. For example, Excel lists a macro named Sum_Expenses in the Personal Macro Workbook as PERSONAL.XLS!Sum_Expenses. Because of this nomenclature, two workbooks can have macros with the same name. In other words, if the macro Sum_Cells exists in both the Budget.xls and Expenses.xls workbooks, Excel treats them as two different macros because they are stored in two different locations. The Macro dialog box lists the macros as Budget.xls!Sum_Cells and Expenses.xls!Sum_Cells.

# Create and Launch
# a Keyboard Shortcut

Excel provides the option of keyboard shortcuts to allow you to quickly launch a command, or even a macro, from the keyboard by pressing a combination of keys. With the use of a keyboard shortcut, you can activate a macro by pressing both the Ctrl key and the macro's shortcut key. You assign keyboard shortcuts to a macro during the macro creation, or at any time after you create the macro. See the section "Record a Macro" for more information on creating a macro.

Keyboard shortcuts in Excel are case sensitive. Excel interprets a lowercase s and an uppercase S as two different keys. By using uppercase and lowercase letters, Excel provides more shortcut keys that you can assign to a macro. To execute a macro that has an uppercase letter for the key, such as M, you press Ctrl+Shift+M.

The downside to assigning shortcut keys to a macro is that you have to remember the assigned shortcut. If you forget your shortcut assignment for a selected macro, you can view it in the Macro Options dialog box, which you access via the Macro dialog box.

Excel allows you to assign any key as the shortcut for your macro. If Excel uses the same key as a shortcut key for a standard Excel option, your shortcut definition overrides the Excel definition. For example, when you press Ctrl+O, Excel opens the Open dialog box, enabling you to select a workbook to open. If you create a shortcut key macro of o, your macro executes whenever you press Ctrl+O instead of displaying the Open dialog box. With this in mind, avoid using shortcut keys that you use for other common Excel tasks.

## Create a Keyboard Shortcut

① On the Macro dialog box, click the desired macro.

You can click Tools→Macro→Macros to display the Macro dialog box.

**Note:** See the section "Run a Macro" for more on the Macro dialog box.

② Click Options.

The Macro Options dialog box displays for the selected macro.

③ Type the desired shortcut key in the Shortcut Key box.

When you type an uppercase character in the field, a message appears, reminding you to type **Ctrl+Shift+shortcut key**.

④ Click OK to save the shortcut key.

## Launch a Keyboard Shortcut

**①** Click the cell where you want the macro to execute.

**②** Press Ctrl and the shortcut key to activate the macro.

- The selected macro executes and makes the appropriate changes to the worksheet.

**③** To run the macro again, repeat steps 1 and 2.

---

### Extra

When you use shortcut keys for macros in other workbooks, you may not always receive the correct macro to execute. Excel does not let you assign a shortcut key if a macro in your current workbook uses the shortcut, but it does not check unopened workbooks. If you open workbooks with the same shortcut key, Excel does not know which macro to execute when you select the shortcut. If you use the shortcut keys for a macro and do not receive the anticipated results, you need to verify what you assigned to the shortcut keys.

If you find that the shortcut keys are the same as another available macro, you can reassign a shortcut key to a macro from the Macro dialog box by clicking the macro and then clicking Options to display the Macro Options dialog box. Type the desired shortcut key and click OK. To make the shortcut key modification permanent, save the workbook that contains the macro. Keep in mind, however, that you may find it easier to simply change a lowercase shortcut to uppercase, or vice-versa.

# Delete a Macro from a Workbook

You can remove macros from any workbook to reduce your list of available macros. Similar to cleaning a closet, you want to eliminate the stuff you no longer need.

When you delete a macro, Excel removes the actual macro without affecting any changes previously applied to the workbook with that macro. For example, if you use the macro to sum a series of cells, the sum remains the same when you delete the macro. Excel immediately applies the macro changes to the worksheet and then no longer relies on it to maintain any futures changes you make.

To delete a macro, you must open the workbook containing the macro because you can only see macros within open workbooks in Excel.

You use the steps in this section to store your macro in unhidden workbooks. If you can open the workbook with the Open command on the File menu, Excel does not hide the workbook. You cannot see hidden workbooks when you view the available workbooks in a folder. A good example of a hidden workbook is the Personal Macro Workbook, which loads automatically when you run Excel.

To delete a macro that you store in the Personal Macro Workbook, you need to perform different steps. See the section "Delete from the Personal Macro Workbook" for more information on working with the Personal Macro Workbook or any other hidden workbook.

Remember that you cannot undo the deletion process. If you delete the wrong macro, you can only restore it by recording it again. If you do not want to re-create an unintentionally deleted macro, try closing the workbook without saving it and then reopen the workbook. This eliminates any changes made since your last save, and restores any deleted macros. Of course, you lose any other changes you made to the workbook if you close without saving.

## Delete a Macro from a Workbook

① Click Tools→Macro→Macros.

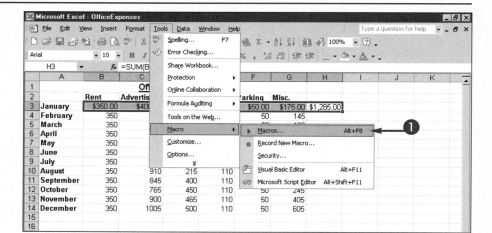

The Macro dialog box displays a list of available macros.

② Click the macro you want to delete.

If the Macro dialog box does not list the macro, click the location of the macro.

③ Click Delete.

A message box appears asking if you want to delete the macro.

④ Click Yes to delete the macro.

If the macro listed is not the one you intended to delete, click No.

Excel deletes the macro from the workbook.

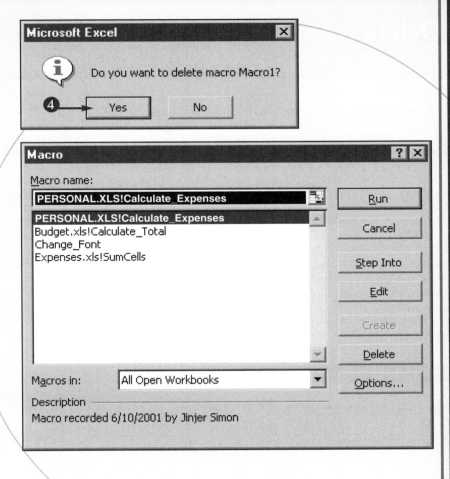

## Extra

When you delete a macro, Excel only deletes the macro. If you add the macro to a menu or toolbar button, it retains the macro reference. If you select one of these options after deleting a macro, an error message displays indicating that Excel cannot find the macro. See the sections "Assign a Macro to a Toolbar Button" and "Assign a Macro to a Menu" for more information about assigning macros to toolbars and menus.

To remove menu options and toolbar buttons, click Tools➔Customize to display the Customize dialog box. You can only modify menus and toolbars within Excel when the Customize dialog box displays on the screen. While the Customize dialog box displays, you can right-click the desired icon or menu option and select the Delete option to remove it, or you can click the button or menu option and drag it onto the Customize dialog box. Keep in mind that dragging a toolbar or menu option onto the Customize dialog box does not add it to the Customize dialog box.

# Delete from the Personal Macro Workbook

You can delete macros that you no longer use from the Personal Macro Workbook. The Personal Macro Workbook stores macros that you want to make available to all workbooks. Excel creates the Personal Macro Workbook when you store your first macro in it. After Excel creates the Personal Macro Workbook, the workbook opens as a hidden file whenever you run Excel. You can only tell that a hidden file exists by viewing the Macro dialog box, where Excel lists the macros used by the Personal Macro Workbook.

Excel stores the Personal Macro Workbook as a file named Personal.xls with a typical path of C:\documents and settings\user_name\Application Data\Microsoft\Excel\ XLSTART folder.

If you try to delete a macro out of the Personal Macro Workbook from the Macro dialog box, Excel displays a message box with the message, "Cannot edit a macro in a hidden workbook. Unhide the workbook using the Unhide

command." By default, Excel does not allow you to delete macros out of hidden workbooks. Because Excel hides the Personal Macro Workbook, you cannot delete the macros in it without first unhiding the workbook using the Excel Unhide command.

After you delete the macro from the workbook, make sure that you hide the workbook again. If you do not hide the Personal Macro Workbook again, the workbook appears as an open workbook. Because you only use this workbook for storing globally used macros, you do not want to make other types of modifications to it. By hiding it, you keep it out of the way and eliminate the possibility of having unwanted changes made to it.

You can also use the Visual Basic Editor to remove macros from the Personal Macro Workbook. See Chapter 2 for more information about removing macros using the Visual Basic Editor.

## Delete from the Personal Macro Workbook

① Click Window→Unhide.

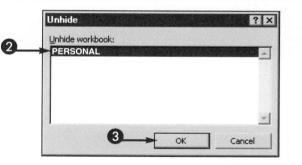

The Unhide dialog box displays a list of open workbooks that are currently hidden.

② Click PERSONAL.

③ Click OK.

The Personal Macro
Workbook is unhidden and
displays in the Excel Window.

④ Click Delete to remove the
macro from the workbook.

**Note:** For information about
deleting a macro, see the
section "Delete a Macro from
a Workbook."

⑤ After modifications are
complete, click
Window➔Hide.

The workbook is hidden.

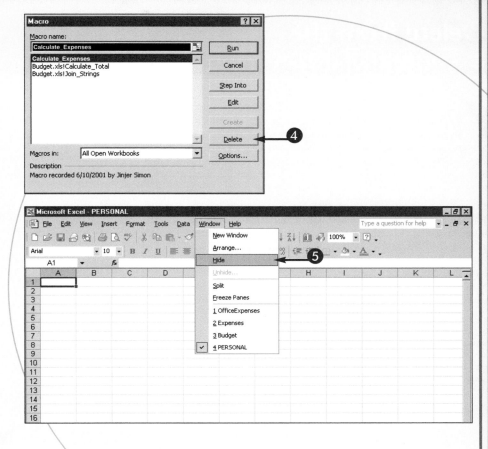

---

## Extra

Typically, you do not share the Personal Macro Workbook with other users. Excel creates a
different Personal Macro Workbook for each username on a machine. If you have multiple
users on your computer with different usernames, Excel creates a different Personal Macro
Workbook for each user. You can share a Personal Macro Workbook between different users,
even on the same computer, by copying the workbook. You can use Windows Explorer and
copy the workbook from one user to another if you want to make the macros in that
workbook available to other users. To do so, make sure you copy the PERSONAL.XLS file to
the C:\documents and settings\user_name\Application Data\Microsoft\Excel\XLSTART folder
from the user workbook you want to share to each user's corresponding folder. Keep in mind,
you can only have one PERSONAL.XLS file for each user. If a user already has a Personal
Macro Workbook, you can overwrite it with the new one. Of course, if you overwrite an
existing Personal Macro Workbook, Excel no longer makes any macros you store in the
workbook available. To eliminate potential problems, you should rename the existing
workbook so that a user can still access it if necessary.

# Assign a Macro to a Toolbar Button

**Y**ou can assign any macro to an Excel toolbar. Excel uses toolbars to provide quick access to commonly used commands. You can make macros more accessible by creating a button on a toolbar to execute a macro. By doing this, you also do not have to remember the shortcut key that launches the macro. If you create a macro toolbar button, each time you want to run the macro, you simply click the appropriate button.

When you add a button to a toolbar, it remains on that toolbar for all workbooks that you open in Excel. In other words, even if the active workbook does not have access to the macro because you closed the corresponding workbook, the Toolbar button still displays. For that reason, you should assign a macro that exists in your Personal Macro Workbook to a toolbar button to make the macro available

from all workbooks. Rememer that the Personal Macro Workbook stores commonly used macros, and opens as a hidden file each time you run Excel. Excel always keeps the Personal Macro Workbook open and, therefore, makes any macros you have in the Workbook always available for use by other workbooks that you open. For more on macro storage, see the section "An Introduction to Macros."

You can add buttons to any of the existing Excel toolbars, or you can create new toolbars for your buttons. By creating a separate toolbar for your macros, you keep your custom macros together in one location and you avoid ruining existing toolbars. You can select the toolbars to display in Excel on the Customize dialog box. Of course, you need to display a toolbar in Excel before you can add buttons to it. You also display the Customize dialog box to add buttons to toolbars.

---

### Assign a Macro to a Toolbar Button

① Click Tools→Customize.

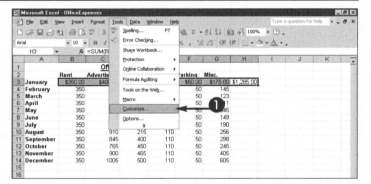

The Customize dialog box displays options for updating menus and toolbars.

② Click the Commands tab.

③ Click Macros.

④ Click the Custom Button option.

⑤ Drag the option to the desired location on the toolbar.

● As you drag the button across the toolbar, Excel inserts a line to indicate the location.

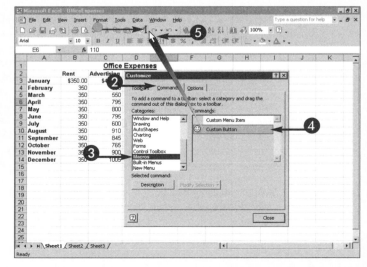

6 Release the mouse button.

The button appears on the toolbar.

7 Right-click the toolbar button to display a menu of options.

**Note:** You must have the Customize dialog box open to customize the button on the toolbar.

8 Click Assign Macro.

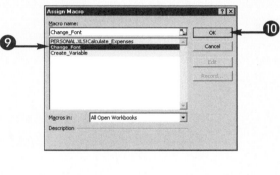

The Assign Macro dialog box displays a list of currently available macros.

9 Click the name of the macro you want to assign to the new button.

10 Click OK.

The macro runs each time you select the button.

---

## Apply It

Chances are you do not want to keep the default smiley face button image Excel inserts on the toolbar. You can change the image by using one of two different options on the menu that appears when you right-click the mouse over the toolbar button when you have the Customize dialog box open. If you want to select an image from a list of existing images, you can click the Change Button Image option. If you do not like the images on the Change Button Image menu, you can also create your own button image on the Button Editor dialog box. To change the button image, click the Edit Button Image option on the menu.

Changing the button image is similar to a paint-by-number exercise you did as a kid. You have 16 different colors you can use to create the new image. Click the desired color and then click the pixel of the image that you want to modify. You can also move the image within the window by clicking and dragging it. But the maximum size of the button image is 16x16 pixels or the contents of the window. When you close the dialog box, the button image updates.

# Assign a Macro to a Menu

Y ou can assign a macro to any existing Excel menu. If you do not want to use existing menus, you can even create a new menu. By assigning a macro to a menu, you make the macro as accessible as any menu option. Assigning macros to menus eliminates the need to remember the shortcut key required to launch the macro.

When you add a macro to a menu, it remains on the menu for all workbooks that you open in Excel. For that reason, you should assign a macro that exists in your Personal Macro Workbook to a menu to ensure that all workbooks can access the macros. The Personal Macro Workbook stores commonly used macros for the current user, and opens as a hidden file each time you run Excel. Because the Personal Macro Workbook is always open, any workbook

can use all of the macros it contains. To learn more about the Personal Macro Workbook, see the section "An Introduction to Macros."

You can assign the macro to any available menu; however, to keep your macros easy to find, you may want to place them all on one custom menu. You can create a new Excel menu using the Customize dialog box. Of course, whatever menu you decide to use as a home for your macro must exist on the Excel window before you can add the macro option to it.

You add options to a menu by dragging them onto the menu from the Customize dialog box. In fact, you can modify menus only while the Customize dialog box displays. You can remove menu options in a similar fashion by dragging them from the menu back to the Customize dialog box.

## Assign a Macro to a Menu

① Click Tools→Customize.

The Customize dialog box appears.

② Click the Commands tab.

③ Click Macros.

④ Click the Custom Menu Item option.

⑤ Drag the item to the desired menu.

The menu expands and a line indicates your position in the menu.

⑥ Release the mouse button.

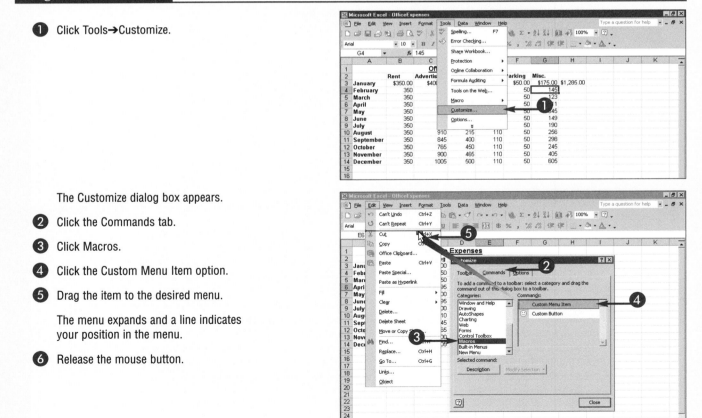

7 Right-click the menu option.

8 Click Name.

9 Type the desired name for the macro menu option in the field.

10 Click Assign Macro.

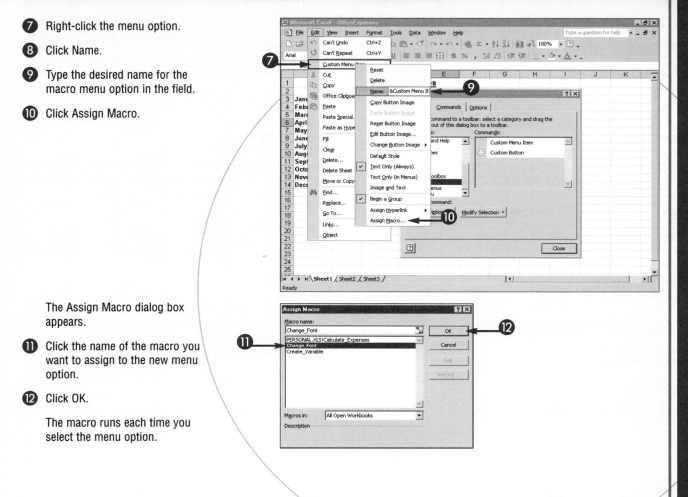

The Assign Macro dialog box appears.

11 Click the name of the macro you want to assign to the new menu option.

12 Click OK.

The macro runs each time you select the menu option.

## Extra

You can create a custom menu for macros you place on a menu. This keeps all the macro references in one location and prevents clutter on the existing Excel menus. To create a new menu, open the Customize dialog box as described in the steps on this page. On the Customize tab select the New Menu option as the desired category. A New Menu option displays as the available command. Click the New Menu option and drag it to the desired menu location. After you add the menu, you can right-click it, and change the name, which makes it ready to receive your macros.

When you name a menu option, you can also create a shortcut key that corresponds to the menu option. Similar to the shortcuts you create for macros, the menu option shortcut launches whatever command you assign to the menu option. Also, these shortcuts launch with the Alt key. To create a menu shortcut, you need to type a & before the character in the menu item name that corresponds to the shortcut key. For example, if you want Alt+T to launch the menu option "Determine Total," you place the & before the letter T: "Determine &Totals."

# Set Macro Security

D ue to the increasing problem with computer viruses, specifically macro viruses, by default, Excel disables all macros in worksheets that you open, except those with a signature from a trusted source. You can Excel open all macros regardless of source, or prompt you before opening unsigned macros, by modifying the macro security level.

Digital signatures, which a creator uses to verify a macro's safety, remain attached to a macro or other file so long as no one modifies the macro or file. Macro modifications require you, as the creator, to reattach the signature. A macro with a valid digital signature confirms the macro's origins and that no one altered it.

Depending how you use Excel — and whether you open workbooks from other sources — you may want to modify the security type that Excel uses to open workbooks containing macros. The three security settings include:

- **High:** The default, selecting this level disables all unsigned macros, even ones you create. You have the option of selecting macros from other trusted sources when you run Excel.

- **Medium:** With this level you can specify whether you want to run macros from trusted and unsigned sources when you load Excel. Select this level if you want to eliminate the hassle of signing the macros you create.

- **Low:** Excel automatically loads all workbooks and macros without checking to see if they are from trusted sources. With this setting, the only protection from macro viruses is a good virus scanner.

To eliminate the hassle and expense of acquiring a digital certificate, you can personally sign your macros by running SelfCert.exe, an Office XP program. Creating and attaching your personal signature indicates that you certify the security of a macro, identifies macros you create, and distinguishes your macros from other macros.

## Set Macro Security

### SET SECURITY

① Click Tools→Macro→Security.

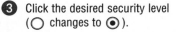

The Security dialog box displays.

② Click the Security Level tab.

③ Click the desired security level (○ changes to ◉).

④ Click OK.

Excel assigns a security level.

## CREATE A PERSONAL SECURITY CERTIFICATE

1. Open Microsoft Windows Explorer.

2. Click the Office10 subfolder of the Microsoft Office folder.

**Note:** If you performed a typical Office XP installation, Excel locates your program files in C:\Program Files\Microsoft Office.

3. Double-click the SelfCert.exe program file.

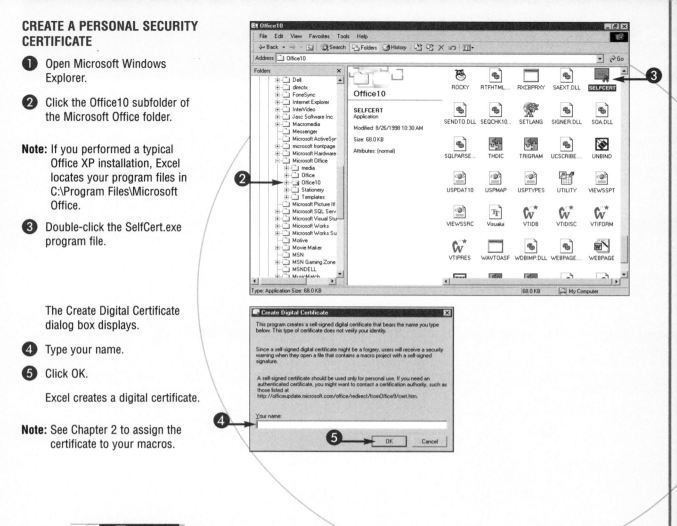

The Create Digital Certificate dialog box displays.

4. Type your name.

5. Click OK.

Excel creates a digital certificate.

**Note:** See Chapter 2 to assign the certificate to your macros.

---

### Extra

Assigning a certificate you create with SelfCert.exe to a project indicates the project is self-signed and not authenticated. This option works well for personal workbooks. However, if you plan to distribute your workbook to other users, you probably want to consider acquiring a true digital signature file. When you use a commercial digital signature file, the digital ID attaches to the macro. The Digital ID remains with the macro, and — if someone alters the macro in any way — notifies the user when the user should not trust the macro. This ensures that a macro you create is not altered to harm another person's machine.

The most common location for obtaining a digital certification is from VeriSign, Inc. Of course, to obtain a commercial certification, you have to submit an application and pay the appropriate fee. You can find out more about obtaining a digital certification for your macro at www.verisign.com. Another company that you can contact for a digital ID is Thwate Consulting. You can find out about their digital signature options at www.thwate.com.

# An Introduction to the Visual Basic Editor

Y ou write Visual Basic Applications, or VBA code, required to create complex macros, using the Visual Basic Editor, acessible via all Microsoft Office applications, including Excel. Arranged in a series of windows, which you can move around with your mouse to obtain the desired development layout, the VBE contains

project information. The Visual Basic Editor remembers the window locations you set up each time you open it. By default, not all windows display when you initially open the Visual Basic Editor, but you can select the windows you want to view from the View menu.

## View of the Visual Basic Editor

**C OBJECT LIST BOX**

Lists objects associated with the selected project.

**D PROCEDURE LIST BOX**

Lists the procedures associated with the selected object.

**A PROPERTIES WINDOW**

Displays properties for the currently selected object.

**B PROJECT EXPLORER WINDOW**

Displays the list of the open projects and corresponding modules, objects, and forms, using nodes to represent each item type.

**E CODE WINDOW**

Displays the VBA source code in the selected module.

**F IMMEDIATE WINDOW**

Provides immediate results for statements typed in the window.

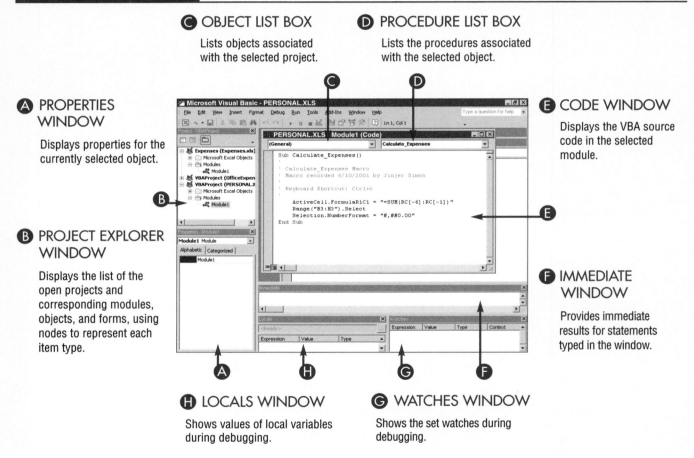

**H LOCALS WINDOW**

Shows values of local variables during debugging.

**G WATCHES WINDOW**

Shows the set watches during debugging.

## Nodes of the VBE Project Window

The Project Explorer window, or Project window, resembles the treelike structure used by the Windows Explorer folders pane. The Visual Basic Editor refers to each entry in the Projects window as a node. The top nodes, which display in bold, represent the Excel VBA projects currently open. Excel opens a new VBA project for each workbook that opens in Excel. Because the Personal Macro Workbook also opens when you run Excel, you see it listed as one of the open projects in Project Explorer. Under each project are three nodes containing project elements:

### Microsoft Excel Objects

This folder contains a node for each sheet within the selected workbook. Each sheet node represents either a worksheet or a chart sheet. When you double-click a particular node, the corresponding code module opens. You can place independent procedures within a specific sheet module, but typically, these procedures are placed in the standard modules. You can place code that triggers upon the occurrence of a specific event, such as opening a workbook, in the ThisWorkbook node.

### Forms

This folder node displays only if you create custom forms for the specific project. If so, Excel creates a node for each form in the selected project. Forms are also referred to as UserForms or custom dialog boxes. You can create custom forms or dialog boxes that resemble the dialog boxes used throughout Excel. Macros use these forms to enable the user to interact with the macro. See Chapter 13 for more information about creating custom forms.

### Modules

Project Explorer lists a node for each module within the project. Modules contain general procedures, either functions or subroutines. Excel creates a new module for a project each time you add a new macro to the corresponding workbook. You can add other modules within the Visual Basic Editor, as outlined later in this chapter. Not all modules contain macros that are visible within Excel. You can create hidden procedures that are called by other functions and subroutines.

## Properties Window

The Properties window displays the properties for the selected object. If you select a module in Project Explorer, the only properties you will see in the Properties window is the module name. If you select a specific sheet, however, you can view and modify properties for a sheet such as whether page breaks display.

To change the properties for an object, you simply click the property and make the desired changes. Some property fields, such as Name, require you to type a value. Other fields have drop-down lists where you can select the appropriate value. If you find that you cannot change its property, it is probably read-only and you cannot modify it.

## VBE and IntelliSense Technology

To make adding VBA code easier, the Visual Basic Editor uses Microsoft's IntelliSense technology, which helps you find the properties and methods for the objects you use in your macro scripts. As you type the name of an object, a list of available properties and objects displays from which to select. You can select from this list by clicking the selection with the mouse. Any property or method that you select appears in your code in the Code window.

# Activate the
# Visual Basic Editor

Y ou can only run the Visual Basic Editor from a Microsoft Office application. The Visual Basic Editor provides the ability to create and modify Excel macros using Visual Basic for Applications, or VBA. You can activate the Visual Basic Editor by editing a macro that you recorded with the Macro Recorder, or you can open the editor directly from the Tools menu via the Visual Basic Editor option. Whether you create a macro using the Macro Recorder or in the Visual Basic Editor, you write all source code using VBA. Of course, with the Macro Recorder, Excel takes the key strokes that you record and coverts them all to VBA.

When you open the Visual Basic Editor, Project Explorer, if displayed, indicates your location within the project. If you open an existing macro from the Macro dialog box within Excel, Project Explorer highlights the corresponding module in the tree, and the VBA code for the macro appears in the

Code window. When you select the Visual Basic Editor directly, however, Project Explorer highlights the name of the current project, which is the name of the workbook open in Excel. You can select a specific module in a project by double-clicking the module node in Project Explorer. To learn more about nodes and the structure of Project Explorer, see the section, "An Introduction to the Visual Basic Editor."

Keep in mind that if the Personal Macro Workbook, Personal.xls, contains macros, the project for the Personal.xls project always opens when you access the Visual Basic Editor. Although the Personal Macro Workbook is hidden within Excel, in the Visual Basic Editor you can view and modify all macros in the Personal Macro Workbook.

See Chapter 3 for more information on using Visual Basic for Applications (VBA).

## Activate the Visual Basic Editor

### OPEN THE VBE USING THE MENU

① Click Tools→Macro→Visual Basic Editor.

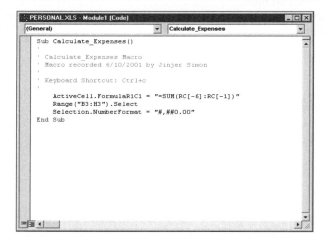

The Visual Basic Editor displays with the window layout you last used.

## OPEN THE VBE FROM THE MACRO DIALOG BOX

**①** Open the Macro dialog box by clicking Tools➔Macro➔ Macros.

**②** Click to highlight the macro you want to modify.

**③** Select Edit.

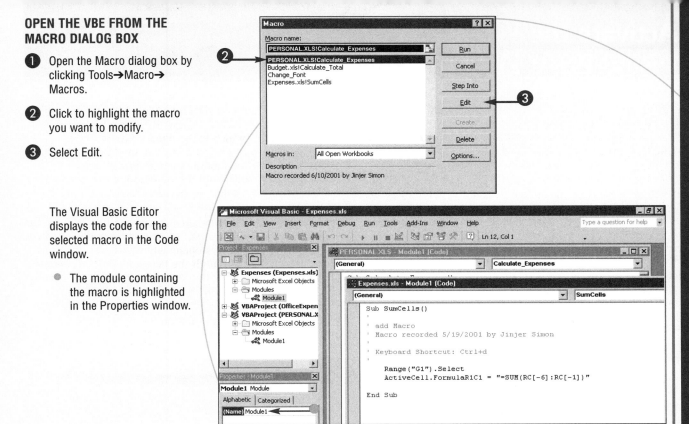

The Visual Basic Editor displays the code for the selected macro in the Code window.

● The module containing the macro is highlighted in the Properties window.

---

### Extra

To make the Visual Basic Editor easier to navigate, Microsoft provides different shortcut keys. These shortcuts work when the Visual Basic Editor window has focus. A window has *focus* when it is the selected window. For example, you can only type text in the selected window.

| SHORTCUT KEY | DESCRIPTION |
|---|---|
| F7 | Switches to the Code window for the object (node) in Project Explorer. If the Code window for that object is not open, it opens and displays on top of any other code windows. |
| F4 | Switches to the Property window and displays the properties for the selected object. If the Property window is not open, the Visual Basic Editor opens it in the location where you last viewed it. |
| Ctrl+R | Switches to Project Explorer. If the Project Explorer window is not open, the Visual Basic Editor opens it in the location where you last viewed it. |
| Alt+F11 | Toggles between the Visual Basic Editor and Excel. This shortcut is useful when you step through a macro. See Chapter 8 for more information on stepping through a macro to debug it. |
| F1 | Displays online help on the item selected in the Code window. |
| Shift+F2 | Displays a definition of the selected function or subroutine in the Code window. |

# Arrange the Visual Basic Editor Windows

The Visual Basic Editor contains several different windows that you use when developing macros. Although Microsoft provides a basic window setup, like most development environments, you can customize this setup by rearranging, resizing, removing, and adding windows. The most commonly used windows are Project Explorer, the Properties window, and the Code window. You may also find the Immediate window useful for quickly testing a statement before adding it to your code. You can only access some windows, such as the Toolbar and UserForm windows, from specific locations, such as when you create a userform.

You can select which windows display and the locations where they display. The View menu lists the available Visual Basic Editor windows. For example, you can only view the Toolbox from a UserForm window. When you select a window from the menu, it displays in the location

where you last placed it. In other words, if you placed the Project Explorer window in the upper-left corner during your last session, that window reopens in that same location.

You can move windows using the standard drag-and-drop features inherent to Microsoft Windows. You can also resize the windows via the edges of the window.

You can also attach windows to specific locations of the Visual Basic Editor by using the docking feature. When you dock a window, it becomes part of another window attached at the specified location. Keep in mind that docking a window does not mean that the window always displays in the Visual Basic Editor. If you set a window to dock, Excel docks in the location you specified each time it displays. You can only dock the windows on the top, bottom, left edge, or right edge of the Visual Basic Editor.

## Arrange the Visual Basic Editor Windows

### SELECT THE DISPLAYED WINDOWS

**1** Click View.

The View menu lists the available windows for the selected window.

**2** Click the menu option for the window to display within the Visual Basic Editor.

● The selected window displays in the last viewed location.

You can click and drag the window to a new location.

You can close a window by clicking the Close button (☒).

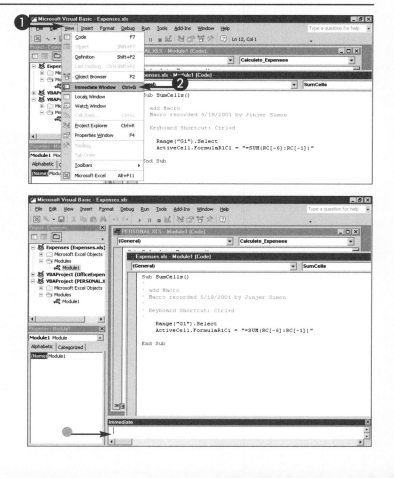

## DOCK INDIVIDUAL WINDOWS

**①** Click Tools➔Options.

The Options dialog box displays.

**②** Click the Docking tab.

**③** Click the windows you want to dock
(☐ changes to ☑).

**④** Select OK to close the Options dialog box.

**⑤** Dock the window by clicking and dragging
it to an edge.

● Excel moves the window to its new
location. You cannot place other
windows on top of a docked window.

## Extra

The number of windows you can open within
the Visual Basic Editor depends on the
resolution of your monitor. The higher your
monitor resolution, the more viewing space
you have available. When writing code for your
macro, you typically need to have only the
Properties window, the Project Explorer
window, and the corresponding code module
window open.

If you have a large high-resolution monitor,
you may want to consider sizing the Visual
Basic Editor and Excel windows so that you
can see both simultaneously. You can
accomplish this by sizing the Excel window to
fit on the top half of the screen and then sizing
the Visual Basic Editor for the bottom half.
This setup works well for stepping through the
execution of the macro to see the results, as
described in Chapter 8, "Debugging Macros."

If you cannot fit both applications on your
monitor effectively, you can switch between the
two by using the Alt+F11 shortcut.

You can move windows around in the Visual
Basic Editor with the same techniques you use
with all Microsoft Windows programs. To
move a window, click the title bar and drag it
to the desired location. To resize a window,
click a corner of the window and drag it to the
desired size.

# Set Properties for a Project

You can set the properties, such as the project name and the lock status of a project, for each project that you view in the Visual Basic Editor. When you lock a project, the project is password protected so that only people who know the password can view and modify the contents of the project. You set both the project name and password information in the Project Properties dialog box.

Excel considers each open workbook a project when you access the Visual Basic Editor. By default, the Visual Basic Editor gives each project the name of VBA Project (WorkbookName), but you can customize the name of the project, if desired, within the Visual Basic Editor. Doing this can help distinguish between different projects, especially if

you have several different workbooks open simultaneously. For example, you can change the project name to match the name of the corresponding workbook.

If you plan to distribute your workbook to other users, you may want to consider password protecting your projects. If a project is password protected, the user must specify the password in order to view or modify any portion of the project. This step can help protect macro code that you do not want others to view or modify. Password protecting the project does not affect the way the corresponding workbook behaves within Excel, but it effectively keeps others from viewing your macro source.

## Set Properties for a Project

**CHANGE A PROJECT NAME**

① Click Tools➔VBAProject Properties.

The Project Properties dialog box displays.

② Click the General tab.

③ Type the desired name for the project.

④ Click OK.

The project name changes within the Project Explorer window.

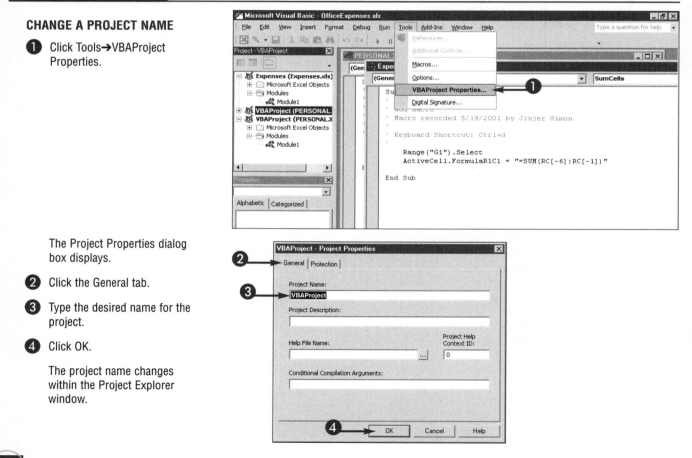

## LOCK PROJECT FROM EDITING

⑤ Click the Protection tab.

⑥ Click the Lock project for viewing option (☐ changes to ☑).

⑦ Type the password required to unlock the project.

⑧ Type the password again.

⑨ Click OK.

Excel applies your settings

## OPEN A LOCKED PROJECT

⑩ Close the Visual Basic Editor.

⑪ Open the Visual Basic Editor.

**Note:** See the section "Activate the Visual Basic Editor" to open the VBE.

⑫ Click the locked project.

A Password dialog box displays.

⑬ Type the password.

⑭ Click OK.

Excel opens the project.

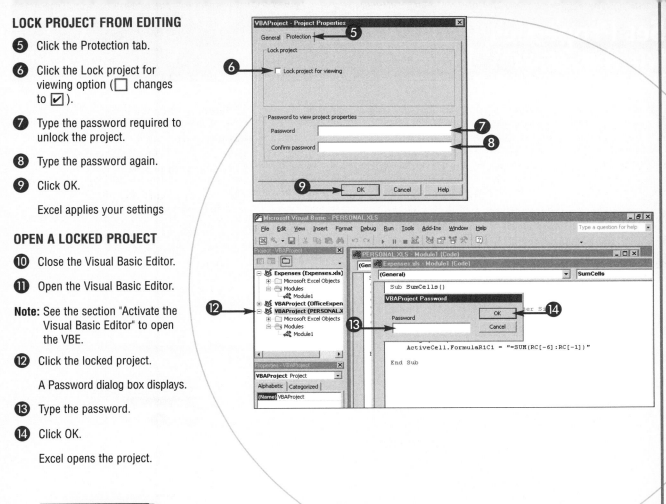

---

### Apply It

If you have multiple workbooks open in Excel, you can copy modules and UserForms between them by using the Project Explorer window. To copy an object, click the desired object and drag it to another workbook. When you release the mouse button, the Visual Basic Editor creates a copy of the selected module in the specified project. By default, the Visual Basic Editor names the copied module the same as the module in the original project. When you copy an object to another project, if one already exists with that name, the Visual Basic Editor renames the object by adding a 1 to the end of the name. For example, if you copy Module2 to a different project and that project contains a Module2 object, the copied object name becomes Module21. If you have a Module21, the Visual Basic Editor names the copied object Module22.

You can change the name of the copied module on the Properties window. To do so, you type a new name in the Name field and then press Enter. The Name of the module changes on the corresponding node in the Project Explorer window.

# Set Display Options for the Code Window

You can modify the display settings for the text that displays on the Code window in the Visual Basic Editor. You can change the text color, font type, and font size for the text that displays in the Code window. You can not only specify the text color but also the background color. Just like any basic editor, the Code window has predefined formatting for the type of text that displays in the window. For example, there is a definition for comments and a different definition for normal text. You may not, however, always find these settings the most appealing. Fortunately, the Visual Basic Editor lets you customize the text settings for the Code window.

For font styles, the Visual Basic Editor enables you to select from the fonts installed on your machine. When dealing with source code (VBA), you may find code easier to read if

you use a fixed-width font such as the Courier New font, the default font. This type of font is preferable because the characters in the code align veritically, making it easier to detect any spacing problems with the code.

The Margin Indicator Bar check box indicates whether a vertical indicator bar displays in the margin when you debug your code. Make sure that this option remains selected, because it helps to quickly spot the appropriate line of code when debugging. The Visual Basic Editor places symbols in the vertical indicator bar to indicate errors and break points. See Chapter 8 for more information on debugging.

As you make changes to the font settings for each of the formatting types, a sample of the font selections displays on the Editor Format tab.

## Set Display Options for the Code Window

① Click Tools→Options.

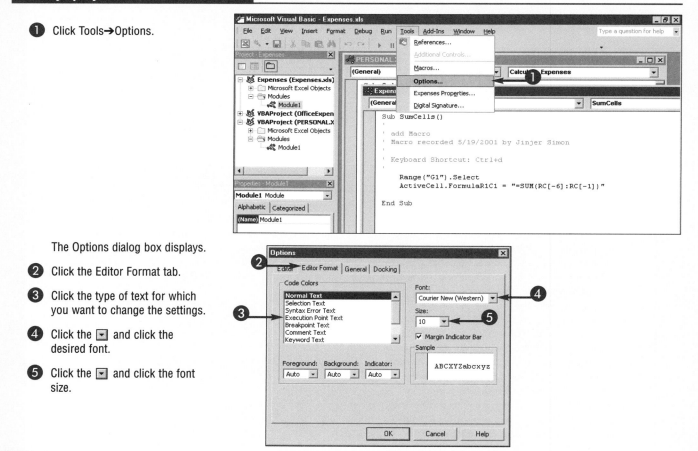

The Options dialog box displays.

② Click the Editor Format tab.

③ Click the type of text for which you want to change the settings.

④ Click the ⏷ and click the desired font.

⑤ Click the ⏷ and click the font size.

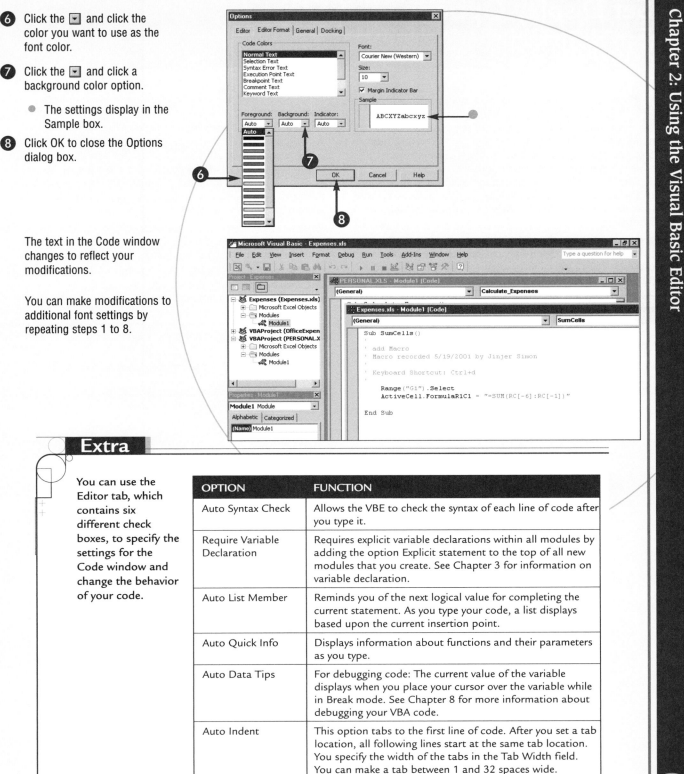

6 Click the ▼ and click the color you want to use as the font color.

7 Click the ▼ and click a background color option.

● The settings display in the Sample box.

8 Click OK to close the Options dialog box.

The text in the Code window changes to reflect your modifications.

You can make modifications to additional font settings by repeating steps 1 to 8.

## Extra

You can use the Editor tab, which contains six different check boxes, to specify the settings for the Code window and change the behavior of your code.

| OPTION | FUNCTION |
|--------|----------|
| Auto Syntax Check | Allows the VBE to check the syntax of each line of code after you type it. |
| Require Variable Declaration | Requires explicit variable declarations within all modules by adding the option Explicit statement to the top of all new modules that you create. See Chapter 3 for information on variable declaration. |
| Auto List Member | Reminds you of the next logical value for completing the current statement. As you type your code, a list displays based upon the current insertion point. |
| Auto Quick Info | Displays information about functions and their parameters as you type. |
| Auto Data Tips | For debugging code: The current value of the variable displays when you place your cursor over the variable while in Break mode. See Chapter 8 for more information about debugging your VBA code. |
| Auto Indent | This option tabs to the first line of code. After you set a tab location, all following lines start at the same tab location. You specify the width of the tabs in the Tab Width field. You can make a tab between 1 and 32 spaces wide. |

# Add a New Module

Y ou can create new code modules directly within the Visual Basic Editor. VBA uses modules to store variable declarations and all procedures, including functions and subroutines. Whenever you create a new macro using the Macro Recorder, Excel generates a new module within the corresponding project to house the new macro. Excel places the macro code in a subroutine with the same name as the macro. See Chapter 3 for more information on procedures, including functions and subroutines.

You do not need to rely on Excel to create the new modules for your macros because you can create them directly within the Visual Basic Editor. After creating a module, you can create a subroutine within the module and add the desired code so that the Macro dialog box lists your macro within

Excel. Of course, in order for Excel to make the macro visible, you must create a public subroutine. See Chapter 3 for more information about working with subroutines.

As you add new modules to a project, Excel gives them the name Module#. The Visual Basic Editor assigns the number to the macro, sequentially increasing the number by one each time you add a macro. For example, the Visual Basic Editor names the first module in the project Module1, the second Module2, and so on.

Project Explorer lists all the modules within a specific project. When you add a new module, Excel selects that module on Project Explorer and creates a blank Code window.

You do not have to create a new module for each procedure that you add to a workbook. You can add multiple procedures to the same module, if desired.

## Add a New Module

① Click the project where you want to add a new module.

② Click Insert→Module.

Excel creates a blank Code window.

③ Type **Sub NewSubroutine** replacing `NewSubroutine` with the name of the new subroutine.

**Note:** See Chapter 3 for information on creating subroutines.

④ Type the code for your macro.

⑤ Type **End Sub**.

⑥ Click the View Microsoft Excel button (🔲) to switch to Excel.

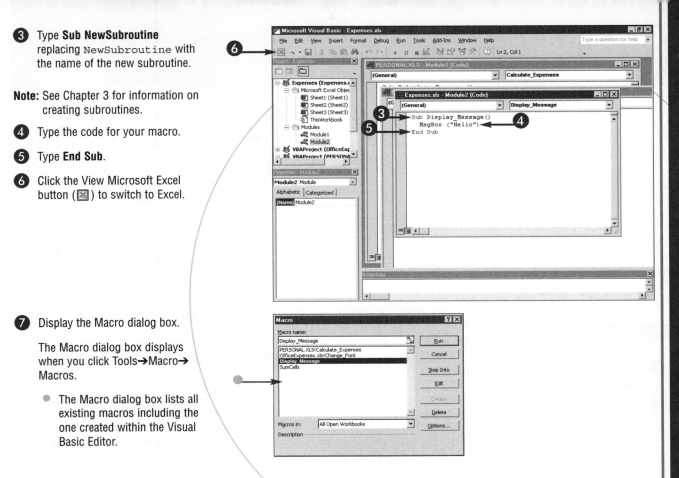

⑦ Display the Macro dialog box.

The Macro dialog box displays when you click Tools→Macro→ Macros.

● The Macro dialog box lists all existing macros including the one created within the Visual Basic Editor.

## Extra

You can easily change the name of a module within the Visual Basic Editor. When you create a new module, the Visual Basic Editor automatically names the module Module# with the number sequentially following the last module you created. For example: Module1, Module2, and so on. If you have a project with several different modules, it becomes difficult to distiguish one module from another without reviewing the source code. You can name modules so they are easier to distinguish. You do so by assigning the name of the main subroutine of function in the module as the module name. This allows you to quickly determine which module contains the desired macro. The name of the macro changes on the Properties window. To change the name, simply change the value in the Name field on the Properties window for the module that you have selected in Project Explorer. As soon as you press Enter, the name of the module changes on the corresponding node on the Project Explorer window.

# Remove a Module

Y ou can remove modules from the Visual Basic Editor rather quickly. As you work within the Visual Basic Editor, you may find that you have modules that you want to remove from a selected project. Typically, you delete modules that contain subroutines and functions that you no longer need for your project.

When you remove a module that contains code for a macro used within Excel, remember that you can no longer access the macro. Also, if you remove a module that contains code referenced by a procedure in another module, including an Excel macro, an error message displays when you run the code in the other module. To avoid error messages, you may want to consider saving the module to another file before you delete it.

When you remove a module, the Visual Basic Editor provides the opportunity to export the module to a file so you can reload it again, either in the same project or a different project. If you do not export the module to a file before deleting it, you cannot restore it later. Even if you do not intend to use the module again, to make sure that you do not cause problems with other procedures or subroutines in the project, again, you should save the module to a file before deleting it. After you ensure that everything works, you can delete the exported file. When you export the module to a file, the Visual Basic Editor saves this module in a .bas file that you can import back into a project again at any time.

When you delete macros within Excel, Excel removes the corresponding VBA subroutine code. If the only code contained in the VBA module is the Excel macro, Excel removes the entire module.

## Remove a Module

① In Project Explorer, click to highlight the module that you want to remove.

If Project Explorer is not displayed, you can summon it by clicking View→Project Explorer.

② Click File→Remove ModuleName where ModuleName is the name of the selected module.

The Remove command always contains the name of the selected module.

The Visual Basic Editor displays a message to verify the delete selection.

③ Click Yes to save the module to a file.

● If you click No, the Visual Basic Editor removes the module permanently.

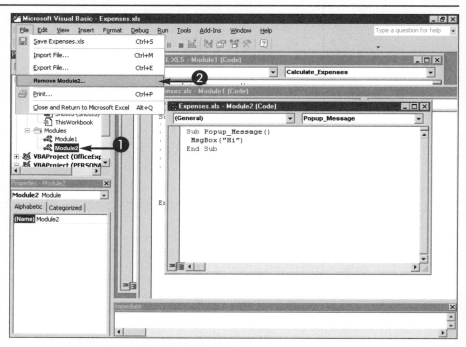

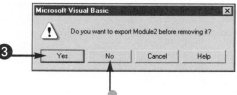

④ Select the folder in which you want to save the module code.

⑤ Type a name for the module code in the File name field.

⑥ Click Save.

● The Visual Basic Editor removes the module from the project.

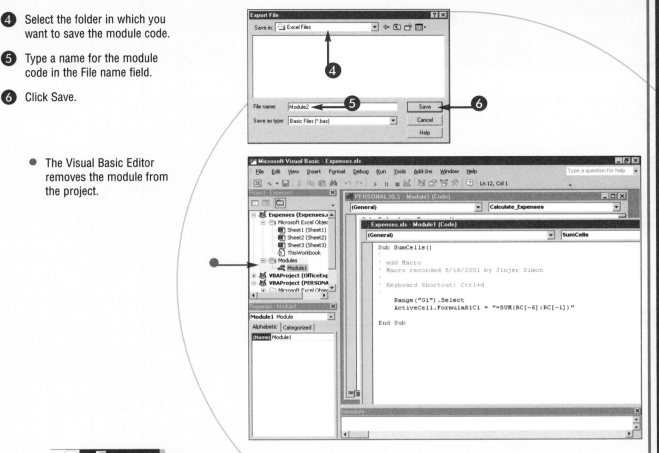

# Rename
# a Macro

You can very easily rename a macro that you created either with the Macro Recorder or in the Visual Basic Editor. Doing so, however, does require accessing the actual macro code within the Visual Basic Editor.

When you create a macro in Excel using the Macro Recorder, Excel automatically writes the code for the macro in Visual Basic for Applications (VBA). When you create a macro using the Macro Recorder, the only way that you can make changes to the macro code, or the macro name, is by modifying the VBA code for the macro using the Visual Basic Editor.

To rename the desired macro, you need to open the Visual Basic Editor and change the name of the subroutine that Excel uses to run the the macro. From Excel you can

accomplish this for nonhidden workbooks via Edit on the Macro dialog box to display the corresponding subroutine.

You can also rename a macro in the Personal Macro Workbook within the Visual Basic Editor. Because Excel opens the Personal Macro Workbook as a hidden file, the steps to rename the macro are slightly different from a regular macro. Essentially, the difference centers on how you access the macro code. Excel does not allow you to edit a macro in the Personal Macro Workbook from the Macro dialog box. To modify a macro in the Personal Macro Workbook, you must access the Visual Basic Editor directly and then make modifications to the corresponding module in the Personal.xls project.

## Rename a Macro

### RENAME A MACRO VIA THE MACRO DIALOG BOX

1 In the Macro dialog box, click the macro you want to rename.

**Note:** See Chapter 1 for information on opening the Macro dialog box.

2 Click Edit.

The Visual Basic Editor displays the source code for the selected macro.

3 After the Sub keyword, type the new macro name.

**Note:** See Chapter 3 for more information about subroutines.

4 Close the Visual Basic Editor.

The name of the macro changes in the Macro dialog box.

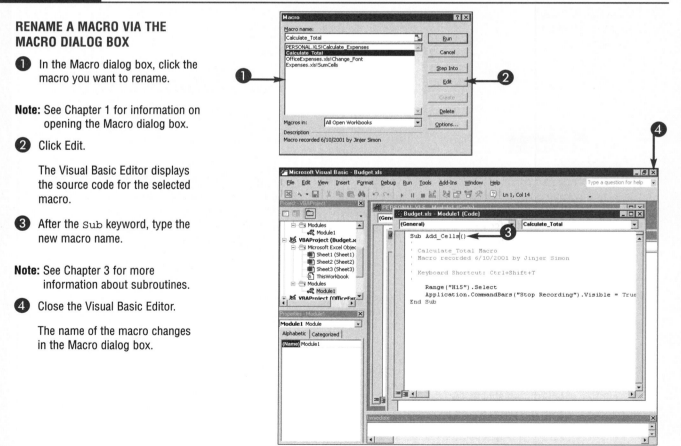

## RENAME A MACRO IN THE PERSONAL MACRO WORKBOOK

① Click Tools→Macro→Visual Basic Editor.

The Visual Basic Editor displays the source code for the current workbook.

② Click the PERSONAL.XLS project.

③ Click the module containing the macro you want to modify.

④ After the Sub keyword, type the new macro name.

⑤ Close the Visual Basic Editor.

The name of the macro changes in the Macro dialog box.

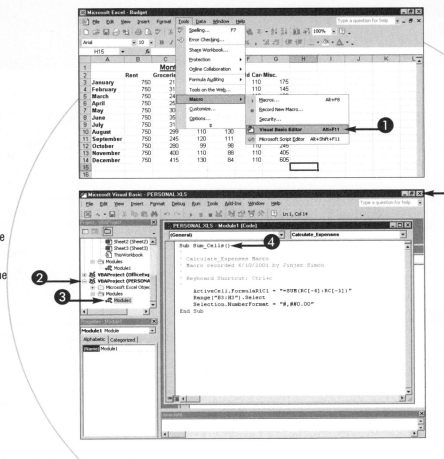

### Extra

When you change the name of a macro, Excel updates the Macro dialog box, but it does not update toolbar buttons and menu options that refer to the macro. Because you changed the name of the macro, you need to change the macro reference for each item to continue using the same button or menu option to reference the macro. To change the macro reference for these items, click Tools→Customize to display the Customize dialog box, and then right-click the menu option or toolbar button to display a menu of options. Click the Assign Macro option to display the Assign Macro dialog box. On this dialog box, click to highlight the name of the macro that you want to use for the corresponding toolbar button or menu option, and then click OK.

Because the name of the macro changes, you may also want to change the name of the toolbar button or menu option to correspond to the macro name. To do this, you need to change the value of the Name field on the Customize menu. You can also change the hot key reference for the macro by typing & in front of the hot key for the macro.

# Create a
# Startup Macro

You can easily create macros that execute whenever you open a specific workbook in Excel. If you want the macro to execute every time you run Excel, you can place the macro in the Personal Macro Workbook. Of course, this type of macro executes only once, which makes it best suited for steps that you perform each time you run Excel.

A startup macro works great for setting the basic layout of your Excel window, such as the toolbars that you want to display and the desired locations. When it comes to the window layout, Excel always opens with the settings you used the last time you ran it. Therefore, any toolbars you closed during the last session are closed when you open Excel again.

By creating a macro that sets the toolbars that you want to view, Excel opens these same toolbars and places them in the same location each time you run Excel.

The simplest method for creating this type of macro is to place the macro in the Personal Macro Workbook. Because Excel loads the Personal Macro Workbook each time you run it, the macro you create executes when Excel opens because that is when the workbook opens. You need to make the macro a part of the Personal Macro Workbook as well as part of the `ThisWorkbook` object.

You must name the macro that you create `Workbook_Open`. If you have a macro with this name, Excel knows that whenever the object — the corresponding workbook — opens, the macro needs to run. See Chapter 4 for more information about Excel objects.

## Create a Startup Macro

① Click Tools→Macro→Record New Macro.

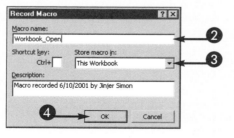

The Record Macro dialog box displays.

② Type **Workbook_Open** in the Macro name field.

③ Click the ▼ and then click This Workbook location in the Store macro in field.

④ Click OK to record the macro.

⑤ Open the Visual Basic Editor.

**Note:** See the section "Activate the Visual Basic Editor" to open the editor.

⑥ Click the current project.

⑦ Double-click the last module in the list.

⑧ Highlight the entire macro code from Sub Workbook_Open() to the End Sub command.

⑨ Click the Copy button (🖺).

⑩ Double-click the ThisWorkbook object on the tree in Project Explorer under PERSONAL.XLS.

⑪ Place the cursor in the Code window for the selected object, under any existing macros.

⑫ Click the Paste button (🖺).

⑬ Close the Visual Basic Editor.

When you open Excel again, the Workbook_Open macro runs and executes the specified code.

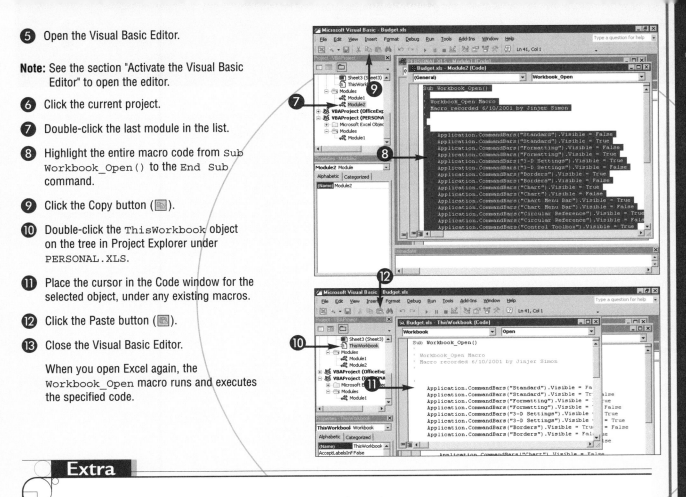

## Extra

Instead of copying the macro code to the ThisWorkbook object, you can create a macro in the ThisWorkbook object code module that calls the macro code in the appropriate code module. For example, if you have a subroutine in a module called SetToolbars that you recorded with the Macro Recorder, you can create another subroutine called Workbook_Open() in the ThisWorkbook object that calls the recorded macro, as shown in the following sample code.

**Example:**
```
Sub Workbook_Open()
      Call SetToolbars
End Sub
```

From the Workbook_Open() subroutine, you can call any other procedure within the same workbook project. To call another procedure, you need to use the Call statement before the name of the procedure you want to call. When Excel executes the main procedure, if it encounters a Call statement, it executes that procedure and returns back to the main procedure.

When you create a Workbook_Open macro, you actually create a subroutine that captures the Open event for the corresponding Workbook object. Events occur in Excel whenever anything occurs, whether initiated by you or the application. You can capture many different events to trigger specific code. See Chapter 15 for more detailed information on working with Excel events.

# Hide a Macro

You can hide macros so that they do not appear on the Macro dialog box in Excel. If you create workbooks that you intend to share with other users, you may find that you want to hide specific macros within your workbook. This can help to ensure that an unknowing user does not inadvertently delete the macro from your workbook.

Because Excel cannot execute a hidden macro from the Macro dialog box, the only method of execution for a hidden macro involves assigning a toolbar button or menu option. When you hide a macro, shortcut keys no longer execute the macro. If you do not assign the macro to a toolbar button or menu option, Excel cannot execute the macro.

If you want to hide a macro, you need to open the module containing the corresponding macro within the Visual Basic Editor and place the `Private` statement in front of the `Sub`

statement for the subroutine. For example, you type the following to hide a `ChangeText` subroutine: **Private Sub ChangeText()**.

Keep in mind that hiding a macro does not prevent users from viewing or modifying it in the Visual Basic Editor. If you want to keep another user from accessing the macro, you need to lock the project containing the macro by changing the properties of the project. See the section "Set Properties for a Project" for more details on specifying the project properties. Locking the project prevents a user from viewing and modifying all the VBA code within that project in the Visual Basics Editor. To open the project, the user must specify the correct password. Although locking a project prevents user accessibility, Excel can still execute any macros within the project.

## Hide a Macro

① Click Tools→Macro→Macros.

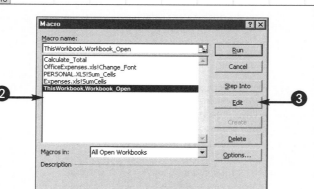

The Macro dialog box displays a list of available macros.

② Click the macro that you want to hide.

③ Click Edit.

The Visual Basic Editor opens and displays the module containing the macro you selected.

④ Type **Private** before the Sub statement.

⑤ Close the Visual Basic Editor.

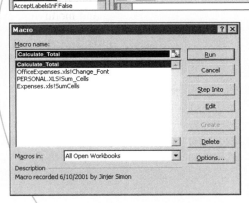

⑥ Open the Macro dialog box.

The macro no longer displays on the Macro dialog box.

---

## Extra

You should hide macros that are called by other macros if you do not want the macros to execute alone from the Macro dialog box. For example, if you have a macro named ChangeCells that calls another macro named AddCellValues, you can hide the AddCellValues macro so that a user cannot select that macro from the Macro dialog box. When you mark a procedure as private by placing the Private statement in front of the Sub statement for the subroutine, you can only access the subroutine within the same code module. In other words, you must place the subroutine that corresponds to the macro calling the hidden macro within the same code module as the hidden macro. See the sections "Create a Subroutine" and "Create a Function" in chapter 3 for more information on using the Private statement.

To make a hidden macro visible again, you need to access the module containing the corresponding subroutine within the Visual Basic Editor and delete the Private statement in front of the Sub statement. Because you cannot access a hidden macro from the Macro dialog box, the only way to access the Visual Basic Editor is to click Tools→Macro→ Visual Basic Editor.

# Assign a Digital Signature to a Macro

Y ou can assign a *digital signature* to any of your macros. You attach signatures to code in a macro, or file, to signify that the code is valid and that no one has modified it since you applied the signature.

You can create two types of digital signatures: certified digital signatures and personal digital signatures. You acquire certified digital signatures from commerical agencies, such as VeriSign, Inc., the signatures of choice when you distribute your code to other users, commercial agencies require you to pay a fee to obtain them. You can also create your own personal digital signature, but Excel does not consider this type of signature certified. Personal digital signatures work well for indicating that no one has altered the macro since you assigned the signature, but they do not certify it like the ones you acquire from a commercial agency. For more on creating a personal digital signature, see Chapter 1.

No matter how you acquire a digital signature, it does not do you any good until you attach it to a macro. Attaching a digital signature is similar to sealing an envelope: If it arrives sealed, no one has tampered with the contents. Keep in mind that the digital signature stays attached to the macro only until someone modifies it. Excel even removes the digital signature if you modify the VBA code. Therefore, if you make any modifications at all to the macro code, you need to re-attach the digital signature.

If you are not sure whether you have modified a macro since attaching the digital signature, you can check to see if the signature is attached on the Digital Signature dialog box. If a digital signature is attached, the name of the signature displays in the Certificate Name field.

## Assign a Digital Signature to a Macro

① Click the module that contains the macro you want to sign.

The macro code displays in the Code window.

② Click Tools→Digital Signature.

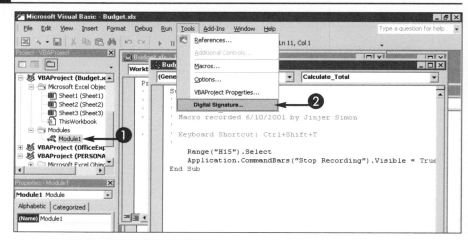

The Digital Signature dialog box indicates whether or not a digital signature certificate is currently assigned to the selected macro.

③ Click Choose.

The Select Certificate dialog box displays a list of available digital signature certificates.

④ Click the desired certificate.

⑤ Click OK.

⑥ Click OK in the Digital Signature dialog box to save the settings.

⑦ Close the workbook in Excel.

⑧ Reopen the workbook containing the macro.

Depending upon the type of certificate loaded, you see a message indicating that Excel is loading a signed macro.

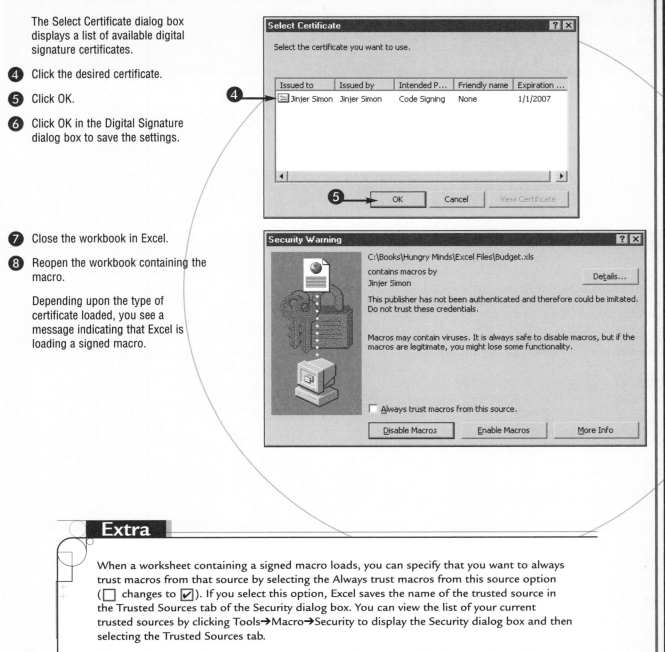

## Extra

When a worksheet containing a signed macro loads, you can specify that you want to always trust macros from that source by selecting the Always trust macros from this source option (☐ changes to ☑). If you select this option, Excel saves the name of the trusted source in the Trusted Sources tab of the Security dialog box. You can view the list of your current trusted sources by clicking Tools➜Macro➜Security to display the Security dialog box and then selecting the Trusted Sources tab.

If at any time you no longer want to trust macros from a source listed on the Trusted Sources tab, you simply highlight the name of the source and click Remove. If you remove the source from the list, the next time you open a workbook with that source Excel prompts you to see if you want to open macros from that source.

Also on the Trusted Source tab you have two other options. To have Excel also warn you before opening installed add-ins and templates, remove the check mark for the Trust all installed add-ins and templates check box. To allow Excel to access all macros with your project without warning you, select Trust access to Visual Basic Project.

# Update a Recorded Macro

You can update macro code at anytime by adding or removing VBA code. Of course, after you record a macro, you can record over the top of it to replace it, but you cannot modify it directly within Excel. The only method you can use to actually modify the macro code is to change the corresponding subroutine within the Visual Basic Editor. If you do not know how to read and write VBA code required for the step you want to add to the macro, this can become quite an undertaking.

Typically, modifying a macro, even one you create with the Macro Recorder, requires manually specifying the new VBA code you want to add to the macro. A quick and dirty method for updating a macro involves recording another macro containing the steps you want to add to the first one, and then using Copy and Paste buttons within the Visual Basic Editor to add the new steps to the old macro.

For example, if you create a macro to sum a column of values but forget to change the formatting of the column to Currency, you can record a second macro in Excel that formats the column and then add that source to the first macro. After you do this, you open the Visual Basic Editor and copy the formatting code of the second macro and paste it into the subroutine for the first macro. Keep in mind, however, that when you copy the code, you only want to copy the portion of the subroutine between the Sub and the End Sub statements.

When you copy the code from the new macro into the old macro, you should delete the new macro. You can find out more about deleting macros in Chapter 1.

## Update a Recorded Macro

① On the Macro dialog box, click to the macro that contains the source you want to add to the original macro.

   To open the Macro dialog box, click Tools→Macro→Macros.

② Click Edit.

   The Visual Basic Editor displays the code for the selected macro.

③ Press the Shift key and click the start of the source you want to copy.

④ Continue pressing the Shift key and click the end of the source to copy.

   Excel highlights the code between the Sub and End Sub statements.

⑤ Click the Copy button (🗎).

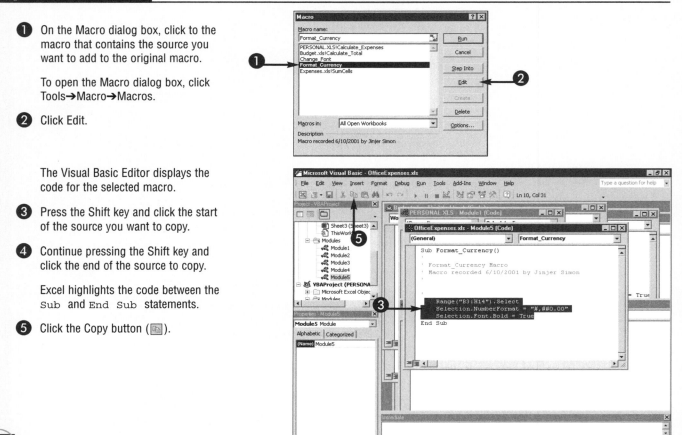

⑥ In Project Explorer click the module that contains the code for the macro you want to update.

⑦ Place the cursor between the last line of code and the `End Sub` command.

You may need to insert a blank line.

⑧ Click the Paste button (📋).

⑨ Close the Visual Basic Editor.

⑩ In the Macro dialog box, click the second-to-last-macro.

⑪ Click Delete to remove the macro.

⑫ Close the Macro dialog box.

When you run the macro, Excel executes the original and copied code.

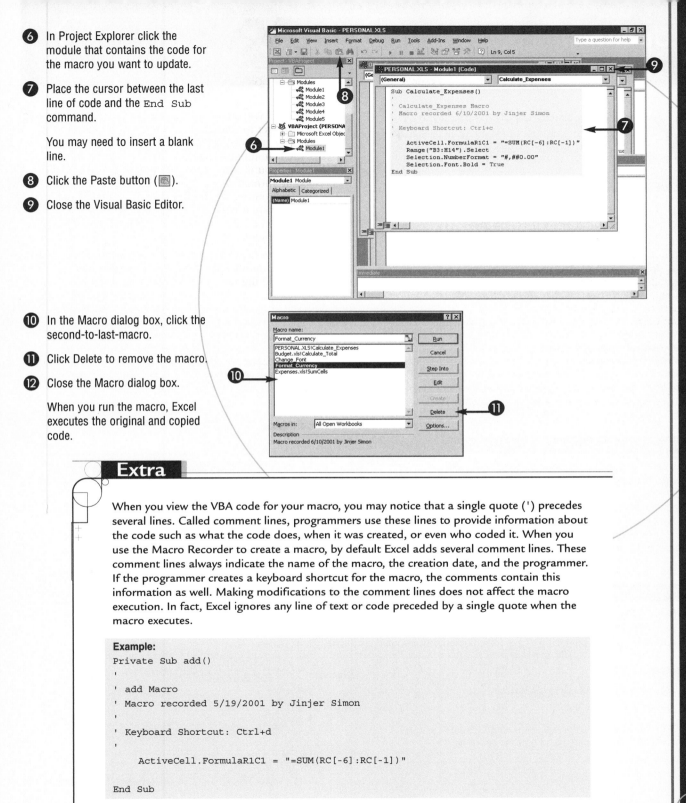

## Extra

When you view the VBA code for your macro, you may notice that a single quote (') precedes several lines. Called comment lines, programmers use these lines to provide information about the code such as what the code does, when it was created, or even who coded it. When you use the Macro Recorder to create a macro, by default Excel adds several comment lines. These comment lines always indicate the name of the macro, the creation date, and the programmer. If the programmer creates a keyboard shortcut for the macro, the comments contain this information as well. Making modifications to the comment lines does not affect the macro execution. In fact, Excel ignores any line of text or code preceded by a single quote when the macro executes.

**Example:**
```
Private Sub add()
'
' add Macro
' Macro recorded 5/19/2001 by Jinjer Simon
'
' Keyboard Shortcut: Ctrl+d
'
    ActiveCell.FormulaR1C1 = "=SUM(RC[-6]:RC[-1])"

End Sub
```

# An Introduction to VBA

You use the Visual Basic for Applications (VBA) programming language to create all macros within Excel. Although most people use VBA for macro development, VBA is actually much more powerful than just a macro language.

## Understand the VB/VBA Relationship

A member of the Visual Basic (VB) family, VBA sits between Visual Basic and VBScript as far as overall functionality. Amazingly enough, VBA actually provides a large portion of the language elements that VB uses, including forms, controls, objects, modules, and data-access technologies. The code for the three languages resemble each other so much that you may find it difficult to differentiate between VB, VBA, and VBScript when looking at a line of code.

One of the big differences between VB and VBA programs is the fact that VBA code runs within the host environment, which means that VBA code for Excel runs within Excel. Also, VBA code is interpreted as it runs, which means that each line converts to machine code prior to execution. VB code, on the other hand, compiles into an executable file that runs independent of any other applications. Therefore,

programmers consider VBA an *interpreted language* because as it runs, the environment in which it runs interprets the code to determine what to do next.

Microsoft Office XP provides VBA in all its applications. Many non-Microsoft applications also use VBA as the platform for developing code that interfaces with the object model for the specific application. By interfacing with the application object model, VBA can manipulate different objects directly, such as changing the value in a cell within Excel. You interface with the particular application object mode by writing macros, but you can also use VBA to develop applications that interface with the corresponding Microsoft application. Each Microsoft Office XP application has its own object model for interfacing with the program functionality. See Chapter 4 for more on the Excel object model.

## Comparing VBA to Other Macro Languages

To call VBA a macro language severely limits your understanding of its overall capability. VBA actually has many features lacking in other macro languages. Historically strong in their ability to capture a series of keystrokes to repeat simple tasks, many macro languages types of macros lack the capability of creating conditional statements or conditionally repeating a series of steps.

Because VBA replaced XLM, the original macro language of Excel, developers commonly refer to it as a macro language. Although the book uses VBA only to work with Excel macro concepts, you should know that you have the option of using it for application development. Such application development, however, is limited to the Microsoft Office program environment, in which VBA runs.

## Understanding VBA Terminology

The remaining chapters in this book deal with the basics of the VBA language in respect to Excel macros and how you can use VBA to add complex functionality to a macro. To perform the tasks, you need to grasp the common VBA terminology that this book utilizes.

### User-Defined

You create user-defined data types as a combination of standard VBA data types.

You can review Chapter 5 to learn about the process of creating a User-Defined data type for your macros.

**Example:**
```
Type BookReview
        Title as String
        Pages as Byte
        ReviewDate as Date
End Type
```

## Data Types

A Data Type refers to how VBA stores data in memory. VBA provides an assortment of built-in data types that you can use to handle your macro data, along with user-defined data types that you create.

In VBA, you do not specify the type of data you store in a variable when you declare it. You can enable VBA to automatically determine the data type, but this can slow down your code for large macros.

The size of a data type refers to the number of bytes it takes to store it. A *byte* is a group of bits, with a *bit* being the smallest storage unit and having a binary value or either 1 or 0. Realizing the number of bytes you require to store a data type can help you use memory more efficiently. Keep storage issues in mind when you create complex macros.

The following table lists the various data types for VBA integers.

| DATA TYPE | BYTES | RANGE OF VALUES |
|-----------|-------|-----------------|
| Byte | 1 | 0 to 255 |
| Integer | 2 | -32,768 to 32,767 |
| Long | 4 | -2,147,483,648 to 2,147,483,647 |

## Numeric

VBA provides several different numeric data types, depending upon the type of numeric value you want to save.

VBA provides three different integer data types. Integers are numeric values that do not include a decimal portion of the value. VBA uses three different types of floating-point data. The one you select depends upon the size of the numeric values you want to store in the variable. The following table lists VBA floating-point values:

| DATA TYPE | BYTES | RANGE OF VALUES |
|-----------|-------|-----------------|
| Single | 4 | -3.402823E38 to -1.401298E-45 for negative values |
| | | 1.401298E-45 to 3.40283E38 for positive values |
| Double | 8 | -1.79769313486232E308 to -4.94065645841247E-324 for negative values |
| | | 4.94065645841247E-324 to 1.79769313486232E308 for positive values |
| Currency | | 8-922,337,203,685,477.5808 to 922,337,203,685,477.5807 |

## Object

You use the Object data type to define a variable as one of the objects that are part of the Excel Object Model. These data types are 4 bytes in size.

Excel provides an abundance of objects, including the Workbook, Window, Chart, and PivotTable. You can assign each of the objects that the Excel Object Model provides as a data type.

For example:

```
Dim chrt as Chart
Dim sheet1 as Worksheet
```

For more information on objects, see Chapter 4.

## Boolean

You use a Boolean data type to store a value of True or False A Boolean data type takes two bytes of data storage. Programmers use Boolean data when working with logical data. VBA predefines the keywords `True` and `False` as Boolean values. To assign them to a variable, you simply specify the value `BoolValue = True`.

You should not use quotes when assigning a Boolean value. When you place quotes around the word `True`, VBA treats the variable as a string instead of a Boolean value.

## Date

The Date data type provides the ability to store dates and times so that you can use them in calculations. VBA accepts a date range from January 1, 100 to December 31, 9999. Unfortunately, the date range within Excel is much smaller — January 1, 1900 to December 31, 9999. If you place a date value in an Excel worksheet that is outside this date, Excel produces an error message.

The Date data type is an 8-byte value that stores as a decimal number. Because Dates are numeric, calculations can use them.

When you specify dates and times in VBA, you enclose them in pound signs instead of the quotation marks used by strings.

```
Const StartDate As Date = #6/12/2001#
```

continued ➔

## Understanding VBA Terminology *(continued)*

### String

You can use a string data type to store a sequence of characters. A string can contain any combination of letters, numbers, punctuation marks, and spaces. In order for VBA to recognize the start and stop of your string, you must enclose it in quotes, for example:

```
SampleString = "This is a sample"
```

You can declare strings in one of two different types: variable length and fixed length. As the names state, you declare *fixed-length* strings with a maximum number of characters, and *variable-length* strings with as many as 2 billion characters.

To declare a fixed-length string, you need to specify the string length as part of the definition. When you declare a string length, the string is always that size, even if you assign a smaller string to it. For example, you declare a string of 25 characters as follows:

```
Dim FixedString As String * 25
```

Variable-length strings have no length specified:

```
Dim VarString As String
```

### Variant

Variant data type is the default data type used by VBA. Because a variant can contain any type of data, VBA treats all variables you do not assign a data type as variants. But because of the processing required by VBA to determine the data type, variants work best when you use them for values that you cannot type with the standard VBA data types. The following table lists VBA variant data types:

| DATA TYPE | BYTES | RANGE OF VALUES |
|---|---|---|
| Decimal | 14 | +/-79,228,162,514,264,337,593,543,950,335 with no decimal point or +/-7.9228162514264337593543950335 with 28 places to the right of the decimal |
| Variant | 16 | -1.79769313486232E308 to -4.94065645841247E-324 (with numbers) for negative values, 4.94065645841247E-324 to 1.79769313486232E308 for positive values |
| Variant | 22 + string length | 0 to 2,000,000,000 (with characters) |

## Variables

Variables are essentially user-defined storage spaces. You can declare a variable to contain a specific type of data value.

This chapter describes the process of declaring a variable to use within a macro. Chapter 5 provides additional information about dealing with variables.

You can make variable names almost anything including any combination of alphabetic characters, numbers, and some punctuation characters — such as #, $, %, ., and ! — as long as the first character is alphabetic. You cannot use spaces as part of the name.

VBA is not case sensitive. You can make the names upper- or lowercase characters, or any combination.

You should make variable names descriptive so you can easily determine what the variable contains. For example, `Cell_Total` indicates that the variable contains the total of adding cells. Keep in mind that the name cannot exceed 254 characters.

## Procedures

A *procedure* is simply a block of code that performs specific actions. Typically, when using VBA with Excel macros, you perform the actions with or on Excel objects.

VBA provides essentially two types of VBA procedures: Functions and Subroutines. The only real difference between the two types of procedures is that a function returns a value.

If, up to this point, you have created all of your VBA code with the Macro Recorder, you have probably seen only subroutines. Because you cannot call functions from Excel as macros, the only way a macro uses a function is when it is called by a subroutine.

To use functions with your macros, a subroutine must call the functions. See "Create a Subroutine" for more information on working with subroutines.

You can make procedure names almost anything, as long as they do not resemble a worksheet cell reference. For example, VBA cannot accept a subroutine named A3 because it resembles a cell reference. You can create procedure names using the same rules as those discussed in the Variables section.

## Arrays

An *array* is a group of variables with the same name and data type. For example, if you have a list of the 50 U.S. states, you can place the state names in an array called States. You refer to each value in an array as an *element.* You access elements of the array using an index number that corresponds to their position in the array.

Using an array reduces the number of variables required in your code because you only have to declare one variable to manage all of your data values. Otherwise, storing our 50 states could require declaring and managing 50 different variables.

```
Dim States(50)
States(43) = "Texas"
```

You refer to an array with one list of data as a *one-dimensional array.* VBA provides the ability to declare multidimensional arrays. With a multidimensional array, each array element has

a corresponding array. For example, with the aforementioned States array, you can have a corresponding list of cities in each state. If a user selects Texas, a list of the cities in Texas becomes available.

```
States(43,5) = "Dallas"
```

VBA allows for up to 60 dimensions in an array, but most developers rarely use more than 2 or 3 dimensions.

You can declare arrays either as *fixed-length,* where you specify the number of elements, or as *dynamic* with an unknown number of elements.

```
Dim States()
```

Chapter 5 provides several examples for working with arrays in your VBA code.

## Constants

Constants, as the name implies, represent specific values that do not change within your code. You declare constants using the Const statement.

```
Const MyName As String = "Jinjer"
```

As with variables, if you do not specify the data type for the constant, Excel treats the constant as a variant.

Using constants enables you to have only one place in the code to modify if the value of the constant changes. For example, suppose that you have the following constant declaration:

```
Const SalesTax As String = ".075"
```

If your state raises the sales tax, you simply have to modify the constant value — .075 in the example — and not each calculation. Using constants helps to eliminate potential errors that can arise from mistyping a value.

continued →

VBA provides several different operators that you can use in your code. You can group these operators into four general categories: arithmetic, concatenation, comparison, and logical. You should find most of these operators quite familiar.

## Arithmetic Operators

VBA accepts seven different arithmetic operators. When a statement contains multiple arithmetic operators, VBA uses precedence order to determine how to evaluate the statement. For example, VBA always calculates exponents first. The only exception to the precedence order is parentheses. When parentheses separate portions of a statement, VBA evaluates the contents of the parentheses first, still using the precedence order. In the following statement, Val2 is added to Val3, and the sum is multiplied by Val1.

```
Value = Val1 * (Val2 + Val3)
```

The following table lists arithmetic Operator Precedence Order:

| OPERATOR | PRECEDENCE | PURPOSE |
|---|---|---|
| ^ | 1 | Raises the number before the operator to the power of the exponent. For example, 2^3 = 8. |
| - | 2 | Denotes a negative value. |
| * | 3 | Multiplies to numerical values. |
| / | 3 | Divides two numerical values and returns the entire result, including any decimal places. For example, 5 / 2 = 2.5. |
| \ | 3 | Divides two numerical values and returns the integer portion of the result. For example, 5 \ 2 = 2. |
| Mod | 4 | Divides two numerical values and returns the remainder. For example, 5 MOD 2 = 1. |
| + | 5 | Adds two numerical expressions. |
| - | 5 | Finds the difference between two numerical expressions by subtracting the second expression from the first. |

## Concatenation Operator

You can use the concatenation operator `&` to join together two or more strings. For example, `ap & ple` creates a new string `apple`. VBA also enables you to use the + operator for concatenating strings, but for consistency you should always use & operator with strings.

## Comparison Operators

You use comparison operators between two expressions to determine if the expressions are equal, greater than, or less than each other.

VBA uses these operators to compare numerical or string values. If comparison operators compare a numerical and string value, Excel always evaluates the numeric expression as less than the string expression.

If you compare two string expressions, Excel looks at the characters in the string and not the string length to determine which string is longer. For example, if you compare *abcd* with *cd,* Excel considers *cd* to be greater because the letter *c* comes after *a.* This is true even though it has fewer characters.

The following table lists comparison operators:

| OPERATOR | PURPOSE |
|---|---|
| = | Determines if expressions are equal. |
| > | Determines if first expression is greater than second expression. |
| < | Determines if first expression is less than the second expression. |
| <> | Determines if expressions are not equal. |
| >= | Determines if first expression is greater than or equal to second expression. |
| <= | Determines if first expression is less than or equal to second expression. |

## Logical Operators

Logical operators evaluate expressions and return a logical value of `True` or `False`. For example, you can use a logical operator to compare two comparison expressions.

```
If val1 > 10 And val2 = 5 Then
```

With this expression, the `If` statement can execute only if both expressions are true.

VBA supports six different logical expressions.

The following table lists logical operators:

| OPERATOR | PURPOSE |
|---|---|
| Not | Negates the value of the expression. If the expression is `True`, the operator causes it to be false, or vice versa. |
| And | Performs a logical conjunction of two expressions. If they are both `True`, the result is `True`. If either of the expressions is `False`, the result is `False`. If either expression is `Null`, the result is `Null`. |
| Or | Performs a logical disjunction of two expressions. If the value of either expression is `True`, the result is `True`; otherwise, the result is `False`. Just like the `And` operator, if either expression is `Null`, the result is also `Null`. |
| Xor | Performs a logical exclusions (exclusive or) on two expressions. The result is the converse of the `Eqv` operator. If both expressions are `True` or if both are `False`, the result is `False`. If one expression is `True` and the other is `False`, the result is `True`. |
| Eqv | Performs a logical equivalence on two expressions. If both expressions are `True` or if both are `False`, the result is `True`; otherwise the result is `False`. |
| Imp | Performs a logical implication on two expressions. If both expressions are `True` or if both are `False`, the result is `True`. If the first is `True` and the second is `False`, the result is `False`, but if the first is `False` and the second is `True`, the result is `True`. |

# Create a Subroutine

You can easily create a *subroutine* within the Visual Basic Editor that executes a series of VBA commands. Each macro that runs in Excel is actually just a subroutine that contains blocks of VBA code. That said, a single subroutine can call other subroutines and functions, creating a macro that is much more complex than just a simple subroutine.

VBA provides essentially two different types of subroutines: *private* and *public*. When you create a macro with the Macro Recorder, the subroutine it creates is public, meaning that all procedures, including the Macro dialog box, can access and see it. Conversely, only other procedures within the same module can access a private subroutine. Excel hides all Private subroutines from the Macro dialog box and you cannot activate them with key combinations. You should mark subroutines as private if you do not want them

accessible as macros. You mark a subroutine as private by placing Private before the `Sub` statement, for example: `Private Sub SampleSub()`. Typically, other subroutines within the same module call private subroutines. A subroutine is called using the `Call` statement: `Call SampleSub()`. Excel considers any subroutines that do not have the `Private` keyword to be public. That being said, the use of the `Public` keyword is really unnecessary because a subroutine with no keyword is the same as one with the `Public` keyword.

VBA does allow a subroutine to be called without the `Call` statement. Even though VBA does not require it, you should always use the `Call` statement to remind you that another procedure is being called. Using the `Call` statement makes your code much more readable because another user can quickly look at the code and see that another subroutine is being called.

## Create a Subroutine

**①** In the Project window, click the project where you want to add a new module.

**②** Click Insert→Module.

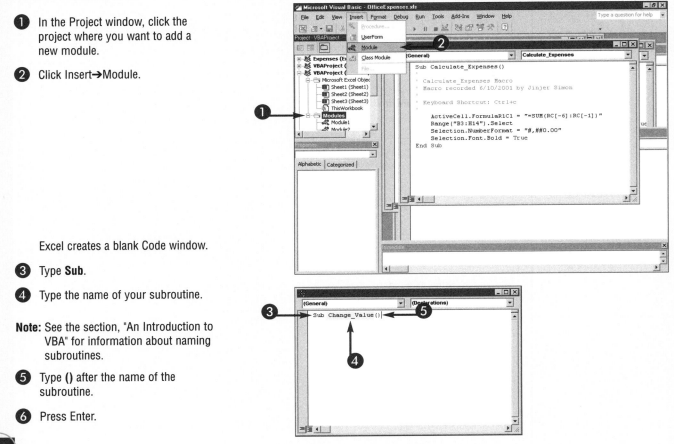

Excel creates a blank Code window.

**③** Type **Sub**.

**④** Type the name of your subroutine.

**Note:** See the section, "An Introduction to VBA" for information about naming subroutines.

**⑤** Type **()** after the name of the subroutine.

**⑥** Press Enter.

The Visual Basic Editor inserts the `End Sub` command when you press Enter.

**7** Type the Macro code.

**8** Switch to Excel and open the Macro dialog box.

**Note:** To open the Macro dialog box, see Chapter 1.

● The new subroutine appears as a macro along with the other available macros.

```
(General)                          Change_Value

Sub Change_Value()
  Cells(1,1) = "45"
End Sub
```

```
Macro name:
Change_Value                                    Run

PERSONAL.XLS!Calculate_Expenses                 Cancel
Budget.xls!Calculate_Total
Change_Font                                     Step Into
Change_Value
Expenses.xls!SumCells                           Edit

                                                Create

                                                Delete

Macros in:   All Open Workbooks                 Options...
Description
```

## Extra

You may have situations where you want to pass parameters to subroutines. A *parameter* is essentially a variable that receives an argument from the statement that you use to call the subroutine. Just like standard variables, you want to specify the data type for the subroutine parameters to avoid converting them into variants.

In the example, the `Call` statement calls the `AddValues` subroutine and passes in the values contained in the `Value1` and `Value2` variables. You can call a subroutine that has parameters from the Macro dialog box. Other procedures typically call subroutines with arguments.

**Example:**
```
Sub AddValues (Val1 As Integer, Val2 As Integer)
    Dim Total As Integer
    Total = Val1 + Val2
    MsgBox (Total)
End Sub
```

Because you cannot call the subroutine as a macro from Excel, you must create a separate subroutine that calls the `AddValues` subroutine. Within this subroutine you need to specify the values for the `Value1` and `Value2` parameters that pass to the `AddValues` subroutine.

**Example:**
```
Sub TotalValues
  Dim Value1 As Integer
  Dim Value2 As Integer
  Value1 = 5
  Value2 = 7
  Call AddValues (Value1, Value2)
End Sub
```

# Create a Function

You can create *functions* to return a value to the procedure that calls them. Unlike subroutines, you cannot call functions directly from the Macro dialog box. When working with macros, only a subroutine can call a function. Like subroutines, functions consist of blocks of VBA code grouped together to perform a common task or series of tasks.

At first glance the value of a function may appear somewhat limiting. But unlike a subroutine, which does not return a value, a function always returns a value making them ideal for performing calculations. For example, you can create a function that always calculates the sales tax for an item and returns that amount.

There are essentially two different types of functions: private and public. All modules within the workbook can access a *public* function. However, only other procedures

within the same module can access a *private* function. A function is marked as private by placing `Private` before the `Function` statement as in the example: `Private Function SampleFunc(Param) As Integer`. Excel considers any functions that do not have the `Private` keyword to be public. That being said, using the `Public` keyword is redundant because a function with no keyword is the same as one with the `Public` keyword.

Other functions and subroutines within the same module typically call private functions. Because functions return a value, they are typically called as part of an expression. For example, you can assign the value returned by a function to a variable: `FunctionValue = SampleFunc(Param)`. This line of code exists in a subroutine that calls the function. When Excel encounters this code, the function executes using the value of the `Param` parameter and the result of the function is placed in the `FunctionValue` variable.

## Create a Function

① In the Project window, click to highlight the project where you want to add a new module.

② Click Insert→Module.

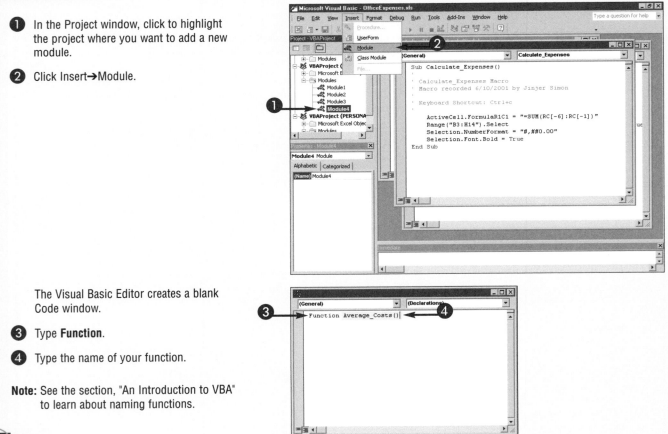

The Visual Basic Editor creates a blank Code window.

③ Type **Function**.

④ Type the name of your function.

**Note:** See the section, "An Introduction to VBA" to learn about naming functions.

⑤ In parentheses, type the names of the function parameters.

⑥ Type **As**.

⑦ Type the data type to be returned by the function.

**Note:** See the section, "An Introduction to VBA" for more information about VBA data types.

⑧ Press Enter.

The Visual Basic Editor inserts the End Function command when you press Enter.

⑨ Type **FunctionName = FunctionVar** replacing FunctionName with the function name and FunctionVar with the value of the function.

The function is created.

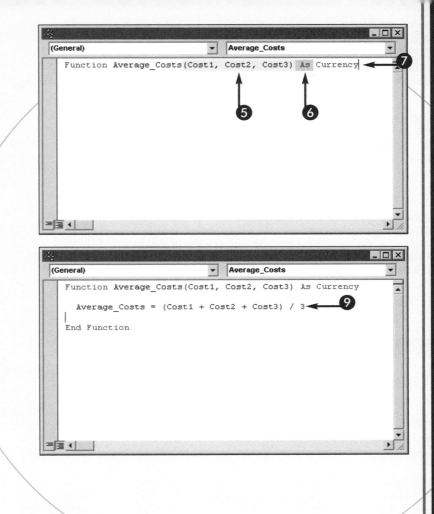

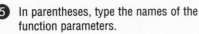

## Extra

You can create VBA functions that you can use within Excel directly to create formulas. When you create a public function in the Visual Basic Editor, it appears in the Insert Function dialog box that displays when you click Insert→Function within Excel. The VBE places the functions that you create under the User Defined category on the Insert Function dialog box. You can use these VBA functions directly in your worksheet to create formulas in the same fashion that you use the built-in functions that come standard with Excel. Keep in mind that the VBA functions you create are available only on the Insert Function dialog box when the corresponding workbook containing the function is open within Excel. Therefore, if you create a specific function that you want to use with all your workbooks, you must add the function to the Personal Macro Workbook, Personal.xls, to ensure that it is always available from within Excel. The Personal Macro Workbook always opens with Excel, so any macros and functions it contains are always available. See Chapter 1 for more information on the Personal Macro Workbook.

# Declare a Variable

You can use variable declaration to make your VBA code run much more efficiently. By definition, *variable declaration* means that you specify the data type of the variable when you declare the variable. In other words, if you intend for the variable to contain only integer values, you declare an integer variable.

Unlike some programming languages, VBA lets you use variables that have not been declared. However, if you misspell a variable within your code, VBA may treat the misspelled variable as a totally different variable. For example, if you use the variable MthRent throughout your code and inadvertently type it as MnthRent, VBA sees it as a new variable and assumes that MthRent and MnthRent are two different variables. To ensure that variables are always properly declared, use the Option Explicit statement as the first statement in a module before you type any procedure code.

You can set the Require Variable Declaration option in the Visual Basic Editor to ensure that variables are always declared for all created procedures. If you select this option, the Visual Basic Editor places the Option Explicit statement at the top of each created module. You can select the Require Variable Declaration check box on the Editor dialog box within the Visual Basic Editor.

Even if the variable is declared, you should also type it as part of the declaration. VBA treats all variables without a data type as *variants.* A variant is VBA's all-purpose data type because it can essentially contain any type of data. In fact, the same variable can contain an integer value at one point and a string value at another location within the same module. Because VBA is forced to interrogate the value in the variant variables to determine the type of data, your code becomes less efficient when you do not specify the data type.

## Declare a Variable

① Type **Option Explicit** at the top of the module.

② Position the cursor after the Sub statement.

③ Type **Dim**.

④ Type the name of the variable.

⑤ Type **As** after the variable name.

⑥ Type your variable data type.

**Note:** See the section "An Introduction to VBA" for more on Variable names and Data types.

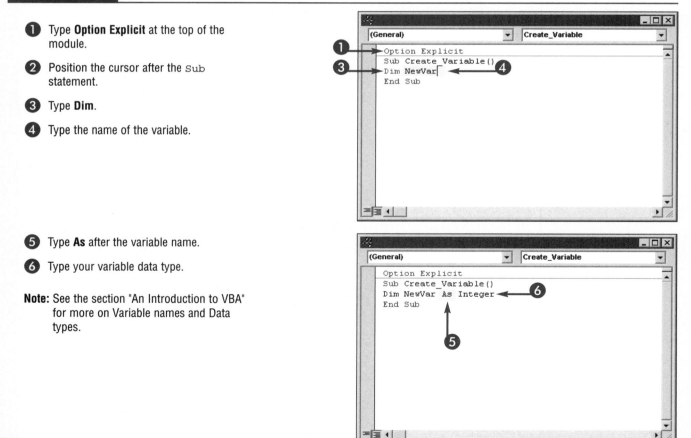

7 Press Enter.

8 Type your variable name.

9 Type an equal sign (=) and a starting value for your variable.

10 Type **MsgBox(*VarName*)**, replacing VarName with the name of your variable.

The MsgBox function displays a dialog box.

11 Switch to Excel and run the corresponding macro.

The message box displays the value to the variable you specified in step 8.

```
(General)                        Create_Variable

Option Explicit
Sub Create_Variable()
Dim NewVar As Integer

NewVar = "45"
MsgBox(NewVar)
End Sub
```

| | A | B | C | D | E | F | G | H | I | J | K |
|---|---|---|---|---|---|---|---|---|---|---|---|
| 1 | | | | Office Expenses | | | | | | | |
| 2 | | Rent | Advertising | Phone | ISP | Parking | Misc. | | | | |
| 3 | January | $350.00 | $400.00 | $200.00 | $110.00 | $50.00 | $175.00 | $1,285.00 | | | |
| 4 | February | 350 | 350 | 240 | 110 | 50 | 145 | | | | |
| 5 | March | 350 | 550 | 310 | 110 | 50 | 123 | | | | |
| 6 | April | 350 | 795 | 250 | 110 | 50 | 211 | | | | |
| 7 | May | 350 | 800 | 245 | 110 | 50 | 345 | | | | |
| 8 | June | 350 | 795 | 310 | 110 | 50 | 149 | | | | |
| 9 | July | 350 | 600 | 340 | | | 190 | | | | |
| 10 | August | 350 | 910 | 215 | | | 256 | | | | |
| 11 | September | 350 | 845 | 400 | 45 | | 298 | | | | |
| 12 | October | 350 | 765 | 450 | | | 245 | | | | |
| 13 | November | 350 | 900 | 465 | OK | | 405 | | | | |
| 14 | December | 350 | 1005 | 500 | | | 605 | | | | |
| 15 | | | | | | | | | | | |
| 16 | | | | | | | | | | | |

## Apply It

You can quickly specify a variable's data type by using the VBA type declaration characters within the declaration statement. Using this method is basically a shortcut for typing the variable.

**Example:**
```
Dim NewVar%
```

Excel provides six different characters that you can use to specify the data type for a variable. In the sample declaration, which declares a variable containing integer values, the type declaration statement replaces the As datatype portion of the declaration statement.

| CHARACTER | DATA TYPE |
|---|---|
| % | Integer |
| & | Long |
| ! | Single |
| # | Double |
| @ | Currency |
| $ | String |

You can shorten your VBA code by declaring variables using one Dim statement. In other words, you declare multiple variables on one line by typing **Dim** followed by each variable and the appropriate data type.

**Example:**
```
Dim Int1 As Integer, Int2 As Integer, Int3 As
Integer
```

Although VBA allows you to lump a group of variables together using one Dim statement and one data type, it does not assign the data type you would expect. For example, you typically declare all three variables as integer.

**Example:**
```
Dim Int1, Int2, Int3 As Integer
```

In reality, VBA only assigns an integer data type to Int3. VBA assigns the other variables a data type of variant.

# Perform Mathematical Calculations

Y ou can perform many types of mathematical calculations within your macros. VBA provides several different operators for performing mathematical calculations within your procedures. Because Excel typically contains numeric values, you frequently use VBA operators to create Excel macros.

VBA includes eight different arithmetic operators for performing calculations. These operators include + (addition), – (subtraction), ^ (exponential), * (multiplication), / (division), \ (integer division), and MOD (Modulo - return remainder).

You typically use operators to perform a mathematical operation on a specific variable. For example, you frequently use the + operator with a For Next loop to increment the loop counter variable. For example, you can read the statement i = i + 1 to mean: "Take the value of the variable i, add 1 to it, and place the result back in the

variable." You frequently encounter this type of mathematical calculation in source code for all programming languages.

VBA provides three different operators that deal with dividing one value by another: /, \, and MOD. Each of these operators returns a different type of value. The /, or division, operator divides two values and returns the entire result, including any decimal portion that results when the numbers do not divide evenly. The \, or integer division, operator divides two values and returns only the integer portion of the result. Any remainder is discarded with this operator. Finally, the MOD operator divides two numbers and returns only the remainder. This operator works well for predetermining if two numeric values divide evenly. If a zero is returned, the values divided evenly and no remainder exists.

See "Arithmetic Operators" in the section "An Introduction to VBA" for more information about the available operators and the precedence order in which calculations take place.

## Perform Mathematical Calculations

① Create a subroutine.

**Note:** See "Create a Subroutine" earlier in this chapter for more information.

② Declare two variables as numeric data types.

**Note:** See "Declare a Variable" earlier in this chapter.

③ Assign initial values to each variable.

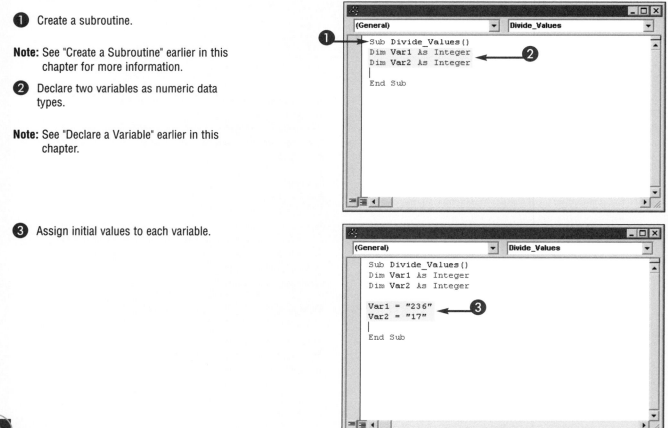

④ Type **Cells(1,1) = Var1/Var2**, replacing Cells(1,1) with the location for the result and Var1 and Var2 with the variables declared in step 2.

⑤ Press Enter.

You can replace the / (division operator) with any of the VBA mathematical operators.

⑥ Switch to Excel and run the macro.

The result of the mathematical calculation displays in the location specified in step 4.

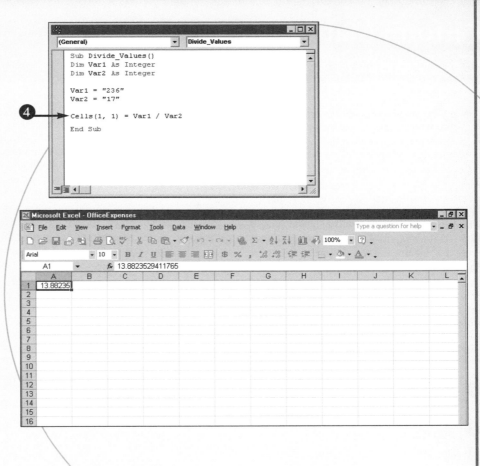

## Extra

You can reference a specific cell in a worksheet with the Cells property. With this property, you can reference a specific cell in a worksheet using one of two methods. The first method enables you to specify the row and column number of the appropriate cell. By specifying the row and column number to reference cell A5, you can type Cells(5,1). This is intepreted as the cell in the fifth row and the first column. Using the cell reference method, you can reference rows from 1 to 65,536 and columns from 1 to 256.

The second method numbers each cell on the worksheet between 1 and 16,777,216 (65,536 rows by 256 columns). With this method you specify one numeric value for the cell, which may confuse you, at first. For example, cell M1 is referenced as Cells(13).

| EXCEL CELL | COLUMN/ROW REFERENCE | NUMERIC REFERENCE |
|------------|---------------------|-------------------|
| A1 | Cells(1,1) | Cells(1) |
| A2 | Cells(2,1) | Cells(257) |
| C5 | Cells(5,3) | Cells(515) |

# Create a Constant

You can create constants to refer to a value, or a string that never changes. For example, given that a week always contains seven days, you can declare a constant with a value of 7 when you place that value in a procedure.

Just as you do with variables, you declare constants with a specific data type. In fact, constants use the same data types that variables use. If you do not specify a data type for a constant, VBA treats the value as a variant. Because constants never change, the functionality of your code to specify a data type improves. For more information, refer to the section "An Introduction to VBA."

Unlike a variable, you cannot alter a constant's value after you declare that constant. For example, if you assign the constant NewVar a value of 32 and attempt to reassign it a value of 45, you receive an error message when your code executes.

Although VBA allows you to declare constants anywhere in your code, consider declaring them at the beginning of the procedure. You can declare multiple constants on one line of code by placing a comma between each constant definition. For example, the following code declares two constants:

```
Const NewString = "Excel Macros", Version As
Integer = 2002.
```

You can name constants using the same naming rules as variables. Essentially a constant can contain as many as 255 characters in length and use both alphabetical and numeric characters. For more information, see the section "An Introduction to VBA" earlier in this chapter.

By default, a constant value is private and only available for use within a particular procedure or module for constants declared at the code module level. You can make constants public and therefore useable by other procedures within the same workbook project by placing the Public keyword before the Const statement.

## Create a Constant

① Position the cursor after the Sub statement of a subroutine.

② Type **Const**.

③ Type the name of the constant.

**Note:** See the section "An Introduction to VBA" for more information on naming variables and constants.

④ Type **As** after the constant's name.

⑤ Type your constant data type.

**Note:** See the section "An Introduction to VBA" for more information.

⑥ Type an equal sign (=) and a starting value for your variable.

⑦ Press Enter.

⑧ Type **MsgBox(Const*Name*)**, replacing `ConstName` with the name of your Const.

**Note:** See Chapter 7 for more information on the `MsgBox` function.

⑨ Run the corresponding macro in Excel.

The message box displays the value to the variable you specified in step 6.

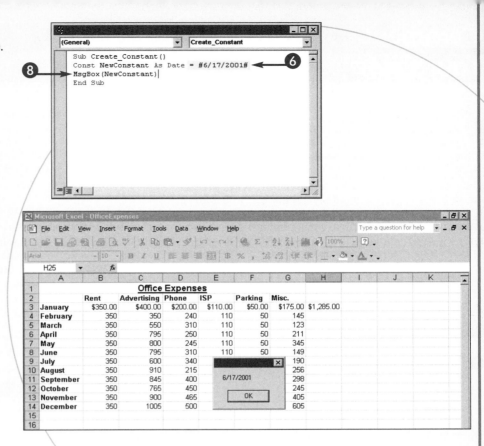

---

## Extra

VBA provides over 700 built-in constants, which you can insert into your code at any point without declaring them. The Excel VBA object model adds another 1,266, all of which begin with either xl or vb. You can use these constants anywhere, and you do not need to know their actual values in order to use them. Two of the most commonly used VBA constants deal with inserting carriage returns, `vbCrLf`, and tab characters, `vbTab`, in your output. Although each of these constants has a numeric equivalent, you simply type the name of the appropriate constant value in your code. To find a list of all VBA and Excel VBA Object Model constants, press F2 to view the Object Browser and search for Constant. Most of the constant values are self-explanatory, based upon the name. Appendix A also includes many of the constant values that you use throughout this book. Many parameter values require a specific type of constant value. For example, with the `MsgBox` function you use one of the `vbMsgBoxStyle` constants for the value of the `Buttons` parameter to indicate the type of buttons on the message box, as follows:

**Example:**
```
MsgBox("Select button", vbYesNoCancel)
```

# Comment
# Your Code

Y ou can provide your reader an explanation of how you intend your code to function by commenting your code. A *comment* adds descriptive text to your code that provides the reader some sense of the functionality of the referenced code.

Whenever a subroutine or function executes, VBA ignores comment lines, so you can and should use them liberally. It may seem monotonous to describe your code today, because you already know what it does. However, comments help you quickly determine code functionality, especially a few months from now when you come back to work with the code again. Of course, comments only help if they provide enough information to describe the code. A reader should be able to read the comments only, without studying the code, and get a good sense of what the code does. For

example, a comment like "sums the values" does not provide any information about the code other than stating that the code adds some values together. A better comment is "Sums the values in cells A1 and A2 and places the result in cell A3" because it describes the actual process.

You can add comments as entire lines of text or place them at the end of a line of code. To indicate a comment, type an apostrophe at the beginning of the comment line. VBA ignores all text from the apostrophe to the end of the line.

The only time that VBA does not treat an apostrophe as a comment is when you type the apostrophe within quotation marks as part of a string of text. For example, VBA does not treat the following statement as a comment: Book = "Jinjer's Book".

## Comment Your Code

① In the Project window, double-click to select the module that contains the procedure you want to document.

The selected module code displays in a Code window.

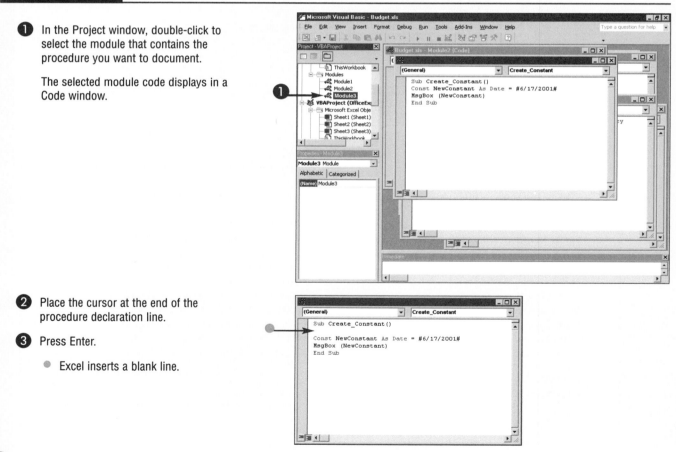

② Place the cursor at the end of the procedure declaration line.

③ Press Enter.

● Excel inserts a blank line.

④ Type an apostrophe (') at the beginning of the line.

⑤ Type comments describing the selected procedure.

Start each comment line with an apostrophe.

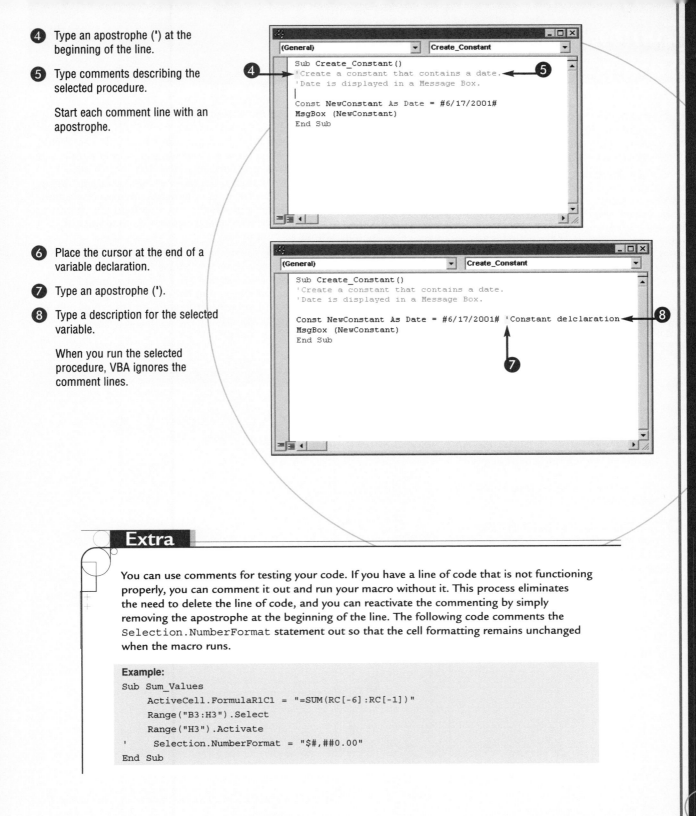

```
Sub Create_Constant()
'Create a constant that contains a date.
'Date is displayed in a Message Box.

Const NewConstant As Date = #6/17/2001#
MsgBox (NewConstant)
End Sub
```

⑥ Place the cursor at the end of a variable declaration.

⑦ Type an apostrophe (').

⑧ Type a description for the selected variable.

When you run the selected procedure, VBA ignores the comment lines.

```
Sub Create_Constant()
'Create a constant that contains a date.
'Date is displayed in a Message Box.

Const NewConstant As Date = #6/17/2001# 'Constant delclaration
MsgBox (NewConstant)
End Sub
```

## Extra

You can use comments for testing your code. If you have a line of code that is not functioning properly, you can comment it out and run your macro without it. This process eliminates the need to delete the line of code, and you can reactivate the commenting by simply removing the apostrophe at the beginning of the line. The following code comments the `Selection.NumberFormat` statement out so that the cell formatting remains unchanged when the macro runs.

**Example:**
```
Sub Sum_Values
    ActiveCell.FormulaR1C1 = "=SUM(RC[-6]:RC[-1])"
    Range("B3:H3").Select
    Range("H3").Activate
'    Selection.NumberFormat = "$#,##0.00"
End Sub
```

# Join Two Strings

Y ou can join the contents of two string variables — actually multiple strings — together to create one string. You commonly refer to the process of joining strings together as *concatenation*.

The only real limitation to joining strings together is the potential of exceeding the declared or maximum length of the string variable receiving the joined string. When you declare a fixed-length string variable using the Dim statement, you also typically specify that string's maximum length. A combined set of strings can contain a maximum of 65,535 characters. Variable-length string variables, on the other hand, can hold up to 2 billion characters, and you do not have to specify their length.

Each character in a string takes 1 byte of storage plus additional storage for the string header. When you declare a string, you specify the size for a fixed-length string. VBA

does not extend the size of a fixed-length string to store a larger string. If two joined strings form a string larger than the space allows, VBA truncates the string to fit the alloted space. For example, if you name a string variable Name with a fixed-length of ten characters, and you specify Name = "Hungry " & "Minds", the Name variable contains string Hungry Min. VBA truncates the remaining two characters, ds, because the string variable can only hold ten characters. Keep in mind that VBA also treats spaces that you add to the strings as characters.

Although the concatenation operator (&) joins strings together, VBA also allows you to use the + (addition) operator to combine strings. Using the concatenation operator to show a distinction between a string concatenation and an arithmetic addition statement adheres to better coding standards.

## Join Two Strings

① Create a subroutine.

② Press Enter.

③ Type **Dim TestString1 As String * 10**, replacing TestString1 with the first string variable and 10 with the string length.

You can repeat step 3 to create a second string variable.

④ Type **Dim TestString3 As String * 20**, replacing TestString3 with the variable to contain the concatenated string and 20 with the string length.

⑤ Type **TestString1 ="Excel"**, replacing TestString1 with the variable in step 4 and "Excel" with the string value.

Repeat step 5 for the second variable.

```
Sub Join_Strings()
Dim TestString1 As String * 10
Dim TestString2 As String * 10
Dim TestString3 As String * 20

End Sub
```

```
Sub Join_Strings()
Dim TestString1 As String * 10
Dim TestString2 As String * 10
Dim TestString3 As String * 20

TestString1 = "Excel"
TestString2 = "Macros"

End Sub
```

⑥ Type **TestString3 = TestString1 & TestString2** replacing `TestString3` with the variable to contain the concatenated string and `TestString1` and `TestString2` with the string variables.

⑦ Type **Cells(1,1) = TestString3**, replacing `TestString3` with the variable containing the concatenated string.

⑧ Run the corresponding macro in Excel.

● The value of the first cell becomes the concatenated string created in step 7.

```
Sub Join_Strings()
Dim TestString1 As String * 10
Dim TestString2 As String * 10
Dim TestString3 As String * 20

TestString1 = "Excel"
TestString2 = "Macros"

TestString3 = TestString1 & TestString2
Cells(1, 1) = TestString3

End Sub
```

## Extra

To ensure that a string has the desired length, you can use the Len function to determine the number of characters in the string. Based upon the value returned by the built-in VBA function, you determine whether you can concatenate the strings without VBA truncating them. For example, if each string you want to join is ten characters in length, you must make the variable that receives the concatenated string at least 20 characters in length, or VBA truncates the string.

If you check the length of a fixed-length variable, it always returns the declared string length, even if the number of characters saved in the string is less than the declared length, as illustrated in the following examples.

**Example**
```
Dim StringTest1 As String * 15
StringTest1 = "SampleString"
Len(StringTest1)
```

In the above, the `StringTest1` string variable has a fixed-length of 15 no matter what you add to the variable. When you add the string `"SampleString"` to the variable — even though the string only has 12 characters — the Len function returns a value of 15.

**Example**
```
Dim StringTest2 As String
StringTest2 = "SampleString"
Len(StringTest2)
```

The `StringTest2` string variable has a variable length. When you add the string `"SampleString"` to the variable, the length of the variable adjusts to fit the string. Because the length of the string is 12 characters, the Len function returns a value of 12.

# An Introduction to the Excel Object Model

**D**esigned around the ability to access and manipulate objects, VBA has access to an *Object Model* in each Microsoft Office product, including Excel, that enables you to interact with each application. Using the Object Model, you can access everything from the entire application to an individual cell in a worksheet.

*Objects* represent the individual pieces of each application. Every object has specific properties and methods associated with it. You use properties and methods to capture events and changes that occur with the selected object.

With such an enormous number of objects, properties, and methods, you may find remembering them all is virtually impossible. Luckily, the Visual Basic Editor provides the Object Browser, with which you can quickly locate and determine the corresponding properties and methods available for an object. You can learn how to use the Object Browser by performing the tasks in this chapter.

## Excel Objects

The Excel Object Model provides nearly 200 different objects and more than 5,000 corresponding properties and methods for use in your VBA code. Each object represents an element of the Excel application. For example, the `Application` object refers to the entire Excel application, but a `Worksheet` object refers to an individual worksheet.

Most objects have *child objects*. A child object is an object that is part of a larger object. For example, a `Worksheet` object is a child object to a `Workbook` object because worksheets are part of a workbook. All objects in the Excel Object Model are the children of at least one other object, except the `Application` object. All objects are under the `Application` object either as children or children of another `Application` object. Because

of this hierarchy within the Object Model, you typically need to reference the parent object with a child object. For example, to access the second worksheet in the current workbook you type **ThisWorkbook.Worksheets(2).**

The Object Model groups common objects into *collections*. For example, the `Workbook` object identifies an individual workbook, but the `Workbooks` collection refers to all open workbooks.

Although the list of available objects is rather extensive, you use only about six frequently: `Application`, `Workbook`, `Worksheet`, `Chart`, `Range`, and `Dialog`. Because you use these objects extensively when you work with Excel Macros, it is a good idea to familiarize yourself with these objects, which the remainder of this book covers.

### Application Object

The `Application` object represents the entire Excel program. All other objects are children of the `Application` object on the Excel Object Model.

The `Application` object has several different properties and methods. Those that return the most common user-interface values, such as the `ActiveCell` property, do not require the use of the `Application` object in the statement. Both of these statements are valid:

**Example:**
```
Application.ActiveCell

ActiveCell
```

### Workbook Object

The `Workbook` object represents an individual workbook that you have open in Excel. You can use the `Workbooks` property of the `Application` object to return a `Workbooks` collection, which contains all of the `Workbook` objects for the workbooks that you currently have open in Excel. See Chapter 9 for more information about dealing with the `Workbook` object.

## Worksheet Object

The `Worksheet` object represents an individual worksheet that you have open in Excel. You can use the `Worksheets` property of the `Workbook` object to return a `Worksheets` collection that contains all of the `Worksheet` objects for worksheets available in a particular workbook. See Chapter 10 for more information about working with the `Worksheet` object.

## Chart Object

The `Chart` object represents an individual Excel chart. You can use this object to create and reference charts that you embed in individual worksheets or that reside in chart sheets. See Chapter 13 for more information about working with charts.

## Range Object

The `Range` object enables you to reference an individual cell or range of cells. `Range` objects are returned by several different properties and methods, including the `Range` property.

**Example:**

```
Range("B3")
```

See Chapter 11 for more information about dealing with the `Range` object.

## Dialog Object

The `Dialog` object references each of the built-in dialog boxes available in Excel. Excel stores these dialog boxes in the `Dialogs` collection. You can use the constant value associated with each Excel dialog box object to view the dialog box. You can view individual dialog boxes by using the `Show` method.

The names for each of the dialog boxes begin with `xlDialog` followed by a unique value that references the appropriate dialog box. For example, `xlSaveAs` references the Save As dialog box in Excel.

This object refers only to existing Excel dialog boxes. It does not refer to any new dialog boxes that you may create. For information about creating dialog boxes, see Chapter 12.

## Excel Properties

Each object in the Excel Object Model has corresponding properties. Use of these properties enables you to view or change the characteristics of the object. For example, you can use the `Value` property to change the value of a range in a `Range` collection.

You can also use properties to change an aspect of behavior for an object. For example, you use the `Hidden` property to hide or unhide an object.

To specify a property for an object, combine the object name with the property name, as follows:

**Example:**

```
Range.Value = 45
```

## Excel Methods

Each object in the Excel Object Model corresponds to certain methods. You can use the available methods to perform actions on or for the selected object. For example, you can use the `Copy` method to copy the worksheet specified by the `Worksheet` object and place it in another location in the corresponding workbook.

To specify a method for an object, combine the object name with the method name, as in the following example:

**Example:**

```
Worksheets(1).Copy After:=Worksheets(3)
```

## Object Collections

The Excel Object Model allows for multiple objects of the same type, such as multiple open `Worksheet` objects in a workbook. To make these objects more accessible, Excel groups them together in an object *collection*. For example, each `Workbook` object contains a `Worksheets` collection. You access a collection similar to an array where an index value is used to reference the desired value in the collection. The following code accesses the second worksheet in the `Worksheets` collection:

**Example:**

```
Worksheets(2)
```

# Using the Object Browser

Eliminating the need to remember required syntax, the Object Browser enables you to quickly search for an object, property, or method that matches a desired keyword. For example, to add a new worksheet when you do not remember the appropriate method, you can use the search option on the Object Browser to find all objects that deal with the Add method.

The Object Browser refers to each object as a class and lists them within the Classes list box. The Object Browser lists all properties and methods associated with an object selected in the Classes list box within the Members list box. You view the associated properties and methods of an object by selecting the object. The Members list box also shows which VBA functions you can use to return the selected object.

The Object Browser has six different object libraries, which you can use to view object information: Excel, MSForms,

Office, Stdole, VBA, and VBA project. You can view all information by selecting the All Libraries option, or you can select an individual object library.

The Excel object library contains all of the objects, methods, and properties in the Excel Object Model. These are the objects discussed throughout this book.

Select the MSForms object library to view objects that you can use to create custom dialog boxes for your macros.

The Office object library contains objects that are common to all Microsoft Office products.

Select the Stdole object library to find objects that you can use for OLE automation.

The VBA object library contains specific Visual Basic for Applications objects.

Each open workbook and the corresponding modules are listed as available objects under VBAProject.

## Using the Object Browser

### OPEN THE OBJECT BROWSER

① Open the Code window for the desired module.

**Note:** See Chapter 2 for more information on working with modules.

② Select View→Object Brower.

Alternately, you can press F2.

### SEARCH THE OBJECT BROWSER

The Object Browser dialog box displays.

③ Click ▾ to display a list of available libraries.

④ Click the desired library.

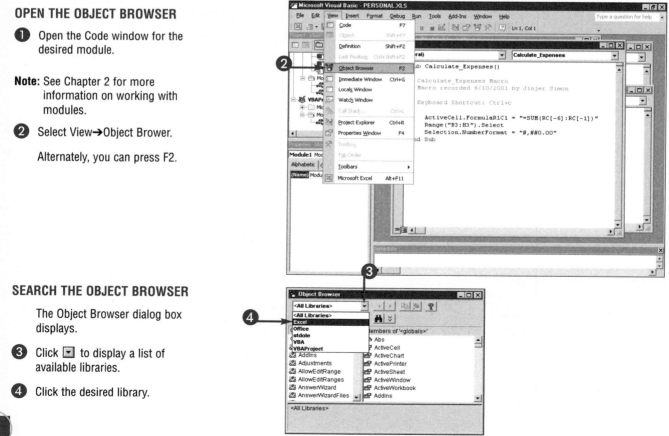

⑤ Type the search string in the field under the libraries.

⑥ Click the Search button (🔍).

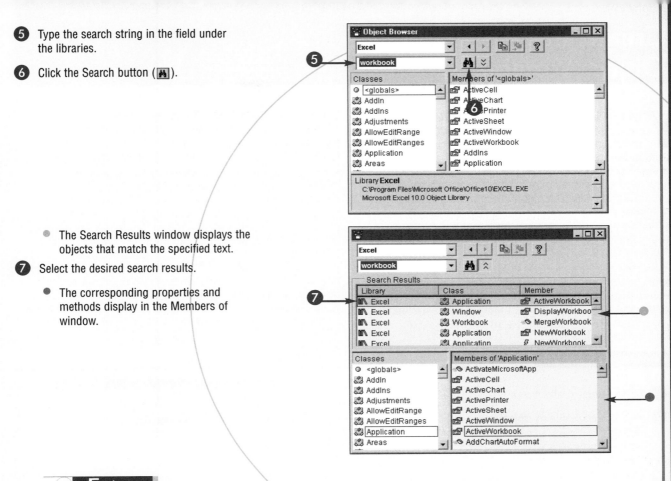

● The Search Results window displays the objects that match the specified text.

⑦ Select the desired search results.

● The corresponding properties and methods display in the Members of window.

---

## Extra

Besides maintaining a list of all objects with their corresponding properties and methods, the Object Browser keeps track of the constant values assigned to object properties. It also keeps track of parameter values for various object methods and VBA functions. For example, the ChartType property enables you to specify the type for a chart. You need to use one of the XlChartType constant values as the value for this property. For example, ThisWorkbook. Chart.Type = xlPie creates a pie chart. The ChartType property accepts only one of these constant values. You can view the list of available XlChartType constants within the Object Browser by typing ChartType in the Search Text field and clicking the Search button (🔍). If you select the XlChartType value in the Classes list box, you see all of the chart type constant values within the Members list box.

You can quickly find more information about an object, property, or method selected on the Object Browser window by pressing F1. When you press F1, the Microsoft Visual Basic Online Help displays help for the item selected on the Object Browser window.

# Create an Object Variable

You can simplify your VBA code by creating object *variables.* Creating object variables enables you to reference a specific object within your code. Although you do not need to use an object variable, VBA enables you to reference objects directly by typing the complete object reference each time you want to work with an object; not only is this method more cumbersome, but it also makes your code run more slowly. Using object variables, on the other hand, greatly simplifies your code because object variables are typically shorter than complete object references. Also, VBA code typically runs faster when you use object variables in your code.

You declare object variables in much the same fashion as a standard variable. You use the Dim statement to declare the variable and the As statement to identify the variable as an object variable. The data type for the variable is the corresponding object type.

For example, the statement Dim ObjectVar As Worksheet creates an object variable named ObjectVar that is a Worksheet object. You can create object variables for each of the objects in the Excel Object Model.

After you create an object variable, you assign a specific object reference to the variable. You assign an object to a variable in basically the same fashion as with standard variables. The difference is that the Set statement must precede the assignment statement. The following statement sets the value of ObjectVar to point to Sheet1 in the workbook: Set ObjectVar = ActiveWorkbook. Worksheets("Sheet1"). Also, when you assign an object to a variable, you are only assigning a reference to the object to the variable and not the actual object value. In other words, in the sample line of code, ObjectVar simply points to Sheet1 within the active workbook.

## Create an Object Variable

① Click to place ⊺ after the Sub statement.

② Type **Dim VarName As ObjectType**, replacing VarName with the name of the object variable and ObjectType with the Excel object type.

③ Press Enter.

④ Type **Set VarName = ExcelObject**, replacing VarName with the variable name and ExcelObject with the object assigned to the variable.

⑤ Press Enter.

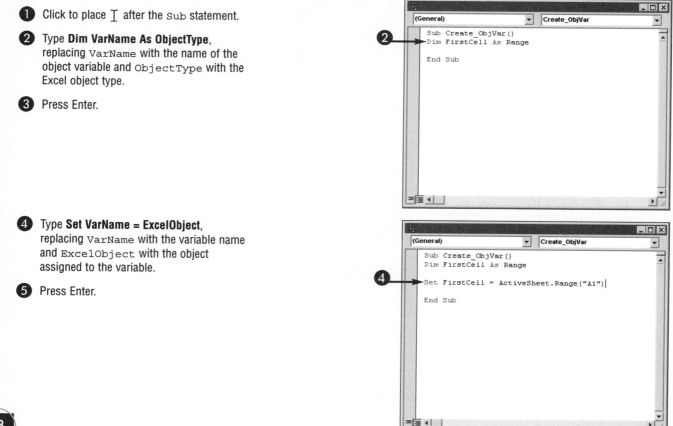

**6** Type **MsgBox(VarName)**, replacing
VarName with the variable created in step 2.

**7** Switch to Excel and run the corresponding
macro.

The message box displays the contents of
the object variable.

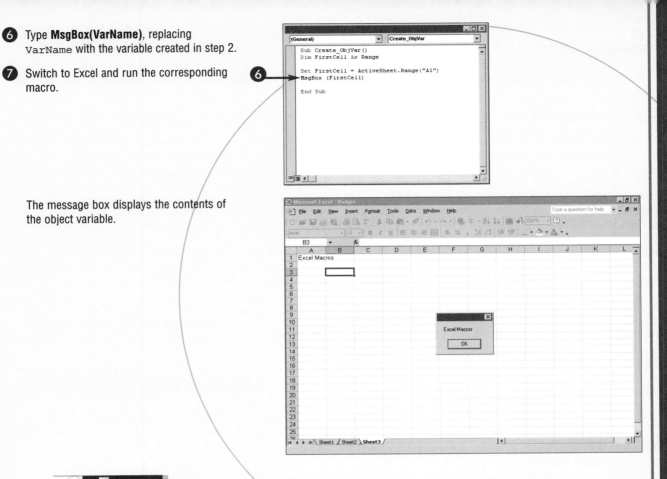

If you want to refer to the currently selected
worksheet in a workbook, you can do so by
using the ActiveSheet property. You use
this property in place of an object reference to
a specific worksheet, such as Worksheets(1),
which refers to the first worksheet in a
workbook. Using the ActiveSheet property,
you can reference whichever worksheet is active
at the time your procedure executes. For
example, SheetName = ActiveSheet.Name
assigns the name of the currently active
worksheet to the SheetName variable.

The ActiveSheet property refers to any type
of sheet within a workbook. Therefore, if the
currently selected sheet is actually a Chart
sheet, the ActiveSheet property returns a
reference to the appropriate chart sheet. See
Chapter 10 for more information on working
with worksheets.

When you create object variables you are
essentially just creating object pointers. Unlike
a standard variable that is the name of a
memory location containing the variable's
value, an object variable actually points to the
memory location that stores a pointer to the
object. For example, in the following code
ObjVar stores the pointer to cell B2 in the
worksheet.

**Example:**
```
Dim ObjVar As Range
Set ObjVar = ActiveSheet.Cells(2, 2)
```

# Change the Properties of an Object

Y ou can change the value of an object, its appearance, and so on, by modifying the properties associated with an object. When working with objects, you do not change the object directly; instead, you make changes to the object by altering the values of the properties associated with the object. For example, when working with a cell on a worksheet, you use the `Value` property to change the value of the cell. If you change to the font style, however, you modify the properties for the `Font` object, such as the `Bold`, `Italic`, `Underline`, and `Size` properties.

When you make several property changes to the same object, doing so typically requires repeating the name of the object each time. Even if you have assigned the object to an object variable, you must repeat the variable name. For example, if you use the statement `Set CellFont = ActiveSheet.Cells(1,1).Font` as the object variable for the `Font` object, you still need to reference the `Font` object

variable each time you change a font attribute. To set the font to bold, you type **CellFont.Bold = True**. Then, if you want to set the font size, you again reference the `Font` object by typing **CellFont.Font.Size = 12**.

Even with the use of an object variable, you must repeat the object variable name each time you change a font setting, making the code complex. You can simplify this type of code with the `With` statement. Instead of typing the object variable reference, you simply type **With CellFont** followed by each property statement. For example, to underline values in the cell you type **.Underline = True**. When you complete you list of property settings, you type **End With** to mark the end of the `With` statement.

The `With` statement enables you to specify statements that refer to the same object. You need only to specify the object name with the `With` statement to apply all statements to that object.

## Change the Property of an Object

① Type **Dim FirstCell  As Range**, replacing
FirstCell with the variable to be used
as the range object.

② Type **Set FirstCell =
ActiveSheet.Cells(1,1)**, replacing
FirstCell with the variable in step 1
and ActiveSheet.Cells(1,1) with
the appropriate range of cells.

**Note:** See the section "Create an Object
Variable" for more information.

③ Type **With FirstCell**, replacing
FirstCell with the variable created in
step 1.

④ Press Enter.

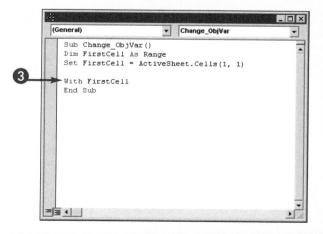

**5** Change the object's properties.

You can type a cell value.

You can type **Font.X = True**, replacing x with Bold, Italic or Underline.

You can type **.Font.Color = RGB(X, Y, Z)**, replacing x, y, and z with RGB values.

You can type code to specify a desired line style constant.

**6** Type **End With**.

**7** Switch to Excel and run the macro.

● The content of the first cell is changed to specified value and the specified font and border attributes are applied.

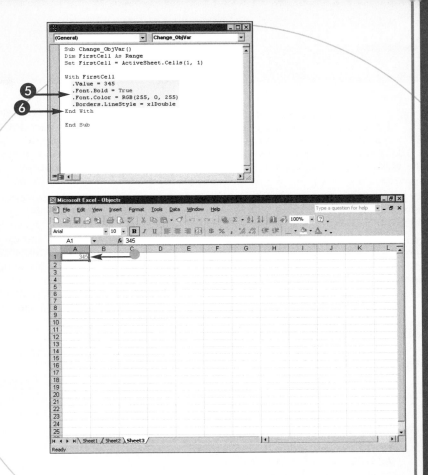

```
Sub Change_ObjVar()
Dim FirstCell As Range
Set FirstCell = ActiveSheet.Cells(1, 1)

With FirstCell
    .Value = 345
    .Font.Bold = True
    .Font.Color = RGB(255, 0, 255)
    .Borders.LineStyle = xlDouble
End With

End Sub
```

## Extra

Some objects, such as the Font object, provide a Color property that determines the color of the object. The RGB function works well for specifying the font color. When you use this function, you select the desired color by indicating the amount of red, green, and blue in the color. You specify the color values with an integer value between 0 and 255. For example, you type **(0,0,0)** for the color black.

| COLOR | RED VALUE | GREEN VALUE | BLUE VALUE |
|-------|-----------|-------------|------------|
| Black | 0 | 0 | 0 |
| Blue | 0 | 0 | 255 |
| Cyan | 0 | 255 | 255 |
| Green | 0 | 255 | 0 |
| Magenta | 255 | 0 | 255 |
| Red | 255 | 0 | 0 |
| White | 255 | 255 | 255 |
| Yellow | 255 | 255 | 0 |

# Compare Object Variables

You can use object comparison to determine if two object variables reference the same object. Unlike standard variables, which actually contain values that you can compare, the object variable does not contain the object, but references it. That being the case, when you compare two object variables, you are really checking if they point to the same object. For example, you may want to check if the currently active workbook is the first workbook. You accomplish this using object comparison.

When you compare standard variables, you use the = (equals sign) operator to determine if they are the same. For example, If Value1 = Value2 Then compares two standard variables. See Chapter 3 for more information on working with standard variables.

When comparing objects, instead of the = operator, you use the Is operator. For example, you write an If Then statement to compare two variables as follows: If ObjVal1 Is ObjVal2 Then. This statement looks at the object referenced by ObjVal1 and checks if it is the same as the object referenced by ObjVal2.

Besides comparing the values of two different operators, you can also use the Is operator to determine if an object variable has an assigned value. To do this, the Is operator checks if the variable has a value of Nothing, as shown in the following example: If ObjVal1 Is Nothing Then. When you use this type of comparison, the comparison statement returns a value of True if the object variable does not point to an object. If the object variable references a specific object, the comparison statement returns a value of False.

## Compare Object Variables

① Create a new subroutine.

**Note:** See Chapter 3 for information on creating subroutines.

② Type **Dim WSRef1 As Worksheet**, replacing WSRef1 with the variable name and Worksheet with the object type.

③ Type **Dim WSRef2 As Worksheet**, replacing WSRef2 with the variable name and Worksheet with the object type.

④ Type **Dim Result As Boolean**, replacing Result with the comparison variable.

⑤ Assign each variable object to point to the same object using the Set command.

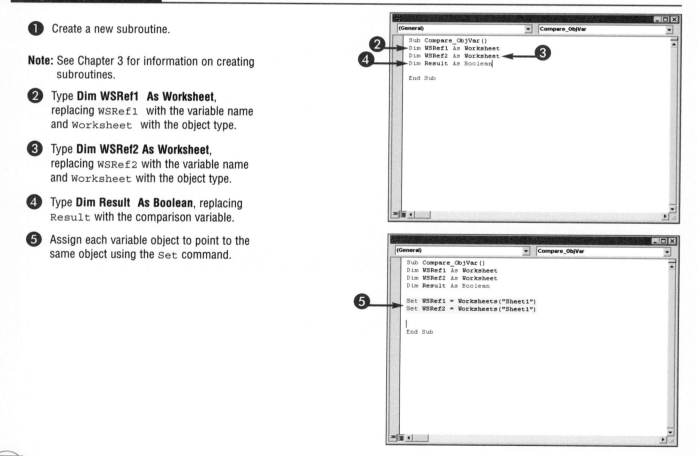

**6** Type **Result = ObjVar1 Is ObjVar2**, replacing `ObjVar1` and `ObjVar2` with the object variables.

**7** Type **MsgBox (Result)**, replacing `Result` with the variable in step 4.

**8** Switch to Excel and run the macro.

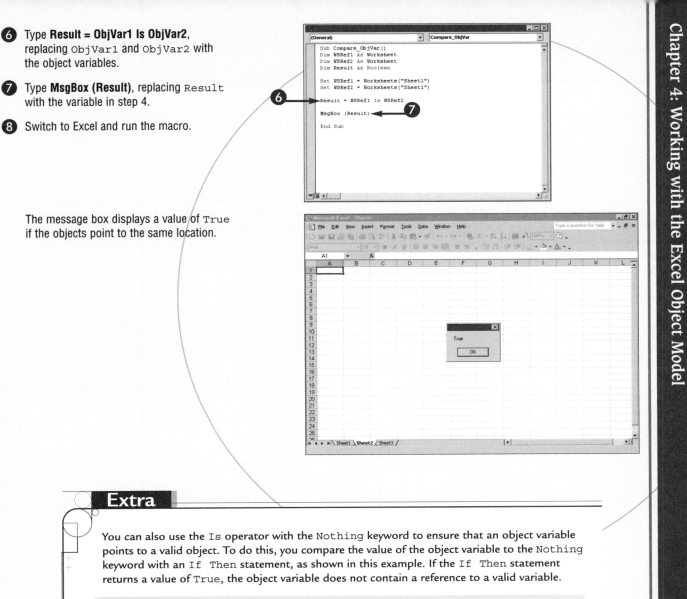

The message box displays a value of `True` if the objects point to the same location.

## Extra

You can also use the `Is` operator with the `Nothing` keyword to ensure that an object variable points to a valid object. To do this, you compare the value of the object variable to the `Nothing` keyword with an `If Then` statement, as shown in this example. If the `If Then` statement returns a value of `True`, the object variable does not contain a reference to a valid variable.

**Example:**
```
If objvar Is Nothing Then
    -MsgBox ("Variable does not point to a valid object")
End If
```

You use the `Nothing` keyword to free an object variable. By doing so, you free up the memory required to store the object pointer in the object variable. When an object has no variable references pointing to it, VBA destroys it. Therefore, if you have multiple object variables pointing to the object, you need to set each one of them to `Nothing`, as shown in this example:

**Example:**
```
Set objvar = Nothing
```

# Using an Object Method

You typically use Excel Object methods to modify to objects. For example, you use a `Delete` method with a `Range` object to remove the values within a specific range of cells. You typically create actions using the methods associated with a particular object.

The Excel Object Model contains nearly 200 different objects, and provides several different methods that correspond to each of the objects that you use to perform an action either to or on behalf of the corresponding object. For example, you can use the `Copy` method to copy a `Worksheet` object and place the copy in another location within the same `Workbook` object.

You use methods with Excel objects in much the same fashion as properties. To use an object method, you specify the appropriate object followed by a period and then the method you want to use. If the selected method has any

arguments, you place these after the method: `Worksheet ("Sheet2").Copy Before:=Worksheet("Sheet1")`. In this example, the code copies the specified worksheet, `Sheet2` and places a copy of it before `Sheet1` in the current workbook.

Most methods require different arguments, which specify how to modify the corresponding object. When you use a method that has arguments, typically at least one of the arguments is required, but the other arguments can be optional. In the example, the `Copy` method requires that you use either the `Before` or `After` argument value to specify the location for placing the copied worksheet. In this situation, although both arguments are optional, you must specify at least one of the two arguments. You use the `Before` argument to specify the sheet in front of which you want to place the copied worksheet, or the `After` argument to specify behind which sheet you want to place the copied worksheet. See Chapter 10 for more information about copying Excel worksheets.

## Using an Object Method

① Create a new subroutine.

② Type **Dim WSNum  As Integer**, replacing WSNum with the variable to store worksheet count.

③ Type **WSNum = Worksheets.Count**, replacing WSNum with the variable in step 2.

The `Count` property returns the number of worksheets in the Worksheet collection.

④ Type **ActiveSheet.Move After:=Worksheets(WSNum)**, replacing WSNum with the variable in step 2.

Alternately, you can type **Before** instead of **After**.

⑤ Switch to Excel and run the macro.

```
(General)                    ▼    Move_Worksheet          ▼

Sub Move_Worksheet()
Dim WSNum As Integer

WSNum = Worksheets.Count
ActiveSheet.Move After:=Worksheets(WSNum)|
End Sub
```

● Excel moves the currently selected worksheet per your specifications.

| | A | B | C | D | E | F | G | H |
|---|---|---|---|---|---|---|---|---|
| 1 | | | | Monthly Expenses | | | | |
| 2 | | Rent | Groceries | Fuel | Electricity | Child Care | Misc. | |
| 3 | January | $750.00 | $214.00 | $75.00 | $87.00 | $110.00 | $175.00 | $1,411.00 |
| 4 | February | 750 | 311 | 88 | 89 | 110 | 145 | 1493 |
| 5 | March | 750 | 245 | 90 | 99 | 110 | 123 | 1417 |
| 6 | April | 750 | 256 | 79 | 103 | 110 | 211 | 1509 |
| 7 | May | $750.00 | $307.00 | $100.00 | $110.00 | $110.00 | $345.00 | $1,722.00 |
| 8 | June | 750 | 350 | 85 | 120 | 110 | 149 | |
| 9 | July | 750 | 310 | 94 | 145 | 110 | 190 | |
| 10 | August | 750 | 299 | 110 | 130 | 110 | 256 | |
| 11 | September | 750 | 245 | 120 | 111 | 110 | 298 | |
| 12 | October | 750 | 280 | 99 | 98 | 110 | 245 | |
| 13 | November | 750 | 400 | 110 | 88 | 110 | 405 | |
| 14 | December | 750 | 415 | 130 | 84 | 110 | 605 | |

Sheet2 / Sheet3 \ Sheet1 /

**Extra**

VBA enables you to use named arguments with procedures (functions and subroutines), properties, and methods. With a named argument, the name of the parameter passes along with the argument value. Named arguments are most useful when calling a procedure that has optional arguments. With a procedure that has optional arguments, if you do not indicate the argument, a comma (,) indicates a placeholder for the argument. For example, the Protect method that protects charts, worksheets, and workbooks has 16 different optional arguments when used to protect a worksheet. Typically, calling this property requires a placeholder for each argument to specify a value for the last parameter, as shown in the example.

**Example:**
```
Worksheets(1).Protect(, , , , , , , ,
, , , , , , True)
```

If you use named arguments, you specify the name of the arguments you want to use followed by a colon and equals sign (:=) and finally the value.

**Example:**
```
Worksheets(1).Protect Password:=
"Excel", AllowSorting:=True
```

You can place named arguments in any order, and you do not have to specify a value for every argument. This means, that even though the Password parameter comes before the AllowSorting parameter in the list of parameters for the Protect method, you can specify them in any order.

# Display a
# Built-in Dialog Box

You can display all of the dialog boxes available in Excel in your macros by using VBA. By displaying a particular dialog box, you can incorporate that Excel functionality directly into your procedure. The Excel Object Model contains a `Dialog` object for each of the Excel dialog boxes. These objects are part of the `Dialogs` collection.

You can access each of the Excel dialog box objects by specifying the corresponding constant value. The constant value for each dialog box begins with `xlDialog` followed by the name for the dialog box. For example, the constant for the Excel Save As dialog box is `xlDialogSaveAs`.

You can use the `Show` method only when working with the `Dialogs` collection. This method essentially displays the dialog box that you specified.

Although you can open a specific dialog box, you cannot access the values that a user specifies on the dialog box.

You can only determine what the user selects by looking at the results after the user dismisses the dialog box. You can, however, use the arguments available with the dialog box to indicate how the dialog box opens. For example, the Properties dialog box (`xlDialogProperties`) has the following arguments: `title`, `subject`, `author`, `keywords`, and `comments`. You can specify custom values for these arguments when you open the dialog box.

Excel provides more than 200 different dialog boxes, and the Excel Object Model provides a constant value to access each one. You can find a complete list of the dialog box constants in the online help that comes with the Visual Basic Editor. Another good method for viewing the dialog box constants is using the Object Browser and searching for the `XlBuiltinDialog` constants. See the section "Using the Object Browser" for more information.

## Display a Built-in Dialog Box

① Type **Sub Open_DialogBox()**.

② Press Enter.

   The `End Sub` statement appears.

③ Type **Application.Dialogs(xlDialogProperties)**, replacing `xlDialogProperties` with the constant for the desired dialog box.

④ Type **.Show "Expenses", "2000 Expenses"** replacing "Expenses" and "2000 Expenses" with the arguments associated with the selected dialog box.

⑤ Switch to Excel and run the Open_DialogBox() macro.

The Properties dialog box displays with the specified argument in the appropriate fields on the dialog box.

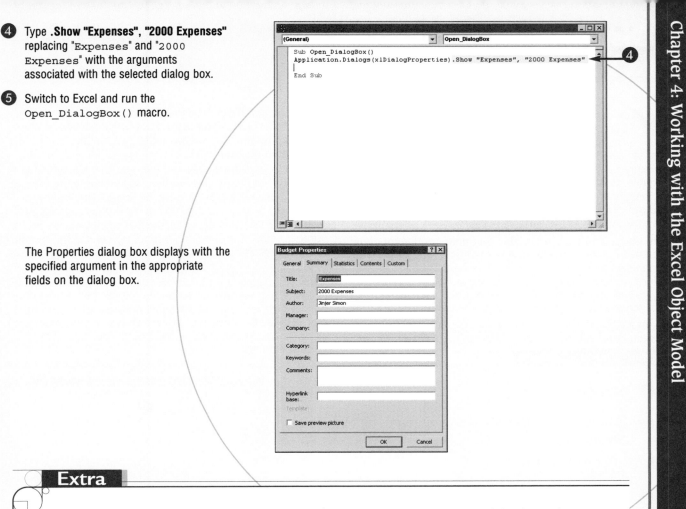

```
Sub Open_DialogBox()
Application.Dialogs(xlDialogProperties).Show "Expenses", "2000 Expenses"

End Sub
```

## Extra

You can capture the results of a button pressed on a displayed dialog box by assigning the Show property statement to a variable. The value of this variable is True if the user clicks OK, and False if the user clicks Cancel in the dialog box.

Excel has over 240 different dialog boxes that display throughout its application. You can display any of these dialog boxes using the appropriate constant. The following table lists a few of the most commonly used Excel dialog boxes:

| CONSTANT | DISPLAYS |
|---|---|
| xlDialogFIleDelete | The Delete dialog box, where you select files to remove. |
| xlDialogInsert | The Insert dialog box for adding additional cells to a worksheet. |
| xlDialogNew | The New Document task pane. |
| xlDialogOpen | The Open dialog box. |
| xlDialogPrint | The Print dialog box. |
| xlDialogSaveAs | The Save As dialog box. |

# Assign Values to Variables

You can assign values to variables at any point within a procedure after declaring the variable using the `Dim` statement. VBA uses variables as storage locations for data values. By using a variable you can change the value of an expression by simply assigning a different value to the variable. Most programmers commonly initialize, or assign an initial value, immediately after declaring the variable, but you can change the value of the variable at any location in the code as long as the variable is valid.

You assign a value to a variable that matches the data type specified for the variable. In other words, if you declare the variable as an integer value, you can only assign integer values to the variable. If you attempt to assign a value other than an integer to the variable, such as a string of text, you receive an error message when you run the macro.

If you assign a string value to a variable declared as an integer, Excel returns a "Type Mismatch" error when you

run the macro. If you assign the variable a decimal value, such as 45.67, VBA truncates the decimal portion of the value and retains the integer value. See Chapter 3 for more information on data types.

When working with values that you type in a worksheet or dialog box, you need to check them before assigning them to variables to ensure that they are the proper data type. You can use the `IsNumeric` function to check the value before assigning it to a variable to ensure that a cell contains a numeric value. The `IsNumeric` function looks at the specified value and returns a Boolean value of `True` for numeric values.

The Variant data type works well in situations where the returned value is a different data type than the variable needs. When you use a Variant data type, VBA accepts any type of data value in the variable. Because VBA code runs more efficiently when you declare an actual data type, such as `Integer`, or `Long`, you should limit your use of the Variant data type.

## Assign Values to Variables

1 Create a new subroutine.

**Note:** See Chapter 3 for information on creating subroutines.

2 Declare variables using the `Dim` statement.

3 Initialize the variables to zero.

4 Type **If IsNumeric(Value) Then**, replacing `Value` with the assigned variable.

**Note:** See Chapter 6 for information on using the `If Then` statement.

5 Assign the value to the variable.

6 Type **End If** to end the `If Then` statement.

7 Repeat steps 4 to 6 for each value.

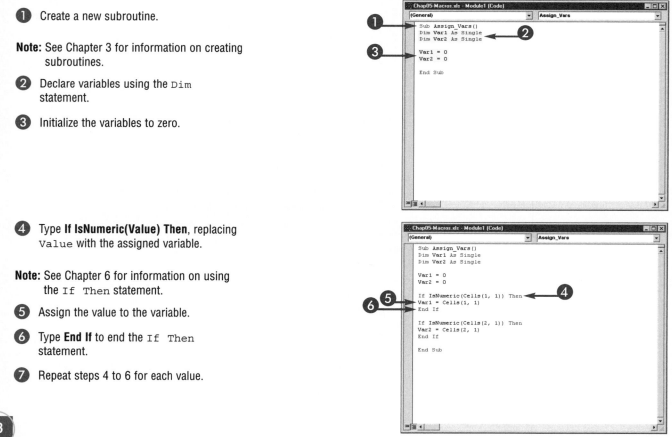

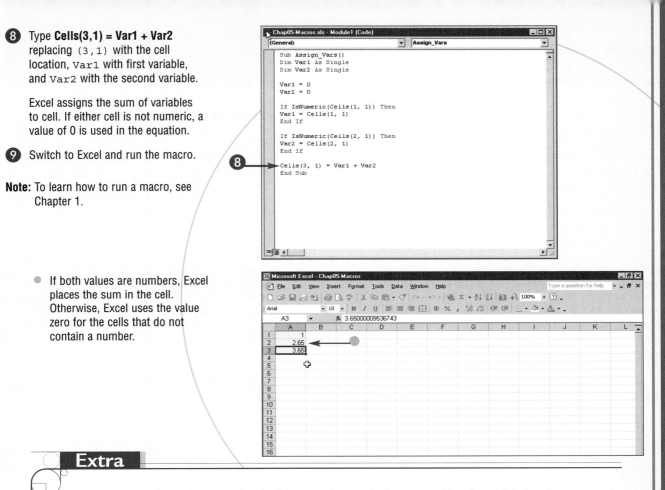

**8** Type **Cells(3,1) = Var1 + Var2** replacing (3,1) with the cell location, Var1 with first variable, and Var2 with the second variable.

Excel assigns the sum of variables to cell. If either cell is not numeric, a value of 0 is used in the equation.

**9** Switch to Excel and run the macro.

**Note:** To learn how to run a macro, see Chapter 1.

● If both values are numbers, Excel places the sum in the cell. Otherwise, Excel uses the value zero for the cells that do not contain a number.

## Extra

VBA provides different functions for checking a value to make sure that it is the desired data type. You should check the data type of a value before assigning it to a variable or performing any type of operation. These functions ensure that no error messages occur if the wrong data type passes to a variable. Each of these functions returns a Boolean value of True or False, indicating whether the value is the specified type.

| FUNCTION | DESCRIPTION |
| --- | --- |
| IsArray | Checks to see if the specified value is an array. |
| IsDate | Checks to see if the specified value is a date. |
| IsNull | Checks to see if the specified value is Null. |
| IsNumeric | Checks to see if the specified value is numeric. |
| IsObject | Checks to see if the specified value is an object. |

Typically you combine these VBA functions with an If Then statement that performs an action if the value is the appropriate data type. See Chapter 6 for more information on using If Then statements. For example, the following code only executes if the value of the NumVal variable is a number.

```
If IsNumeric(NumVal) Then
    Total = Total + NumVal
End If
```

# Using Global Variables

Y ou can declare global variables that all modules in a project can access. When you talk about where you can use a variable, you refer to the *scope* of the variable. When creating Excel macros in VBA, you can use variables on three different levels: procedure level, private module level, and public module level. Of these three variable types, the private module level and public level are two different types of global variables.

Available only to other procedures within the same module, you declare private module-level variables at the top of the module with the use of the `Private` keyword. In other words, they are global within the module, but not available to other modules in the procedure. If the module only contains one procedure, declaring a private module-level variable is the same as a procedure-level variable.

You declare the other type of global variable, public module-level variables, at the top of a module, which makes

them available *globally,* or to all modules within the corresponding procedure. You declare these variables using the `Public` keyword.

Keep in mind that you can use the `Dim` keyword at the module level to declare variables. When you use the `Dim` keyword at the module level, it has the same effect as the `Private` keyword and creates a private module-level variable. Because the `Dim` keyword is more confusing than using `Public` and `Private` keywords, you typically avoid it with module-level variables.

Keep in mind, you declare procedure-level variables within a specific subroutine or function using a `Dim` statement. Because you can use them only within the procedure, you typically refer to the variable as a local variable. Because a local variable is only valid within that procedure, other procedures can have variables with the same name, and you have no conflict.

## Using Global Variables

① At the top of a module, type **Public PubVar As DataType**, replacing `PubVar` with the variable and `DataType` with the variable's data type.

**Note:** For more information on Data types, see Chapter 3.

② Create a new subroutine.

● You can type **Private** in front of the subroutine so it does not appear on the macro list.

③ Set the value of the `PubVar` variable.

④ Create another subroutine in the same module.

⑤ Set the value of the variable to be the current value plus a value.

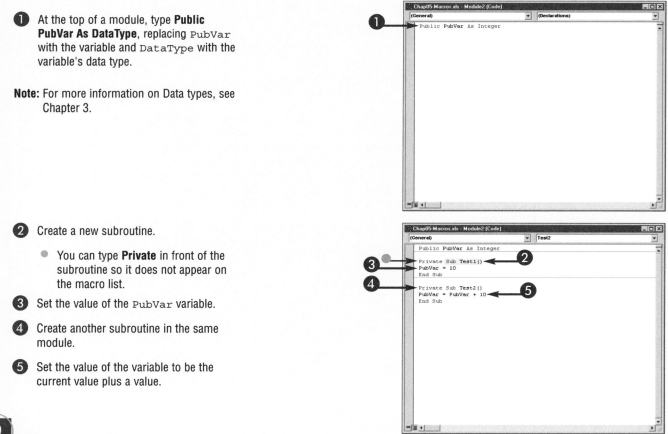

**6** Create a third subroutine.

**7** Type **Call Sub1**, replacing Sub1 with the first subroutine.

**8** Type **Call Sub2**, replacing Sub2 with the second subroutine.

**9** Use the MsgBox function to display the contents of the PubVar variable.

**Note:** See Chapter 7 for more information on using the Msg function.

**10** Switch to Excel and run the macro.

The message box displays the contents of the PubVar variable after being passed between each subroutine.

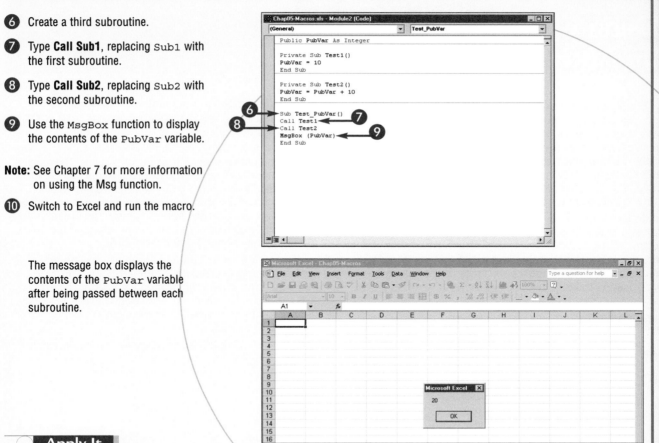

## Apply It

VBA enables subroutines and functions to call other subroutines and functions. When you call another function or subroutine, control passes from the current procedure to the procedure that is called. Upon completion of that procedure, control returns to the next line of code in the original procedure. You call a procedure using the Call statement before the procedure name.

**Example:**
```
Sub Main_Proc()
   Dim LocalVar As Integer
   LocalVar=1
   Call New_Proc
   LocalVar = LocalVar + 1
End Sub
```

In this example, the Main_Proc subroutine executes and creates a variable called LocalVar. The New_Proc subroutine is called. When that subroutine completes, control returns to the Main_Proc subroutine and LocalVar is incremented by one. While the New_Proc subroutine has control, the LocalVar variable is not available.

When one subroutine calls other functions and subroutines, you typically hide those functions and subroutines so that you cannot separately call them. All subroutines that you do not hide display on the Macro dialog box for the corresponding workbook. To hide a subroutine or function, place the word Private before the procedure declaration statement.

**Example:**
```
Private Sub New_Sub()
End Sub
```

81

# Declare
# an Array

You can declare an array a group of the same type of data values. You declare an array in the same fashion as you declare any other variable. Just like other variables, you declare arrays as either local or global variable arrays. You specify the scope of an array with either the `Dim`, `Private`, or `Public` statements. See the section "Using Global Variables" for more information about setting the scope of a variable.

You declare arrays to store a group of related data. The array stores data with the same data type; for example, integers, strings, and so on. Use of arrays greatly simplifies your code because you only declare one variable to store several values. For example, you can declare an array to store a list of students in a class. Instead of creating a

separate variable for each student, such as student1, student2, and so on, you can create one array that contains all student names.

When declaring an array, you can also specify its size, where size is the number of elements in the array, as in the example: `Dim Students(1 To 50) As String`. An element is an individual data value in the array, such as a student name. You specify the size of the array by placing the value in parentheses after the name of the array. In the example, the Students array has a size of 50 elements with the lower bound of the array of 1 and the upper bound of the array of 50.

You refer to each value you add to an array as an array element. You access elements of the array with an index value, which represents the desired element of the array. To access the second element of the Students array, the index value is 2, as in Students(2), for example.

## Declare an Array

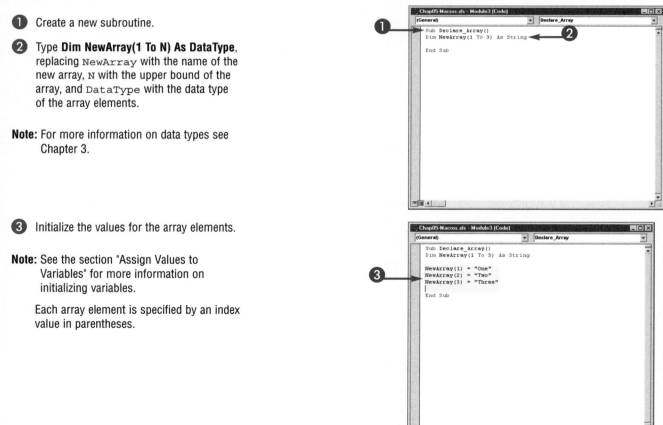

① Create a new subroutine.

② Type **Dim NewArray(1 To N) As DataType**, replacing `NewArray` with the name of the new array, `N` with the upper bound of the array, and `DataType` with the data type of the array elements.

**Note:** For more information on data types see Chapter 3.

③ Initialize the values for the array elements.

**Note:** See the section "Assign Values to Variables" for more information on initializing variables.

Each array element is specified by an index value in parentheses.

④ Use the `Cells` property to assign the values of the array to cells in the spreadsheet.

**Note:** For more information on the Cells property, see Chapter 11.

⑤ Switch to Excel and run the macro.

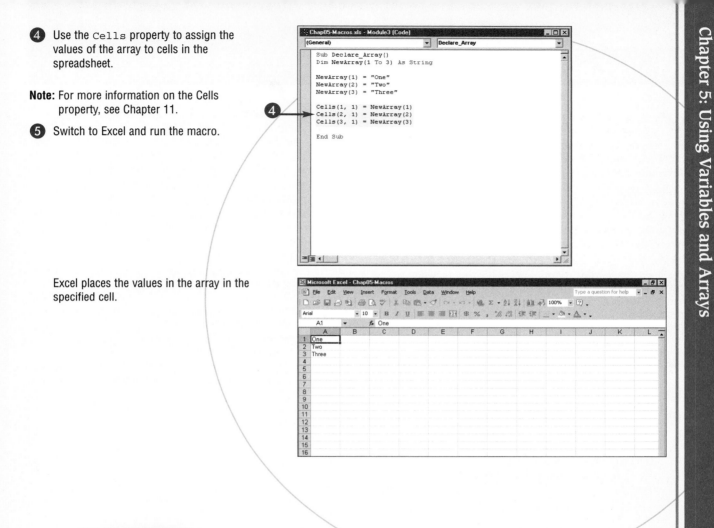

Excel places the values in the array in the specified cell.

---

## Extra

When you specify the size of an array, you indicate the upper and lower bounds of the array, or the first and last index value. In the example, `Dim NewArray(1 To 45)`, the statement creates an array with 45 elements with the lower bound of the array of 1 and the upper bound of 45. If desired, you can omit the lower bound value when you declare an array, as in the example `Dim NewArray(45)`. When you do not specify the lower bound of the array, VBA assigns a lower bound value of 0. Therefore, the specified array, `NewArray`, actually has 46 elements starting with the first element at 0 and the final element at 45.

If you want to give all the arrays you declare a lower bound value of 1, you do so by placing the following statement before any procedures in your module: `Option Base 1`. With this statement, you only have to specify the upper bound of the array. You can specify any number as the lower bounds for the arrays within the module. Keep the lower bounds in mind when declaring the array.

# Declare a Multidimensional Array

Y ou can declare a multidimensional array to store related values within one array. VBA allows you to create arrays with up to 60 dimensions, although dealing with arrays that have more than two or three dimensions can become rather confusing.

Multidimensional arrays provide the ability to store related values in one location, such as the test score for each student in the class. The first dimension of the array may contain the student's name, and the second dimension may contain the student's score.

To help you envision a somewhat overwhelming multidimensional array, try thinking of a two-dimensional array as a worksheet, with rows and columns. You access each element of the array by specifying two different index values. For example, MultiArray(2,4) accesses the value whose first dimension index is 2 and whose second dimension is 4.

As you add a third dimension to an array it gains depth. Using the worksheet example, you can add a third dimension to the two-dimensional array to make it resemble a cube. Accessing an element of the array now requires three index values, as in the example: MultiArray(2,4,2).

As with other variables, you use the Dim statement to declare procedure-level arrays, the Private statement for arrays available to other procedures within the module, and finally the Public statement for arrays that are accessible to the entire project.

When you declare a multidimensional array, you need to indicate the size of each dimension in the array. You do not have to make the dimensions of the array, as in the example: Dim MultiArray (1 To 4, 1 To 5, 1 To 3). In this example, the array contains four elements in the first dimension, five in the second, and three in the third.

See Chapter 3 for more information on VBA data types.

## Declare a Multidimensional Array

① Create a new subroutine.

② Type **Dim ArrayName(1 To N, 1 To M) As DataType**, replacing ArrayName with the name of the array, N and M with the upper bounds of each dimension, and DataType with the data type of the array elements.

③ Type **Dim CellRange As Range**.

④ Type **Set CellRange = Range(Cells(1,1), Cells (3,3))** replacing Range(Cells(1,1), Cells (3,3)) with the range of cells.

Set the range of cells for the Range object.

⑤ Type **ArrayName(1,1) = Value** replacing ArrayName(1,1) with the array element reference and Value with the value of the first element of the array.

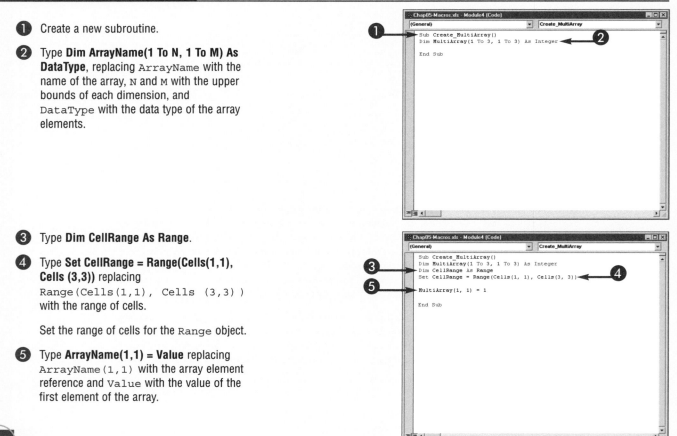

6 Assign values to the remaining array elements.

7 Type **CellRange.Value=ArrayName**, replacing `ArrayName` with the name of the array containing the values.

The contents of the array are assigned to the cells in the `Range` object.

8 Switch to Excel and run the new macro.

● The values in the array appear in cells in the worksheet.

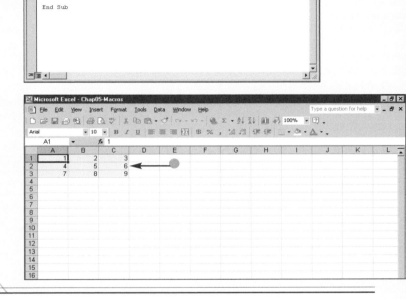

## Extra

You can assign the contents of an array to a series of cells in a worksheet by using the `Value` property of the `Range` object. When you create a `Range` object, you can specify the cells that you want to include in the range by using the `Set` statement. As the macro runs, any values that you assign to the `Range` object are placed in the corresponding cells in your worksheet.

**Example:**
```
Dim CellRange As Range
Set CellRange = Range(Cells(1,1),
Cells(3,3))
CellRange.Value = MultiArray
```

The `Set` statement assigns the range of cells to the specified `Range` object. You specify the range using the `Cells` property to determine the starting and ending cells for the desired range. After you specify the desired range, you assign the contents of an array to the cells in the range using the `Value` property.

When you declare a multidimensional array, all elements of the array have the same data type. If you plan to use the array to store different types of values, such as strings and numeric values, you must store all values as variants.

**Example:**
```
Dim MultiArray (1 To 4, 1 To 5, 1 To 3)
As Variant
```

# Convert a List into an Array

**B** y converting a list of common values to an array, you can access the individual values quickly using one variable. You can convert a list of values to an array using a variety of different methods. You assign values to arrays by referencing the index values of each element. Arrays use index values to identify each of their elements. For example, if an array has 10 elements with lower bounds of 1, the third element in the array has an index value of 3. In order to assign a value to an array, you need to specify the index values that correspond to the appropriate array element. For example, this code assigns a value of 45 to the third array element: SampleArray(3) = 45.

With large arrays, assigning values to each element of the array using the above statement can become rather cumbersome. After all, the purpose of using an array is to simplify your code by storing all related values in one variable, instead of a series of different variables. For Next loops work well for adding a series of values to an array.

You simply declare a For Next loop to cycle through the entire array. See Chapter 6 for more information about working with For Next loops.

For Next loops work best for adding values either from a series of cells or when you can increment values equally. When you have a specific list of values to add to an array, you can also use the Array function, which enables you to add a list of values to an array. The function adds values to the array starting at the lower bounds of the array, the first element, and then adds consecutively. For example, the following code adds the values "One", "Two", "Three" to the SampleArray: SampleArray = Array("One", "Two", "Three").

You can produce the same results when you specify each element individually, for example, when you assign a value to the first element of the array: SampleArray(1) = "One".

The biggest disadvantage of the Array function is that you can only use it with a Variant data type variable. In other words, you cannot declare the variable to which you assign the list of values as an array.

## Convert a List into an Array

① Create a new subroutine.

② Type **Dim ArrayVar As Variant**, replacing ArrayVar with the name of the variable to receive the list of values.

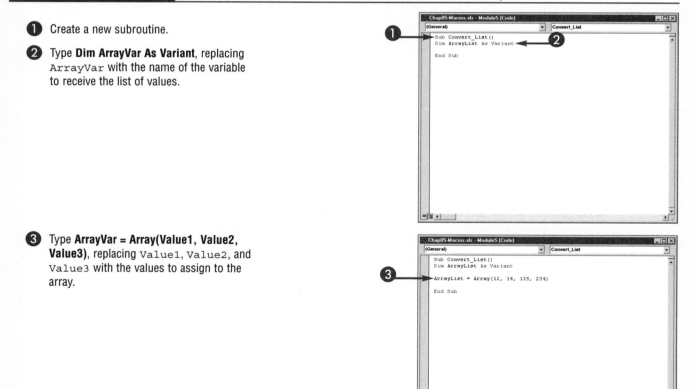

③ Type **ArrayVar = Array(Value1, Value2, Value3)**, replacing Value1, Value2, and Value3 with the values to assign to the array.

④ Type **MsgBox(ArrayVar(N))**, replacing `ArrayVar` with the name of the variable and `N` with the index of the array element.

**Note:** See Chapter 7 for more information on using the `Msg` box function.

⑤ Switch to Excel and run the macro.

The message box shows the array element specified in step 4.

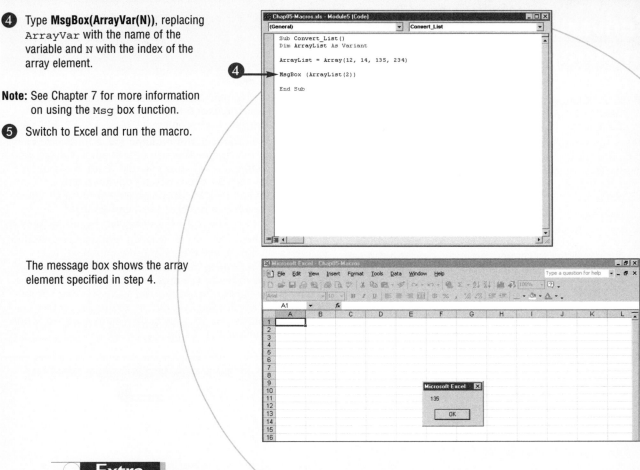

## Extra

The `Array` function works well when you specify a number of items to place in the array. Although all elements you add to the array are variants, you can have a mixture of different data types. For example, you can add both strings and numeric values to the same variable using the `Array` function.

Because you create dynamic arrays with the `Array` function, you can use the `Redim` statement to change the size of the array after you create it. You can also use the `Array` function again within the same procedure to reassign the values in the array. See the section "Redimension an Array" for more information on resizing an array.

The `Option Base` statement does not change the lower bounds for arrays you create with the `Array` function. All arrays have a lower bounds index value of 0. Therefore, if you add three items to the array using the `Array` function, the upper bounds value is 2. The following code adds three values to `TestArray` with the first element having an index value of 0.

**Example:**
```
TestArray = Array("One", "Two", "Three")
MsgBox(TestArray(2))
```

The message box displays a value of `Three` because the first element of the array has an index value of 0.

# Redimension an Array

You can change the size of an array by redimensioning it using the ReDim statement. You can change the size of a dynamic array at any time within a procedure.

VBA lets you declare two different types of arrays, *fixed-size* and *dynamic* arrays. When you declare a fixed-size array, you specify the number of elements in the array. For example, the following code statement creates a fixed array with 15 elements: Dim NewArray(15) As Integer.

If you do not know how large to make the array when you declare it, you can use a dynamic array. A dynamic array does not have a size until you use the ReDim statement within your procedure to change the array size. You can use the Dim statement, without a size to create the array, as in the example: Dim NewArray() As Integer.

When you are ready, you can use the ReDim statement to size the array so you can add values. For example, in the code ReDim NewArray(1 To 15), the array is initially

declared as a dynamic array with an unknown number of elements. The array is redimensioned to contain 15 elements using the ReDim statement.

VBA does not enable you to redimension a fixed-size array. If you attempt to change the size of a fixed-size array, you receive an "Array already dimensioned" error message. If the array was initially declared as a dynamic array, however, you can use the ReDim statement multiple times within a procedure to change the size of an array.

Each time you redimension an array, you destroy the existing elements in that array. If you want to preserve the existing values in the array, use the Preserve statement. For example, the statement ReDim Preserve NewArray(10) instructs VBA to resize the array to 10 elements and maintain any existing values. If the array has five values, those values remain the first five values in the resized array. If the array has 15 values, the first ten values in the array are maintained.

## Redimension an Array

① Create a new subroutine.

② Type **Dim ArrayName() As DataType**, replacing ArrayName with the name of the array variable and DataType with the type of values the array will store.

③ Type **ReDim ArrayName(N)**, replacing N with the upper bounds of the array.

④ Specify the values for each element of the array.

⑤ Use the MsgBox function to view an element of the array.

**Note:** See Chapter 7 for more information on using the MsgBox function.

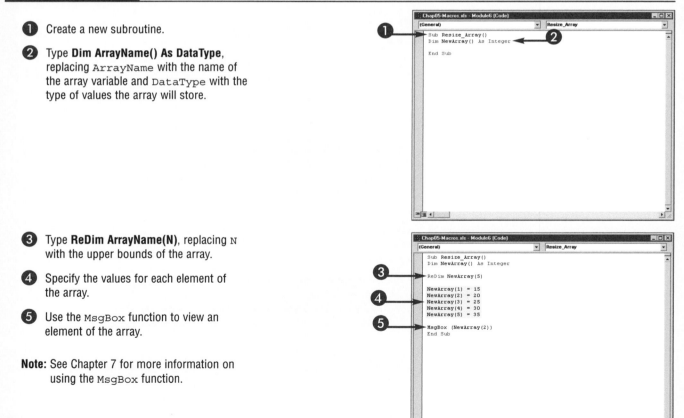

**6** Type **ReDim Preserve ArrayName(M)**, replacing M with the new upper bounds for the array.

**7** Use the MsgBox function to view the same element of the array.

**8** Switch to Excel and run the macro.

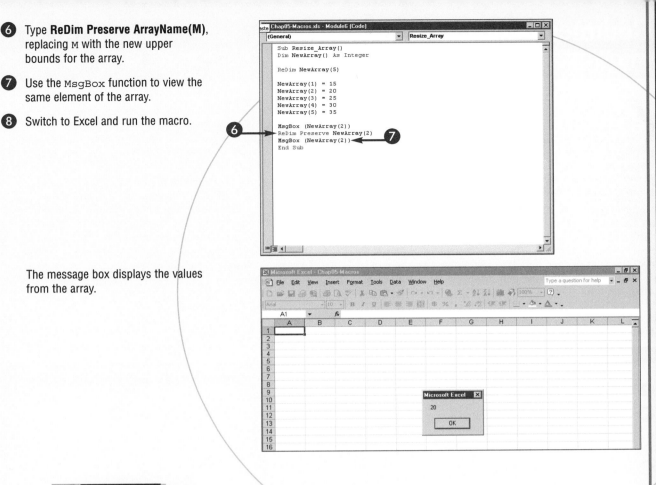

The message box displays the values from the array.

---

**Extra**

Because you may not always know the size of the array, VBA provides functions for determining an array's upper and lower bounds. When working with dynamic arrays, you frequently need to know the upper and lower bounds of the array to correctly code your procedure. To find the upper and lower bounds of an array, VBA provides the UBound and LBound functions. The sample code finds the lower and upper bounds and assigns them to variables.

**Example:**
```
UpperBound = UBound(EmployeeArray)
LowerBound = LBound(EmployeeArray)
```

Each of these functions returns a Long data type indicating the upper or lower bounds of the specified array. If the array is multidimensional, you need to specify the dimension for which you want the bounds.

**Example:**
```
UpperBounds = UBound(MultiArray, 2)
```

# Create a User-Defined Data Type

Y ou can create *user-defined data types* to deal with specific types of data. User-defined data types resemble multidimensional arrays in that you can store related values using one variable name. However, because you construct it from other data types, you can create a user-defined data type containing multiple data types, while all elements in the array must contain the same data type.

You declare user-defined data types at the top of your module in the same location as your public and private module variables. You specify a user-defined data type with the Type and End Type statements. The Type statement indicates the start of the user-defined data type definition, and the End Type statement specifies the end. After the Type statement, you indicate the name of the new data type; for example, Type ItemInfo creates a data type called ItemInfo. To create a user-defined data type to store an item price and description, you can specify a user-defined data type with two components.

After you create the data type, you can declare variables that use the specified data type. You typically use user-defined data types as the data type for an array. For example, to create an array of the ItemInfo data type, you type: Dim NewItems(10) As ItemInfo.

To assign values to a user-defined array, you not only specify the array element, but you also indicate the component you want to change. For example, this code changes the value of the first component in the array: NewItems(1).ItemDescription = "15 inch Monitor".

Similiarly, you can copy the entire contents of one element to another by simply referring to the array element. The following code copies ItemDescription and ItemPrice of the first element of the array to the third array element: NewItems(3) = NewItems(1).

## Create a User-Defined Data Type

① Create a new module.

② Type **Type DataType** replacing DataType with the name of the user-defined data type.

③ Declare the data type components.

④ Type **End Type**.

⑤ Create a new subroutine.

⑥ Type **Dim NewArray(N) As DataType,** replacing NewArray with the name of the array, N with the number of elements, and DataType with the user-defined data type name you used in step 2.

Typically, you create an array using the new data type.

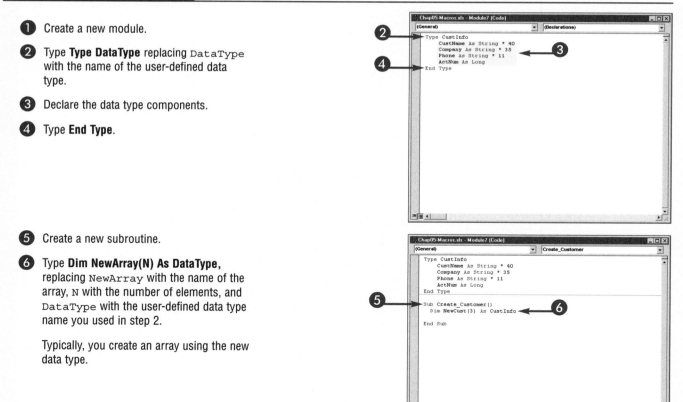

**7** Specify the values for each element of the array.

You can specify a component value by typing **NewArray(N).ComponentName**.

```
Type CustInfo
    CustName As String * 40
    Company As String * 35
    Phone As String * 11
    ActNum As Long
End Type

Sub Create_Customer()
    Dim NewCust(3) As CustInfo

    NewCust(1).ActNum = 135
    NewCust(1).Company = "ABC Corp"
    NewCust(1).CustName = "John Smith"
    NewCust(1).Phone = "888 555 1414"

End Sub
```

**8** Copy the contents of one array element to another array element.

The user-defined data type is created.

```
Type CustInfo
    CustName As String * 40
    Company As String * 35
    Phone As String * 11
    ActNum As Long
End Type

Sub Create_Customer()
    Dim NewCust(3) As CustInfo

    NewCust(1).ActNum = 135
    NewCust(1).Company = "ABC Corp"
    NewCust(1).CustName = "John Smith"
    NewCust(1).Phone = "888 555 1414"

    NewCust(2) = NewCust(1)

End Sub
```

## Extra

As you develop macros using VBA, the complexity of your code may make it difficult to keep track of different variables. To simplify the process, many developers use a standard naming convention where the variable name reflects the variable type. To use this type of naming convention, you preface each variable name with a standard lowercase prefix that identifies the data type of the variable. For example, you can identify an integer variable by prefixing it with i, to create the variable name iNumVisits. Using the integer prefix makes it clear at any location in the code that the variable holds an integer value. This naming convention is useful if you share your macro code with other people. The following table lists the standard variable-naming conventions for Visual Basic and VBA.

| PREFIX | DATA TYPE |
|--------|-----------|
| b | Boolean |
| c or cur | Currency |
| dt | Date/Time |
| d | Double |
| i or int | Integer |
| l or lng | Long |
| obj | Object |
| s or sng | Single |
| str | String |
| u | User-defined |
| v or var | Variant |

# Execute a Task While a Condition Is True

Y ou can execute a task or a series of tasks as long as a specific condition is true by using the Do While loop statement in VBA. A Do While loop provides a great means for repeating a series of statements. For example, a Do While loop lets you apply changes to a series of cells as long as the cells contain a numeric value.

When you use the Do While loop, the statements specified between the Do and Loop statements execute as long as the condition is true. As soon as the looping structure determines that the condition is no longer true, control moves to the next statement outside the loop.

The Do While loop consists of four basic parts. The Do statement initiates the loop. You can locate the While condition statement following the Do statement, or at the

end of the loop. The body of the loop contains a series of statements to perform as long as the condition is true. Finally, the Loop statement marks the end of the loop.

When you locate the While condition following the Do statement, the Do Loop verifies that the condition is true before executing. If the condition is not true, the loop does not execute. With this form of the Do Loop, the loop may never execute.

When you locate the While condition at the end of the loop, the Do Loop always executes once and then checks the condition. If the condition evaluates false at that point, the Do Loop stops execution, and control passes to the next VBA statement in your macro.

## Execute a Task While a Condition Is True

① Create a new subroutine.

**Note:** See Chapter 3 for information on creating subroutines.

② Type **Dim N As Integer**, replacing N with the name of the variable to use as the counter for your loop.

③ Initialize the value of the counter variable.

④ Type **Do**.

⑤ Type **While N < M**, replacing M with the maximum value for the counter variable and N with the variable specified in step 2.

Alternately, you can skip to step 6 and perform steps 6 to 8 to place the While condition at the end of the loop.

6  Type the body of the loop.

7  Type **N = N + 1** to increment the counter variable.

8  Type **Loop** to mark the end of the Do While loop.

If you skipped step 5, type **While N < M** to specify the condition of the loop, replacing M with the maximum value for the counter variable and N with the variable specified in step 2.

9  Switch to Excel and run the macro.

**Note:** To learn how to run a macro, see Chapter 1.

● The body of the macro repeats until the maximum counter value is met.

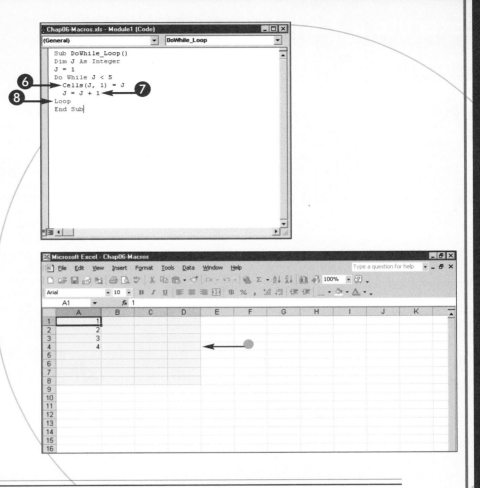

## Extra

Because the body of the loop typically contains at least one statement that affects the results of the loop, you can use incremental statements, such as *counter variables,* within the body of a loop to change the condition of the loop. A counter variable has a specific constant added to it each time the loop executes. Typically, you declare a counter variable as an integer data type and initialize it with a start value outside the loop. Within the loop, you increment the variable by a constant value.

In the following example, the macro assigns the counter variable J an initial value of 1. The Do While loop verifies that it is less than 5, and then executes the loop. The loop assigns a value of 1 to the first cell on the worksheet, cell A1. The counter variable J increments to 2 and the loop retests the condition. The looping continues until the condition is false. In this instance, the loop repeats only four times. When J has a value of 5, the looping stops.

**Example:**
```
Dim J As Integer
J = 1
Do While J < 5
  ActiveSheet.Rows(J).Cells(1).Value = J
  J = J + 1
Loop
```

93

# Perform Multiple Tasks Until a Condition Is Met

You can execute a task or a series of tasks until a specific condition is met by using the Do Until loop statement in VBA. A Do Until loop provides a great means for repeating a series of statements. For example, a Do Until loop lets you apply changes to a series of cells until you encounter an empty cell.

When you use the Do Until loop, the statements you specify between the Do and Loop statements execute until the specified condition is met. As soon as the looping structure determines that the condition is true, control moves to the next statement outside the loop.

The Do Until loop consists of four basic parts. The Do statement initiates the loop. The Until condition statement typically follows the Do statement, although you can also specify the Until condition at the end of the loop. The

body of the loop contains a series of statements that perform until the value of the statement meets the condition of the loop. Finally, the Loop statement marks the end of the loop.

When the Until condition follows the Do statement, the Do Until loop checks to see if the condition is true before executing. If the condition is not true, the loop executes. With this form of the Do Until loop, the loop may never execute if the statement meets the condition of the loop before the loop executes the first time.

When you place the Until condition at the end of the loop, the Do Until loop always executes once and then checks the condition. If the condition is true at that point, the Do Until loop stops execution, and control passes to the next VBA statement in your macro.

## Perform Multiple Tasks Until a Condition Is Met

① Create a new subroutine.

② Type **Dim N As Integer**, replacing N with the name of the variable to increment in the loop.

③ Initialize the value of the variable.

④ Type **Do**.

⑤ Type the **Until** condition, followed by the condition of the loop.

Alternately, you can skip step 5 and perform steps 6 to 9 to place the Until condition at the end of the loop.

In this example, the loop repeats until it encounters an empty cell.

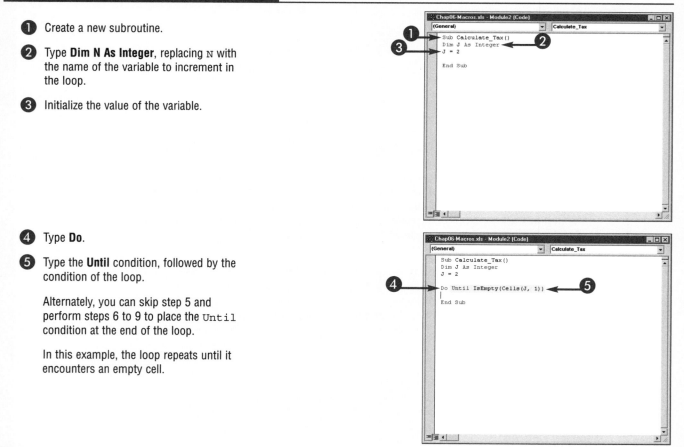

**6** Specify the body of the loop.

**7** Increment the variable.

**8** Type **Loop** to end the Do
Until loop.

If you skipped step 5, type
**Until** followed by the condition
of the loop.

**9** Switch to Excel and run the
macro.

● The macro repeats until
the specified condition
is true.

```
Sub Calculate_Tax()
Dim J As Integer
J = 2

Do Until IsEmpty(Cells(J, 1))
    Cells(J, 2).Value = Cells(J, 1) * 1.15
    J = J + 1
Loop

End Sub
```

| | A | B |
|---|---|---|
| 1 | Total | Total with Tax |
| 2 | $5.00 | $5.75 |
| 3 | $6.50 | $7.48 |
| 4 | $17.65 | $20.30 |
| 5 | $385.00 | $442.75 |
| 6 | $52.00 | $59.80 |
| 7 | $683.00 | $785.45 |
| 8 | $14.50 | $16.68 |
| 9 | $3.00 | $3.45 |
| 10 | $11.45 | $13.17 |

## Apply It

When working with Do While and Do Until loops, you may have situations where you want to
jump out of a loop before executing the remaining statements in the loop. You can do this by using
the Exit Do statement. You can place an Exit Do statement anywhere within the body of the
loop, which can contain multiple Exit Do statements. When VBA encounters an Exit Do
statement, the control immediately transfers out of the current loop to the next statement outside
the loop.

Typically a conditional statement such as If Then appears before the Exit Do statement. The
conditional statement looks for a condition to meet and then executes the Exit Do statement. The
following code uses an If Then statement to check a second condition, as indicated. This code
continues to execute as long as Condition1 is true. Each time the loop executes, the If Then
statement checks to see if the value of Condition2 has changed. When the value of Condition2 is
true, the loop exits immediately, and processing continues with the next statement outside the loop.

**Example:**
```
Do While Condition1 = True
        If Condition2 = True
                Exit Do
        End If
Loop
```

# Execute Tasks a Specific Number of Times

You can use the For Next loop to execute a statement or a series of statements a specific number of times in your macro. For example, using a For Next loop lets you add the values in a specific number of cells.

When you use the For Next loop, the statements you specify between the For and Next statements execute until the counter variable reaches the specified maximum value. As soon as the looping structure determines that the maximum value is met, control moves to the next statement outside the loop.

The For Next loop consists of four basic parts. The For statement initiates the loop. You specify a counter variable with an initial and maximum value, such as A = 1 To 5. The inside of the body of the loop consists of a series of

statements that perform until the counter meets the maximum value of the loop. Finally, you mark the end of the loop with the Next statement.

When the For Next loop starts, it checks to make sure the value of the counter variable has not met the maximum value. If the variable is less than the maximum, the loop executes. The counter variable is a numeric value that is incremented by 1 each time the loop executes.

The loop continues to execute as long as the Minimum value is less than the Maximum value specified for the counter variable. If the Minimum value is initially greater than the Maximum value, the body of the loop never executes.

## Execute Tasks a Specific Number of Times

① Create a new subroutine.

② Declare the loop variable and any other variables needed for the subroutine.

③ Type **For N = 1 To Max**, replacing N with the variable declared for the For Next loop and Max with the maximum value of the loop.

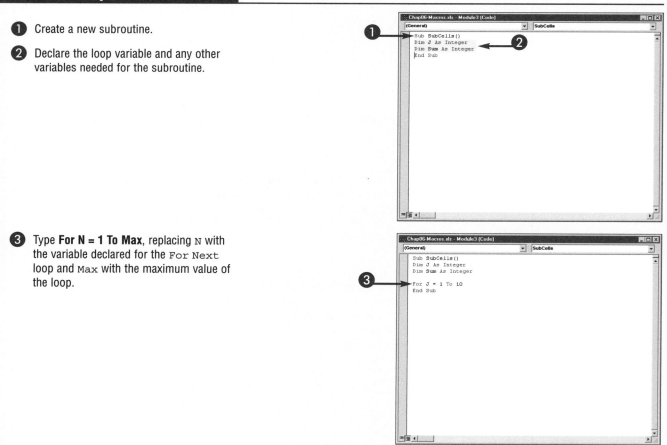

④ Type the VBA statements for the body of the loop.

⑤ Type **Next** to indicate the end of the loop.

⑥ Type any additional code needed for your subroutine.

⑦ Switch to Excel and run the associated macro.

The macro executes the contents of the For Next loop the specified number of times.

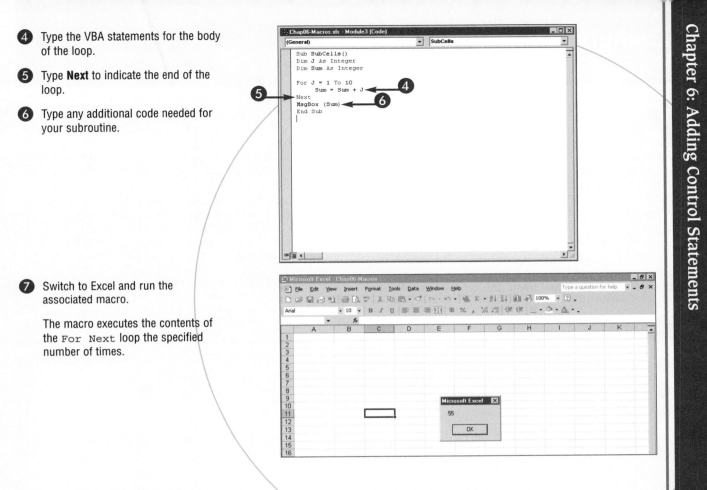

## Apply It

You can specify a different value to increment the Counter variable. By default, the Counter variable for the For Next loop increments by one each time the loop executes. If you want to increment or decrement the Counter variable by a different numeric value, you can use the Step statement and specify the increment value. If you specify a positive value, the Counter variable increments by that value each time the loop cycles. If you specify a negative value, the Counter variable decrements by that value each time the loop cycles. In the following example, the For loop starts with an initial counter variable J of 2 and a maximum value of 20. Each time the loop cycles, the counter variable increments by 2. The TotalVal variable increments by the value of the loop. The loop executes ten times. When the initial and maximum values of the counter are equal, the loop executes a final time before it passes control to the next statement outside the loop.

**Example:**
```
For J = 2 To 20 Step 2
     TotalVal = TotalVal + J
Next
```

# Using the For Each Next Loop

You can use the `For Each Next` loop to repeat a series of statements for each element in an array or each object in a collection. When you use the `For Each Next` loop, the statements you specify between the `For` and `Next` statements execute for each element in the specified array or collection. As soon as the looping structure finds the last element, control moves to the next statement outside the loop.

The `For Each Next` loop consists of four basic parts. The `For Each` statement initiates the loop. The statement `Element In Group` follows the `For Next` statement.

The body of the loop contains a series of statements to perform for each element. Finally, the `Next` statement marks the end of the loop.

The `Element In Group` statement consists of two parts: `Element` represents a variable of the same data type as the items in the array or collection, and `Group` names the array or collection. For example, if you want to loop through the elements of an array, you can have the statement `For Each Student In StudentNames`.

The `For Each` loop continues to execute as long as the specified group contains values. The `Element` variable contains a copy of a group element each time the loop executes, not a reference to the element in the array. Therefore, changing the `Element` variable does not modify the array. For example, when dealing with an array of student names, Excel copies the name of the student in the array element to the value specified as the `Element`. Because of that, changing the value of the `Student` variable does not modify the contents of the array.

## Using the For Each Next Loop

① Create a new subroutine.

② Type a **Dim** statement to declare an array, N.

③ Type a **Dim** statement to declare the count variable for the `For Next` loop.

④ Type **Dim Element as Variant**, replacing `Element` with the variable for the `For Each` loop.

⑤ Declare any additional variables needed by the subroutine.

⑥ Type a **For Next** loop to add values to the array.

**Note:** For more information on creating For Next loops see the section "Execute Tasks a Specific Number of Times."

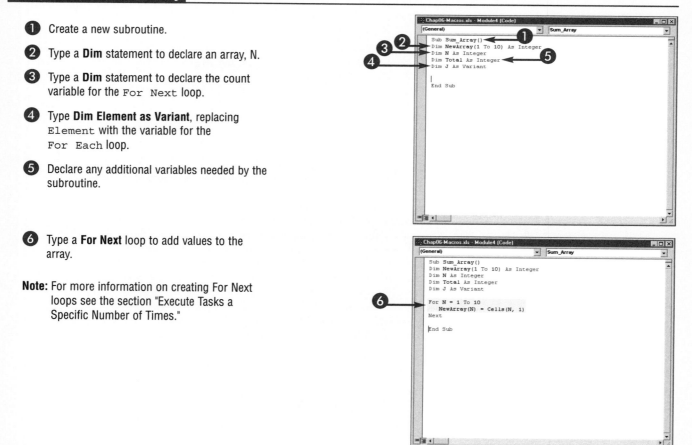

**7** Type **For Each Element in Group**, replacing `Element` with the variant variable declared and `Group` with the name of the array.

**8** Type the VBA code to execute as the body of the loop.

**9** Type **Next** to close the loop.

**10** Type any additional statements for the subroutine.

**11** Switch to Excel and run the macro.

The `For Each` loop executes for each element in the specified array.

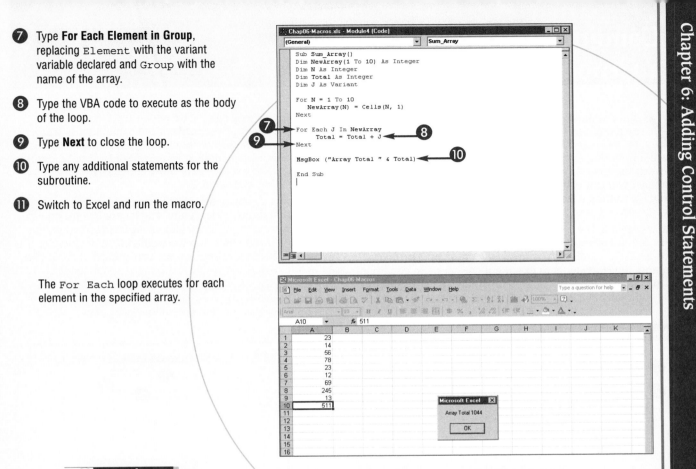

## Apply It

You commonly nest loops to populate a multidimensional array. When you nest loops, you place one loop completely inside another loop. To work with a multidimensional array, you create a separate loop for each dimension of the array. The following code uses two nested `For Next` loops to access elements of the array. Notice that the inside loop, with the `L` counter variable, completely cycles each time the loop with `K` runs once. Each `Next` statement has a variable following it. This code works well when you nest loops because you can determine which loop ends. Remember, you must exit the inside loop before you can exit outside loops.

**TYPE THIS:**

```
Sub Build_Array()
Dim NewArray(1 To 3, 1 To 3) As Integer
Dim K As Integer
Dim L As Integer
For K = 1 To 3
        For L = 1 To 3
NewArray (K, L) = K+L
        Next L
 Next K
End Sub
```

**RESULT:**

The code creates a two-dimensional array with values as outlined in the following table:

| 2 | 3 | 4 |
|---|---|---|
| 3 | 4 | 5 |
| 4 | 5 | 6 |

# Conditionally Execute a Group of Statements

You can conditionally execute a group of statements by using the If Then conditional statement. The If Then conditional statement checks to see if a specific condition is true and, if so, executes all statements between the Then keyword and the End If statement. For example, you can use the If Then statement to make sure variables contain a numeric value before summing.

The If Then conditional statement always consists of three different parts. The If keyword always initiates the If Then conditional statement. A condition always follows, such as A = 5, followed by the keyword Then. The body contains the statements to execute if the specified condition is true. Finally, the End If statement indicates the end of the conditional statement.

The statements you specify between the If Then and End If statements only execute if the condition is true. If the condition is false, your macro ignores the statements. The If Then statement also enables you to specify a group of statements to execute only if the condition is false, by using the Else statement.

You can nest If Then statements together to check multiple conditions. Nesting the statements together means that you place one If Then statement inside another. For example, you can check the value of a cell to make sure it is numeric and that it contains a number greater than 0. You can accomplish this with nested If Then statements.

With nested If Then statements, the first If Then statement must be True, or your macro never sees the condition specified by the second If Then statement.

## Conditionally Execute a Group of Statements

① Create a new subroutine.

② Type **If Condition Then**, replacing Condition with the statement to check.

③ Type the statements to execute if the condition is true.

④ Type **Else**.

⑤ Type the statements to execute if the condition is false.

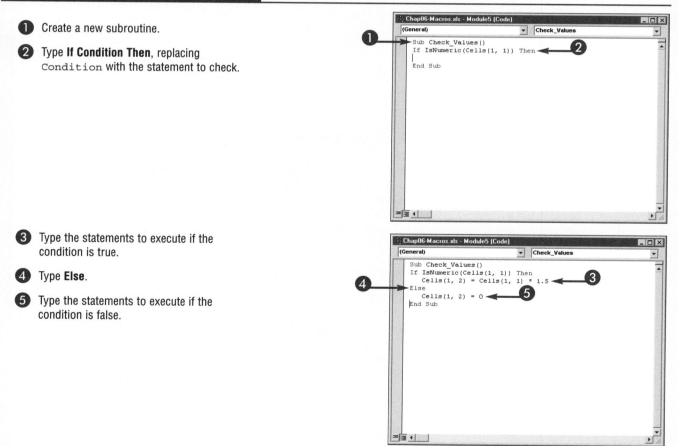

**6** Type **End If**.

**7** Switch to Excel and run the associated macro.

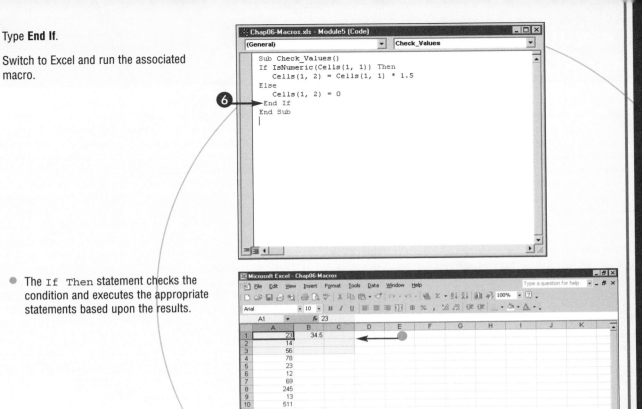

```
Chap06-Macros.xls - Module5 (Code)

(General)                              Check_Values

Sub Check_Values()
If IsNumeric(Cells(1, 1)) Then
    Cells(1, 2) = Cells(1, 1) * 1.5
Else
    Cells(1, 2) = 0
End If
End Sub
```

● The `If Then` statement checks the condition and executes the appropriate statements based upon the results.

## Extra

Although VBA does not require you to indent your code, you can use indentation to improve readability. Indenting enables you to more easily look at the layout of the code without reading each line. When dealing with conditional statements, such as `If Then` statements and looping statements, most programmers typically indent the code within these statements for readability. The following example shows how you can indent the code body of a `For Next` loop to let people easily locate the loop's beginning and end. The example also indents the `If Then` statement body code to show its location.

**Example:**
```
For I = 1 To 5
        If J < 10 Then
            J = J + 1
        End If
Next
```

If you have an `If Then` statement that consists of only one body statement, you can combine the `If Then` statement with the body statement and eliminate the `End If` statement.

**TYPE THIS:**
```
If Sum <10 Then Sum = Sum + 1
'This is equivalent to typing the following:
If Sum < 10 Then
    Sum = Sum + 1
End If
```

**RESULT:**

The code adds 1 to the sum as long as the sum is less than 10.

# Execute a Statement Based upon the Value

You can create code to execute a specific block of code based upon the value of a statement using the `Select Case` statement. The `Select Case` statement is similar to specifying multiple `If Then` statements to check the value of the same expression. The `Select Case` statement works well if you have different conditions to execute based upon the value of a variable, such as determining in which state a user lives in order to calculate sales tax. For example, if you want to execute a different statement depending upon which value a user selects, you can either use multiple `If Then` statements to check the value of the response, or you can use one `Select Case` statement.

The `Select Case` statement is best suited for situations where you need to check one expression for several different values. The `Select Case` statement consists of

four different parts. The `Select Case` statement includes the expression you want to check. For example, if you determine the value of the `UserVal` variable, your initial statement is `Select Case UserVal`. Each `Case` statement indicates a value for the expression. For example, `Case 4` determines if `UserVal = 4` is True. Under each `Case` statement are statements to execute if the expression equals the specified value. Finally, the `End Select` statement specifies the end of the `Select Case` statement.

When the `Select Case` statement finds a match to the value of the expression, the corresponding statements execute and exit the `Select Case` statement. You can also add a `Case Else` statement that tells the statement to run if none of the other `Case` statements are valid. For example, you can add a `Case Else` statement that executes if the value of `UserVal` is not one of the `Case` statement values.

## Execute a Specific Statement Based upon the Value

① Create a new subroutine.

② Declare any variables needed for the subroutine.

③ Initialize variables.

You can type a loop to pass values to subroutine.

● In this example, `Do While Not (IsEmpty(Cells(R,2)))` loops through values in column B as long as they are not empty.

④ Type **Select Case Expression**, replacing `Expression` with the expression to check for values.

⑤ Type **Case Value1**, replacing `Value1` with the first value to check for the specified expression.

⑥ Type the code statements to execute if expression equals specified value.

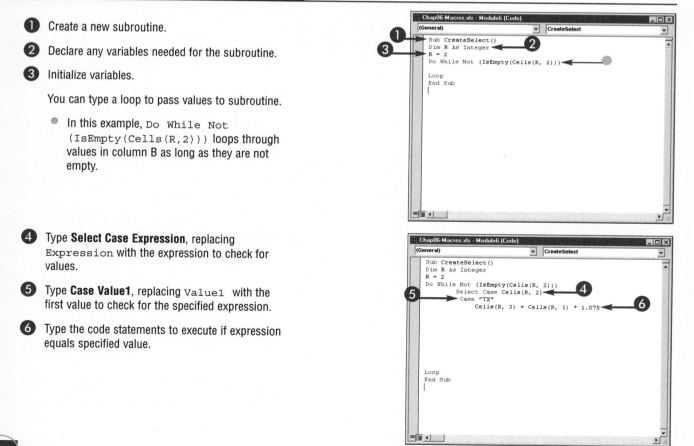

⑦ Repeat steps 5 and 6 for each expected value of the expression.

⑧ Type **Case Else**.

⑨ Type the code statements to execute for all other values of the expression.

⑩ Type **End Select**.

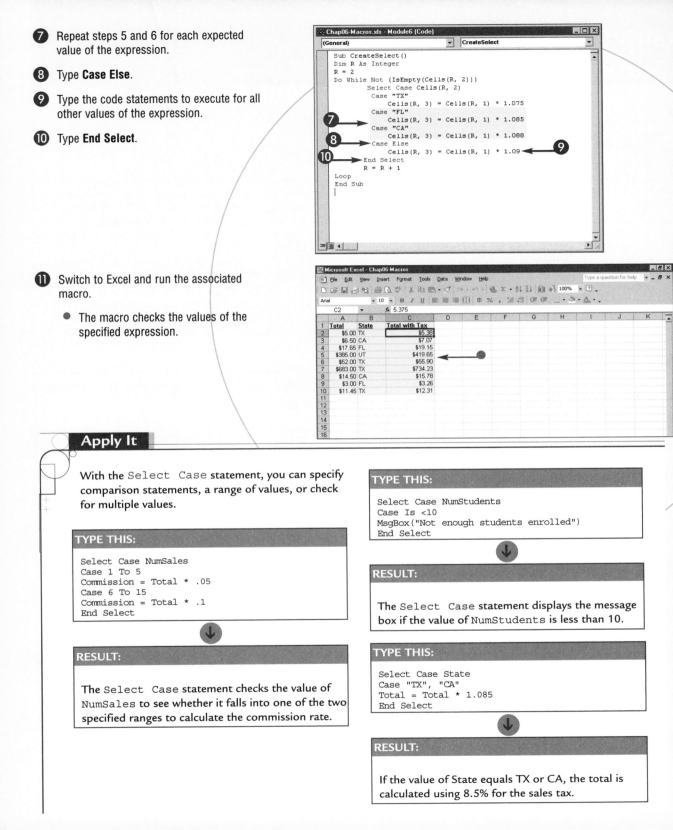

```
Chap06-Macros.xls - Module6 (Code)
(General)                                    CreateSelect

Sub CreateSelect()
Dim R As Integer
R = 2
Do While Not (IsEmpty(Cells(R, 2)))
        Select Case Cells(R, 2)
        Case "TX"
            Cells(R, 3) = Cells(R, 1) * 1.075
        Case "FL"
            Cells(R, 3) = Cells(R, 1) * 1.085
        Case "CA"
            Cells(R, 3) = Cells(R, 1) * 1.088
        Case Else
            Cells(R, 3) = Cells(R, 1) * 1.09
        End Select
        R = R + 1
Loop
End Sub
```

⑪ Switch to Excel and run the associated macro.

● The macro checks the values of the specified expression.

| | A | B | C |
|---|---|---|---|
| 1 | Total | State | Total with Tax |
| 2 | $5.00 | TX | $5.38 |
| 3 | $6.50 | CA | $7.07 |
| 4 | $17.65 | FL | $19.15 |
| 5 | $385.00 | UT | $419.65 |
| 6 | $52.00 | TX | $55.90 |
| 7 | $683.00 | TX | $734.23 |
| 8 | $14.50 | CA | $15.78 |
| 9 | $3.00 | FL | $3.26 |
| 10 | $11.45 | TX | $12.31 |

## Apply It

With the `Select Case` statement, you can specify comparison statements, a range of values, or check for multiple values.

**TYPE THIS:**

```
Select Case NumSales
Case 1 To 5
Commission = Total * .05
Case 6 To 15
Commission = Total * .1
End Select
```

**RESULT:**

The `Select Case` statement checks the value of NumSales to see whether it falls into one of the two specified ranges to calculate the commission rate.

**TYPE THIS:**

```
Select Case NumStudents
Case Is <10
MsgBox("Not enough students enrolled")
End Select
```

**RESULT:**

The `Select Case` statement displays the message box if the value of NumStudents is less than 10.

**TYPE THIS:**

```
Select Case State
Case "TX", "CA"
Total = Total * 1.085
End Select
```

**RESULT:**

If the value of State equals TX or CA, the total is calculated using 8.5% for the sales tax.

# Jump to a Specific Location in a Macro

You can jump to a named location within your macro using the GoTo command. In order to use a GoTo statement, you need to have a label within your procedure that the GoTo statement can reference. The label is just a text string followed by a colon. The GoTo command references that label and passes control from the current location in the procedure to the labeled section.

GoTo commands date back to the days when you performed programming on mainframe computers and each line of code had a specific line number. The GoTo command jumped directly to the specified line of code. Now, you only use GoTo commands in situations where you cannot obtain the desired results using other conditional statements and loopings structures. Although you frequently use the command for trapping errors in VBA, the hardcore programming community considers using the GoTo command too frequently bad programming. See Chapter 8 for more information on debugging your macro code.

The GoTo command actually consists of two pieces: the GoTo statement and the name of the source label, which follows the statement. You can place the label anywhere in the code of your procedure. Excel often references the labeled area of code as a subprocedure.

The GoTo command can only jump to subprocedures within the same procedure. It cannot reference a subprocedure you place outside the current procedure, even if they both are in the same module. For example, if you have the code GoTo ChangeValue, somewhere else within the same procedure you need to have a ChangeValue statement. When Excel encounters the GoTo ChangeValue statement, it jumps from that location to the statements that follow the ChangeValue statement.

You can add multiple GoTo commands to the same procedure. Each GoTo command can jump to the same labeled command, or to separate commands.

## Jump to a Specific Location in a Macro

① Create a new subroutine.

② Type the code that determines when the GoTo statement is needed.

③ Type **GoTo Label**, replacing Label with the name of the subprocedure to which you want to jump.

④ Type additional code for the procedure.

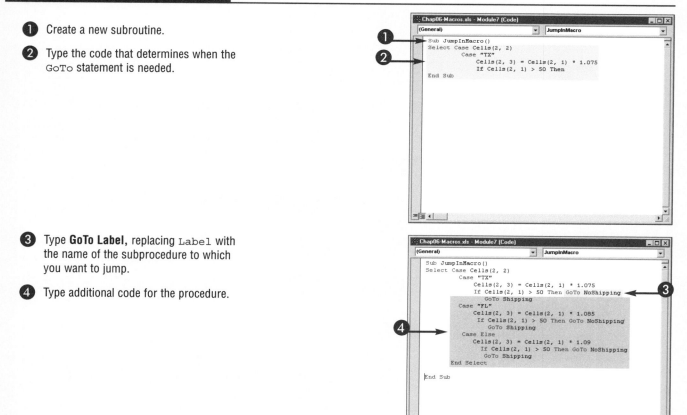

⑤ Type **Label** followed by a colon (:) replacing `Label` with the name typed in step 3.

⑥ Type statements to execute when label is called.

⑦ Type **Exit Sub** to exit the procedure after running statements.

⑧ Switch to Excel and run the macro.

● The appropriate `GoTo` statement executes.

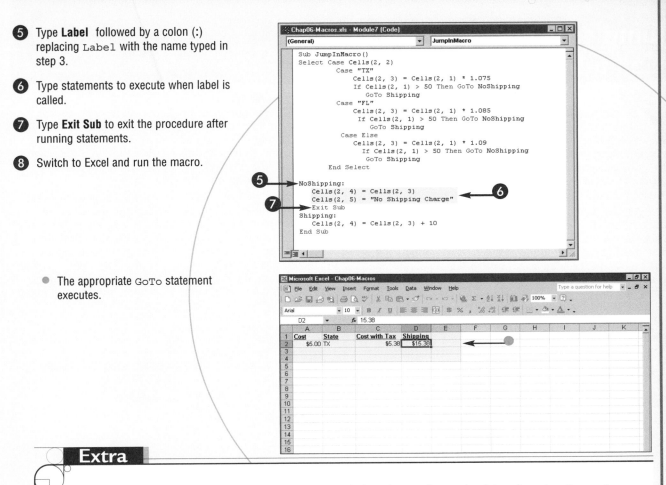

## Extra

You place labels within the code of a procedure to mark the subprocedure code. Other than signaling to the `GoTo` statement the location of the code to run, Excel ignores the label. Labeling the code does not change how it executes. Code within a loop or conditional statement executes only when a condition is met. Labeled code executes when the `GoTo` statement jumps to it, or when control passes to that area of the code.

If you have multiple areas of labeled code, you may not want it all to execute. To avoid execution of code that follows a labeled section, you can either use another `GoTo` statement or an `Exit Sub` statement to terminate the current subroutine.

The following example uses the `Exit Sub` command before the label subprocedure to avoid execution of the `T =50` statement. If the `GoTo` command jumps to the `IncreaseValue` labeled subprocedure, the `T = T * 5` statement does not execute.

**Example:**
```
Sub TestGoTo()
Dim T As Integer
T = Cells(1,1)
If T < 5 Then GoTo IncreaseValue
T = T * 5
Exit Sub
IncreaseValue:
T = 50
End Sub
```

# Conditionally Call a Subroutine

Y ou can conditionally move out of any location in a subroutine to run another subroutine or function. You can accomplish this by using a conditional VBA statement, such as an `If Then` statement, and combining it with a procedure call statement. When you combine the `Call` statement with a conditional statement, the other procedure is only called if the condition is met.

When you use this type of structure, the `If Then` statement checks the specified condition. If the value of the condition is true, the control passes to the specified subroutine or function. After the subroutine completes processing, control returns to the next line of code in the original subroutine. If you do not want to continue processing the first subroutine after calling the second, you need to use an `Exit Sub` statement at that point to exit the subroutine without running any other statements.

When VBA encounters an `Exit Sub` statement, it stops processing of the subroutine and does not process any VBA statements that follow the statement. Remember to place the `Exit Sub` statement directly after the `Call` statement to ensure that VBA immediately exits the subroutine after control returns from the other procedure.

Keep in mind, you can only use the `Call` statement to call another subroutine or function within the same project. VBA does not provide a method for calling subroutines and functions that exist in other projects. To access functions and subroutines that exist in other projects, you must copy the modules that contain them and insert the copies in your current project. You can copy a module using the Project Explorer window. See Chapter 2 for more information about working with the Project Explorer window.

## Conditionally Call a Subroutine

① Create a new subroutine.

② Declare and initialize any variables for the subroutine.

③ Type code required to determine when to jump to another macro.

④ Type **If Condition Then**, replacing `Condition` with the condition to check.

⑤ Type **Call NewProc()**, replacing `NewProc()` with the name of the procedure to call.

⑥ Type **Exit Sub**.

⑦ Type any additional VBA commands required for the subroutine.

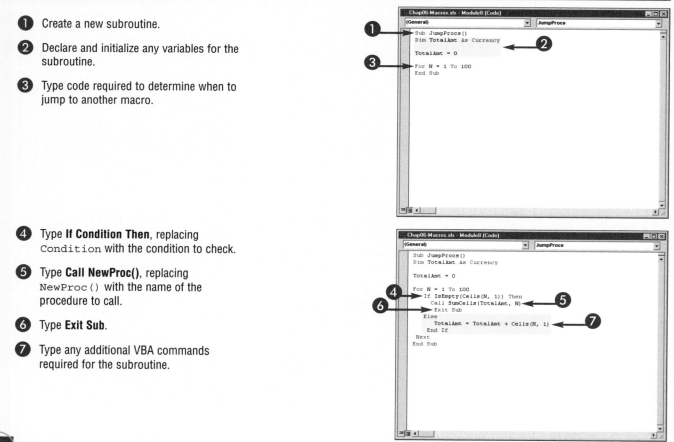

8 Create another new subroutine.

9 Type code to run when the subroutine is called.

10 Switch to Excel and run the macro.

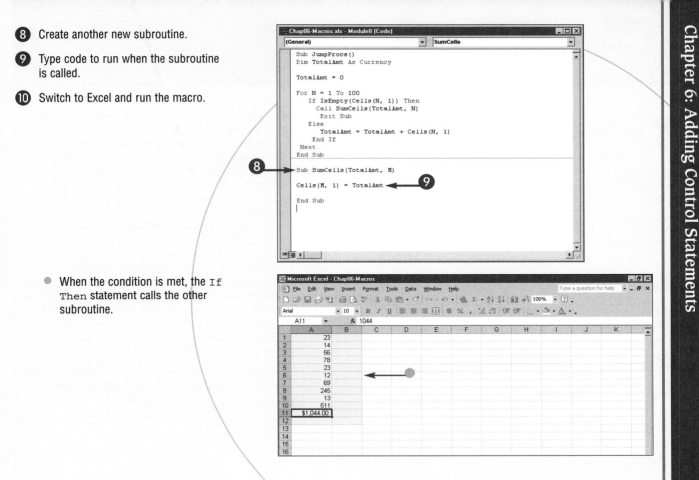

● When the condition is met, the If Then statement calls the other subroutine.

## Extra

You can place an entire If Then statement on one line in VBA to create cleaner code. When you do this, VBA does not require the End If statement. You can only use one line for an If Then statement if you only have one statement to execute when the condition is true. For example, you can type the following code in just one line:

**THIS CODE**
```
If A>B Then
    MsgBox("A is larger")
End If
```
**IS EQUIVALENT TO**
```
If A > B Then MsgBox("A is larger")
```

Although using the Call keyword eliminates any potential confusion by indicating that an outside function or subroutine is being called, you do not need to specify the Call keyword when you call another procedure, subroutine, or function. When you use the Call keyword, you must enclose any arguments passed in parentheses. Conversely, if you call a procedure without the Call statement, you must omit the parentheses around the argument list.

**THIS CODE**
```
Call NewProc(Var1, Var2).
```
**IS EQUIVALENT TO**
```
NewProc Var1, Var2.
```

# Using Excel Worksheet Functions

You can add almost all of the Excel worksheet functions to your VBA code. VBA provides a very limited number of built-in functions. By using the various functions available within Excel, you can add functionality that is not available with the existing VBA functions. For example, Excel provides several different financial functions that you can use within your macros.

To place an Excel worksheet function in your VBA subroutine or function, you use the `WorksheetFunction` property along with the name of the function.

One of the properties available for the Application object, the `WorksheetFunction` property is part of the Excel Object Model that VBA uses to access features of Excel. The Application object refers to the actual Excel program. The `WorksheetFunction` object stores all of the Excel Worksheet functions. To access one of the functions in the `WorksheetFunction` object, you use the

`WorksheetFunction` property and precede the name of the function with the statement: `Application.Worksheet Function`. The function follows with any arguments required by the function enclosed in parentheses. For example, the code `Application.WorksheetFunction. Max(Num1, Num2, Num3, Num4)`, uses the `Max` Excel worksheet function to compare the values in four different variables to determine which variable contains the largest value. See Chapter 4 for more information on the Excel Object Model.

You cannot call Excel worksheet functions that have equivalent VBA functions. For example, both VBA and Excel have functions called `Cos` that return a numeric value that represents the cosine of an angle. If you try to use the Excel worksheet function `Cos` in your VBA procedure, you receive an error message stating "Object doesn't support this property or method." This message displays indicating that Excel does not recognize the function call.

## Using Excel Worksheet Functions

① Create a new subroutine.

**Note:** See Chapter 3 for information on creating subroutines.

② Type **Dim WSVar As Datatype**, replacing `WSVar` with a variable to contain results of the function call and `Datatype` with the data type.

③ Declare any additional variables for the subroutine.

④ Initialize values of variables.

⑤ Type **WSVar = Application.WorksheetFunction**, replacing `WSVar` with the name of the variable.

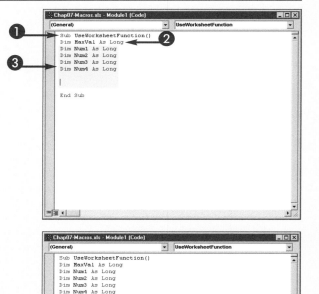

**6** Type **.FunctionName(arguments)**, replacing FunctionName with the Excel function and corresponding arguments within the parentheses.

As you type the argument list, Microsoft IntelliType displays a list of required arguments for the function.

**7** Type additional code required to display the results of the Excel function.

**8** Switch to Excel and run the macro.

**Note:** See Chapter 1 for more on running a macro.

The Excel worksheet function returns the appropriate results.

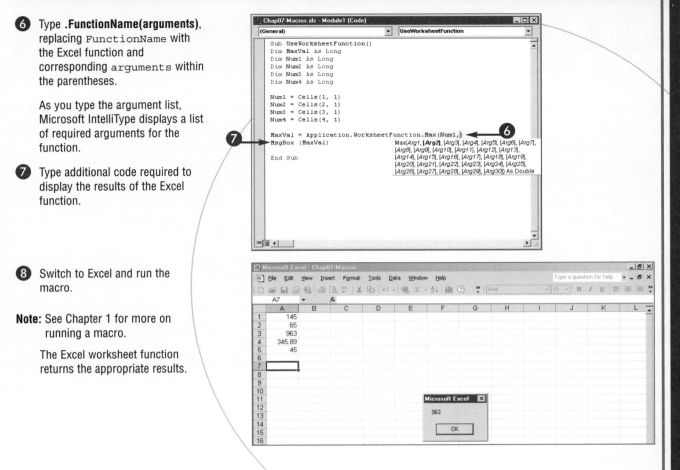

---

## Extra

You can use the built-in Excel functions to add functionality to your Excel macros. VBA provides a limited number of built-in functions for use within the subroutines and functions you create. Because of this, it is not unusual to use the Excel worksheet functions within your VBA procedures. On the other hand, Excel provides an enormous number of functions for doing everything from performing statistical calculations to manipulating text. Even if you are an avid Excel user, you may find the sheer number of functions that Excel provides somewhat intimidating.

The Object Browser lists the functions that are part of the WorksheetFunction object. You can use these Excel worksheet functions within your VBA function or subroutine. You can view this list using WorksheetFunction as the search criteria. See Chapter 4 for more information on the Object Browser.

If you do not know the purpose of a particular Excel function, you can view the Insert Function dialog box in Excel, which displays when you click Insert→Function. The Insert Function dialog box lists all of the available Excel functions. When you click a function, a short description of the function appears under the function list.

# Using the
# MsgBox Function

Y ou can use the MsgBox function to display pop-up message boxes when a VBA procedure executes. The MsgBox function does two things: It displays a dialog box to provide information to the user and it returns a value that indicates the response from the user. You capture the user response by assigning the results of the MsgBox function to a variable. For example, the code UserResponse = MsgBox("Do you want to continue?") assigns a value between 1 and 7 indicating the user response to the UserResponse variable. For example, if the user clicks OK, the MsgBox function returns a constant value of vbOK or 1.

The MsgBox function has five different arguments: Prompt, Buttons, Title, Helpfile, and Context. All but the first argument are optional.

The Prompt argument indicates the value that displays in the message box. You can make this argument a text string and enclose it in quotes or use a variable. You can combine values by using the concatenation operator (&), as in the example: MsgBox("Total Sum: " & TotalSum).

The optional Buttons argument enables you to specify a constant value indicating the buttons and icons to display on the message box. If you do not specify a button constant, the MsgBox function uses the default vbOKOnly that displays only the OK button.

The optional Title argument contains the text that displays on the title bar of the message box. If you omit this argument, Excel displays a default value of Microsoft Excel.

The final two optional arguments are available for adding help to the message box. The Helpfile argument specifies the name of the help file and the Context argument specifies the context ID of the help topic to display.

## Using the MsgBox Function

① Create a new subroutine.

② Type **Dim MsgVar As Integer**, replacing MsgVar with the variable to receive the MsgBox return value.

③ Declare other variables needed for the subroutine.

④ Type **MsgVar = MsgBox("Text Prompt", buttons, "Text Title")**, replacing "Text Prompt" with the prompt for the message box, buttons with the button constant, and "Text Title" with the title for the message box.

You can type **+** to separate multiple button constant values.

**⑤** Type a conditional statement to test the value returned from the `MsgBox` function.

In this example, the `If Then` statement determines if a value of 6 or 7 returns.

**⑥** Type additional code for the subroutine.

You can type **&** to join the text string with a variable value.

```
Sub DisplayMsgBox()
Dim Msg As Integer
Dim Result As Integer
Dim N As Integer
Dim CellSum As Long

Msg = MsgBox("Do you want to sum cells?", vbYesNo + vbQuestion, "Sum Cells")

If Msg = 6 Then
  N = 1
  Do While Not IsEmpty(Cells(N, 1))
        CellSum = CellSum + Cells(N, 1)
        N = N + 1
  Loop
End If
If Msg = 7 Then
  Exit Sub
End If

Result = MsgBox("The Sum is: " & CellSum, vbInformation, "Cell Total")

End Sub
```

**⑦** Switch to Excel and run the macro.

The message box displays and the macro processes the value of the button pressed.

You can use twenty different constant values as the `Buttons` value for the `MsgBox` function. You can use these values separately, or combine them by adding an addition sign (+) between each constant value. For example, the following code creates a message box containing Yes, No, and Cancel buttons as well as the Warning Query icon. For a list of the constants that you can use for the `Buttons` argument, refer to Appendix A.

**Example:**
```
MsgBox("Select button", vbYesNoCancel +
vbQuestion)
```

The `MsgBox` function returns an integer value between 1 and 7 that indicates which button the user selects. You can determine this selected button with the value that the `MsgBox` function returns, either by looking at the integer value, or by using the constant value that represents the button. The following table shows the integer values returned by the `MsgBox` function and the equivalent constant value.

| MSGBOX RETURN VALUE | CONSTANT | DESCRIPTION |
| --- | --- | --- |
| 1 | vbOK | OK button pressed |
| 2 | vbCancel | Cancel button pressed |
| 3 | vbAbort | Abort button pressed |
| 4 | vbRetry | Retry button pressed |
| 5 | vbIgnore | Ignore button pressed |
| 6 | vbYes | Yes button pressed |
| 7 | vbNo | No button pressed |

# Using the InputBox Function

Y ou can use the InputBox function to prompt for specific user input during the execution of a procedure. The InputBox function displays a dialog box requesting specific input and returns the user response. You capture the user response by assigning the results of the InputBox function to a variable.

The InputBox has seven different arguments, but only the first is required: Prompt, Title, Default, xPos, yPos, Helpfile, and Context.

The Prompt argument indicates the user prompt on the dialog box. You can make this argument either a text string enclosed in quotes, or a variable. You can combine values using the concatenation operator (&), as in this example, UR = InputBox("Sum:" & TSum).

The optional Title argument contains the text that displays on the title bar of the dialog box. If it is omitted,

Excel displays a default value of Microsoft Excel. The optional Default argument specifies the default value to display in the text box on the dialog box.

You specify the display position of the dialog box using the optional arguments xPos and yPos. If you omit them, the dialog box displays in the center of the screen. These arguments use units of measurement called *twips*. One twip equals ½₀ of a point or ¼,₄₄₀ of an inch. The xPos argument indicates the distance from the left side of the screen to the left side of the dialog box. The yPos indicates the position from the top of the screen to the top of the dialog box.

You use the final two optional arguments for adding help capability to the dialog box. The Helpfile argument specifies the name of the help file and the Context argument specifies the context ID of the help topic to display. If you specify one argument, you must specify both.

## Using the InputBox Function

① Create a new subroutine.

② Type **Dim UserInput As Variant**, replacing UserInput with the variable to receive value from InputBox function.

③ Declare and initialize any other variables for the subroutine.

④ Type the initial VBA code.

The example uses a Do While loop to request values from a user until Done is typed.

⑤ Type **UserInput = InputBox("Text Prompt")** replacing "TextPrompt" with the text to display on the Input Box.

You can type **&** to join the text string with a variable value.

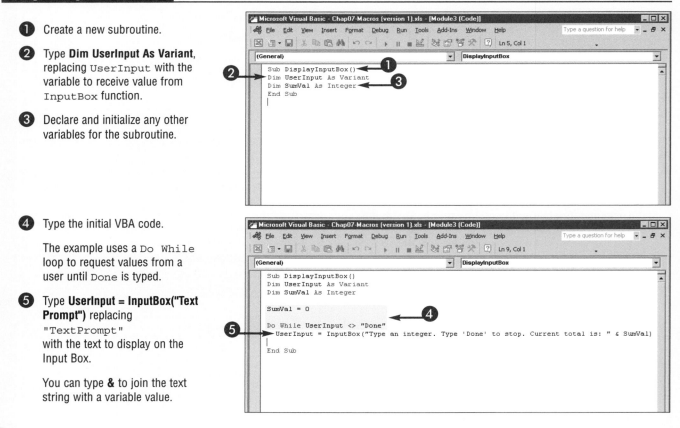

112

**6** Type additional code to process the value returned from the `InputBox` function.

**7** Switch to Excel and run the associated macro.

The `InputBox` function requests specific input from the user.

```
Microsoft Visual Basic - Chap07-Macros (version 1).xls - [Module3 (Code)]
File  Edit  View  Insert  Format  Debug  Run  Tools  Add-Ins  Window  Help          Type a question for help

(General)                                          DisplayInputBox

Sub DisplayInputBox()
Dim UserInput As Variant
Dim SumVal As Integer

SumVal = 0

Do While UserInput <> "Done"
  UserInput = InputBox("Type an integer. Type 'Done' to stop. Current total is: " & SumVal)
  If IsNumeric(UserInput) Then
    SumVal = SumVal + Int(UserInput)
  End If
Loop
MsgBox ("Total Sum = " & SumVal)
End Sub
```

```
Microsoft Excel - Chap07-Macros (version 1)  [Recovered]
File  Edit  View  Insert  Format  Tools  Data  Window  Help          Type a question for help

Microsoft Excel
Type an integer. Type 'Done' to stop. Current total is: 34      OK
                                                                 Cancel
```

---

## Apply It

You can use named arguments to simplify your function calls. When you work with built-in VBA functions, you see that many of the functions have optional arguments. For example, although the `InputBox` has seven different arguments, only the first one is required. If you want to include any additional arguments, you need to specify the argument values in order, leaving a placeholder for any you do not want to use.

**Example:**
```
UserInput = InputBox("Type a value",  , "test")
```

Instead of specifying a placeholder for each value, VBA enables you to use named arguments with the built-in procedures. With a named argument, you specify the name of the argument along with the corresponding value. To specify a named argument, you type the name of the argument followed by a colon, an equals sign, and the value of that particular argument. You can place named arguments in any order, and you do not have to specify a value for every argument.

**Example:**
```
UserInput = InputBox(prompt:="Type a value.", default:="5")
```

# Retrieve Current Date and Time

VBA gives you the ability to retrieve the current date and time information from your system using some of its built-in functions. VBA includes several date-related built-in functions that you can add to subroutines and functions that you create. You use these functions to return a system date or time, perform date calculations, set a date, and even time a specific process.

If you want to include the current date and time information, you can select from three different functions. The Date function returns the current system date, the Time function returns the current system time, and the Now function returns both the date and time.

VBA formats the date and time information to match your system's short date format. You can modify the date and time settings via the Start menu.

When working with dates, you can avoid displaying a date outside a range by remembering the date range that Excel accepts. VBA accommodates a much larger date range than Excel by accepting dates between January 1, 100, and December 31, 9999. Excel for Windows, however, only accepts dates between January 1, 1980, and December 31, 1079. If you happen to use Excel on a Macintosh, the date range is even smaller with the acceptable dates being January 1, 1904, to February 5, 2040. Hopefully none of these date limits pose any issues for you as you work with dates in the macros you create. If you need to display dates outside the range, you can do so by placing the date in a string variable.

You can assign the results of the Date or Time function to another variable, a worksheet cell, or another function, such as the MsgBox function, as in this example:
MsgBox("Current Date and Time: " & Now()).

## Retrieve Current Date

① Create a new subroutine.

② Type **MsgBox("Current date:" & Date)**.

③ Switch to Excel and run the macro.

The current system date displays in the message box.

You can modify the date setting by clicking Start→Settings→ Control Panel→Regional Options.

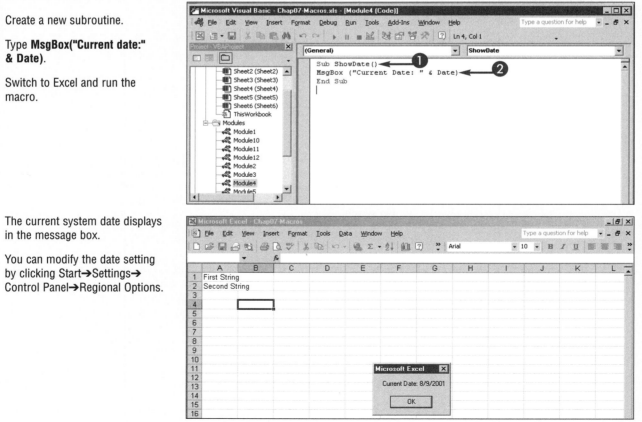

① Create a new subroutine.

② Type **Cells(1,1) = "Current Time:" & Time()** replacing `Cells(1,1)` with the location for the time and `"Current Time"` with the text string to display.

③ Switch to Excel and run the macro.

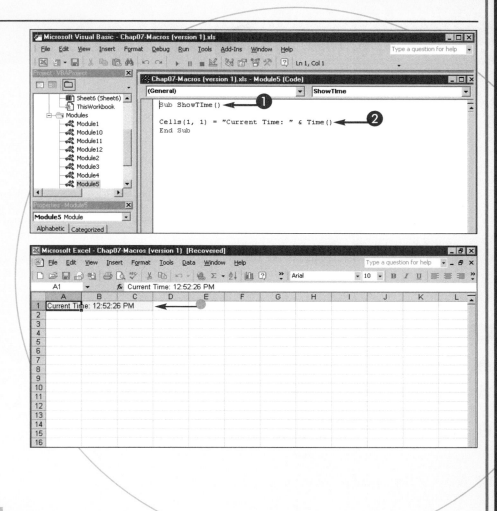

● The current system time displays in the first cell.

You can modify the time setting by clicking Start→Settings→Control Panel→ Regional Options.

## Extra

VBA uses the same serial number system for dates and times as Excel, which stores each date as a numeric value. You can express each date and time as a sequential number starting at 0. You can express the date portion of the number as the integer portion of the number and the time portion of the date as a decimal value between 0 and 0.99999999 representing times from 0:00:00 (12:00 Midnight) to 23:59:99 (11:59:99 PM). Because Excel stores dates and times as numeric values, you can easily manipulate them by adding and subtracting them.

Excel uses the Western calendar to determine the number of days in each month and which month is the first month of the year. Using this calendar, the first month of the year, January, has 31 days and the second month has 28 days with the exception of years divisible by 4, which have 29 days. All other months have 31 or 30 days. One exception to the leap year rule, century years must be divisible by 400 to be a leap year; therefore 2000 is a leap year, but 3000 is not.

# Determine the Amount of Time between Dates

You can determine the amount of time between two different dates by using the `DateDiff` function. With this function you can return almost any time interval between the specified date values, such as months, days, hours, minutes, or even seconds.

The `DateDiff` function has five different arguments of which the first three are required: `Interval`, `Date1`, `Date2`, `Firstdayofweek`, and `Firstweekofyear`.

You can use the `Interval` argument to express, in units of time, the difference between the two dates. There are ten different values that you can specify for this argument.

The `Date1` and `Date2` arguments specify the two dates you want to compare. You can use a date string, the value returned by a function, or the contents of a cell, as long as it is a valid date. To ensure the date is valid, consider using the `IsDate` function to check the date.

You can utilize the optional `Firstdayofweek` argument if you want to use a day other than Sunday as the first day of the week. To specify a constant value for this argument, you simply include vb before the appropriate day of the week. For example, to use Monday as the first day of the week, you specify `vbMonday` as the value of the argument. See Appendix A for `Firstdayofweek` constant values.

Finally, you can use the optional `Firstweekofyear` argument to indicate what you want to treat as the first week of the year. If you omit this argument, VBA considers the first week that contains the date January 1 as the first week of the year, even if it falls on Saturday. For example, if you want to have the first week containing at least four days of January, you specify a value of `vbFirstFourDays`. See Appendix A for `Firstweekofyear` constant values.

## Determine the Amount of Time between Dates

① Create a new subroutine.

② Type **Dim Date1 As Variant**, replacing `Date1` with the variable for the first date.

③ Type **Dim Date2 As Variant**, replacing `Date2` with the variable for the second date.

④ Declare and initialize other variables for the subroutine.

⑤ Type initial VBA code.

⑥ Type **Date1 = datevalue1**, replacing `Date1` with the variable in step 2 and `datevalue1` with the first date.

⑦ Type **Date2 = datevalue2**, replacing `Date2` with the variable in step 3 and `datevalue2` with the second date.

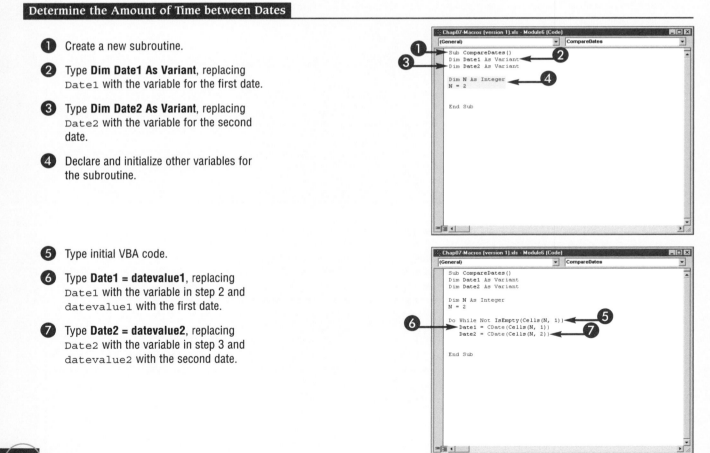

**8** To verify that both dates are valid, type **If IsDate(Date1) And IsDate(Date2) Then** replacing `Date1` and `Date2` with the date variables.

**9** Type **Diff = DateDiff(interval, Date1, Date2)**, replacing `Diff` with the variable to receive the results of the function and `Date1` and `Date2` with the date variables.

**10** Type the remaining VBA code.

**11** Switch to Excel and run the associated macro.

● The `DateDiff` function compares the specified date and returns an interval value.

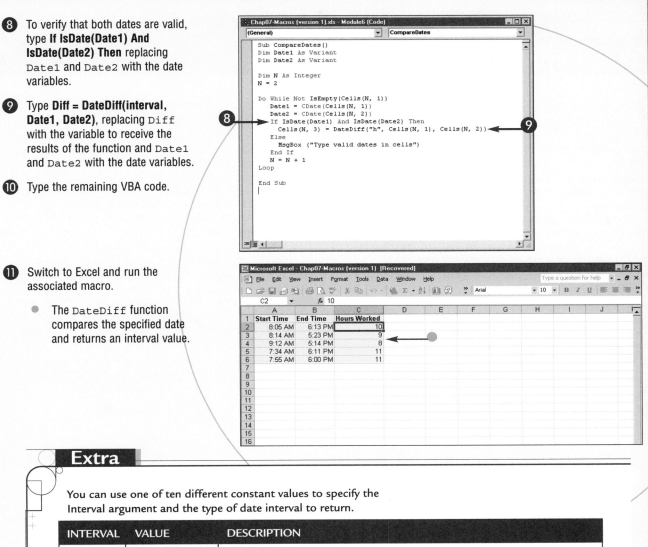

## Extra

You can use one of ten different constant values to specify the Interval argument and the type of date interval to return.

| INTERVAL | VALUE | DESCRIPTION |
| --- | --- | --- |
| yyyy | year | Only compares the year portion of both dates. 12/31/1999 and 1/1/2000 return a value of 1 year. |
| q | Quarter | Divides year into four quarters and returns number of quarters between dates. |
| m | Month | Only compares the month portion of both dates. 12/31/1999 and 1/1/2000 return a value of 1 month. |
| y | Day of Year | Same results as using d. |
| d | Day | Number of days between two dates. |
| w | Weekday | Determines the day of the week of the first date, for instance, Wednesday, and then counts the number of Wednesdays between the dates. |
| ww | Week | Relies on the value specified as the `firstdayofweek` argument to determine the number of weeks between two dates. |
| h | Hour | If a time is not specified, uses midnight or 00:00:00. |
| n | Minute | Number of minutes between two times. |
| s | Second | Number of seconds between two times. |

# Format a
# Date Expression

You can custom format an expression using a specific date or time with the `FormatDateTime` function. Doing so returns a `Variant` data type value with the specified formatting. See Chapter 3 for more information on data types.

The `FormatDateTime` function uses two different arguments, of which only the first argument is required: `Date`, and `NamedFormat`. The `Date` argument identifies the date expression that you want to format and accepts cell references, variable references, string expressions, or numeric values. If you reference a cell, the cell must have default formatting. In other words, the cell must have Default, and not Date, or some other formatting value, when you view the formatting.

You can reference a cell using any of the cell range reference options discussed in Chapter 11. For example, if the date you want to format is located in cell A1, you can

type the following code using the `Cells` property to reference that cell: `FormatDateTime(Cells(1,1))`.

The `NamedFormat` argument specifies the formatting of the expression. You can use one of the predefined formatting constants. If you omit the `NamedFormat` argument, the `FormatDateTime` function uses the `vbGeneralDate` constant as the default value. The `vbGeneralDate` constant instructs Excel to format the date expression with the system date settings and formats the time portion with the system long time settings.

Windows maintains your default date and time settings on the Regional Options dialog box, which you can access through the Start menu. When you use a constant with the `NamedFormat` argument, you specify the combination of these settings that you want for formatting your date and time values. By changing the values on this dialog box, you affect how the dates and times display when you use the `FormatDateTime` function.

## Format a Date Expression

① Create a new subroutine.

② Type the `Dim` statement to define variables for the subroutine.

③ Type **DateVar = DateExp**, replacing `DateVar` with the variable to hold the date expression specified by `DateExp`.

The example assigns date values from the corresponding worksheet.

④ Type **DateVar2 =
FormatDateTime(DateVar,
vbformat)**, replacing `DateVar2`
with the result and `vbformat`
with the constant that indicates
the desired format.

⑤ Type the remaining VBA code.

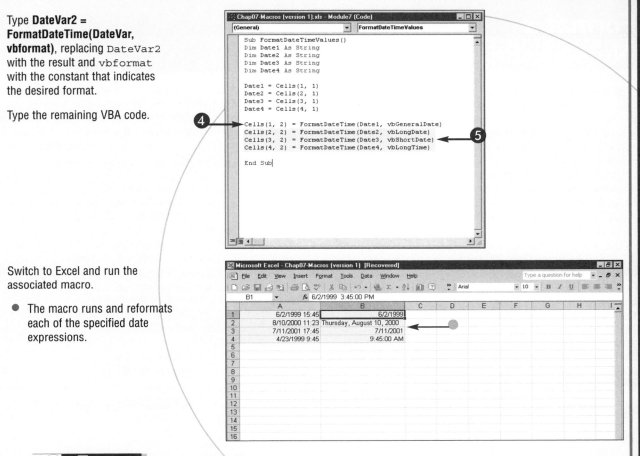

⑥ Switch to Excel and run the
associated macro.

● The macro runs and reformats
each of the specified date
expressions.

## Extra

You can specify the formatting of the specified date and time with `NamedFormat` argument.
If it is omitted, Excel uses the `vbGeneralDate` constant. When you use the `NamedFormat`
argument, you can pass it either the constant value or the numeric value that corresponds
to the constant, as outlined in the following table. Keep in mind, the actual formats used as
a result of specifying these constant values are based upon the system date and time settings
on the Regional Options dialog box. You display the Regional Options dialog box by clicking
Start➔Settings➔Control➔Regional Options. You can then select the corresponding tab, either
Date or Time.

| CONSTANT | VALUE | DESCRIPTION |
|---|---|---|
| vbGeneralDate | 0 | Default value if `NamedFormat` argument is omitted. Displays the date using the system short date format and the time using the system long time format. |
| vbLongDate | 1 | Displays the date using the system long date format. |
| vbShortDate | 2 | Displays the date using the system short date format. |
| vbLongTime | 3 | Displays the time using the system time format. |
| vbShortTime | 4 | Displays the time using a 24-hour clock format commonly referred to as Military time. For example, 6:00 p.m. formats as 18:00. |

# Format a Numeric Expression

You can custom format a numeric expression so that it displays with specific formatting by using either the `FormatNumber`, `FormatCurrency`, or `FormatPercentage` functions. These functions all take a numeric value and return a formatted number based upon the values you specify for each argument. The `FormatNumber` function returns a formatted number, whereas the `FormatCurrency` function returns a number that begins with a currency symbol, and the `FormatPercentage` function returns a number followed by a percentage sign.

Each of these functions has the same five arguments with the first being required: `Expression`, `NumDigitsAfterDecimal`, `IncludeLeadingDigit`, `UseParensForNegativeNumbers`, and `GroupDigits`.

`Expression`, the first argument, specifies the numeric value to format. The `NumDigitsAfterDecimal` argument indicates the number of decimal places to display on the right side of the decimal. The `IncludeLeadingDigit` argument determines whether a zero displays before the decimal for numbers between -1 and 1. The

`UseParensForNegativeNumbers` argument specifies whether to place parentheses around negative numbers. Finally, the `GroupDigits` argument determines how Excel groups numbers to make them more readable. For example, with this argument, you express fifty thousand as 50,000.

The last three arguments, `IncludeLeadingDigit`, `UseParensForNegativeNumbers`, and `GroupDigits`, all use the same three constant values. Use `vbTrue` as the value of the argument to perform the corresponding formatting. Use `vbFalse` if you do not want that type of formatting. If you do not specify a value, or specify `vbUseDefault`, the function utilizes the corresponding value from your computer's regional settings.

Windows stores all default settings for your system on the Regional Options dialog box. You can modify these settings at anytime, but modifications affect all Windows applications. You can view and modify your regional settings by selecting them via the Regional Options dialog box. To access this dialog box, see the section "Format a Date Expression."

## Format a Numeric Expression

① Create a new subroutine.

② Type **Dim NumberVar As Variant**, replacing `NumberVar` with a variable for use with a number format function.

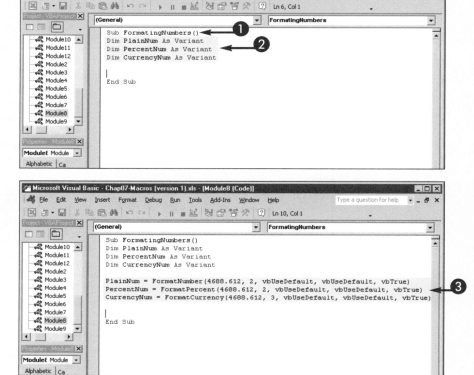

③ Type **NumberVar = FormatNumber(123, 2, vbUseDefault, vbUseDefault, vbTrue)**, replacing the first two arguments with the number to convert and number of decimal places.

④ Type the remaining VBA code to work with the formatted number.

⑤ Switch to Excel and run the associated macro.

● The macro runs and reformats the number using the specified formatting function.

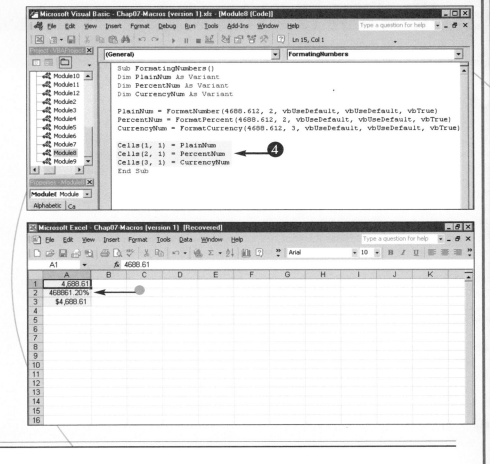

If you want to further customize the way a number displays, you use the Format function. You can create your own number formats by combining specific characters along with symbols that represent the numbers, for example: Format(NumVal, "##.##").

| NUMERIC CHARACTERS | DISPLAYS |
|---|---|
| 0 | A numeric digit or a zero if the number does not have a digit in that place. Use this character to ensure that a digit appears in a specific place. For example, 0000 always displays a four-digit number. If there are fewer digits, a zero displays for the non-specified digits. |
| # | A numeric digit if the number has a digit in that place. If there is no digit, a value does not display in that place. |
| . | Decimal point placeholder. |
| % | An expression as a percentage by multiplying by 100 and adding a percent sign. |
| , | Thousands separator. |
| E-, E+, e-, e+ | Numeric expression in scientific format. The number of digits on the right side of the symbol indicates the number of digits in the exponent. |
| \ or " " | The character that follows that backslash or enclosed in quotes. For example, to place a plus sign (+) in the number string you would type \+ in the desired location. |

# Remove Extra Spacing from a String

You can remove excess spaces from the front or the end of a specific string using one of the built-in trim functions in VBA. Extra spacing at the beginning or end of strings can affect the way the string displays. You have three different functions for trimming excess spacing. The RTrim function removes the excess spacing at the end of the string. The LTrim function removes the excess spacing at the beginning of the string. If you want to remove the extra spaces from both ends of a string simultaneously, you can use the Trim function.

Each function requires just one argument: the string containing the excess spacing. Typically, you pass the string to the function as the value of a variable or the contents of a cell in a worksheet. For example, LTrim(LongString) trims the excess spacing at the beginning of a string.

When you call any one of these functions, the function returns a Null value if the value of the string expression passed to the function is Null.

Each function returns a Variant data type with a subtype of String. See Chapter 3 for more information on data types in VBA. If you want the function to return a String data type value, you need to place the String type declaration symbol, a dollar sign, at the end of the function. When you use the dollar sign at the end of the function to return a String value, make sure the variable to which you assign the results is declared as a string.

None of these functions remove excess spacing within a string. For example, Trim(" This          is a          sample string      ") removes the spacing only before the word This and after string. The extra spacing within the string remains untouched.

## Remove Extra Spacing from a String

① Create a new subroutine.

② Type **Dim StringVar As String**, replacing StringVar with the variable containing the string.

③ Declare other variables needed for the subroutine.

④ Assign the string expression to StringVar.

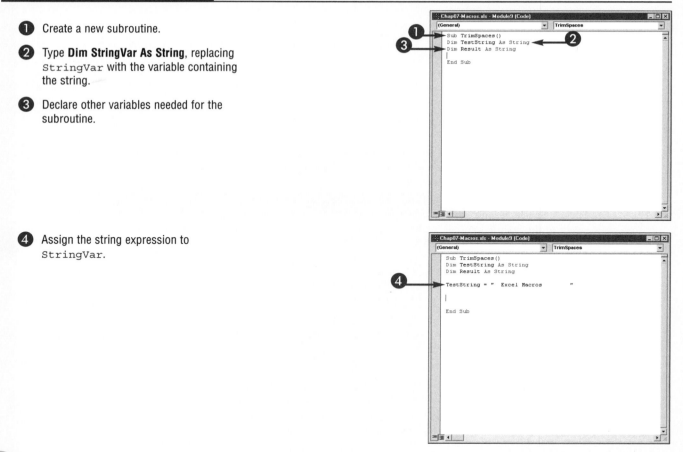

**5** Type **Result = Trim$(StringVar)**, replacing `StringVar` with the variable to receive the trimmed string.

**6** Type additional VBA code.

**7** Switch to Excel and run the associated macro.

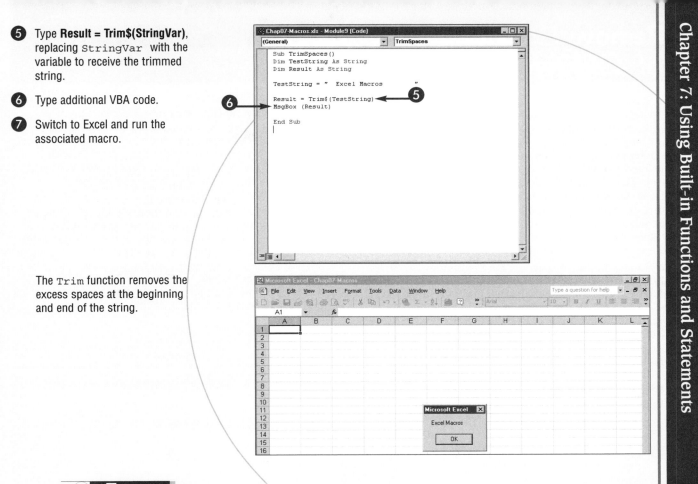

The `Trim` function removes the excess spaces at the beginning and end of the string.

## Extra

Many of the built-in functions in VBA return a `Variant` data type value. Good for simplifying code because their data types can handle any type of data, Variants still are not as efficient as Strings, which require less memory to store than Variants. For this reason, you can modify most of the built-in VBA functions that return a Variant to return a String data type by simply adding a dollar sign symbol ($) to the end of the function name. You can use the dollar sign with the following functions:

| | | |
|---|---|---|
| Chr | ChrB | CuDir |
| Date | Dir | Error |
| Input | InputB | Lcase |
| Left | LeftB | Ltrim |
| Mid | MidB | Oct |
| Right | RightB | Rtrim |
| Space | Str | String |
| Time | Trim | UCase |

# Return a Portion of a String

nstead of an entire string, you can use the built-in functions available in VBA to return only a portion of a string. These functions work well when you only want a smaller portion of a string. You can use three different functions to return a portion of a string. The Left function returns the specified number of characters starting at the left side, or beginning, of the string. The Right function returns the specified number of characters starting at the right side, or end of the string. Each of these functions has the same two required arguments: Left(string, length) and Right(string, length).

The string argument specifies the string from which you want to return the specified number of characters. You can make the argument an actual string enclosed in quotes, a variable that contains a string, or a cell reference. The length argument indicates the number of characters to return from the string.

The third built-in function for returning a portion of a string is the Mid function. This function works well for retrieving characters from the center of a string. When you use this function, you indicate the first character with which to start and how many characters to return. There are three different arguments for the Mid function: Mid(string, start, length).

Similar to the Left and Right functions, the Mid function string argument specifies the string to use with the function. The start argument indicates the position of the first character in the string to return. The length argument is the only optional argument with the Mid function. If you omit the length argument, the function returns the remaining portion of the string. Otherwise, the length argument indicates the number of characters to return.

## Return a Portion of a String

### USING THE LEFT/RIGHT FUNCTION

① Create a new subroutine.

② Type **Dim StringVar As String**, replacing StringVar with the string variable.

③ Type **StringVar = "String"**, replacing "String" with the string to assign to the variable.

④ Type **Result = Left(StringVar, #)**, replacing Result with the shortened string and # with the number of characters.

To return characters from the right side of the string, you can replace Left with Right.

⑤ Switch to Excel and run the associated macro.

● The function returns the shortened string.

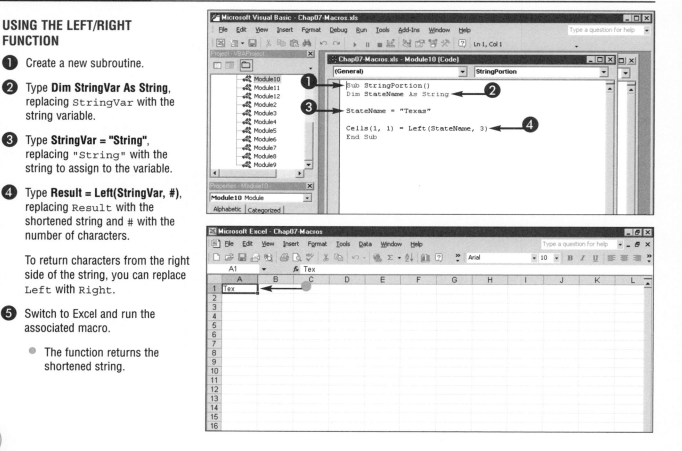

## USING THE MID FUNCTION

**1** Create a new subroutine.

**2** Type **Dim IB As String**, replacing IB with the string variable.

**3** Declare additional variables for the subroutine.

**4** Type **IB = InputBox ("Text")** replacing IB with the variable in step 2, and `"Text"` with the input bpx text.

**5** Type **Cells(1,1) = Mid(IB, MS, NC)** replacing `Cells(1,1)` with the result's location, `MS` with the start number, and `NC` with the number of characters.

**6** Switch to Excel and run the associated macro.

● The Mid function returns the specified number of characters from the string.

```
Chap07-Macros.xls - Module11 (Code)
(General)                    MidString

Sub MidString()
Dim IB As String
Dim NC As Integer
Dim MS As Integer

IB = InputBox("Text")

NC = Len(IB)

MS = Int(NC / 2)

Cells(1, 1) = Mid(IB, MS, 3)

End Sub
```

Microsoft Excel - Chap07-Macros

A7

| | A | B | C | D | E | F | G | H | I | J | K | L |
|---|---|---|---|---|---|---|---|---|---|---|---|---|
| 1 | mpl | | | | | | | | | | | |

---

## Apply It

With the Mid, Right, and Left functions, you do not always know the length of the strings and may need to check the string length to determine the number of characters to return before calling one of these functions. You can determine the length of a string with the Len function: Len(string), which uses only one argument, string, to identify the string to check. You can make the string argument an actual string, or the name of a variable that contains a string. You can use a conditional statement along with the Len function to determine the number of characters to return from a string. The If Then statement in the following example checks to see if the length of the string is longer than ten characters. If so, the Right function returns a portion of the string.

**Example:**
```
Dim NewStr As String
Dim NewStr2 As String
Dim CharNum As Integer
Dim NewLength As Integer
NewStr = "This is a Sample String"
CharNum = Len(NewStr)
If   CharNum > 10 Then
     NewStr2 = Right(NewStr, CharNum - 10)
End If
```

# Compare
# Two Strings

You can compare two strings to see if they are alike using the built-in StrComp function in VBA. When you compare two strings, the StrComp function returns a value indicating whether the strings are the same. If the strings are different, the function returns a value that shows which string is larger.

The StrComp function has three different arguments, of which the first two arguments are required: string1, string2, and compare. The string1 and string2 arguments indicate the strings to compare. You can use a string enclosed in quotes, a string variable, or a reference to a cell containing a string as the argument value.

An optional constant value, the compare argument, determines how the function compares the strings. If you omit the argument, the function uses a binary comparison of the strings, or the comparison specified by the Option Compare statement. The vbBinaryCompare constant

indicates that you want to compare the strings based upon the ANSI character code for each character in the string. On an ANSI character chart, lowercase letters have a larger value than uppercase characters.

Use the vbTextCompare constant if you want to compare strings based upon the actual text, regardless of the case. With this comparison, the StrComp function sees an *M* and *m* as the same character.

You can use the vbUseCompareOption to indicate that you want to use the type of comparison specified by the Option Compare statement. If the statement does not exist, a binary comparison is performed.

The StrComp function returns a value of 0 if the strings are the same. If the first string is larger, it returns 1. If the second string is larger, the function returns -1. If either string is Null, the function returns Null.

## Compare Two Strings

① Type **Option Compare Text** at the top of the module.

② Create a new subroutine.

③ Type **Dim String1 As String** replacing String1 with the first string to compare.

④ Type **Dim String2 As String** replacing String2 with the second string to compare.

⑤ Assign values to String1 and String2.

**6** Type **If StrComp(String1, String2) = 0 Then**, replacing String1 and String2 with the strings in steps 3 and 4.

**7** Type VBA statements to perform if strings match.

**8** Type VBA statements to perform if strings do not match.

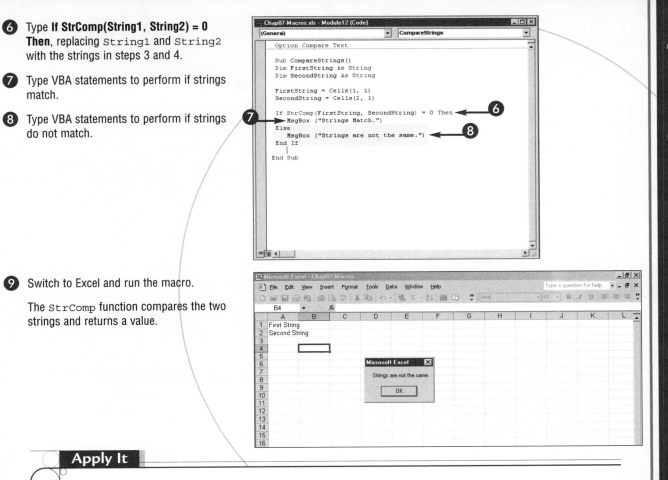

**9** Switch to Excel and run the macro.

The StrComp function compares the two strings and returns a value.

## Apply It

When comparing strings, the StrComp function treats upper- and lowercase characters differently for a binary comparison. In other words, the StrComp function considers a J and j the same. If you want to compare strings to see if they contain the same characters, you must convert the strings to the same case — either all uppercase or all lowercase — before making the comparison. VBA provides two built-in functions that you can use to convert strings. The UCase function, UCase(string), converts the lowercase characters in a string to uppercase. The LCase function, LCase(string), converts all uppercase characters in the string to lowercase. Both functions ignore numbers and symbols in the string and require one argument to convert the string. You can make the string argument an actual string enclosed in quotes, or a reference to a string such as a variable name. If the string contains a Null value, the function returns a value of Null.

You can place the Option Compare statement at the top of a module to indicate the type of comparison to make between strings. To perform a binary comparison of all strings, type:

```
Option Compare Binary
```

If you want to compare all strings as text, type:

```
Option Compare Text
```

# Debugging Basics

N o matter how adept you are at writing VBA code, sooner or later you encounter an error when running your macro. Not all errors are the result of bad code; you may, for example, encounter errors because the procedure may anticipate a different data type. Whatever the cause of the error, you need to determine the source of the error and how to resolve the issue. The process of finding errors is referred to as *debugging*.

As you work with the Visual Basic Editor, you can encounter *design*, *compile*, *runtime*, and *logical* errors. Although you normally fix design-time errors immediately

upon the creation of the procedure, compile and runtime errors do not show up until the procedure executes, and may require some debugging to locate. The most difficult errors for you to locate typically consist of logical error, because you only know that you did not receive the anticipated results. Because logical errors do not produce an error message, you have to rely on debugging options to trace through your code and determine the error location.

## Design Errors

Predominantly created when you write your code, most design errors consist of syntax errors that occur when you mistype a statement. You create design errors when you omit an argument for a function, or forget to use parentheses. The code `MsgBox ("Sample Text"`, for example, produces a syntax error due to the omission of the closing parenthesis.

As long as you use the Code Settings of the Visual Basic Editor, you immediately know when a syntax error occurs in your code. The Options dialog box includes an Auto Syntax Check

option that instructs the Visual Basic Editor to check the syntax of each line of code that you type. If the Visual Basic Editor encounters an error, a Syntax Error message box displays immediately, highlighting the error and indicating what you need to correct it. You should always have this option selected. For more concerning the Visual Basic Editor, see Chapter 2.

## Compile Errors

If you have done any other programming, you know that *compiling* is the process of converting or translating your VBA code into a format that your computer can understand. With other programming languages, you compile a program before you run it. With VBA and Excel, the compile occurs automatically each time you run a procedure. This is true whether you run the procedure within the Visual Basic Editor or

you select the corresponding macro in Excel. Because this process occurs so quickly, you are typically unaware that a compile even occurs.

If any errors occur during the compile process, an error message box pops up, and the Visual Basic Editor highlights the location of the error.

## Runtime Errors

You encounter runtime errors as your code executes. As with the other types of errors, when the Visual Basic Editor encounters an error, a message box displays with a description of the error. Also, when the Editor encounters a runtime error, if you have not placed any error handling in the code, execution of the procedure stops.

You typically receive errors when you pass invalid data to your procedure, such as when you pass the wrong data type value to a variable. If you pass a string to an expression that expects a numeric value, a runtime error occurs.

To avoid having your code stop due to a runtime error, you need to use the `On Error Resume Next` statement at the beginning of your procedure. The statement causes VBA to skip over the error and continue processing the procedure. Although the code no longer halts abruptly due to an error, the error still exists, and you need to handle it. VBA places the information for the error in the `Err` object. As you write your code, you should check the `Err` object to ensure that runtime errors do not occur. If you encounter an error, you need to write code to resolve the error situation as quickly as possible.

The VBA Object Model includes the `Err` object that captures information about a runtime error. You can use the properties of the `Err` object to capture a runtime error and return a message providing information on how to resolve the error situation without abruptly halting the procedure. The following table lists the three different properties of the `Err` object and their descriptions.

| ERR OBJECT PROPERTY | DESCRIPTION |
| --- | --- |
| Description | Contains a VBA description of the runtime error |
| Number | Contains the VBA error number of the runtime error |
| Source | Indicates the name of the current procedure that caused the error |

You can create code similar to the following that executes if VBA encounters an error. This code creates a message box containing the description of the error and places the VBA error number in the title bar of the message box. See Chapter 7 for more information on working with message boxes. The generated code appears as follows:

**Example**
```
If Err.Number <> 0 Then
    MsgBox Err.Description, vbCritical, "Error # " & Err.Number
End If
```

## Logical Errors

Unlike the other types of errors, logical errors do not produce any type of error message. Instead a logical error returns unexpected results. For example, although the following code is syntactically correct, it has a logical error in calculating the sales tax. The sales tax rate is 7.5 percent, but the code is charging 75 percent because of a misplacement of the decimal point:

**Example**
```
Price1 = 4.45
Price2 = 6.95
TotalCost = (Price1 + Price2) * 1.75
```

Simple logical errors such as mistyping a value or placing a decimal in the wrong place are sometimes the most difficult errors to spot. Because logical errors normally are not obvious, you typically need to use break points or step throughout the code to find the location of the error. As you step through your code, you can monitor the value of each variable to determine when the value changes to something unexpected. See the sections "Insert a Break Point in a Procedure," "Step through a Procedure," and "Using Watch Expressions to Debug a Procedure" for more information on inserting a break point and stepping through a macro.

# Debug a Procedure with Inserted Break Points

You can insert *break points* in a procedure to stop execution at the specified line of code. Break points enable you to quickly debug problems with a subroutine or function as well as to determine whether a procedure executes correctly up to the specified location.

You can display the Locals window in the Visual Basic Editor to view the current values of the local variables. When you debug your code, consider docking this window to the bottom of the screen so that you can view the local variables while you debug. After you set a break point, the procedure executes until it reaches the specified break point, and Visual Basic Editor highlights the break point and stops the execution.

The Locals window, which displays in the last opened location, shows the current values of all local variables at each break point. If a variable does not have the appropriate

value when you reach a break point, you know that the coding error occurred prior to the current break point. See Chapter 2 for more information on using the Visual Basic Editor windows.

When your procedure stops at a specified break point, VBA places you in Break mode and stops the execution of the current procedure. You can continue executing your procedure until it encounters another break point or end the procedure. Each time VBA encounters a break point, the values of the local variables update in the Locals window.

You can set a break point for a code statement in the margins of the Code window. The Visual Basic Editor inserts a dark circle next to the code and highlights the line of code based upon the formatting settings you specify. See Chapter 2 for more information on setting the display settings for the Code window.

## Debug a Procedure with Inserted Break Points

① In the Projects window, open the module containing the procedure you want to debug.

**Note:** See Chapter 2 for information on opening VBA modules.

② Click View→Locals Window.

The Locals window displays in the last viewed location.

③ Click in the margin next to the line of code to add a break point.

● You can add additional break points as needed.

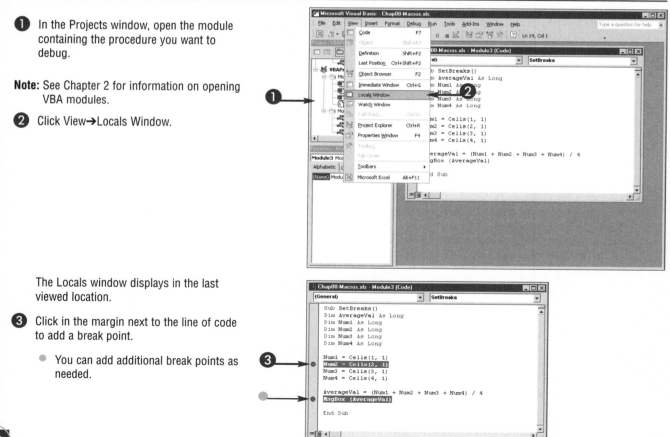

④ Click the Run Sub/UserForm button (▶).

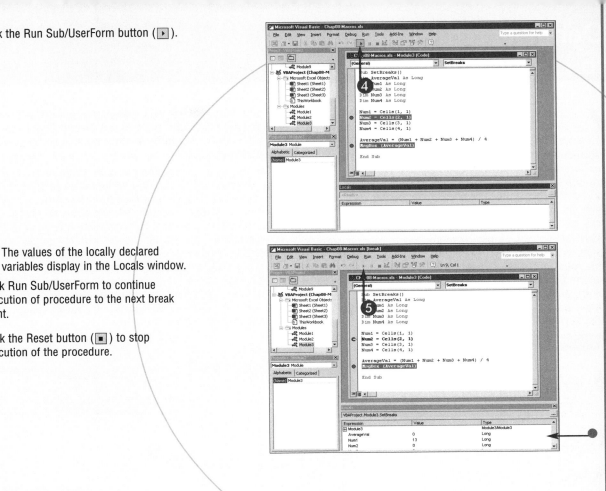

● The values of the locally declared variables display in the Locals window.

⑤ Click Run Sub/UserForm to continue execution of procedure to the next break point.

Click the Reset button (■) to stop execution of the procedure.

## Extra

Visual Basic Editor has three different modes in which it operates. In the Design mode, you can create new VBA procedures. You activate the Run mode, and thus execute the currently selected procedure, by clicking the Run Sub/UserForm button (▶), or by pressing F5.

VBE places you in the Break mode whenever the execution of a procedure stops due to a break point, a Stop statement in the code, a Watch statement, or when it encounters an error during execution. Whatever the cause of the break in execution, the Visual Basic Editor highlights the line of code that caused the error. To remind you that the Editor is in Break mode, the word *break* appears in the caption of the title bar at the top of the window. To exit out of Break mode, click the Reset button (■).

You can clear a break point from your code by simply clicking it with the mouse. You should remember to clear all break points after you complete debugging your code.

# Using Watch Expressions to Debug a Procedure

You can use *watches* to monitor the value of specific expressions or variables as you step through the VBA code in a procedure. VBA code watches work well for debugging code to determine why a variable or expression does not return the anticipated value. Programmers commonly refer to this type of error as a logical error. When you set watches, the Visual Basic Editor displays each watch along with the value of the specified expression or variable in the Watches window.

The Watches window, which displays in the same location as you last viewed it, lists the active watches along with the current value of the expression or variable being watched. If the selected procedure is not running or is in break mode, the expression has a value of `<Out of context>`. See Chapter 2 for more information on displaying windows in the Visual Basic Editor. You set a watch expression using

the Add Watch dialog box, where you specify the expression that you want to watch in the Expression field. Typically, the expression you specify checks for the value of a variable to meet specific criteria, as in the example n > 8.

After you specify the expression to watch, you must select an option to specify the type of watch to perform. When you select the Watch Expression option, the value of the expression displays in the Watches window as the procedure executes. The value of the expression is always a Boolean value of `true` or `false` to indicate whether the expression is true. The Break When Value is True option instructs VBA to break execution of the procedure as soon as the condition is true, whereas the Break When Value Changes option breaks the execution of the procedure as soon as the value of the expression changes from `true` to `false`, or vice versa.

## Using Watch Expressions to Debug a Procedure

① In the Projects window, open the module containing the procedure you want to debug.

**Note:** See Chapter 2 for information on opening VBA modules.

② Click View→Watch Window.

The Watches window displays in the last viewed location.

③ Click Debug→Add Watch.

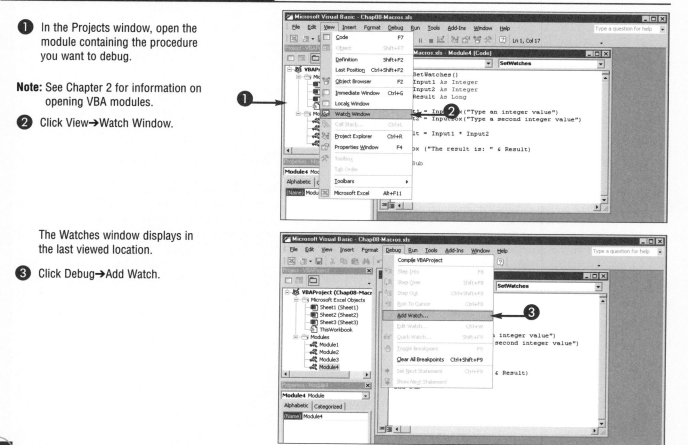

The Add Watch dialog box displays.

④ Type the expression to watch in the Expression field.

⑤ Click an option for the desired type of watch ( ○ change to ⦿ ).

⑥ Click OK to close the dialog box.

The Watches window lists each watch.

⑦ Click ▶.

● The value of the watch expression displays in the Watches window.

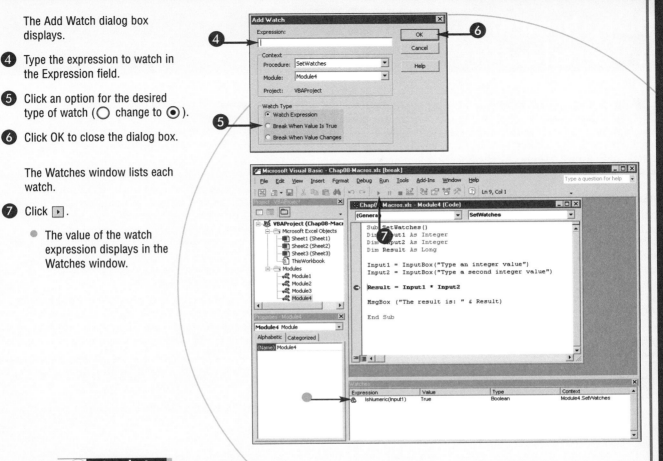

## Apply It

Instead of specifying an expression to watch using the Add Watch dialog box, you can set watches on expressions within your code or on the values of variables using the Quick Watch dialog box. The Quick Watch option works well for checking the value of a particular expression or variable while in Break mode.

To use the Quick Watch option to check the value of a variable, click next to the variable name and then press Shift+F9 to display the Quick Watch dialog box. The Quick Watch dialog box displays the selected expression and indicates the value of the expression at the current break point. If you want to continue to monitor the variable value, click Add to add the watch to the Watches window.

When dealing with a specific code expression, such as X > 5, the value on the Quick Watch dialog box is either true or false, indicating whether the expression is valid. For example, if the current value of X is 6, the expression has a value of true because 6 is greater than 5.

# Step through a Procedure

You can debug your procedure by stepping through the execution of the code one line at a time. Stepping through the code in this fashion is commonly referred to as *tracing*. Unlike break points, which execute the code until a break is encountered, tracing literally executes a line and waits for you to indicate that you want to execute the next line of code. This method of debugging works well for locating logical errors in your code.

When you step through your code, you can also use watches to monitor the value of different expressions. A *watch* is an expression for which you monitor the value. As you step through the procedure, the values of the watches update. You can quickly see at what point in the procedure your watches are valid. See the section "Using Watch Expressions to Debug a Procedure" for more information on creating a watch.

As the code executes, the values of each local variable display in the Locals window. Make sure the Locals window displays prior to selecting the option to step through the code. See Chapter 2 for more information about using the Locals window.

When you step into the current procedure, the Visual Basic Editor selects the first line of code in the procedure, the Sub or Function statement. Continue stepping through the code using the Step Into option. As you select the option, the Visual Basic Editor highlights the next line of code to execute. The Locals window updates the values of the local variables each time there is a value change. Finally, the Watches window monitors the values of any watch expressions created for the procedure.

As you step through a procedure, if a code statement calls another procedure, the Visual Basic Editor also steps through the called procedure. After that procedure executes, the control returns to the original procedure.

## Step through a Procedure

① In the Projects window, open the module containing the procedure you want to debug.

**Note:** See Chapter 2 for information on opening VBA modules.

② Click View→Watch Window.

③ Click View→Locals Window.

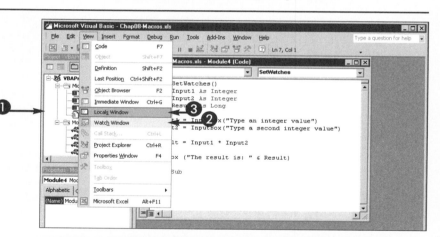

The Watches and Locals windows display in the last viewed location.

④ Click Debug→Step Into.

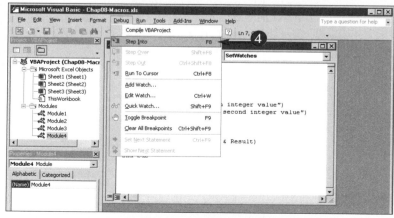

- The first line of code in the procedure is highlighted.

**5** Press F8 to move to execute that code and move to the next line.

**6** Continue pressing F8 to step through the entire procedure.

- As you step through the code, local variable values display in the Locals window and any watches set display in the Watches window.

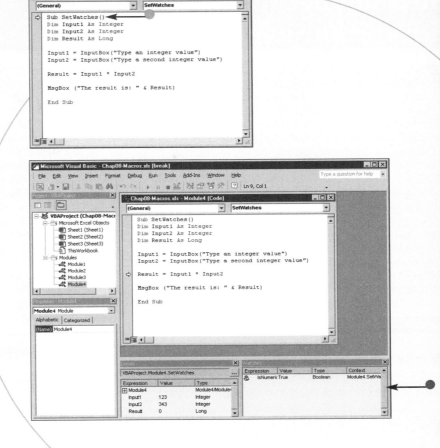

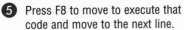

You step into procedures by pressing F8 or by clicking Debug→Step Into. You can continue walking through an entire procedure using the Step Into command. If your procedure contains calls to other procedures, you can step through those procedures by using the Step Into command. If you do not want to step through those procedures, you can step over them and continue processing the current one. To step over the highlighted procedure, click Debug→Step Over or press Shift+F8. Doing this instructs the Visual Basic Editor to execute the entire called procedure without stopping and to return control to the next line in the original procedure.

Even if you decide to step through the called procedure, you still have the option of stepping out of it at any time. To step out of a called procedure, click Debug→Step Out or press Ctrl+Shift+F8. When you select this option, the remainder of the called procedure executes and then control returns to the original procedure. Whenever control returns from a called procedure, the control passes to the next line of code after the procedure that called the outside procedure.

# Resume Execution if an Error is Encountered

You can instruct VBA to continue execution of a procedure when it encounters an error using the `On Error Resume Next` statement. With this statement, VBA skips any runtime errors that occur during the execution of the procedure, and execution continues with the next line of code. By doing this, the procedure continues executing and an error message does not inadvertently display on the screen. Keep in mind, that although the error message no longer displays, an error still exists in the code and therefore the procedure typically does not produce the appropriate results.

You should consider placing the `On Error Resume Next` statement at the top of all procedures you develop, especially procedures that you use in macros that you intend to distribute to another user. The statement ensures that the macro does not stop abruptly due to an error encountered in the code. If you adequately code to trap any potential errors, you can inform the user anytime conditions exist that would cause an error.

If you want to execute specific code when an error is encountered, you can modify the `On Error` statement to be `On Error GoTo Label`. With this statement, control jumps to a labeled section of code within the procedure whenever an error condition is encountered. Typically this code is placed at the end of the procedure. You may want to place an `Exit Sub` prior to the labeled section to keep the procedure from executing the code within the label if an error is not encountered.

For example, you can use `ErrCode:` as a label for the code to run if an error is encountered. Notice that the code label contains a colon. If you add the `Resume Next` statement at the end of the code, control returns to the next line of code in the procedure after the location that produced the runtime error. Although the runtime error appears to have been ignored, it is not. The information about the runtime error is placed in the `Err` object.

## Resume Execution if an Error is Encountered

 Create a new subroutine.

**Note:** See Chapter 3 for information on creating subroutines.

② Type **On Error Goto Label**, replacing `Label` with the label for the code to execute when an error occurs.

③ Type the VBA code for the procedure.

④ Type **Exit Sub** at the end of the main procedure code.

The `Exit Sub` statement causes the procedure to exit without running the error code.

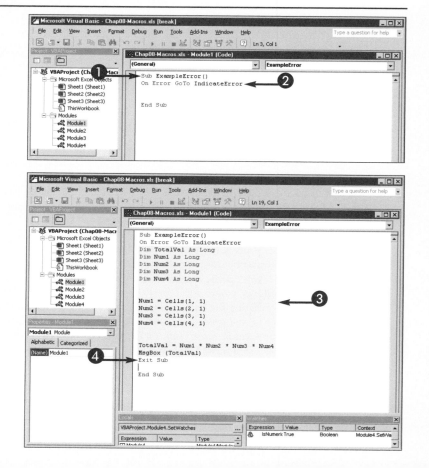

⑤ Type **Label:**, replacing Label: with the appropriate label name for the error-handling code.

⑥ Type the VBA code to execute if an error occurs.

⑦ Type **Resume Next**.

⑧ Switch to Excel and run the macro.

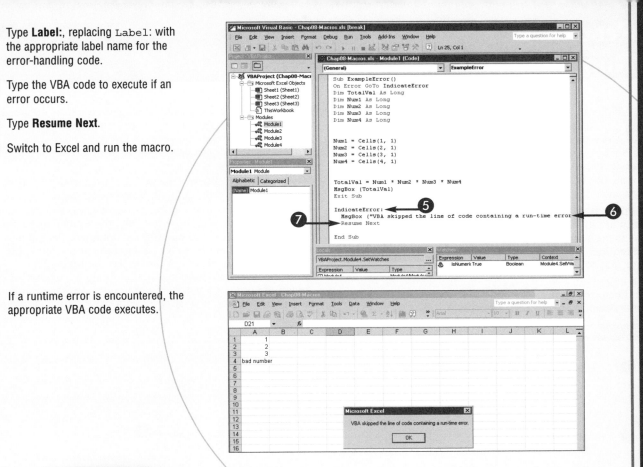

If a runtime error is encountered, the appropriate VBA code executes.

## Apply It

You can actually use three different forms of the Resume statement within your code: Resume, Resume Next, and Resume Label. You typically place each of these statements at the end of the error-handling portion of your code to indicate how to return to the main portion of the code.

You should use the Resume statement, which returns to the line of code that originally caused the runtime error, with caution. If the line of code executes and produces another error, the error-handing code calls again. Use this statement only when you are sure that you corrected the condition that caused the error. For example, if you instruct the user to enter a valid value in a cell, you can resume execution so that the value is verified again.

The Resume Next statement returns control to the next line of code after the line that produced the error, thus continuing execution without that line of code. This option enables you to complete the procedure, but typically does not produce the anticipated results due to the skipped code.

The third form of the Resume statement, the Resume Label statement, transfers control to another labeled area of code.

# Process a Runtime Error

You can use the error code that VBA captures from a runtime error to make corrections so that the procedure executes correctly. Whenever VBA encounters an error during the execution of a procedure, it places the error information, which includes the error code and description, in the `Err` object. You can use this information to process the error and often correct the error situation.

To ensure that you capture the error without halting the execution of your code, place the `On Error Resume Next` statement immediately after the `Sub` statement for your subroutine. This statement instructs VBA to capture the error and continue processing.

The `Err.Number` property contains the error code if a runtime error occurs. The error codes for runtime messages are between 1 and 65,535. Essentially, if the `Number`

property has a value greater than zero, an error occurred. You can quickly check to see if an error exists by checking the `Number` property of the `Err` object with an `If Then` statement as in the following code:

`If Err.Number >0 Then`.

The real power of using the `Number` property comes from the ability to execute different code based upon the error message code returned by the runtime error. You can design your error processing code to react differently depending upon the specific runtime error encountered. For example, if the `Err.Number` property has a value of 13, the value passed to a variable is not the correct data type; for example, you may have specified a string for a variable that required an integer value. If you write code that examines the runtime error, you can prompt for the correct data type.

## Process a Runtime Error

① Create a new subroutine.

**Note:** See Chapter 3 for information on creating subroutines.

② Type **On Error Goto Label** replacing `Label` with the label for the code to execute.

③ Use the `Dim` statement to declare subroutine values.

**Note:** See Chapter 3 for more information on declaring variables.

④ Type VBA code for the subroutine.

⑤ Type **Exit Sub** at the end of the code.

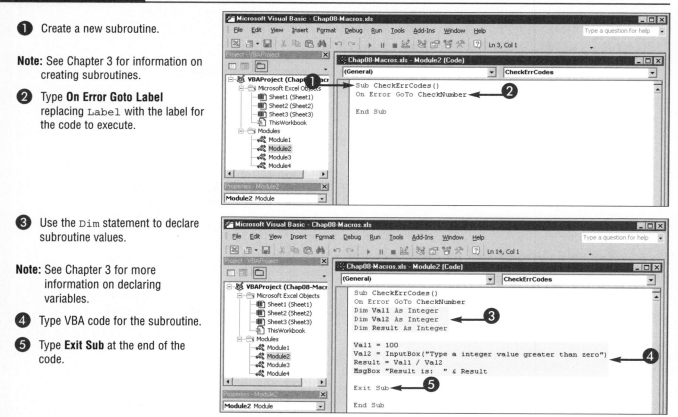

6 Type **Label:**, replacing `Label:` with the appropriate label name for the error-handling code.

7 Type a conditional statement, such as `Select Case`, to check the value of the `Err.Number` object property.

8 Type code to execute if a specific error occurs.

9 Type **Resume** to return to the line of code where the error occurred.

10 Switch to Excel and run the macro.

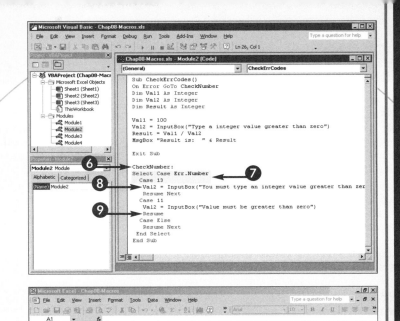

If the value passed to the subroutine is not valid, the error processing occurs.

## Extra

The following table lists some of the most common errors that VBA returns when it encounters a runtime error. Each error code has a description message you can display using the `Err.Description` property, or you can capture the code and display your own custom messages.

| CODE | ERROR | DESCRIPTION |
|------|-------|-------------|
| 3 | Return without GoSub. | Return statement exists without a corresponding `GoSub` statement. |
| 5 | Invalid procedure call. | The call to another subroutine or function cannot be made. Typically due to a problem with the arguments. Either not calling with a valid number of arguments, or the value of an argument is not valid for the procedure. |
| 9 | Subscript out of range. | Attempt was made to access an array element that does not exist. Commonly occurs when you forget that, unless specified, array indexes start at zero. |
| 10 | The array is fixed or temporarily locked. | You cannot redimension a fixed length array. |
| 11 | Division by zero. | You cannot divide by zero. If the value of the divisor is zero, this error occurs. |
| 13 | Type mismatch. | Typically, this means the value passed to a variable is not the correct data type. |
| 35 | Sub, Function, or Property not defined. | Occurs when you attempt to call a subroutine, function, or property that does not exist. |

# Open a Workbook

You can create a procedure to open a workbook in Excel using the Open method of the Workbooks collection. Each time you open another workbook, Excel adds that workbook to the Workbooks collection. Similar to using the Open command on the File menu, opening another workbook using the Open method makes the workbook active.

Sixteen different parameters determine how Excel opens a workbook. Of these parameters, Excel requires only FileName. In addition, you only need to use the FileName, ReadOnly, Password, WriteResPassword, IgnoreReadOnlyRecommended, and AddToMRU parameters to open an Excel workbook. In addition, Excel requires several arguments when you open a text file. For more on opening text files, see the section "Open a Text File as a Workbook."

The FileName argument indicates the name of the workbook to open. You specify the workbook name for a workbook located in the same folder as the current workbook. For a workbook in another folder, you specify the workbook path as part of the file name: `Workbooks.Open("C:\Workbooks\Budget.xls")`.

You can specify a value of True for the ReadOnly parameter to open the workbook as read-only. A False value opens the workbook as editable.

You can use the Password parameter to require users to enter a password to open a workbook. If you omit the password, and the workbook requires one, Excel prompts the user for a password before opening the file. Similar to the Password parameter, WriteResPassword requires users to enter a password to write in a workbook.

If you originally save a workbook with the Read-Only Recommended option selected, each time the workbook opens, Excel prompts you to open it as read-only. If you want to open the workbook without the prompt, you can specify a value of True for the IgnoreReadOnlyRecommended parameter.

Finally, you specify a value of True for the AddToMRU parameter if you want Excel to add a workbook to the recently used files list.

## Open a Workbook

① Create a new subroutine

**Note:** See Chapter 3 for more information on creating subroutines.

② Type **Workbooks.Open**.

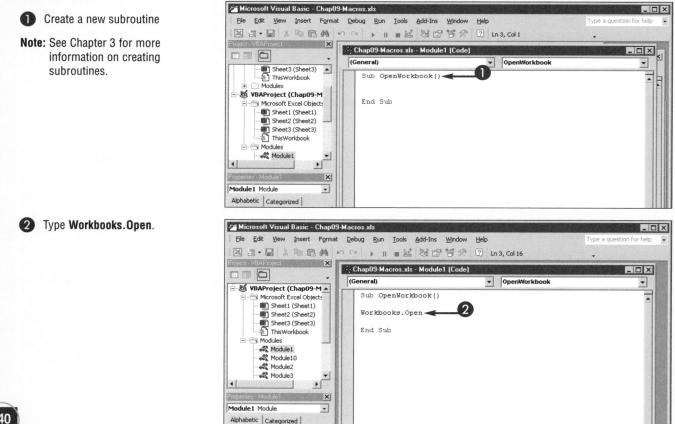

**③** Type **FileName:="WorkbookName"**, replacing `WorkbookName` with the name and path of the workbook to open.

- You can type a comma and a space and then type optional parameters that you want to include with the `Open` method.

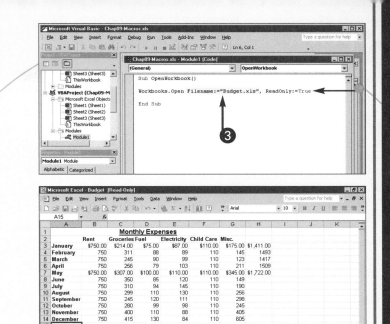

**④** Switch to Excel and run the macro.

**Note:** See Chapter 1 to run a macro.

The specified workbook opens as the active workbook.

---

**Apply It**

You can use several other parameters with the `Open` method if you want to open text files in Excel.

| PARAMETER | DESCRIPTION |
|---|---|
| UpdateLinks | Specifies how to handle links within the workbook. Type **0** for no updates, **1** to update external references, and **2** to update remote references. A value of **3** updates external and remote references. |
| Format | Indicates the delimiter character in the text file to separate data into cells in a worksheet. |
| | Value Delimiter    Value Delimiter<br>1    Tabs    4    Semicolons<br>2    Commas    5    Nothing<br>3    Spaces    6    `Delimiter` parameter value |
| Origin | Indicates original platform of text files and has three constant values. `xlMacintosh`, `xlWindows`, and `xlMSDOS`. If omitted, Excel uses the current operating system. |
| Delimiter | Specifies a delimiter character when the `Format` parameter has a value of 6. |
| Editable | Type **True** to view an Excel Add-in or to edit an Excel template. |
| Notify | Use `True` to add a file that cannot be opened as Read/Write to the notification list. |
| Converter | Index of a file converter to use when opening a file. |
| Local | Use `True` to save a file using the language being used by Excel. `False` saves the file using the language used by VBA. |
| CorruptLoad | Indicates method used to retry a corrupt load of a file. `xlNormalLoad`, `xlRepairFile`, and `xl<Extra>ctData` are the three options. |
| OpenConflictDocument | `True` opens the local conflict document. |

# Open a Text File as a Workbook

You can open a text file within Excel using the `OpenText` method of the `Workbooks` collection. When you use this method, Excel opens the text file as a single worksheet within a new workbook. The file remains a text file, but you can modify it using Excel as the editor.

You can specify how the text file opens using the parameters associated with the `OpenText` method. The list of parameters for this method is pretty extensive, but only the `FileName` parameter is actually required to specify the name of the text file to open.

When you use the `FileName` parameter, you typically want the name to include the complete path of the file to ensure that Excel locates the file. If you place the workbook activating the macro in a different location than the text file, Excel cannot locate it.

Because the list of parameters is so extensive with the `OpenText` method, you should use named parameters with the method to eliminate the need to specify all parameters. With named parameters, you can indicate the name of each parameter along with the associated value, for example:

```
Workbooks.OpenText FileName:="C:\Excel Files\
Sample.txt", DataType:+ xlDelimited, Tab:=True.
```

This code opens the text file using the tab character as the delimiter. The delimiter is the character that indicates a separation of data. In this file, the tab indicates that the data following the tab should be placed in the next cell. As illustrated, the `OpenText` method has parameters for the standard delimiter characters. If you know the delimiter for the text file, you can specify the delimiter character to ensure that the text file opens correctly.

## Open a Text File as a Workbook

① Create a new subroutine.

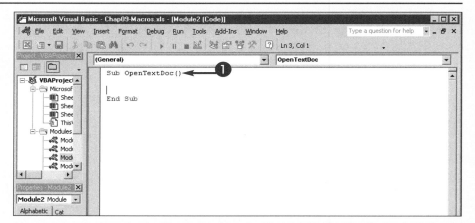

② Type **Workbooks.OpenText**.

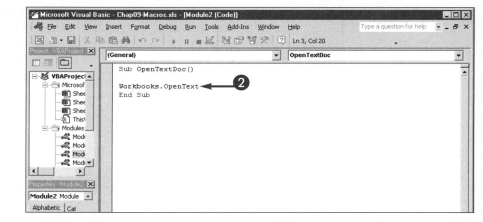

**③** Type **FileName:"TextFile"**, replacing `TextFile` with the name of the text file.

**④** Type **Tab:=True**, followed by a comma.

**⑤** Type **ThousandsSeparator:=","**.

You can type a comma and a space and then type optional parameters that you want to include with the `OpenText` method.

**⑥** Switch to Excel and run the macro.

The specified text file opens in a workbook format.

## Apply It

You can use the following parameters with the `OpenText` method to open a text file as a workbook.

| PARAMETERS | DESCRIPTION |
|---|---|
| FileName | Name and location of the text file. |
| Origin | Use xlMacintosh, xlWindows, or xlIMSDOS to indicate the original file platform. |
| StartRow | First row to use from the text file. |
| DataType | The type of data in the text file, either xlFixedWidth or xlDelimited. |
| TextQualifier | The character that identifies text. Use xlTextQualifiedDoubleQuote, xlTextQualifierNone, or xlTextQualifierSingleQuote. |
| ConsecutiveDelimiter | Type **True** to treat consecutive delimiters as one. |
| Tab, Semicolon, Comma, Space | Type **True** if the character is the delimiter. |
| Other, OtherChar | Type **True** for Other if you specify a different delimiter for OtherChar. |
| FieldInfo | Column number followed by an XlColumnDataType constant (see Appendix A for constants). |
| TextVisualLayout | Visual layout of the text. |
| DecimalSeparator, ThousandsSeparator | Characters indicating decimal and thousands location. |
| TrailingMinusNumbers | Character that indicates minus numbers. |
| Local | True saves the file in the Excel language. False saves the file in the VBA language. |

# Open a File Requested by the User

Instead of specifying the file to open in your code, you can retrieve the name of the file by prompting the user with an Open dialog box. To display an Open dialog box from an Excel macro, you use the GetOpenFilename method.

When you use this method, the file selected in the Open dialog box does not open when the user clicks OK. The dialog box passes the name of the file selected back to the variable that receives the statement assignment. If you want to open the selected file, you need to use the Open property.

The GetOpenFilename includes several optional parameters that you can specify to customize the Open dialog box. You can use the FileFilter parameter to allow the user to specify the type of files to open from the dialog box. You specify the file type by listing a value in the Files of Type drop-down box of the Open dialog box. For

example, "XML Files (*.xml)" specifies that Excel should only open XML files. You can specify multiple file types as long as you separate each one by a comma.

You can use the FilterIndex parameter to indicate the default file filtering option. Your choice of parameter depends on what you selected for the FileFilter parameter. You specify a filter value between 1 and the number of filters you selected. If you omit this parameter, VBA uses the first filter specified as the default value.

Use the Title parameter to customize the name of the dialog box. For example, if you want the dialog box to open a text file, you can change the title of the dialog box to "Open Text File".

If you want to select and open multiple files at once, specify a value of True for the MultiSelect parameter.

## Open a File Requested by the User

① Create a new subroutine.

② Type **Dim UserFile As Variant**, replacing UserFile with the variable to receive the name of the file to open.

③ Type **UserFile = Application. GetOpenFilename()**.

④ Type **FileFilter:="TextFiles (*.txt), *.txt"** within the parentheses to specify the type of file to open.

⑤ Type **Title:="Dialog box text"** within the parentheses, replacing Dialog box text with the text for the header of the dialog box.

You can specify additional parameter values.

**6** Type **Workbooks.OpenText Filename:=UserFile** to open the file selected in the Open dialog box.

**Note:** See "Open a Text File as a Workbook" for more information on using the `OpenText` method.

**7** Switch to Excel and run the macro.

The Text Files dialog box requests the workbook to open.

Microsoft Visual Basic - Chap09-Macros.xls - [Module3 (Code)]

File  Edit  View  Insert  Format  Debug  Run  Tools  Add-Ins  Window  Help       Type a question for help

(General)                                    GetUserFileName

```
Sub GetUserFileName()
Dim UF As Variant

UF = Application.GetOpenFileName(FileFilter:="Text Files(*.txt),*.txt", Title:="Text Files")

Workbooks.OpenText Filename:=UF    ◄── 6

End Sub
```

Text Files

Look in:  Excel Files

History

My Documents

Desktop

Favorites

My Network Places

Sales
Salestst
test

File name:

Files of type:   Text Files

Open

Cancel

## Extra

The `FileFilter` parameter enables you to indicate the type of files users can select in the Open dialog box. If you omit this parameter, by default, VBA lists all file types that Excel can open. You limit the file types by specifying the appropriate file types as values for the parameter. To use this parameter, you need to include two different strings for each file type. First indicate the text description of the filter followed by the MS-DOS wildcard file specification. For example: `"Text Files (*.text)` is the first part of the filter string. The second part, `*.txt`, is the MS-DOS wildcard that the dialog box uses to determine what types to display. You can specify any string for the filter description, but you must include the appropriate MS-DOS wildcard values. The table lists common file types Excel can open.

| FILE TYPE | DESCRIPTION |
|-----------|-------------|
| *.txt, *.prn, *.csv | Text files |
| *.xls, *.xlm, *.xl, *.xlc | Microsoft Excel files |
| *.htm | Web pages |
| *.xml | XML files |
| *.odc, *.udl, *.dsn | Data sources |
| *.mdb, *.mde | Access databases |
| *.wk? | Lotus files |
| *.wks | Microsoft Works 2.0 Files |
| *.dbf | dBase files |

# Save a Workbook

Y ou can save the currently selected Excel workbook using either the `Save` or `Save As` methods of the `Workbook` object. Excel has a different workbook object for each workbook you open. You can reference a specific workbook object by name, if you know the name. For example, the code `Workbooks("Sample.xls").Save` saves the Sample.xls workbook.

If you do not know the name of the workbook you want to save, you make the workbook the active workbook in Excel, and use the `ActiveWorkbook` property to save the workbook. For example, the code `ActiveWorkbook.Save` saves whichever workbook is currently active in Excel.

If the workbook you want to save contains the macro currently running, you can use the `ThisWorkbook` property: `ThisWorkbook.Save`. Typically this is the same as the active workbook, but if you open a new workbook during the execution of the macro, the active workbook becomes the new workbook.

To specify how Excel saves the workbook, you need to use the `SaveAs` method which has several different parameters to customize the way the workbook saves: `FileName`, `FileFormat`, `Password`, `WriteResPassword`, `ReadOnlyRecommended`, `CreateBackup`, `AccessMode`, `ConflictResolution`, `AddToMru`, and `Local`.

Use the `FileName` parameter to specify the filename and location where you want to save the workbook. If you omit this parameter value, Excel uses the filename of the workbook as the value for the `FileName` parameter.

You can use the `FileFormat` parameter to specify the file format for the saved workbook. You can save the workbook using any of the file formats Excel supports by listing one of the `XlFileFormat` constant values. See Appendix A for a list of the `XlFileFormat` constant values.

**Save a Workbook**

 Create a new subroutine.

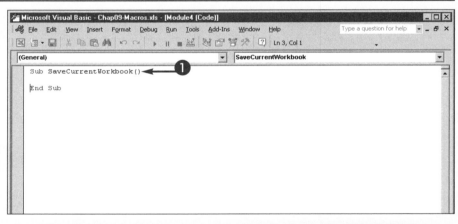

② Type **Workbooks(1).SaveAs.**, replacing `Workbooks(1)` with the workbook that you want to save.

You can also use the `Save` method by typing **Workbooks(1).Save** and skipping the other steps.

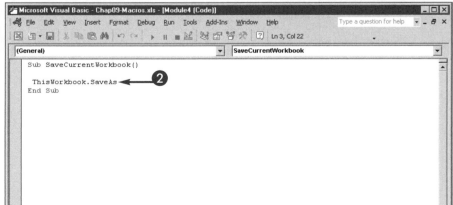

**③** Type **FileName:="NameofFile"**, replacing `NameofFile` with the name and path to save the file.

**④** Type **FileFormat:=xlWorkbookNormal**, replacing `xlWorkbookNormal` with the `xlFileFormat` constant.

**⑤** Type **AddtoMru:=True**.

You can specify additional parameter values.

**⑥** Switch to Excel and run the macro.

Excel saves the workbook file using the specified name and format.

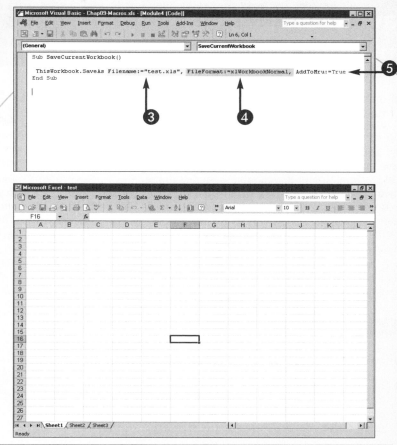

## Extra

The `SaveAs` method has several optional parameters that determine how the file saves.
Remember to use the named parameter option to specify parameter values for the method.

| SAVEAS PARAMETER | DESCRIPTION |
|---|---|
| FileName | Indicates the name and location to save the file. |
| FileFormat | Contains an `XlFileFormat` constant that indicates the format to save the file. See Appendix A for the `XlFileFormat` constant values. |
| Password | Contains up to a 15-character password required to open the file. |
| WriteResPassword | Contains the password for write-restricting the file. |
| ReadOnlyRecommended | Type **True** to display a message that recommends the file be opened as read-only. |
| CreateBackup | Type **True** to create a backup file. |
| AccessMode | Contains a constant value of `xlExclusive`, `xlNoChange`, or `xlShared` indicating access mode. |
| ConflictResolution | Contains a constant indicating how to resolve conflicts. A value of `xlUserResolution` displays a Conflict Resolution box, `xlLocalSessionChanges` accepts local user's changes, or `xlOtherSessionChanges` accepts changes from other users. |
| AddToMru | Type **True** to add a workbook to a list of recently used files. |
| Local | Type **True** to save files in the Excel language and `False` to save files in the VBA language. |

147

# Save Workbook in Format Specified by User

Y ou can request the name, location, and format for saving a workbook file from the user of your macro with the GetSaveAsFilename method. Using this method displays the Save As dialog box into which the user entered information for saving the file. The dialog box does not save the workbook file; instead, Excel returns the user specified information to the variable assigned to the statement. To save the file, you use the SaveAs method. See the section "Save a Workbook" for more information. The GetSaveAsFilename includes several optional parameters for customizing the appearance of the Save As dialog box: InitialFilename, FileFilter, FilterIndex, and Title.

You use the InitialFilename parameter to suggest a different name, other than the active workbook default, in the File name field.

You use the FileFilter parameter to allow only certain file formats for saving the workbook file. If you omit this parameter, Excel lists all formats available. If you include this parameter, you need two different string parts. The first, a text description of the file format, displays in the Save as type drop-down list box. The second indicates the MS-DOS wildcard statement for the file type.

You use the FilterIndex parameter to indicate the default file filtering option, which depends on the options you specify for the FileFilter parameter. You specify a filter value listed between 1 and the number of filters. If you omit this parameter, VBA uses the first filter specified as the default value. You use the Title parameter to customize the name of the dialog box.

## Save Workbook in Format Specified by User

① Create a new subroutine.

② Type **Dim UserFile As Variant**, replacing UserFile with the variable to receive a name for saving the file.

③ Type **UserFile = Application. GetSaveAs Filename()**.

④ Type **FileFilter:="Excel Workbooks (*.xls)"**, replacing *.xls within the parentheses with the type of file to save.

To save only the Excel Workbooks, you can type **"Excel Workbook (*.xls), *.xls"**.

⑤ Type **Title:="Dialog box text"** within the parentheses, replacing "Dialog box text" with the text for the header of the dialog box.

You can specify additional parameter values.

**6** Type **ThisWorkbook.SaveAs Filename:=UserFile** to save current workbook with the specified filename and path.

**Note:** See the section "Save a Workbook" for more information on using the `SaveAs` method.

**7** Switch to Excel and run the macro.

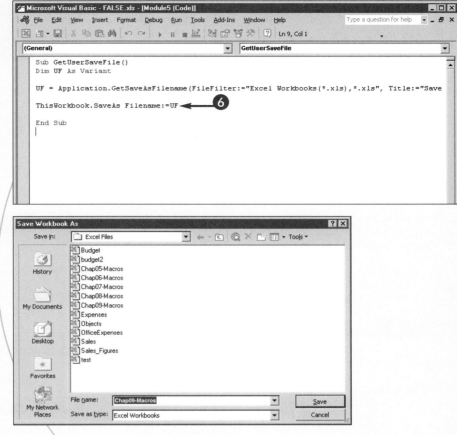

The Save As dialog box requests the information for saving the workbook.

Instead of saving an individual workbook, you can save the entire workspace. You can use workspaces, which have a .xlw extension, if you have multiple workbooks that you need to open simultaneously. If you save them as a workspace, you simply need to open that workspace and all workbooks in the workspace.

To save a workspace, you use the `SaveWorkspace` method from the `Application` object. The `Filename` parameter, the required and only parameter, which you must specify for this method, contains the filename and location where Excel stores the workspace file. For example, if you type **Application.SaveWorkspace "NewWorkspace"**, Excel saves the current workspace, which includes all open files, with the specified name.

Instead of saving the workbooks into a workspace, you can save each open workbook using the `Save` method of the `Application` object and combining it with a looping statement. The example code cycles through all currently open workbooks and saves them one by one. If you have not previously saved a workbook, Excel prompts you via the Save As dialog box for a file name and location.

**Example:**
```
For Each wb in Application.Workbooks
     wb.Save
Next
```

# Determine if a Workbook Is Open

You can determine if a workbook is currently open by viewing the Workbooks Collection, which contains all of the currently open workbooks in Excel. As a new workbook opens, it becomes a workbook object and Excel adds it to the `Workbooks` collection. Excel stores workbooks in the collection sequentially with the first workbook opened being the first workbook in the collection. If you know the order in which a workbook was opened, you can access it using the associated index value.

The code `MyWorkbook = Workbook(1)`.Name uses the `Name` property to return the name of the first workbook in the collection to the `MyWorkbook` variable. The `Name` property, a read-only property, enables you to return the name of a workbook but prohibits you from changing the workbook's name. To change the name of the workbook, see the section "Save a Workbook."

In order to locate the workbook, you look at each workbook within the Workbooks Collection to determine if any of them is the workbook of interest. The `For Each Next` looping statement enables you to cycle through the list of workbooks and determine if the list contains the desired workbook. See Chapter 6 for more information about using a `For Each Next` looping statement.

Within the looping structure you need to compare the name of each workbook with the name of the desired workbook. For this type of VBA statement, you use an `If Then` statement, which enables you to check the value and execute a series of statements if the specified condition is `True`. See Chapter 6 for more information about using the `If Then` statement.

## Determine if a Workbook Is Open

① Create a new subroutine.

② Type **Dim wb As Workbook**, replacing wb with the workbook variable.

③ Type **Dim wbOpen As Boolean**, replacing wbOpen with the variable to track if the file is open.

④ Type **Dim wbFilename As String**, replacing wbFilename with the string containing the name of the workbook to open.

⑤ Type **wbOpen = False**.

⑥ Type **wbFilename = "Budget.xls"**, replacing wbFilename with the workbook variable and "Budget.xls" with the name of the workbook to open.

⑦ Type **For Each wb In Application.Workbooks**.

⑧ Type **If wb.Name = wbFilename Then**.

⑨ Type **wbOpen = True**.

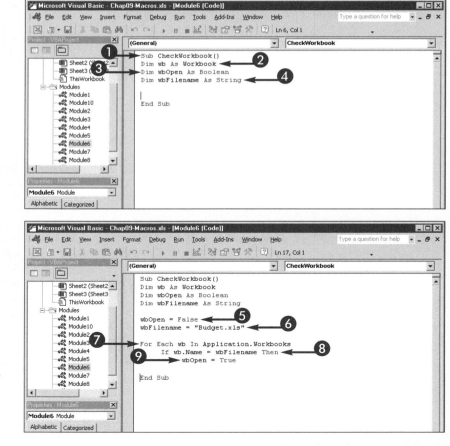

⑩ Type additional statements to perform if the workbook is open.

⑪ Type **Next**.

⑫ Type **If wbOpen = False Then**.

⑬ Type statements to perform if the workbook is not open.

⑭ Switch to Excel and run the macro.

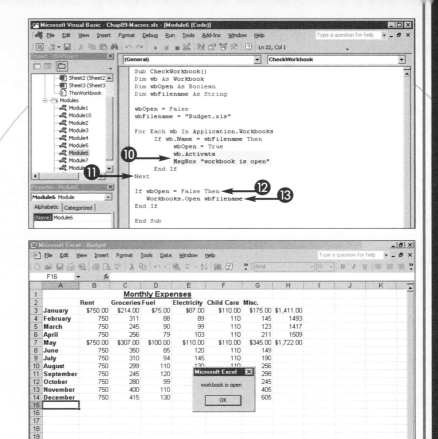

The macro checks to see if the workbook is open. If not, the workbook is opened.

## Extra

If a workbook is open, you can activate it using the `Activate` method of the `Workbook` object. When you activate the workbook, it becomes the currently selected workbook in Excel. The `Activate` method has no parameters. You can use it by specifying the workbook to activate followed by the method, for example:

**Example:**
```
SelectedWorkbook.Activate.
```

If, when you activate a particular workbook, you have the workbook open in multiple windows, the activate statement activates the first window that contains the specified workbook. For example, the code `Workbooks("budget.xls").Activate` activates the first window which has the window title budget.xls.

When you use Application.Workbooks to return the collection of open workbooks, it returns all workbooks, including those that are hidden, but it does not return any open add-ins. In order to return a specific add-in you need to reference the add-in by name. For example, the code `Workbooks ("OpenAddin.xla")`. `Open` opens the specified add-in file. Remember, just like workbooks, if you do not specify the path, Excel looks for the workbook in the current folder. To avoid any problems caused by Excel not locating the specified file, use the complete path statement as part of the name. See Chapter 15 for more information on add-ins.

# Close a Workbook

You can close a particular workbook from your macro using the `Close` method and including a reference to the `Workbook` object that contains the workbook you want to close. The `Workbooks` collection contains all of the currently open workbooks as individual workbook objects. The `Workbooks` collection adds the `Workbook` objects sequentially in the order you opened them. You reference a workbook with an index value, the name of the workbook, the `ActiveWorkbook` property, or the `ThisWorkbook` property.

When you use the `ActiveWorkbook` or `ThisWorkbook` property with the `Close` method, the current workbook running the macro closes. If you have code after the `Close` statement, Excel may ignore it.

There are three different optional parameters that you can use with the `Close` method: `SaveChanges`, `Filename`, and `RouteWorkbook`.

You can use the `SaveChanges` parameter to save changes to a workbook as it closes. If you specify a parameter value of `True`, the workbook saves as it closes; with a value of `False`, however, the workbook closes without Excel saving it, and you lose any changes you made to the workbook.

You can specify a filename and path if you utilize the `FileName` parameter to save the workbook. Keep in mind, if you specify a value of `False` for the `SaveChanges` parameter, Excel ignores the `FileName` parameter because the file is never saved. Excel only saves the workbook if you have made changes to it.

If you set up the workbook to route, you can use the `RouteWorkbook` parameter to route the workbook to the next recipient on the routing list. Specify a value of `True` to route the workbook or a value of `False` if you do not want to have the workbook sent to the next recipient.

## Close a Workbook

 Create a new subroutine.

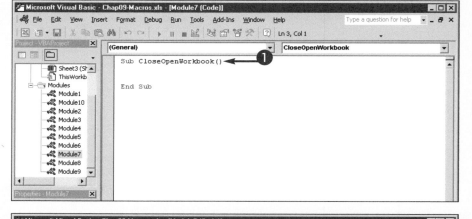

 Type **Workbooks ("workbook.xls").Close**, replacing workbook.xls with the name of the workbook to close.

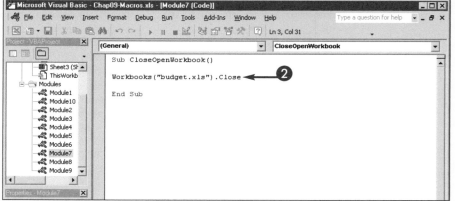

③ Type **SaveChange:=True**.

● If desired, specify additional parameter values.

④ Switch to Excel and run the macro.

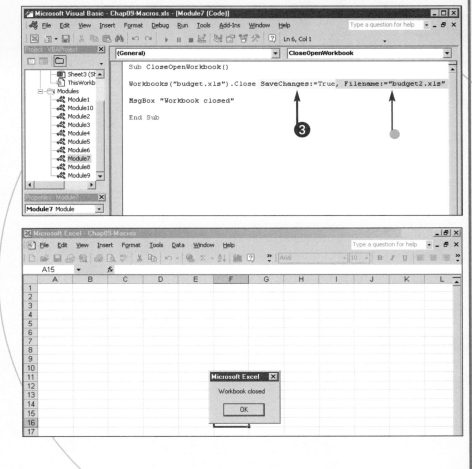

The specified workbook file is closed. If changes have been made, the workbook is saved.

---

## Extra

Using the `Close` method, you can specify that you want to close all workbooks you have open in Excel. If the `SaveChanges` parameter does not have a value specified, Excel checks each workbook to ensure that you have saved it since its last modification. If a workbook contains modifications, Excel prompts you to save the workbook.

When you close all workbooks, the workbooks all close, but the application, Excel, remains running. If you want the Excel application to close, you can use the `Quit` method with the `Application` object: `Application.Quit`.

Before closing Excel, the `Quit` method first closes the open workbooks. If any of the workbooks contain current changes, Excel prompts you to save the changes. If you do not want to save modified worksheets, and you want to avoid the dialog box asking you to save changes, you can use the `DisplayAlerts` property. This property determines whether the alert message displays when Excel closes workbooks or performs any other tasks.

**Example:**
```
Application.DisplayAlerts = False
```

# Create a New Workbook

You can create a new Excel workbook using the Add method of the Workbooks Collection. When you create a new workbook, Excel creates a new Workbook object and adds it to the Workbooks collection. The Add method has one optional parameter that you can use, as shown in the following code: Workbooks.Add(Template).

You can combine the Template parameter with the Add method to specify how Excel creates the workbook. You can use another workbook as the template for the new workbook or one of the four xlWBATemplate constant values.

When you use a workbook as the template, Excel copies all elements of the specified worksheet into the new workbook including all macros, text, and any settings. Be sure to specify the complete path of the workbook so that Excel can locate the file when the macro runs.

The xlWBATemplate has four different constant values that you can use to create a new workbook containing one sheet of the type specified with the constant value. Use xlWBATWorksheet to create a workbook containing one worksheet. If you want a workbook containing a chart, specify a constant value of xlWBATChart. To create an Excel 4.0 macro sheet, use xlWBATExcel4MacroSheet. Use xlWBATExcel4IntMacroSheet to create an international macro sheet.

When you use the Add method, without specifying a template, Excel creates a new workbook with the name Book1.xls. If a workbook already exists with that name, Excel assigns a name of Book2.xls. You can customize the workbook with the different properties of the Workbook object, such as the Title property, to specify the title for the workbook. You can change the name of the new workbook using the SaveAs method. See the section "Save a Workbook" for more information on the SaveAs method.

## Create a New Workbook

① Create a new subroutine.

② Type **Dim NewWB As Workbook**, replacing NewWB with the name of the workbook variable.

③ Type **Set NewWB = Workbooks. Add("Filename.xls")**, replacing Filename.xls with the name of the workbook to use as the template.

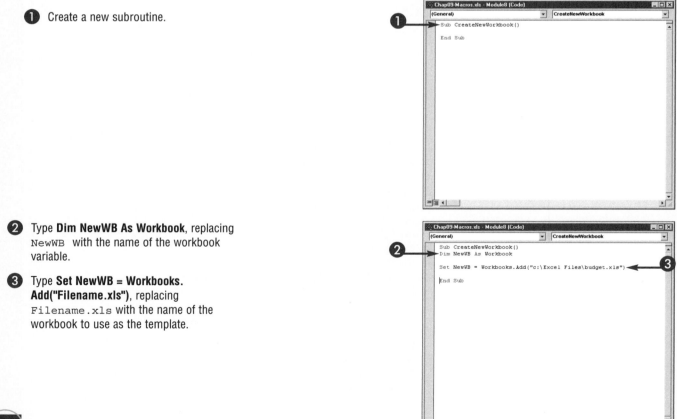

④ Type **NewWB.Title = "2001 Budget"**, replacing 2001 Budget with the text for the workbook title bar.

⑤ Type **NewWB.SaveAs "NewFilename.xls"**, replacing NewFilename.xls with the new name for the workbook.

⑥ Switch to Excel and run the macro.

Excel creates a new workbook using the specified template file and saves the workbook with the specified name.

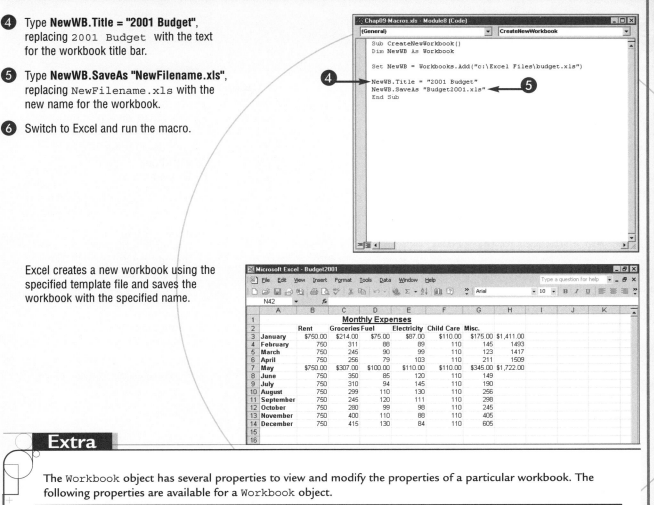

## Extra

The Workbook object has several properties to view and modify the properties of a particular workbook. The following properties are available for a Workbook object.

| PROPERTY | DESCRIPTION |
|---|---|
| ActiveSheet | Read-only string indicating the name of the active sheet in the workbook. |
| FileFormat | Read-only value indicating the format of the workbook. Returns an XlFileFormat constant, see Appendix A. |
| FullName | Read-only string indicating the name and complete path of the workbook. |
| HasPassword | Read-only Boolean value indicating whether the workbook is password protected. |
| Name | Read-only string indicating the name of the workbook. |
| Password | Returns or sets the password string for the open workbook. |
| Path | Read-only value that returns the complete Excel application path. |
| ProtectStructure | Read-only Boolean value indicating whether the order of the sheets in the workbook are protected. If value is True, you cannot move, delete, or add workbooks. |
| ReadOnly | Read-only Boolean value indicating whether the workbook was opened read-only. |
| ReadOnlyRecommended | Read-only Boolean value indicating whether the workbook was saved as read-only. |
| Saved | Contains a Boolean value to indicate whether changes have been made since the workbook was modified. |
| Title | Indicates the title that displays in the Excel title bar for the worksheet. |

# Delete
# a File

**V**BA provides the ability to delete a workbook, or any other file using the `Kill` statement. You can use this statement to delete any file, as long as the user has permission to delete it. The following code illustrates the use of the `Kill` statement: `Kill(pathname)`.

The `Kill` statement requires one argument, the pathname. The pathname argument is a string referencing the files that you want to delete. To assure that Excel locates the files, the pathname argument must include not only the filename but also the folder and drive specification. If you do not specify the path, Excel looks for the specified files within the current directory. Make sure you enclose the path statement within quotes.

You can specify the name of a single file by typing the complete filename, including the extension. You can also remove multiple files at once using the wildcard symbols

supported by VBA to specify multiple characters. You can use an asterisk (*) to represent multiple characters or a question mark symbol (?) to specify a single character. For example, you can remove the entire contents of a folder using the `*.*` specification. For example, the statement `Kill ("c:\Excel Files\*.*")` matches the string to the files within the folder. Because `*.*` matches all filenames, Excel removes all files within the folder. If you only want to remove the Excel workbooks within the folder, you use `*.xls`.

Keep in mind that you cannot delete files that are open. If you attempt to do so, a Permission Denied error appears and tells you that you cannot delete the file. You also cannot delete files that have a read-only property. If you attempt to delete a read-only file, Excel displays a Path/File access error message.

## Delete a File

 Create a new subroutine.

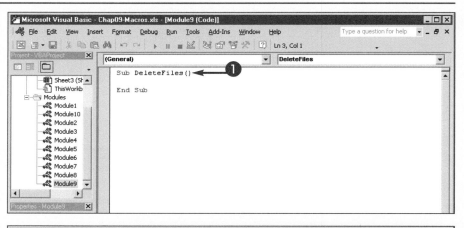

 Type **Dim DeleteWB As String**, replacing `DeleteWB` with the name of the workbook variable.

Type additional VBA Code to determine the name of the file(s) to delete.

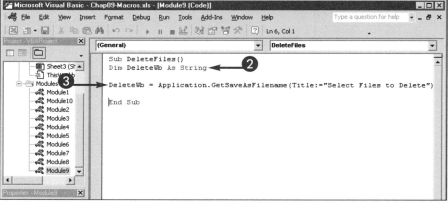

④ Type **Kill(DeleteWb)**.

⑤ Switch to Excel and run the macro.

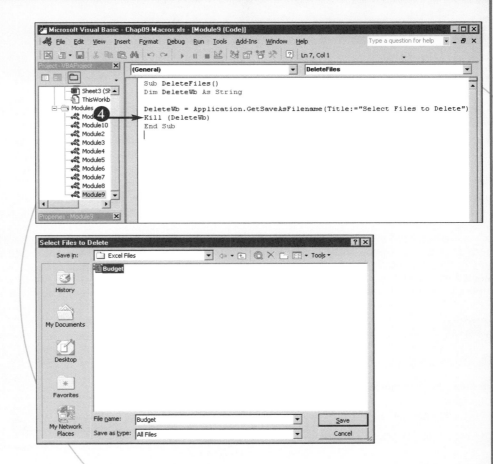

Excel removes the specified files from your computer.

You can only use the `Kill` statement to remove files; it does not remove folders. To delete a folder you can use the `RmDir` statement. The only argument for the `RmDir` statement — the path argument — is not required. If you attempt to omit the argument, VBA tries to delete the current folder. The path argument consists of a string containing the path specifying the folder location to remove. For example, the code `RmDir("c:\Excel Files")` removes the folder on the specified path. The `RmDir` statement only removes folders; it does not remove any files. If the folder you are deleting contains any files, an error message displays warning you that Excel cannot remove the folder.

When working with folders, you may need to know the current path in order to determine which folder to remove, or whether the folder exists. You can determine the current folder using the `CurDir` function. The `CurDir` function returns a string containing the path for the current folder. Typically, you can assign the value returned by the function to a variable, as shown in the code `CurrentFolder`.

**Example:**
```
= CurDir.
```

# Find
# a File

You can use VBA to create a procedure to find specific files on your computer. By creating this type of procedure, you can ensure that a specific file exists before attempting to reference it. This type of coding is useful for avoiding errrors because it verifies that a file exists, as well as the file's exact location.

In order to search for a file on your system, you use the FileSearch object. This object essentially opens the Excel Open dialog box and attempts to locate the file based upon specified methods and property values. The .Filename property indicates the name of the file for which you want to search. You can search for one, or a series of files, using a wildcard character. You use an asterisk (*) to represent multiple characters or a question mark symbol (?) to

specify a single character. For example, you can find all text files with the *.txt specification.

You stipulate the location where Excel starts the search with the .LookIn property. You can use the SearchSubFolders property to indicate whether you want Excel to look in the subfolders of the location specified by the .LookIn property.

If Excel locates your file, VBA returns a FoundFile object containing the matching filenames. You reference the individual filenames in the FoundFile object using an index value. VBA adds the filenames to the FoundFile object in the order that Excel locates them. You can determine the number of file names in the FoundFile object using the Count method. Using a For Next looping statement enables you to cycle through all of the matches that Excel finds using your search criteria. For example, you can write your code to open each file that matches the specified criteria.

## Find a File

① Create a new subroutine.

② Type **Dim PathInfo As String**, replacing PathInfo with the file location variable.

③ Type **With Application.FileSearch**.

④ Type **.NewSearch**.

⑤ Type **.FileName = "Book.xls"**, replacing Book.xls with the name of the file(s) to locate.

⑥ Type **.LookIn = "C:\"**, replacing C:\ with the path to search.

⑦ Type **.SearchSubFolders = True**.

If you do not want to search subfolders, you can specify a value of False for SearchSubFolders.

⑧ Type **If.Execute()>0Then**.

⑨ Type **For i=1 To .FoundFiles.Count**.

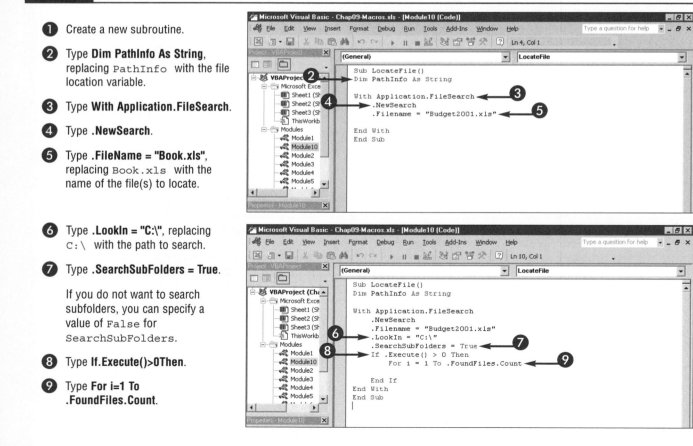

⑩ Type **PathInfo = FoundFiles(i)**.

⑪ Type additional VBA code to execute for each file match.

⑫ Type **Next i**.

⑬ Type **Workbooks.Open Filename:=PathInfo**.

⑭ Switch to Excel and run the macro.

If Excel finds the specified file, it is opened.

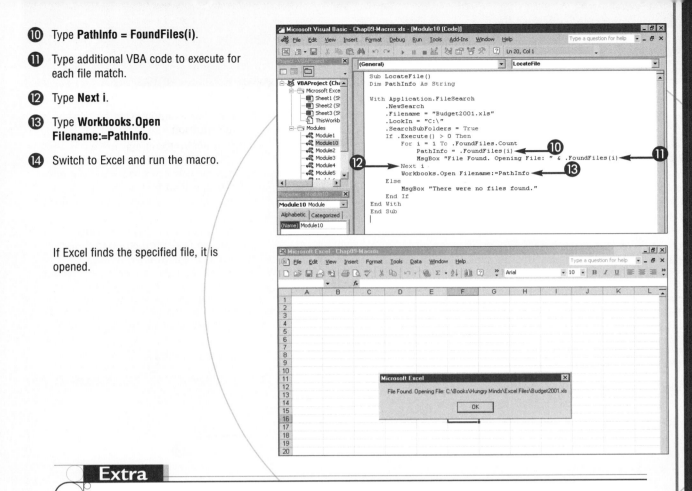

## Extra

You can use different optional properties with the `FileSearch` object to search for specific files on a system. The following table lists the most useful properties.

| FILESEARCH PROPERTY | DESCRIPTION |
|---|---|
| FileName | Indicates the name of the file to locate during the file search. This value can be a specific filename or contain the wildcard symbols * and ?. |
| FileType | A MsoFileType constant value indicating the type of files to look for during the file search. See Appendix A for the available MsoFileType constant values. |
| FoundFiles | Returns a FoundFiles object containing the names of the file matches. |
| LastModified | A MsoLastModified constant value indicating the amount of time since file was last modified. See Appendix A for the MsoLastModified constant values. |
| LookIn | Indicates the folder to search. |
| MatchTextExactly | Boolean value used with TextOrProperty property to indicate if only files containing specified text should be returned. |
| SearchSubFolders | Boolean value indicating whether the subfolders of the folder specified by the .LookIn property should also be searched. |
| TextOrProperty | A string that sets the word or phrase to search for in the body of the file or the file's properties. The string can include the * and ? wildcard symbols. |

# Add a Sheet

You can add a new sheet to a workbook using the `Add` method with the `Sheets` object. You use this method to add any type of sheet to a workbook, worksheet, chart sheet, or macro sheet.

The `Add` method has four optional parameters that specify where in the workbook to place the sheet, the number of sheets to add, and the type of sheet to create: `ThisWorkbook.Sheets.Add(Before, After, Count, Type)`.

You use the `Before` parameter, the parameter Excel applies when you do not specify any parameters, to place the sheet before the currently active sheet in the workbook. You use the `After` parameter to place a worksheet after the active sheet. You reference a sheet either by the sheet name or using the Worksheets Collection with an index value, as in the example: `ThisWorkbook.Sheets.Add Before:=Worksheets(1)`.

Excel references sheets within a Worksheets Collection based on the order of the sheets within the workbook from right to left, with the worksheet on the left being the first sheet with an index of Worksheet(1).

You can add any number of sheets to a workbook at one time using the `Count` parameter. If you do not specify a value for the `Count` parameter, Excel adds only one sheet to the workbook.

By default the `Add` method creates an Excel worksheet when it is called. You can also use this method to create chart or macro sheets. You specify the type of sheet you want to create using one of the four `XLSheetType` constant values. If you specify `xlWorksheet`, Excel adds a new worksheet. Use `xlChart` to create a new chart. If you want to create a macro sheet, you can use `xlExcel4MacroSheet`. Use `xlExcel4IntMacroSheet` to create an international macro sheet.

## Add a Sheet

① Create a new subroutine.

**Note:** See Chapter 3 for information on creating subroutines.

② Type **ThisWorkbook.Sheets.Add**.

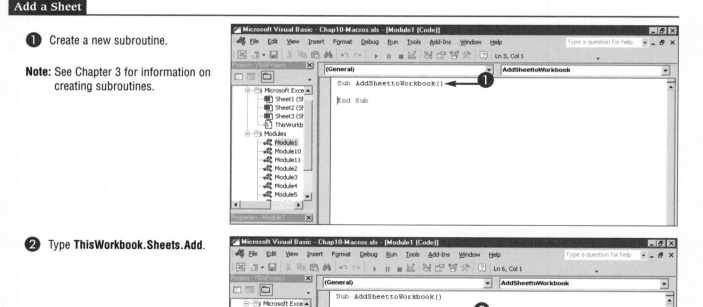

③ Type **Before:=Worksheets(1)**, replacing `Before` with either `Before` or `After`, and `Worksheets(1)` with the sheet in front of which you want to place the new sheets.

④ Type **Count:=2**, replacing `2` with the number of sheets you want to add.

⑤ Type **Type:=xlWorksheet**, replacing `xlWorksheet` with the constant indicating the type of sheet to create.

⑥ Switch to Excel and run the macro.

● Excel adds the specified number of sheets to the workbook.

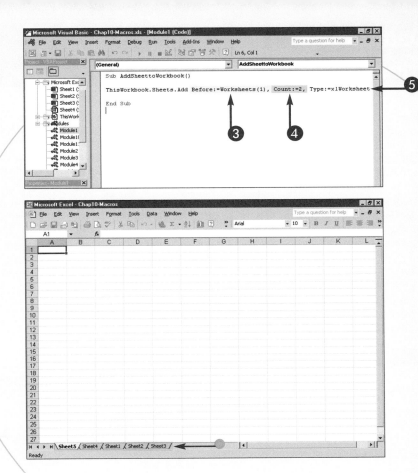

## Extra

When you use the `Before` and `After` parameters to specify the location in the workbook where you want to place the new sheets, you can use multiple methods. If you know you want Excel to add the sheets before the first sheet in the workbook, or after the last sheet, you can easily do so by referencing an element of the Worksheets Collection. Because Excel adds sheets to the Worksheets Collection in the order they exist in the workbook, Excel always makes the first sheet in the workbook the first element of the Worksheets Collection, and references it as `Worksheets(1)`. Because you do not always know how many sheets are in a workbook, you can use the `Count` method with the `Worksheets` object to determine the last sheet in the workbook by typing `Worksheets.Count`.

You can also reference a specific sheet by name. For example, by default Excel names all worksheets as `Sheet1`, `Sheet2`, and so on. If you want to place the new sheets before `Sheet1`, you can type the following for the `Before` parameter: **Before:=Sheet1**.

Alternately, you can add the sheet before the active sheet in the workbook. To do this you use the `ActiveSheet` property. This option is useful because no matter what sheet you select, Excel adds the new sheets before or after that specific sheet.

# Delete a Sheet

Y ou can delete or remove any sheet from a workbook as long as you have the ability to modify it. If you open the workbook in read-only mode or if another user has protected the workbook, you cannot make any modifications to the workbook, including the removal of sheets.

You can delete a sheet using the `Delete` method with the `Sheets` object. This combination enables you to remove any type of sheet from the workbook, including worksheets, chart sheets, and macro sheets. To use this method, you must identify the sheet you want to remove, as illustrated in the following code, which removes the first worksheet in the workbook: `Sheets(1).Delete`.

Although Excel numbers sheets and charts as you add them to the workbook (for example, Sheet1, Sheet2, or Chart1, Chart2, and so on), it does not necessarily reference sheets

in numeric order. If you use a numeric index value to specify the first sheet in a workbook, Excel considers the first sheet to be the one with the tab in the bottom-left corner. If you move sheets within the workbook, Excel reorders them within the `Sheets` object.

You can also reference the sheet you want to delete using the sheet name. If you specify a sheet name, you must enclose the name of the sheet in double quotes, for example: `Sheets("Sheet3").Delete`.

No matter what method you use, Excel displays a message box to verify that you really want to remove the sheet. You remove the specified sheet from the workbook using the Delete button. Remember, if the sheet contains any data, Excel permanently removes all data as well as the specified sheet.

## Delete a Sheet

 ① Create a new subroutine.

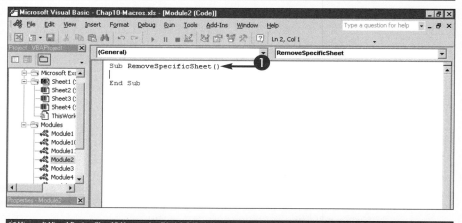

② Type **Dim DeleteWS As String**, replacing `DeleteWS` with the variable name of the sheet to delete.

③ Assign the name of the sheet to remove from the workbook to the `DeleteWS` variable.

This example uses the `InputBox` function to request the sheet name from the user.

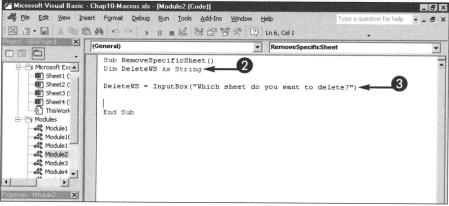

④ Type **Sheets(DeleteWS).Delete**.

⑤ Switch to Excel and run the macro.

**Note:** See Chapter 1 for more on running a macro.

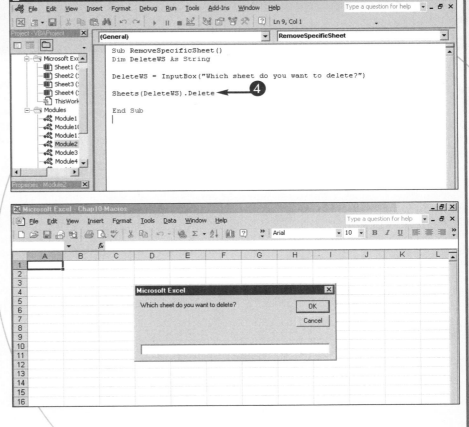

Excel removes the specified sheet from the workbook.

---

## Extra

If you want to create a subroutine that only removes worksheets from the workbook, you can use the Delete method with the Worksheets object instead of the Sheets object. The Sheets object contains all worksheets, chart sheets, and macro sheets open within a workbook, whereas the Worksheets object only keeps track of the open worksheets. If you use the Worksheets object to remove the first worksheet in the workbook, Excel ignores any chart sheets that exist in the workbook before the first worksheet. The following statement finds the first worksheet and ignores anything else that is not a worksheet.

**Example:**
```
Worksheets(1).Delete
```

On the contrary, if you only want to create a subroutine that removes chart sheets from the workbook, you can use the Delete method with the Charts object. The Charts object contains all of the chart sheets contained within the workbook. Keep in mind that this method only works with chart sheets, not charts embedded in worksheets. When you use the Charts object with the Delete method, Excel only considers actual chart sheets, and ignores any worksheets within the workbook, even if they exist before the specified chart sheet. The following code statement deletes the first chart sheet within the workbook, and ignores any other sheet types.

**Example:**
```
Charts(1).Delete
```

# Move a Sheet

You can rearrange sheets within a workbook using the Move method with the Sheets object. When you move a sheet, you indicate the new location by specifying the name of the sheet that you want to place before or after the current sheet.

The Move method has two optional parameters, Before and After. Although both parameters are optional, you can only use one of them. Use the Before parameter to specify the sheet in front of which you want to move the current sheet. Use the After parameter to specify the sheet after which you want to place the current sheet. For example, the following code statement moves the first sheet in a workbook and places it behind the third sheet: Sheets(1). Move After:=Sheets(3).

If you do not specify a Before or After parameter value, Excel creates a new workbook and places the moved

worksheet in that workbook. The moved worksheet becomes the only worksheet in the new workbook.

When you use the Sheets object, you reference all sheets within the workbook including all workbooks, chart sheets, and macro sheets. As shown in the example, you can use index values to reference specific sheets based upon their order within the workbook. You can also reference a sheet using the sheet name that appears on the sheet tab.

Be sure to use all sheet references. Moving a sheet before or after a non-existent sheet causes VBA to display a Subscript out of range error. To avoid error, especially when using index values to reference specific sheets, consider employing the Count method to determine the exact number of sheets in the workbook before attempting to move sheets. When you know the number of sheets, you can proceed with the move by not attempting a move beyond the maximum number of sheets.

## Move a Sheet

① Create a new subroutine.

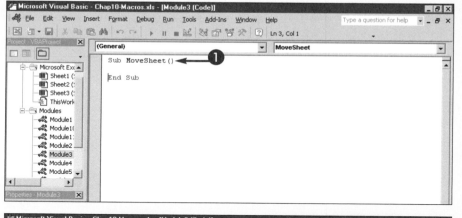

② Type **Dim LastSheet As Long**, replacing LastSheet with the variable to determine the number of sheets in the workbook.

③ Type **LastSheet = Sheets.Count**.

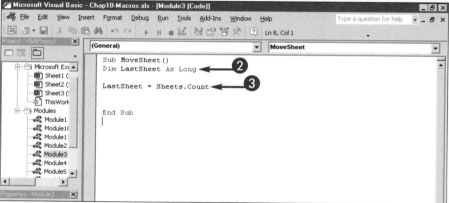

④ Type **Sheets(1).Move**, replacing
`Sheets(1)` with a reference to the sheet
to move.

⑤ Type **After:=Sheets(LastSheet)**, replacing
`After` with `Before` if you want to place
the sheet before the specified sheet.

⑥ Switch to Excel and run the macro.

● Excel moves the specified sheet to the
end of the workbook.

```vba
Sub MoveSheet()
Dim LastSheet As Long

LastSheet = Sheets.Count

Sheets(1).Move After:=Sheets(LastSheet)

End Sub
```

## Apply It

As you work with Excel objects in VBA,
especially collection objects that contain
several values, such as the Sheets Collection,
you frequently must determine the number
of objects within the collection. Because the
number of objects in a collection varies
based upon what you have currently open,
you need to determine the number of
objects as your code runs. The best method
for this is the `Count` property, which works
with virtually all VBA collection objects to
return a value that specifies the number of
objects within the current collection:

**Example:**
`NumSheets = Worksheets.Count`

The `Count` property is read-only, meaning
that you cannot use it to change the
number of sheets in a workbook. But you
should use it at any point where the number
of items in a collection may change. For
example, you may know that the Excel
workbooks on your system all have at least
three pages because you have set up your
defaults to always create a new workbook
with three pages. Even if this is the case,
you should not assume that you always
have that many pages in each workbook
you open.

# Copy and Paste a Sheet

Y ou can copy and paste the new sheets in a workbook using the Copy method with the Sheets object. When you copy a sheet, you indicate the location for the copy by specifying the name of the sheet that you want Excel to place before or after the current sheet.

The Copy method has two optional parameters, Before and After. Although both parameters are optional, you can only use one of them. Use the Before parameter to specify the sheet in front of which you want to place the copy of the sheet. Alternately, you can use the After parameter to specify the sheet after which you want to place the copy of the sheet. The following code statement illustrates copying the first sheet in a workbook and placing the copy behind the third sheet: Sheets(1). Copy After:=Sheets(3). If you do not specify a Before or After parameter value, Excel creates a new workbook and places this lone copy in that workbook.

When you use the Sheets object, you reference all sheets within the workbook, including chart sheets and macro sheets. You can use index values to reference specific sheets based upon their order within the workbook. You can also reference a sheet using the sheet name that appears on the sheet tab.

Be careful with the sheet references that you do use. If you try to place a copy of a sheet before or after a non-existent sheet, VBA displays a Subscript out of range error. To avoid the potential for error, especially when using index values to reference specific sheets, consider using the Count method to determine exactly how many sheets you have in a workbook before attempting to copy and paste. Knowing the number of sheets ensures that you do not attempt to place a sheet beyond the maximum number of sheets.

## Copy and Paste a Sheet

 **1** Create a new subroutine.

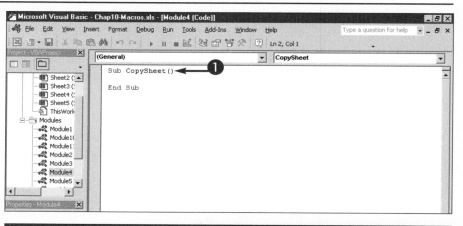

**2** Type **Dim LastSheet As Long**, replacing LastSheet with the variable to determine the number of sheets in the workbook.

**3** Type **LastSheet = Sheets.Count**.

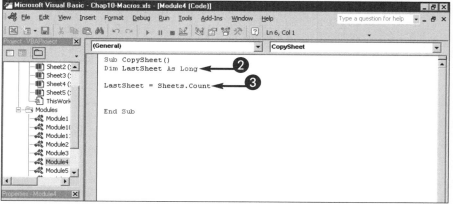

④ Type **Sheets(LastSheet).Copy**, replacing `Sheets(LastSheet)` with a reference to the sheet to copy.

⑤ Type **Before:=Sheets(1)**, replacing `Sheets(1)` with the location for placing the copied sheet before a sheet.

Alternately, you can type **After:=Sheets (1)**, replacing `Sheets(1)` with the location for placing the copied sheet after a sheet.

⑥ Switch to Excel and run the macro.

● The specified sheet is copied and placed in front of or behind the indicated sheet in the workbook.

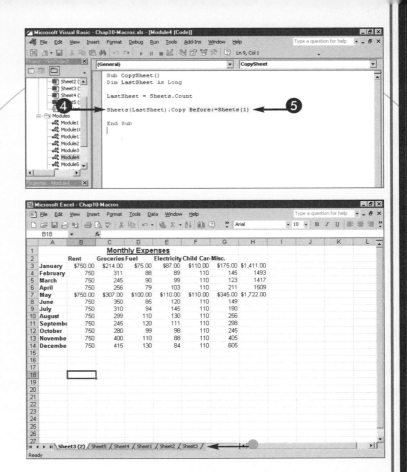

---

The `Copy` method produces the same results when you use it with the `Chart` object, `Charts` collection object, `Worksheet` object, and `Worksheets` collection object instead of the `Sheets` object. You can use these other objects when you only want to work with a specific type of sheet. For example, to place a copy of a worksheet at the beginning of the workbook, you type: `Worksheet(3).Copy Before:=Worksheets(1)`. This code places a copy of the third worksheet in front of the first worksheet. If the first sheet in the workbook is actually a chart, the copied sheet comes after the chart, but still before the first worksheet. The same process holds true for copying chart sheets, but you use the `Charts` collection object to specify the chart sheet to copy.

You can combine your object references with a `Copy` statement. For example, you can place a copy of the first workbook before the first chart sheet:

**Example:**
```
Worksheets(1).  Copy Before:=Charts(1).
```

When you copy a sheet within a workbook, Excel indicates the copy of the sheet by placing a number in parentheses behind the sheet name. For example, for Sheet3, Excel indicates the copied sheet as Sheet3 (2), with the number in parentheses indicating this is the second version. Copying this worksheet again creates Sheet3 (3).

# Hide a Sheet

Y ou can hide specific sheets in a workbook using the Visible property of the Sheets object. You may want to hide sheets in a workbook to prevent others from viewing them. Typically these sheets contain the raw values that you use to calculate data, and which displays on a separate sheet. Keep in mind, hiding a sheet does not keep a user from accessing it. Another user can unhide sheets in Excel using the Unhide option on the Format menu. If you have something that you do not want others to access, consider protecting as well as hiding the sheet. See the section "Protect a Worksheet" for more information about protecting sheets.

Using the Visible property, you can either determine the current state of a sheet — visible or not visible — or you can change the state of a sheet. To determine the

current state of a sheet, you can assign the visible property to a Boolean variable as follows: SheetProps = Sheets(1).Visible.

If you declare the SheetProps variable as a Boolean value, the variable receives a value of True if the specified sheet is visible; otherwise, it receives a value of False. If you forget to declare the variable as Boolean, Excel assigns a numeric value of -1 if the sheet is visible, and 0 if the sheet is not visible.

You change the visibility of a sheet by assigning a Boolean value of True or False to the Visible property for the appropriate sheet. You can hide all but one sheet in a workbook. Excel requires that a workbook have at least one visible sheet. The following code illustrates how to hide a sheet so it is not visible: Sheet(2).Visible = False.

## Hide a Sheet

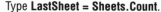

① Create a new subroutine.

② Type **Dim LastSheet As Long**, replacing LastSheet with the variable to contain the number of sheets in the workbook.

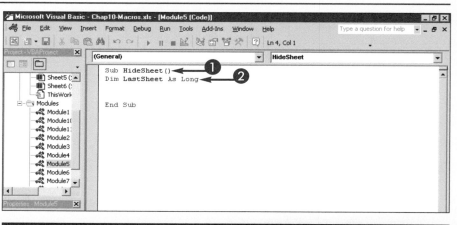

③ Type **LastSheet = Sheets.Count**.

④ Type **For N = 2 To LastSheet**.

The For Next loop sets the Visible property for all but the first sheet.

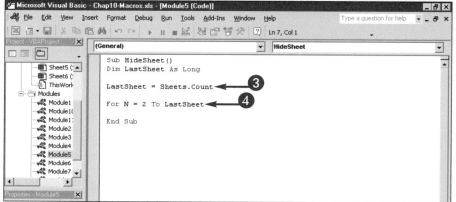

**⑤** Type **Sheets(N).Visible = False**.

**⑥** Switch to Excel and run the macro.

```
Sub HideSheet()
Dim LastSheet As Long

LastSheet = Sheets.Count

For N = 2 To LastSheet
    Sheets(N).Visible = False
Next

End Sub
```

● Excel hides all but the first sheet in the workbook.

| | A | B | C | D | E | F | G | H |
|---|---|---|---|---|---|---|---|---|
| 1 | | | | Monthly Expenses | | | | |
| 2 | | Rent | Groceries | Fuel | Electricity | Child Care | Misc. | |
| 3 | January | $750.00 | $214.00 | $75.00 | $87.00 | $110.00 | $175.00 | $1,411.00 |
| 4 | February | 750 | 311 | 88 | 89 | 110 | 145 | 1493 |
| 5 | March | 750 | 245 | 90 | 99 | 110 | 123 | 1417 |
| 6 | April | 750 | 256 | 79 | 103 | 110 | 211 | 1509 |
| 7 | May | $750.00 | $307.00 | $100.00 | $110.00 | $110.00 | $345.00 | $1,722.00 |
| 8 | June | 750 | 350 | 85 | 120 | 110 | 149 | |
| 9 | July | 750 | 310 | 94 | 145 | 110 | 190 | |
| 10 | August | 750 | 299 | 110 | 130 | 110 | 256 | |
| 11 | September | 750 | 245 | 120 | 111 | 110 | 298 | |
| 12 | October | 750 | 280 | 99 | 98 | 110 | 245 | |
| 13 | November | 750 | 400 | 110 | 88 | 110 | 405 | |
| 14 | December | 750 | 415 | 130 | 84 | 110 | 605 | |

## Extra

Keep in mind that you cannot hide every worksheet in a workbook. If you attempt to do so, Excel displays a Run-time error indicating that it is unable to set the `Visible` property of the `Worksheet` class. This message essentially means that you cannot hide all worksheets. To avoid receiving that message, make sure you leave one worksheet visible. To ensure that another user does not hide the worksheet that you want to keep visible, consider using the `Visible` property. This property checks that a sheet is visible before changing the visibility of the other worksheets.

Sheets that you hide are still accessible to the user from within Excel. You can see which sheets are hidden in a workbook by selecting Format→Sheet→Unhide. The Unhide dialog box lists all of the sheets that are currently hidden. To unhide a sheet, you need to click the appropriate sheet and then click OK. This process is equivalent to setting the `Visible` property for a sheet to `True`.

# Change the Name of a Sheet

You can change the name of a sheet within a workbook using the `Name` property of the `Sheets` object. By default Excel names all worksheets Sheet# replacing # with the order in which you added the sheet to the workbook. For example, a typical workbook contains three worksheets, Sheet1, Sheet2, and Sheet3. If you add an additional worksheet, by default Excel names the sheet Sheet4. Excel uses the name Chart# for chart sheets. Again, Excel assigns chart sheets numbers based upon the order in which you add them with the first chart sheet being Chart1. The other two types of sheets, macro sheets and dialog sheets, also have the same naming conventions. Excel names the first macro sheet you add to a workbook as Macro1 and the first dialog sheet as Dialog1.

You can change the name of a sheet in a workbook by assigning a new string value to the `Name` property of the corresponding `Sheet` object. For example, the following

code illustrates how to change the name of the sheet to Budget2000: `Sheets(1).Name = "Budget2000"`. Remember when assigning a string value, you must enclose the string in parentheses. You can also assign a string as the value of a variable.

The other function of the `Name` property is to provide the name of a specific sheet. For example, you can check that a sheet has the appropriate name. To determine the name of a sheet, you assign the string that the `Name` property returns to a variable, for example: `StringName = Sheets(3).Name`.

After assigning the value to a variable, you perform any of the typical string functions. For example, you can compare it to another string, or just display it using the `MsgBox` function. See Chapter 7 for more information on working with the `MsgBox` function.

## Change the Name of a Sheet

① Create a new subroutine.

② Type **Dim SheetName As String**, replacing `SheetName` with the variable to contain the new sheet name.

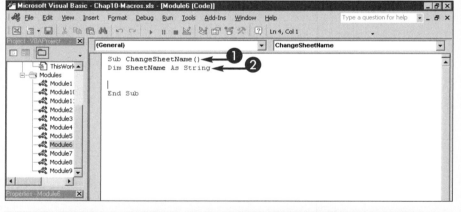

③ Type **SheetName = InputBox("Input Box Text")**, replacing `Input Box Text` with the text to display on the Input Box.

④ Type **ActiveSheet.Name = SheetName**.

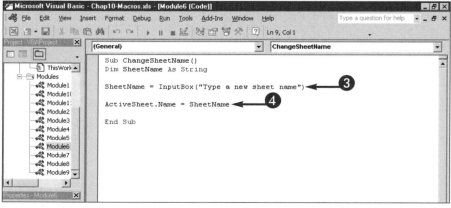

**⑤** Switch to Excel and run the macro.

**⑥** Type the desired sheet name in the input box.

**⑦** Click OK.

● The name of the active sheet changes to the name specified by the user.

---

## Extra

You can manually change the name of a sheet within Excel by clicking Format➔Sheet➔Rename. Excel highlights the sheet name tab. Click the tab and type the new name. After you modify the name, click elsewhere on the sheet and Excel updates the sheet name.

Because users can easily modify the name of a worksheet within Excel, be careful when referencing sheet names with your macros. If you attempt to reference the name of a sheet that has a changed name, Excel returns an error message.

No matter what its name, Excel still keeps track of the sheets based upon the order in which they exist within the Sheet Collection. If you use Project Explorer to view the list of sheets in the workbook, you see listings of Sheet1, Sheet2, and so on, with the corresponding sheet name in parentheses.

You can also use the Name property in conjunction with the Parent property to determine the name of the workbook that contains the current sheet. You can use this Name property function to ensure that you are in the appropriate workbook before executing the contents of a macro. You determine the name of the corresponding workbook using the code CurrentWB = ActiveSheet.Parent.Name.

# Save a Sheet to Another File

You can save a specific sheet in your workbook with the SaveAs method. You can use this property with a Sheets Collection object, which enables you to save any sheet. You can also use the property with a specific Worksheet or Chart object to indicate a specific workbook or chart that you want to save.

With the SaveAs method, you have eight different optional parameters that specify how Excel saves the sheet: FileName, FileFormat, Password, WriteResPassword, ReadOnlyRecommended, CreateBackup, AddToMru, and Local.

You use the FileName parameter to specify the file name and location where you want to save the selected sheet. If you omit this parameter value, Excel utilizes the filename of the corresponding workbook as the value for the FileName parameter. If you do not specify a path as part of the filename, Excel saves the file containing the sheet in the current folder.

You use the FileFormat parameter to specify the file format for saving the sheet to a file. You save the sheet to any of the file formats supported by Excel with one of the xlFileFormat constant values. See Appendix A for a list of the xlFileFormat constant values. If you do not specify a FileFormat parameter value, Excel uses the default value. The default value consists of the last specified file format you used to save a sheet as well as the version of Excel you use for new files. For example, to save a sheet to a Text file, you use the xlTextMSDOS XLFileFormat constant value.

With the Password parameter you can specify up to a 15-character password for opening the file. You use the WriteResPassword parameter to restrict the file to open as read-only without the password. The other parameters accept Boolean values of either True or False.

## Save a Sheet to Another File

① Create a new subroutine.

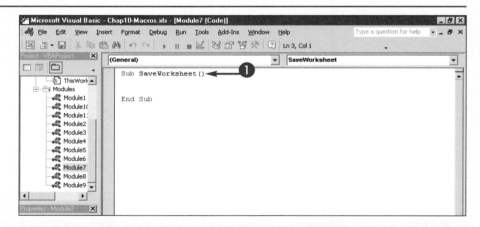

② Type **ActiveSheet.SaveAs**, replacing ActiveSheet with a reference to the sheet you want to save.

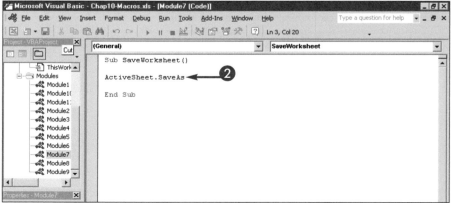

**③** Type **FileName:="NameofFile"**, replacing `NameofFile` with the name and path to save the file.

**④** Type **FileFormat:=xlHtml**, replacing `xlHtml` with the format in which you want to save the file.

**⑤** Switch to Excel and run the macro.

● The current sheet is saved in the specified format.

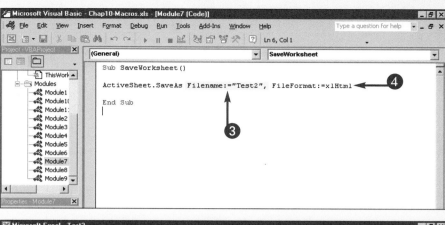

---

The `FileFormat` parameter accepts any of the `XlFileFormat` constant values, as outlined in Appendix A. The list of available file formats is rather extensive. Typically, you save the worksheet in another workbook by specifying the `xlWorkbookNormal` constant. This constant creates a new workbook based upon the default workbook format for the current version of Excel. If you need to save the workbook in a format to be used by an earlier version of Excel, you need to specify the appropriate format parameter. For example, `xlExcel5` saves the workbook in a format that can be opened by Excel 5.0 or later.

As specified, the `Password` and `WriteResPassword` parameters provide two different types of protection for the new workbook. The `Password` parameter protects the workbook from being opened. In other words, you must specify the correct value for the `Password` parameter to open the workbook containing the sheet. You can employ the `WriteResPassword` parameter with or without the `Password` parameter to indicate the password that must be specified to modify the workbook. If the user types a password that does not match the one specified by the `WriteResPassword` parameter, the workbook opens as read-only and the user cannot modify it.

# Protect a Worksheet

You can use the `Protect` method to password protect a worksheet so that other users cannot modify it. You can allow certain types of modifications, such as inserting rows, by specifying the appropriate parameter value for the `Protect` method.

The `Protect` method has several different optional parameters that enable you to customize the type of protection that you assign to the workbook. Most of these parameters accept only `True` or `False` to indicate whether that type of protection is active for the workbook. The parameters include: `Password`, `DrawingObjects`, `Contents`, `Scenarios`, `UserInterfaceOnly`, `AllowFormattingCells`, `AllowFormattingColumns`, `AllowFormattingRows`, `AllowInsertingColumns`, `AllowInsertingRows`, `AllowInsertingHyperlinks`, `AllowDeletingColumns`, `AllowDeletingRows`, `AllowSorting`, `AllowFiltering`, and `AllowUsingPivotTables`.

Although optional, you need to specify the `Password` parameter to really protect the worksheet. You can use any string, but remember it is case-sensitive. In other words, Excel interprets "Password" and "PASSWORD" differently.

All other parameters of the `Protect` method accept only `True` and `False` values. You use the `DrawingObjects` parameter to protect any shapes you add to your worksheet. The default value is `False`. By default, Excel protects the locked cells and scenarios if a worksheet is protected. To remove the protection of locked cells, specify a value of `False` for the `Contents` parameter. To unprotect scenarios, specify a value of `False` for the `Scenarios` parameter. If you do not use the `UserInterfaceOnly` parameter, Excel applies the protection to macros and the user interface options for the worksheet. If you only want the user interface protected, specify a value of `True` for the `UserInterfaceOnly` parameter.

The other parameters all have default values of `False`. If you want to allow any of those options when you protect the worksheet, change the value of the corresponding parameter to `True`.

## Protect a Worksheet

① Create a new subroutine.

② Type **Worksheets(1).Protect**, replacing `Worksheets(1)` with a reference to the worksheet to protect.

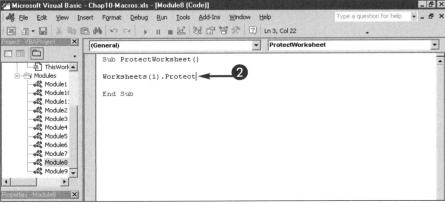

**3** Type **Password:="Excel"**, replacing "Excel" with the password you want to use to unprotect the worksheet.

**4** Type **AllowFormattingCells:=True**.

**5** Specify any other parameters you need to protect the worksheet.

**6** Switch to Excel and run the macro.

Excel no longer allows modifications to the worksheet.

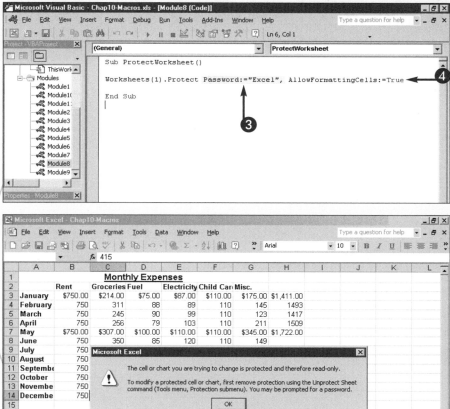

## Extra

After you protect a worksheet, a user must use the appropriate password to make modifications to it. A user specifies the password in Excel by clicking Tools→Protection→Unprotect Sheet and typing the appropriate password for the sheet in the dialog box that appears. When the user types the appropriate password, the worksheet remains unprotected and the user can make any necessary modifications.

You can unprotect the worksheet from within a procedure with the Unprotect method. You use this method with any sheet or workbook that you want to protect. If you use this method with an unprotected worksheet, Excel ignores it and the worksheet remains unaffected.

The only parameter required for the Unprotect method is the Password parameter. You must use this parameter as a string to represent the password of the worksheet you want to unprotect. Remember that the password is case-sensitive and must match the current password of the worksheet. For example, ActiveWorkbook.Unprotect Password:="Excel" unprotects the active worksheet by passing it the correct password.

Remember to keep track of the passwords that you have assigned to worksheets. If you lose a password, you cannot access the password-protected document.

# Protect a Chart

You can protect a chart so that a user cannot modify it using the `Protect` method. When you protect a chart, you typically password protect it to eliminate the ability to modify it.

The `Protect` method uses different optional parameters that enable you to customize the type of protection that you assign to the chart. All but one of these parameters accepts only `True` or `False` to indicate whether or not that type of protection is active for the workbook. The following code illustrates use of the `Protect` method with a chart:

```
Charts(1).Protect(Password, DrawingObjects,
Contents, Scenarios, UserInterfaceOnly).
```

Although optional, to effectively protect the chart, you need to specify the password. You can use any string, but remember that it is case-sensitive. This means that Excel treats uppercase and lowercase letters as different characters. In other words, Excel interprets *Password* and *PASSWORD* differently, even though they are the same word.

All other parameters of the `Protect` method accept only `True` and `False` values. You use the `DrawingObjects` parameter to protect any shapes you add to your chart with the drawing options in Excel. The default value of this parameter is `False`. By default, Excel protects the entire chart and scenarios if you protect a chart. To remove the protection, specify a value of `False` for the `Contents` parameter. To unprotect scenarios, specify a value of `False` for the `Scenarios` parameter. If you do not use the `UserInterfaceOnly` parameter, Excel applies the protection to macros and the user interface options for the chart. If you only want to protect the user interface, specify a value of `True` for the `UserInterfaceOnly` parameter.

You can unprotect a chart using the `Unprotect` method with the corresponding password for the chart.

## Protect a Chart

① Create a new subroutine.

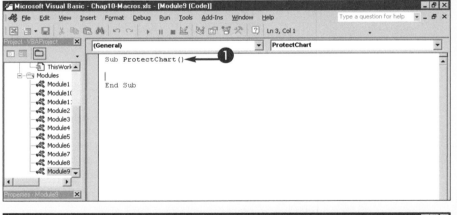

② Type **Charts(1).Protect**, replacing `Charts(1)` with a reference to the chart to protect.

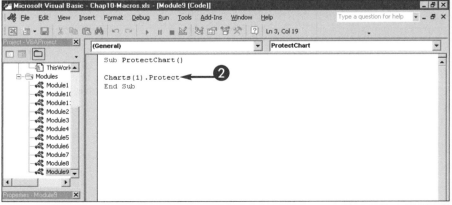

③ Type **Password:="Excel"**, replacing "Excel" with the password you want to use to unprotect the chart.

④ Type **DrawingObjects:=False**.

⑤ Specify any other parameters needed to protect the chart.

⑥ Switch to Excel and run the macro.

Excel no longer allows modifications to the chart.

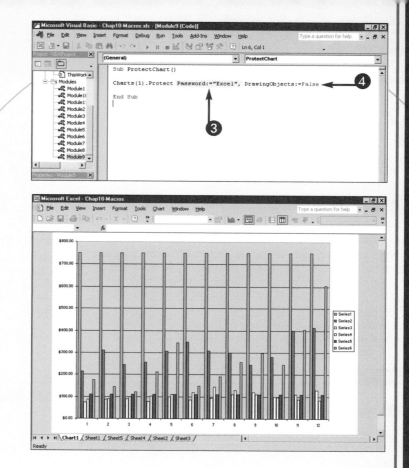

## Apply It

VBA provides different properties that you can use with worksheet and chart objects to determine if parts of a sheet are protected. Doing this helps to eliminate errors caused by attempting to modify a protected sheet. Each of these properties is read-only, meaning you can only use them to determine if the sheet has that type of protection.

| PROPERTY | DESCRIPTION |
| --- | --- |
| ProtectContents | Returns a value of True if the sheet is protected. For a chart, the property looks to see if the entire chart is protected. For a worksheet, the property looks to see if the cells are protected. To turn off this property, set the Contents parameter of the Protect method to False. |
| ProtectDrawingObjects | Returns a value of True if the drawing shapes that were added to the sheet are protected. To turn off this property, set the DrawingObjects parameter of the Protect method to False. |
| ProtectScenarios | Returns a value of True if the scenarios are protected. To turn off this property, set the Scenarios parameter of the Protect method to False. |
| ProtectionMode | Returns a value of True if the user-interface is protected. |

# Print a Sheet

Y ou can create a procedure to print the contents of a sheet using the PrintOut method. Not only do you have the ability to specify what to print, you can also specify the number of copies to print or the method to print the contents of a sheet to a file. The PrintOut method has several different properties available for specifying how Excel prints the sheet: From, To, Copies, Preview, ActivePrinter, PrintToFile, Collate, and PrToFileName.

You use the From and To parameters to indicate the range of pages within the specified sheet to print. You indicate the page number of the first page to print as the value of the From parameter and the page number of the last page as the value of the To parameter. If you omit these parameters, Excel prints the entire sheet.

By default, Excel prints one copy of the sheet. For multiple copies, use the Copies parameter to indicate the desired number. You can specify a value of True for the Collate parameter to have Excel collate the copies.

If you want the Excel preview window to show the contents of the print selection, set the value of the Preview parameter to True. Keep in mind that the Print button on the Print Preview screen actually prints the copy and that the Close button cancels the print.

You can specify the printer Excel uses with the ActivePrinter parameter. To set a default printer, you can specify the name of the printer for this parameter.

You can also send the printout to a file instead of a printer by setting the PrintToFile parameter to True and specifying the name of the file to which you want to send the printout. If you do not specify a filename, Excel prompts you for one when your procedure runs.

## Print a Sheet

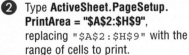

**1** Create a new subroutine.

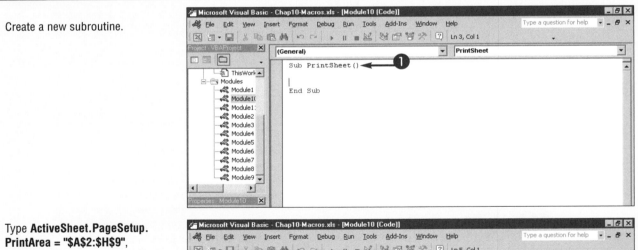

**2** Type **ActiveSheet.PageSetup. PrintArea = "$A$2:$H$9"**, replacing "$A$2:$H$9" with the range of cells to print.

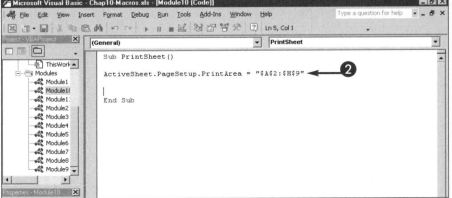

**③** Type **ActiveSheet.PrintOut**.

**④** Type **Preview:= True**.

**⑤** Type **ActivePrinter:= "HP DeskJet 894Cxi"**, replacing HP DeskJet 894Cxi with the name of the printer to use.

**Note:** You need to specify the name of a printer that is defined on your system.

Specify any additional optional parameter values for the Print method.

**⑥** Switch to Excel and run the macro.

The Print Preview screen displays.

**⑦** Click Print to print the specified cells.

Alternately, you can click Close to cancel the print.

Excel prints the cells.

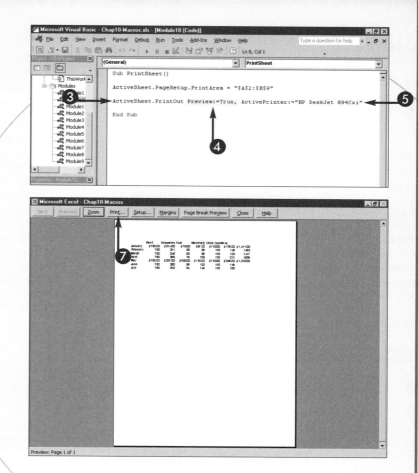

## Apply It

Instead of setting the range, you can set a print area for a worksheet with the PrintArea property. You use this property with the PageSetup object, a child object of the Worksheets collection object. You assign a range of cells as the print area, for example: ActiveSheet.PageSetup.PrintArea = "$A$2:$G$8". This code sets the range of cells in the print area to A2-G8. Even if cells outside that range contain data, Excel does not print them. The dollar signs in front of the row and column references indicates that you use absolute references to the cells you want to add to the range. See Chapter 11 for more information about absolute cell references.

When you use the PrintArea property to set the range of cells to print, you can omit the From and To parameters with the PrintOut method. If you want to clear the print area, you need to use the PrintArea property again and assign it a value of False or an empty string. Both of the following lines of code clear the print area:

**Example:**
```
ActiveSheet.PageSetup.PrintArea = False
ActiveSheet.PageSetup.PrintArea = " "
```

# Sort Worksheets by Name

You can use VBA to sort the order of the worksheets in a workbook based upon the worksheet name. When you first create a new workbook with three worksheets, Excel lists the sheets in order: Sheet1, Sheet2, and Sheet3. But as you add additional sheets, the order of the sheets can change dramatically. For example, if your active sheet is Sheet2 and you instruct Excel to add a new sheet, Excel adds it before Sheet2. If your workbook contains three worksheets, Excel adds the new sheet and names it Sheet4 making the order of your sheets Sheet1, Sheet4, Sheet2, Sheet3. Or course, you can easily resolve this by manually renaming or moving the sheets within the workbook.

Alternately, you can create a subroutine that sorts the worksheets so that Excel lists them in alphabetical order. To do this, you must first determine the number of sheets within the workbook using the Count property.

When you know the number of sheets in a workbook, you need to use For Next looping to cycle through the sheets so Excel can compare the names and move a sheet when one name is greater than another. You can accomplish this with *nested looping,* which is the process of placing one looping statement within another looping statement. The inside loop executes completely and control returns to the outside loop. See Chapter 6 for more information on using For Next looping statements.

Within the second For Next loop you can use an If Then statement to compare the name of a sheet to the currently smallest sheet name. If that name is smaller, it becomes the new smallest name. Remember, Excel does an alphabetical comparison when you deal with strings. Therefore, "apple" is smaller than "bat" even though the word apple has more characters.

## Sort Worksheets by Name

① Create a new subroutine.

② Type **Dim SheetName As String**, replacing SheetName with the variable for storing the smallest sheet name.

③ Type **Dim SheetCount As Integer** replacing SheetCount with the variable to store the number of sheets.

④ Type **SheetCount = Sheets.Count**.

⑤ Type **For N = 1 To SheetCount**.

⑥ Type **SheetName = Sheets(N).Name**.

⑦ Type **For M = N To SheetCount**.

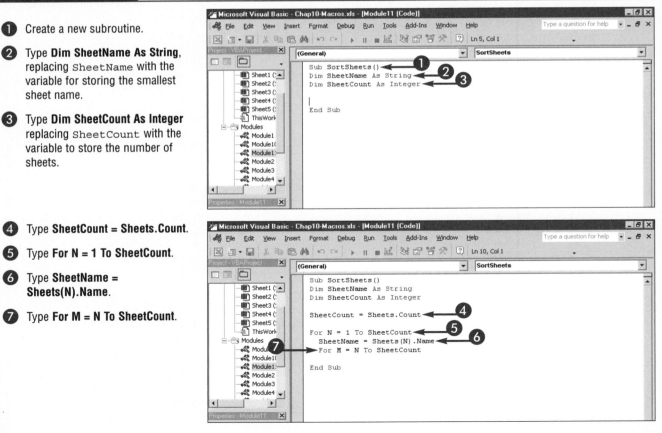

⑧ Type **If Sheets(M).Name < SheetName Then**.

⑨ Type **SheetName = Sheets(M).Name**.

⑩ Type **End If**.

⑪ Type **Next**.

⑫ Type **Sheets(SheetName).Move Before:=Sheets(N)**.

⑬ Switch to Excel and run the macro.

● The sheets are sorted alphabetically within the workbook.

```
Sub SortSheets()
Dim SheetName As String
Dim SheetCount As Integer

SheetCount = Sheets.Count

For N = 1 To SheetCount
    SheetName = Sheets(N).Name
    For M = N To SheetCount
        If Sheets(M).Name < SheetName Then
            SheetName = Sheets(M).Name
        End If
    Next
    Sheets(SheetName).Move Before:=Sheets(N)
Next

End Sub
```

## Apply It

In step 12 of the task example, Excel determines the sheet with the smallest name in the inside loop and places that sheet before the current sheet. Although this code works correctly, it is not the most effective method of sorting a larger list of items. The code attempts to move the sheet without first checking to see if the smallest sheet is the same sheet as the current sheet. Therefore, if the sheets are identical, Excel still attempts to move them. To make the execution of the code more efficient, you can add a conditional If Then statement that compares the two statements, as long as they are not the same sheet, and then performs the move. By adding this statement, the code runs more effectively because it determines that no move is required if the sheet is already in the correct order.

**TYPE THIS:**

```
If Sheets(SheetName) <> Sheets(N) Then
    Sheets(SheetName). Move Before:=Sheets(N)
End If
```

**RESULT:**

This code checks that the sheet you are moving and the sheet before which you intend to move it are not the same sheet. If the sheets are the same, Excel ignores the move statement and continues on with the looping statements.

# Using the Range Property

Y ou can use the Range property to define a range of cells within a worksheet. When you define a range, you create a Range object, which you can make a single cell, an entire column, a row, or a selection of multiple cells. Typically when working with the contents of a worksheet, you need to define a range in order to make any modifications to it.

You can use the Range property with an Application, Worksheet, or Range object. Therefore, the statements Application.Range and ActiveSheet.Range return the same results. If you use the Range property without an object, Excel assumes that the object you reference is the ActiveSheet.

There are two different syntaxes that you can use with the Range property. The first version requires two different parameters, Cell1 and Cell2. With this form of the Range

object, you reference the upper-left corner of the desired range with the Cell1 parameter and the lower-right corner of the range with the Cell2 parameter. For example, to specify a range of cells between A1 and E15 you use the code: Range("A1", "E15").

The other form of the Range property requires the use of a Name parameter. This required parameter indicates a range using the A1-style reference. You use a colon between two cells to specify a range. For example, Range("A3:F5") specifies the range of cells from A3 to F5. You can specify the union between two ranges by placing a comma between the range definitions. You can also specify the location where two ranges intersect by leaving a space between the two range definitions. For example, Range("A3:F3 D2:G5") specifies a range where the range of cells A3 to F3 intersect with the range of cells D2 to G5.

## Using the Range Property

### USING THE RANGE PROPERTY WITH CELL REFERENCES

① Create a new subroutine.

**Note:** See Chapter 3 for information on creating subroutines.

② Type **Range("A1", "B3").Select**, replacing A1 and B3 with the upper-right and lower-left corners of the selection.

Alternately, you can place a space or a colon (:) between the ranges to specify an intersection or union.

③ Switch to Excel and run the macro.

**Note:** To learn how to run a macro, see Chapter 1.

● The specified range of cells is selected.

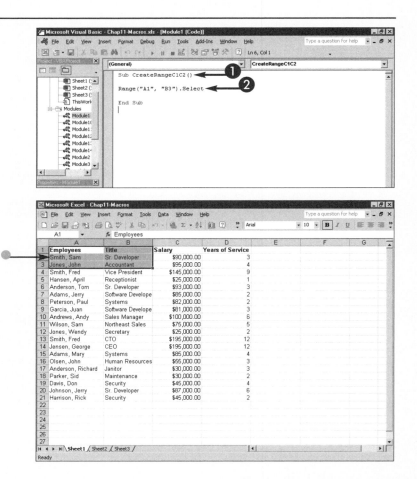

## USING THE RANGE PROPERTY WITH NAMES

**①** Create a new subroutine.

**②** Type **Range("A3:C7, E1:F3").Select**, replacing `A3:C7` with the first range of cells and `E1:F3` with a second range of cells.

**③** Switch to Excel and run the macro.

- The specified range of cells is selected.

### Extra

You can use the `Select` method with a Range object to highlight a cell or range of cells on a worksheet. For example, to select the range of cells from A3 to A6, you type **Range("A3:A6").Select**.

When you use the `Select` method with a `Range` object, the active cell becomes the first cell in the specified range. If you specify individual cells with the `Select` method, the active cell is the first cell specified. For example, `Range("A3, A1, A5").Select` selects cell A3 as the active cell.

You can also use the `Activate` method to highlight a cell or range of cells. With the `Activate` method, the first cell referenced in the range is the active cell, but all of the other cells in the range are highlighted to indicate that they are also selected. For example, in the code `Range("B4:C6").Activate`, Excel marks B4 as the active cell and highlights the remaining cells. Keep in mind, when you use the `Select` method, the first cell in the range is also marked as the active cell. This makes the two methods totally interchangeable when dealing with ranges.

# Using the Cells Property

You can use the `Cells` property to reference specific cells in a worksheet, allowing you to make changes to the values or properties of the cells, such as the font settings. The Excel Object Model does not contain a `Cells` object, so in order to reference specific cells, you use either the `Cells` property or the `Range` property, each of which actually returns a Range object with the specified cells. See the section "Using the Range Property" for more information on the `Range` property. One big difference in the two properties is that the `Cells` property, when you use it with its two parameters, returns only a single cell, whereas you typically use the `Range` property to return a series of cells.

You can use the `Cells` property with the `Application`, `Range`, and `Worksheet` objects. When you use it with the `Application` and `Worksheet` objects, you return the same result. For example, you can type **Cells**, **Application.Cells**, or **ActiveSheet.Cells** to return a `Range` object containing all cells in the active worksheet.

If you use the `Cells` property with the optional parameters, you can reference a specific cell within the worksheet. The first parameter, `row`, contains an integer value between 1 and 65536 indicating the row index. The second parameter, `column`, contains an integer value between 1 and 256 indicating the column index. For example, using this method to reference cell B5, you assign a value of 5 for the `row` parameter and a value of 2 for the `column` parameter, as shown in this code: `Cells(5,2)`.

One big advantage of using the `Cells` property instead of the `Range` property is that you can utilize variables to easily change the integer values. For example, you can use a variable to represent either the row or column, as shown in this code: `Cells(N,1) = 5`, which sets the value of the cell in column A and the row specified by N to 5.

## Using the Cells Property

 **①** Create a new subroutine.

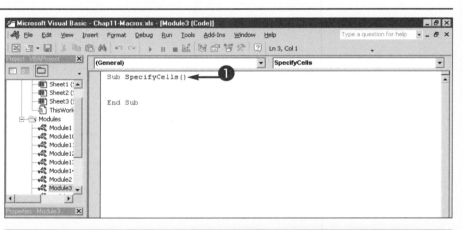

**②** Type **For N = 1 To 10**, replacing `10` with the number of cells to modify.

**③** Type **Cells(N,1) = N**, replacing `N` with the value to assign to each cell.

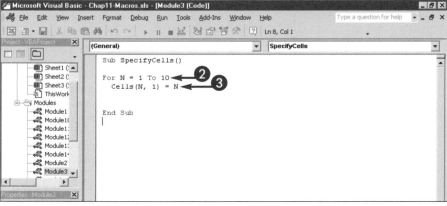

④ Type **Cells(N,1).Font.Bold = True**, replacing `Bold` with the font attribute to assign to the cells.

You can use any properties, methods, or child objects of the `Range` object to customize the selected range of cells.

⑤ Type **Next**.

⑥ Switch to Excel and run the macro.

● The value and font attributes of the specified cells are changed.

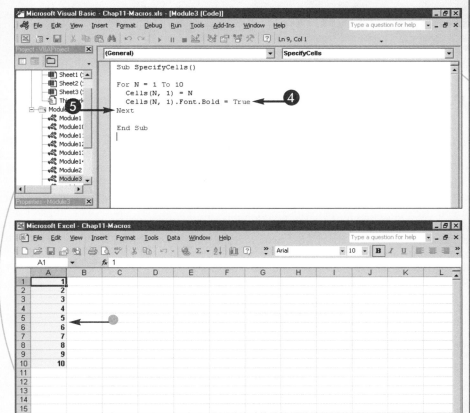

## Apply It

You can use the `Font` object to specify the font attributes for specific objects within Excel. Typically you use it to modify the attributes of a cell or a range of cells. The `Font` object has several properties that allow you to view or modify the attributes of the specified object. The following table lists the common properties you can use with the `Font` object.

| FONT PROPERTY | DESCRIPTION |
|---|---|
| Bold | A Boolean value indicating whether the font for the object is bold. |
| Color | Indicates the color of the font. Use the RGB function to set the font color. |
| FontStyle | Indicates the font style. For example, to set both a bold and underline font style, you specify `Font.FontStyle = "Bold Underline"`. |
| Italic | A Boolean value indicating whether the font for the object is italics. |
| Shadow | A Boolean value indicating whether the font is a shadow font. |
| Size | Indicates the size of the font. |
| Strikethrough | A Boolean value indicating whether a strikethrough font is used. A strikethrough font draws a horizontal line through each character in the font. |
| Subscript | A Boolean value indicating whether the font is subscript. |
| Superscript | A Boolean value indicating whether the font is superscript. |
| Underline | A Boolean value indicating whether the font is underlined. |

# Combine Multiple Ranges

You can use the Union method to create a multiple area range. A multiple area range contains more than one block of cells, which may not be connected. For example, you use the Union method to create a Range object containing the cells A1 through B5 and D1 through E5. Although these two groups of cells are separated within the worksheet, using the Union method you can create one range that references only those cells.

When you use the Range property in conjunction with the Union method, you can assign any number of parameter values, as long as you specify at least two different ranges. Each parameter value must specify a range of cells. You can specify the ranges that you assign to the Union method using any option that returns a valid Range object, such as the Range property or the Cells property. See the sections "Using the Range Property" and "Using the Cells Property" for more information on the Range and Cells properties.

For example, the code Set RangeVar = Union (Range("A1:A3"), Range("A5:A15")) uses the Union method to combine two Range objects created with the Range property and assigns the result to a Range variable. With this sample code, the new range contains the cells A1 through A3 and A5 through 15. When you view this range, you see that cell A4 is not selected as part of the range.

Because you must declare the variable to which you assign the multi-area range as a Range object, you need to use the Set statement as part of the assignment statement. You must use the Set statement whenever you assign an object to a variable. See Chapter 4 for more information on assigning objects.

## Combine Multiple Ranges

① Create a new subroutine.

② Type **Dim Range1 As Range**, replacing Range1 with the name of the first range.

③ Type **Dim Range2 As Range**, replacing Range2 with the name of the second range.

④ Type **Dim NewRange As Range**, replacing NewRange with the name of the combined range.

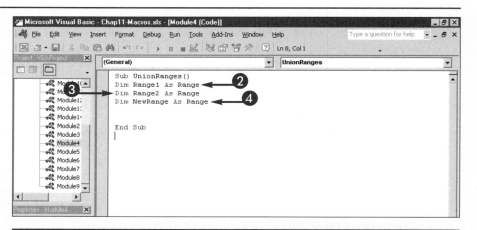

⑤ Declare any additional variables needed for the subroutine.

⑥ Type **Set Range1 = Range ("A1:B3")**, replacing Range("A1:B3") with a reference to the first range.

⑦ Type **Set Range2 = Cells(5,5)**, replacing Cells(5,5) with a reference to the second range.

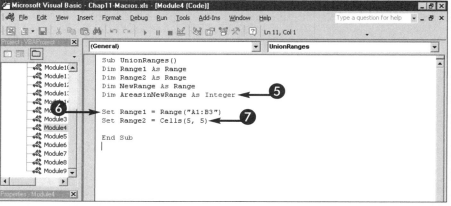

**⑧** Type **Set NewRange = Union(Range1, Range2)**.

**⑨** Type additional VBA code to work with the new combined range of cells.

**⑩** Switch to Excel and run the macro.

● Excel highlights the combined range of cells.

```
Sub UnionRanges()
Dim Range1 As Range
Dim Range2 As Range
Dim NewRange As Range
Dim AreasinNewRange As Integer

Set Range1 = Range("A1:B3")
Set Range2 = Cells(5, 5)

Set NewRange = Union(Range1, Range2)   ⑧

NewRange.Select

AreasinNewRange = Selection.Areas.Count   ⑨
MsgBox "There are " & AreasinNewRange & " selected ranges."

End Sub
```

| | A | B | C | D |
|---|---|---|---|---|
| 1 | Employees | Title | Salary | Years of Service |
| 2 | Smith, Sam | Sr. Developer | $90,000.00 | 3 |
| 3 | Jones, John | Accountant | $95,000.00 | 4 |
| 4 | Smith, Fred | Vice President | $145,000.00 | 9 |
| 5 | Hansen, April | Receptionist | $25,000.00 | 1 |
| 6 | Anderson, Tom | Sr. Developer | $93,000.00 | 3 |
| 7 | Adams, Jerry | Software Develope | $85,000.00 | 2 |
| 8 | Peterson, Paul | Systems | $82,000.00 | 2 |
| 9 | Garcia, Juan | Software Develope | $81,000.00 | 3 |
| 10 | Andrews, Andy | Sales Manager | $100,000.00 | 6 |
| 11 | Wilson, Sam | Northeast Sales | $75 | |
| 12 | Jones, Wendy | Secretary | $25 | |
| 13 | Smith, Fred | CTO | $19 | |
| 14 | Jensen, George | CEO | $19 | |
| 15 | Adams, Mary | Systems | $88 | |
| 16 | Olsen, John | Human Resources | $55 | |
| 17 | Anderson, Richard | Janitor | $30,000.00 | 3 |
| 18 | Parker, Sid | Maintenance | $30,000.00 | 2 |
| 19 | Davis, Don | Security | $45,000.00 | 4 |
| 20 | Johnson, Jerry | Sr. Developer | $87,000.00 | 6 |
| 21 | Harrison, Rick | Security | $45,000.00 | 2 |

Microsoft Excel: There are 2 selected ranges. OK

---

## Extra

When you use the `Union` method, you combine multiple ranges to create one multi-range, or Areas Collection. You can reference the entire range selection using the `Selection` property. This property returns the selected object. You can combine the `Selection` property with the `Areas` property to return an Areas collection representing all of the areas selected after performing a union.

The Areas Collection actually contains a collection of the specific areas, or blocks of cells, within a specific selection. Each individual member of the Areas Collection is actually a `Range` object representing a contiguous block of cells with one `Range` object for each block of cells.

You cannot apply some VBA operations to ranges that contain multiple areas. Therefore, you may need to determine the number of areas within a specific range. In order to do this, you can use the `Count` property. The `Count` property counts the number of areas within the range; if a value greater than 1 is returned, you know there is more than one area selected. The following example uses the `Count` property to determine the number of areas within the selected range.

**Example:**
```
AreasInNewRange = Selection.Areas.Count.
```

# Using the Offset Property

The Offset property provides another method for specifying a range of cells. Using the Offset property you can define a range that is a specific *offset* from another range, with the offset being the distance, in rows and columns, between the new range and the existing range selection.

You use two different parameters with the Offset property. Although both are optional, you specify at least one of the values, or the current selection is returned. Use the RowOffset parameter to indicate the number of rows to offset the range from the current selection. A positive number offsets the range downward. A negative value offsets the range upward. The offset values are based upon the upper-left cell in the selected range. For example, if the active range is cells A1 through B4, the offset values are based upon the number of rows and columns from cell A1.

Use the ColumnOffset parameter to specify the number of columns to offset the range from the current selection. A positive number offsets the range to the right. A negative number offsets the range to the left. The default value for both parameters is 0.

If you only assign a value to one of the parameters, Excel gives the other parameter a value of 0. For example, if you specify a value of 5 for the RowOffset and omit the ColumnOffset parameter value, the property returns the range that is five rows from the current range selection.

If you specify a value outside the valid number of rows and columns in a worksheet — for example, if you specify -1 and the current cell is A1 — Excel returns an error. The acceptable range for columns is 1 to 256 and the acceptable range for rows is 1 to 65536.

## Using the Offset Property

① Create a new subroutine.

② Type **Dim FirstRange As Range**, replacing FirstRange with the current range variable.

③ Type **Dim NewRange As Range**, replacing NewRange with the new range variable.

④ Type **Set FirstRange = Range("A1:B4")**, replacing Range("A1:B4") with the current range.

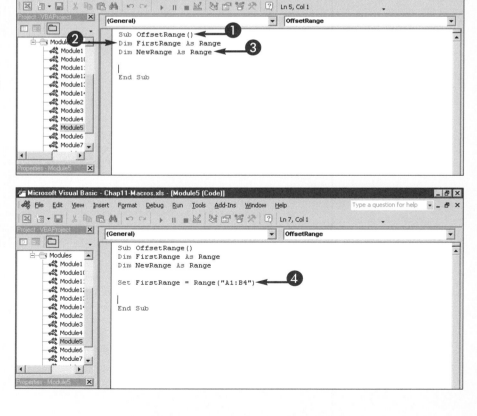

**5** Type **Set NewRange = FirstRange.Offset(3, 3)**, replacing 3, 3 with the offset for the new range.

**6** Type additional VBA code for processing the new range.

**7** Switch to Excel and run the macro.

- Excel highlights the newly created range with the `Offset` property on the worksheet.

## Extra

Besides referencing specific blocks of cells to create `Range` objects, you can specify a `Row` or `Column` as a `Range` object with the `Rows` and `Columns` properties. If you specify an entire column as a range selection, Excel creates a `Range` object containing the specified column. For example, the following code selects Column B and the selected column:

```
SelectedColumn = Columns(2).
```

You can use the `Rows` property to specify a row you want to use as a `Range` object. With this property, Excel selects the entire row as the `Range` object:

```
SelectedRow = Rows(3).
```

You can also use each of these properties separately to refer to the entire group of columns or the entire group of rows within the worksheet. For example, the following code refers to the current columns:

```
Set ColRange = Columns.
```

You can use the `Rows` and `Columns` properties to determine a specific column or row within a range. For example, if you have a range of cells from B5 to G10, using the `Rows` parameter you can select the first row within the specified range. You can accomplish this by specifying the desired row, as shown in this code.

```
Set RngObj = Range("B5:G10")
RngObj.Rows(1).Select
```

# Delete a Range of Cells

You can remove a specific range of cells from a worksheet using the Delete method. When you delete a range of cells, Excel completely removes the specified cells and adjusts the remaining values within the worksheet to fill in the gap left by the deletion. For example, if you remove an entire column of values, such as column B, Excel shifts the values in column C left and they become the new column B values. All remaining column values shift left. Conversely, if you delete a row, Excel shifts all values in the rows below up one row.

Excel easily determines how to shift the cells when you remove entire rows and columns, but if you just remove a block of cells, you must specify how the remaining values fill to ensure you get the anticipated results. You can specify how Excel shifts the cells using the Shift parameter with the

Delete method. When you use the Shift parameter, you assign it one of the XLDeleteShiftDirection constant values. The first value, xlShiftToLeft, tells Excel how to shift values to the left to fill the gap created by the deletion. The xlShiftUp constant value indicates that Excel should shift the values up from below the deletion to fill the gap.

Keep in mind that Excel ignores the Shift parameter value if it is not a valid shift direction for the deleted range. For example, the code Column(2).Delete Shift:=xlShiftUp deletes a specific column, but Excel still shifts the cells left; because you removed the entire column there are no cells to shift up. Although these instances may occur occasionally, for best results, remember to specify how to shift the cells, so that when Excel has a choice, your cells shift in the appropriate direction.

## Delete a Range of Cells

 Create a new subroutine.

 Type **Dim RangeDelete As Range**, replacing RangeDelete with the name of the range to delete.

❸ Type **Set RangeDelete = Range("A1:B4")**, replacing Range("A1:B4") with the range to delete.

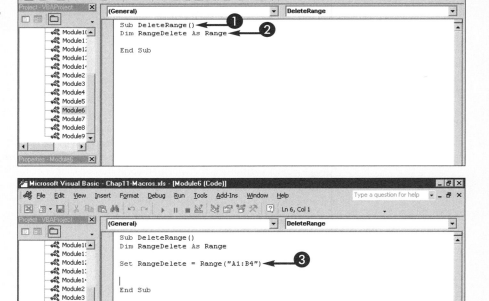

④ Type **RangeDelete.Delete Shift:=xlShiftUp**, replacing `xlShiftUp` with the constant indicating how to shift the remaining cell values.

⑤ Switch to Excel and run the macro.

- Excel removes the specified range of cells adjusts the remaining cells accordingly.

## Extra

If you protect a worksheet, you cannot remove or add cells. To eliminate any errors that may occur from trying to remove a range from a protected worksheet, you can use the `AllowEdit` property to determine if you can modify the range. The `AllowEdit` property returns a Boolean value of `True` if you can modify the specified range. In the example code, you can use the `AllowEdit` property to check the range to make sure you can modify a range before you call the `Delete` method.

**Example:**
```
If RangeDelete.AllowEdit Then
    RangeDelete.Delete Shift:=xlShiftUp
End If
```

Excel checks the `AllowEdit` property for the specified `Range` object. Using the `If Then` statement ensures that the code only attempts to delete the specified range of cells if you can modify the range. Otherwise, Excel ignores the `Delete` statement.

You protect worksheets using the `Protect` method. The type of protection you apply is based upon the parameters you use with the `Protect` method. See Chapter 9 for more information on using the `Protect` method to protect a specific worksheet.

# Hide a Range of Cells

You can hide a specific range of cells using the Hidden property with the Range object that you want to hide. You can use the Hidden property to either change the range of cells that you want to hide or to determine if the range is visible or hidden. You commonly hide portions of a worksheet that contain values that you do not want others to see when they access your worksheet. For example, you may have a worksheet that contains the formulas and the values you use to calculate the displayed data. By hiding the cells that contain the original data, you eliminate a user's ability to view the data you want to keep invisible.

In order to use the Hidden property to hide a range of cells, the range of cells you want to hide must consist of an entire row or column. You make a range hidden by assigning a value of True to the Hidden property for the specified range. Keep in mind that when you hide a range of cells, Excel either sets the width of the columns or the height of the rows to zero making it appear that it is not visible.

You can later verify that the range of cells is still hidden by checking the Hidden property. For example, if you hid column A, you can check to ensure the column is still hidden by typing HiddenRange = Range1.Hidden. If you declare the HiddenRange variable as a Boolean value, the variable receives a value of True if the specified range is hidden; otherwise, it receives a value of False. If you forget to declare the variable as Boolean, Excel assigns a numeric value of -1 if the range is hidden and 0 if the range is visible.

## Hide a Range of Cells

① Create a new subroutine.

② Type **Dim StartColumn As Integer**, replacing StartColumn with the name of the first column to hide.

③ Type **Dim EndColumn As Integer**, replacing EndColumn with the name of the last column to hide.

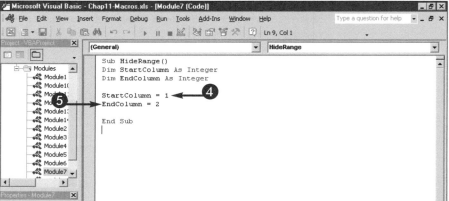

④ Type **StartColumn = 1**, replacing 1 with the first column number.

⑤ Type **EndColumn=2**, replacing 2 with the last column number.

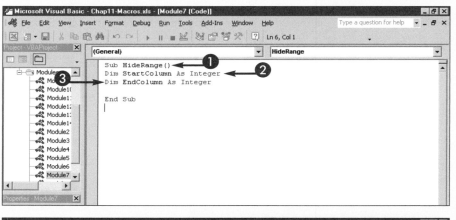

⑥ Type **For N = StartColumn to EndColumn**.

⑦ Type **Columns(N).Hidden = True**.

⑧ Type **Next**.

⑨ Switch to Excel and run the macro.

Excel hides the specified columns.

```
Sub HideRange()
Dim StartColumn As Integer
Dim EndColumn As Integer

StartColumn = 1
EndColumn = 2

For N = StartColumn To EndColumn
    Columns(N).Hidden = True
Next

End Sub
```

| | C | D | E | F | G | H | I | J | K |
|---|---|---|---|---|---|---|---|---|---|
| 1 | Salary | Years of Service | | | | | | | |
| 2 | $90,000.00 | 3 | | | | | | | |
| 3 | $95,000.00 | 4 | | | | | | | |
| 4 | $145,000.00 | 9 | | | | | | | |
| 5 | $25,000.00 | 1 | | | | | | | |
| 6 | $93,000.00 | 3 | | | | | | | |
| 7 | $85,000.00 | 2 | | | | | | | |
| 8 | $82,000.00 | 2 | | | | | | | |
| 9 | $81,000.00 | 3 | | | | | | | |
| 10 | $100,000.00 | 6 | | | | | | | |
| 11 | $75,000.00 | 5 | | | | | | | |
| 12 | $25,000.00 | 2 | | | | | | | |
| 13 | $195,000.00 | 12 | | | | | | | |
| 14 | $195,000.00 | 12 | | | | | | | |
| 15 | $85,000.00 | 4 | | | | | | | |
| 16 | $55,000.00 | 3 | | | | | | | |
| 17 | $30,000.00 | 3 | | | | | | | |
| 18 | $30,000.00 | 2 | | | | | | | |
| 19 | $45,000.00 | 4 | | | | | | | |
| 20 | $87,000.00 | 6 | | | | | | | |
| 21 | $45,000.00 | 2 | | | | | | | |

## Extra

When you hide a row or column in Excel, you can still access the values contained in the cells with references in functions and macros. Excel indicates the existence of hidden rows and columns by skipping over the hidden rows and columns with the row and column headings. For example, if you hide columns C and D, you see the column labels for columns A, B, E, F, and so on.

You can hide the entire worksheet using either the Columns or Rows properties. Either one of the following produces the same results by hiding either all rows or all columns.

**Example:**
```
Columns.Hidden = True
Rows.Hidden = True
```

To unhide rows or columns in a worksheet, you need to set the Hidden property to False. For example, the following code statement unhides all columns in a worksheet.

**Example:**
```
Columns.Hidden = False
```

This statement is useful for ensuring that all cells in a worksheet are visible. If you apply it to a column that is already visible, Excel ignores the statement and the column remains visible. Of course, you can also use the Rows property in the same fashion to unhide any invisible rows.

**Example:**
```
Rows.Hidden = False
```

# Specify the Name of a Range

You can use the `Name` property to assign a specific name to a range of cells. Excel uses names to reference specific ranges of cells on a worksheet. By specifying a named range, you no longer have to know the location of the cells that contain the desired values; you simply need to find the cells with the appropriate range name. For example, if cell B3 contains the sales tax rate, instead of remembering the appropriate cell reference, you can simply assign the name `"Tax_Rate"` to the cell. This allows you to reference the cell by name when you want to use it.

You can use the `Name` property to either assign a name to a range of cells or to determine what the name is for the range. To assign a name to a range, you need to specify the appropriate name. For example, the code

`Columns(3).Name = "May_Sales"` assigns the name May_Sales to Column C in the active worksheet. After you assign the name to the range, you can view it in Excel by highlighting the corresponding range, in this case Column C, to see the name appear in the Name box on the Formula Bar.

You can determine the name of a specific range by assigning it to a string variable. For example, the code `RangeName = Columns(3).Name` assigns the name of Column C to the `RangeName` variable.

After you assign a range name to a specific range, you can use the range name to access the range of cells at any point. The advantage of using a range name is that you do not need to set the range within your current procedure. When you assign a range name to a worksheet, it remains there until you remove it.

## Specify the Name of a Range

① Create a new subroutine.

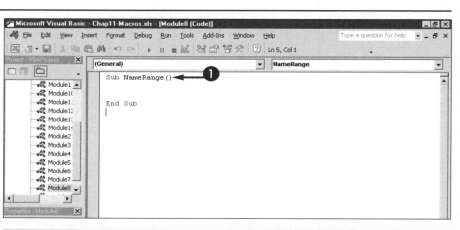

② Type **Columns(3).Name = "Salary"**, replacing `Columns(3)` with the range to name and `"Salary"` with the name for the range.

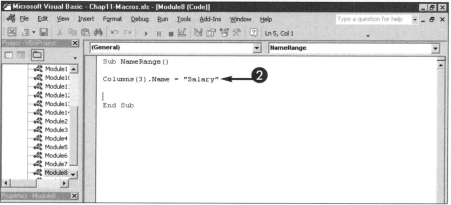

③ Type **Range("Salary").Select**.

④ Switch to Excel and run the macro.

● Excel highlights the named range, and the Name box on the Formula bar contains the range name.

---

**Extra**

You can create named ranges within Excel by highlighting the selected range and clicking Insert→Name→Define to display the Define Name dialog box. Type the appropriate range name in the Names in workbook field and click Add. The list box on the dialog box contains a list of all named ranges within the current workbook.

You can see which cells are part of a specific named range by highlighting the range within the list box and viewing the corresponding range displayed in the Refers To field. Keep in mind that Excel does allow you to assign multiple names to the same range.

If you no longer want to make the named range available within your workbook, you can highlight the range name and click Delete. Keep in mind that if you delete a named range, any macro that references the named range no longer works correctly.

Another method for creating a named range in Excel is to highlight the range and then click the Name box. The Name box lists a reference to the first cell in the range. To assign a name to the range, type the desired range name in the Name box.

# Resize a Range

You can change the size of a range using the `Resize` property. Typically you resize a range because it does not contain the desired number of cells. When you resize a range, you change the number of rows and columns in a range. You can change the size by specifying either more or fewer rows or columns.

The `Resize` property has two optional parameters of which you need to use at least one. If you do not use either parameter, Excel returns the original range. The first parameter, `RowSize`, indicates the number of rows in the new range. The second parameter, `ColumnSize`, indicates the number of columns in the new range.

When you resize the range, the upper-left corner of the original range remains the same. For example, if the original range is B1 through C4 and you resize the range to contain only 2 rows and 2 columns, B1 remains as the upper-left cell value. The range is adjusted based upon that cell creating a new range of cells from B1 to C2.

You need to know how many rows and columns currently exist in a range in order to determine how to resize it. If you are dealing with a range that you defined elsewhere, such as a named range, you can use the `Count` property to determine the number of rows and columns within the range, as shown in the following code: `NumberofRows = Range("Named_Range").Rows.Count`. The `Count` property counts the number of rows in the named range `"Named_Range"` and assigns that value to the `NumberofRows` variable. You can use the same type of syntax with the `Columns` property to determine the number of columns in the range. When you know the size of the range, you can use the `Resize` property to modify the number of rows and columns.

## Resize a Range

① Create a new subroutine.

② Type **Dim NumRows As Integer**, replacing `NumRows` with the variable for the number of rows in the range.

③ Type **Dim NumColumns As Integer**, replacing `NumColumns` with the variable for the number of columns in the range.

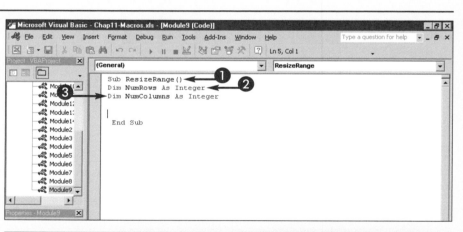

④ Type **NumRows=Range ("EmpInfo").Rows.Count**, replacing `"EmpInfo"` with the range to count.

⑤ Type **NumColumns=Range ("EmpInfo").Columns.Count**, replacing `"EmpInfo"` with the range to count.

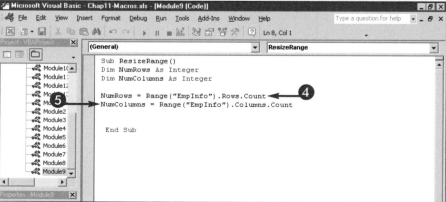

**6** Type an `If Then` statement to determine if the range contains the appropriate number of rows and columns.

**7** Type **NumRows = NumRows + 5**, replacing + with – to subtract and 5 with the number to which you want to change the row number.

**8** Type **NumColumns = NumColumns + 5**, replacing + with – to subtract and 5 with the number to which you want to change the column number.

**9** Type **Range("EmpInfo). Resize(RowSize:=NumRows, ColumnSize:=NumColumns). Select**.

**10** Switch to Excel and run the macro.

● The newly sized range is selected.

## Extra

Besides determining the number of rows and columns within a range, you may also need to know the exact row or column where the range begins. You can accomplish this by using either the `Row` property for rows or the `Column` property for columns. You can determine the number of the first row in a range with the following code:

**Example:**
```
FirstRowNum = CurrentRange.Row
```

This code assigns the integer value representing the first row in the specified range to the `FirstRowNum` variable. You can also determine the first column in the range using the `Column` property, as shown in this code:

**Example:**
```
FirstColNum = CurrentRange.Column
```

When you know what the first row and column are in the range, you can create the first cell in the range using the `Cells` property, as shown in this code:

**Example:**
```
Cells(FirstRowNum, FirstColNum)
```

This statement takes the values returned by the `Row` and `Column` properties and determines the first cell. Typically this cell is also the active cell, if you have just selected the range.

# Insert a Range

You can insert a range of cells into a worksheet using the `Insert` method. When you insert a range of cells into a worksheet, Excel adjusts the values in the existing cells by moving them either down or to the right to allow you to insert into the specified location. For example, if you insert a new row of cells in row 3, Excel shifts the existing values in row 3 down to row 4. Excel shifts all remaining values within the worksheet down. If you add a new column, Excel shifts all existing values right.

It is fairly obvious how the cell values in the worksheet should shift when you add an entire row or column; but, when you insert a smaller block of cells, you must instruct Excel how to shift the cells. You use two optional parameters with the `Insert` method. You use the `Shift` parameter, and

assign it one of the `XLInsertShiftDirection` constant values, to make sure the cells shift correctly. Use the `xlShiftToRight` constant value to have Excel shift the cell values right when you insert a new range of cells. Use the `xlShiftDown` constant value to shift existing cell values down.

The `CopyOrigin` parameter accepts only values of `True` or `False` and indicates whether to insert a copy of the last range of values you placed in the clipboard. You can add cells to the clipboard either using the `Copy` and `Cut` methods or the Copy and Cut options directly in Excel. If the value of the parameter is `True`, Excel only adds the portion of the copied range that fits the insert range. For example, if you copy cells A5:B10 and then insert cells A1:B2, Excel only inserts the values in cells A5:B6 as the new range values.

## Insert a Range

① Create a new subroutine.

② Type **Range("A3:B4").Copy**, replacing `Range("A3:B4")` with the range of cells to copy.

**Note:** See Chapter 10 for information on using the `Copy` method.

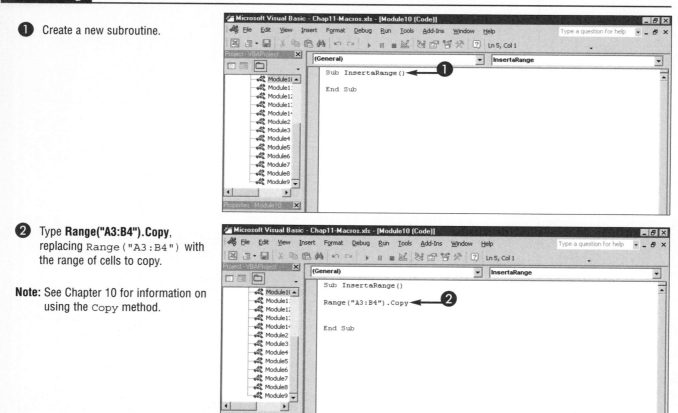

③ Type **Range("A1:B2").Insert**, replacing `Range("A1:B2")` with the range where you want to add cells.

④ Type **Shift:=xlShiftDown**, replacing `xlShiftDown` with the constant value indicating how cells should shift.

⑤ Type **CopyOrigin:=True**.

⑥ Switch to Excel and run the macro.

● Excel copies the specified range of cells and inserts a copy as a new range in the worksheet.

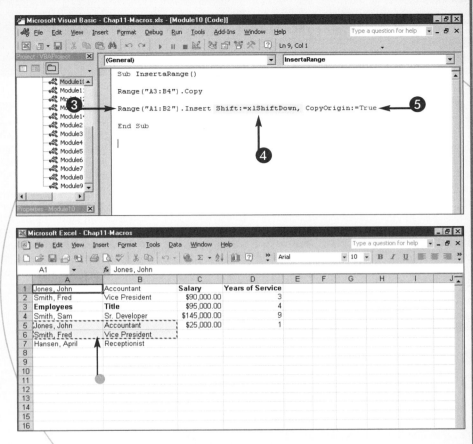

## Extra

You can also use the `Insert` method to add a specific value to a cell. In order to insert a value in a cell, you need to use the `Insert` method with the `Characters` object. You can insert a string of characters at the beginning of the characters in a cell, or at any location within the cell. For example, to insert the string "New String" in cell B1 and replace the contents, you type the following code:

**Example:**
```
Range("B1").Characters.Insert("New String")
```

If you want to place the new string within the existing string of characters, you must indicate the character location to place the new string, and the number of characters to replace at that location. For example, if you have the string "Excel 2000 Worksheet," you can replace the "2000" in the string with "2002" using the `Insert` method. The following code illustrates how to replace the portion of the string when the string is located in cell A1:

**Example:**
```
Range("A1").Characters(7,4).Insert("2002")
```

The `Characters` object has two parameters, `Start` and `Length`. The `Start` parameter indicates the number of the character to start the insert, in this case character 7. The `Length` parameter indicates the number of characters to replace in the string.

# Set the Width of Columns in a Range

You can customize the width of a column using the `ColumnWidth` property. With this property, you specify how wide the specific column displays when you view the worksheet containing the column in Excel. By default, Excel assigns a width of 8.43 characters to each column. Excel bases this width size upon the number of zeros it can place in the cell using the default font style, which is the Normal font style. Excel bases this measurement upon the number of zeros, not characters, that it can place within the cell and still have them visible. Because most fonts that you use within Excel are proportional fonts, the spacing varies based upon each character. For example, you can always fit more of the letter "I" in a cell than you can of the letter "M" when working with a proportional font. When you use a monospaced font, such as Courier, the width is an actual measurement of the number of characters that fit in the column because, with this font, all characters require the same amount of space. Keep in mind, numeric digits 0 through 9 are all the same width regardless of whether you use a proportional or monospaced font.

You can use the `ColumnWidth` property to determine the width of the columns in a range. If all columns in the range have the same width, the width is returned as the number of characters that can display in each column. If the columns within the selected range do not have the same width, a value of `Null` is returned.

## Set the Width of Columns in a Range

  Create a new subroutine.

  Type **Dim NewRange As Range**, replacing NewRange with the name of the range of cells.

  Type **Dim NumColumns As Integer**, replacing NumColumns with the name of variable containing the number of columns.

  Type **Set NewRange = Range("B1:D21")**, replacing Range("B1:D21") with the range of cells.

  Type **NumColumns=NewRange.Columns.Count**.

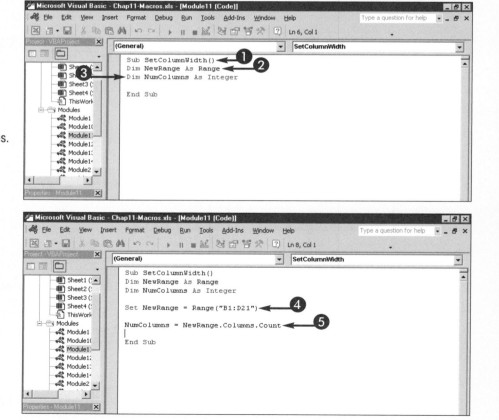

⑥ Type **For I = 1 To NumColumns**.

**Note:** See Chapter 6 for more information on using the `For Next` looping statement.

⑦ Type **NewRange.Columns(I).ColumnWidth = 15**, replacing 15 with the desired column width.

⑧ Type **Next**.

⑨ Switch to Excel and run the macro.

Excel resizes the columns in the specified range to the new width.

```
Sub SetColumnWidth()
Dim NewRange As Range
Dim NumColumns As Integer

Set NewRange = Range("B1:D21")

NumColumns = NewRange.Columns.Count

For I = 1 To NumColumns
    NewRange.Columns(I).ColumnWidth = 15
Next

End Sub
```

---

## Extra

You can also use the `Width` property to determine the width of a particular column. Be aware that the `Width` property returns the measurement of the column width in points, unlike the `ColumnWidth` property, which returns characters. You typically use a point to reference font sizes, with 1 point equivalent to ½ of an inch. For example, the default font size that Excel uses is typically 10 point.

The `Width` property is read-only, meaning that you can only use it to return the width of a column, and not to modify the width. You can return the `Width` property of a column by assigning the value to a variable, as shown in the following code:

**Example:**
```
ColWidth = Column(4).Width
```

Because the only method for changing the width of the column is the `ColumnWidth` property, which uses the number of characters that fit in a column and not a point value, you may not use the `Width` property as frequently as the `ColumnWidth` property. The `Width` property is valuable if you need to compare the column width to the row height, because Excel does store the row height as a point value.

# Set the Height of Rows in a Range

Y ou can modify the height of rows within a range using the `RowHeight` property. When you use this property, you specify how high the specific row displays when you view the worksheet containing the row in Excel. By default, Excel assigns a height of 12.75 points to each row. A point is a measurement Excel uses with font sizes, with each point being approximately ½ of an inch. You measure a font based upon the height of a capital character, such as W, to determine the point size. Because the default font size in Excel is 10 point, typically the default row size of 12.75 points is adequate for displaying text in cells. Of course, if you specify a larger font size, or if you want the text to wrap within the cell, you need to specify a larger row size using the `RowHeight` property.

You can set the height of the row by assigning a numeric value to the `RowHeight` property for the corresponding object. For example, to change the height of row 2 to 25, you use the code: `Rows(2).RowHeight=25`. Keep in mind, when you use the Rows property without referencing the corresponding `Range` object, Excel automatically uses the current active sheet.

If the row height you specify is not high enough to display the entire size of the font, the text appears cut off in the row when you view it in Excel.

You can use the `RowHeight` property to determine the height of the rows in a range. If all rows in the range have the same height, the height is returned as the number of points. If the rows within the selected range do not have the same height, a value of `Null` is returned.

## Set the Height of Rows in a Range

1. Create a new subroutine.

2. Type **Dim NewRange As Range**, replacing NewRange with the name of the range of cells.

3. Type **Dim NumRows As Integer**, replacing NumRows with the name of the variable containing the number of rows.

4. Type **Dim AverageHeight As Long**, replacing AverageHeight with the variable to contain the average row height.

5. Type **Set NewRange = Range("B1:C14")**, replacing Range("B1:C14") with the range of cells.

6. Type **NumRows=NewRange. Rows.Count**.

7. Type **AverageHeight = NewRange.Height / NumRows**.

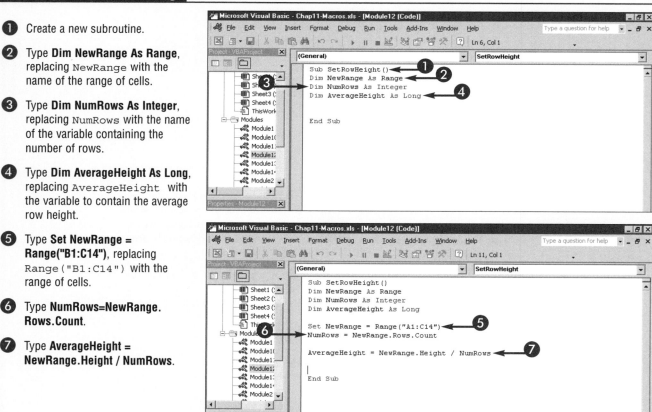

⑧ Type **For N = 1 To NumRows**.

**Note:** See Chapter 6 for more information on using the `For Next` looping statement.

⑨ Type **NewRange.Rows(N).RowHeight = AverageHeight**.

⑩ Type **Next**.

⑪ Switch to Excel and run the macro.

Excel resizes the rows in the specified range to be the same height.

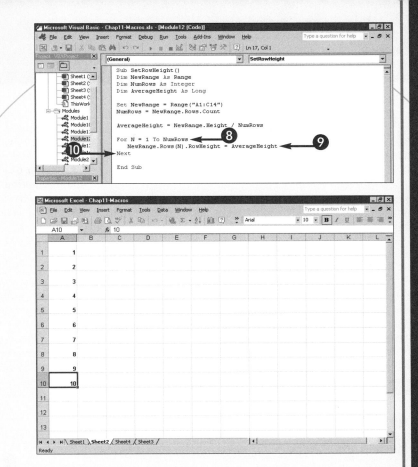

# Convert a Column of Text into Multiple Columns

You can break a column of text into multiple columns using the `TextToColumns` method. For example, if you have a list that contains both the first and last names in one column, you use `TextToColumns` to break that list into two different columns.

You use the `TextToColumns` with the `Range` object containing the columns to parse into multiple columns. This method provides several different optional parameters to specify how to separate the text, including `Destination`, `DataType`, `TextQualifier`, `ConsecutiveDelimiter`, `Tab`, `Semicolon`, `Comma`, `Space`, `Other`, `OtherChar`, `FieldInfo`, `DecimalSeparator`, `ThousandsSeparator`, and `TrailingMinusNumbers`.

You use the `Destination` parameter to specify the range where you want to place the results. If the destination `Range` object contains more than one cell, Excel uses the top-left cell in the range as the initial cell. For the `DataType` parameter, specify a constant value of `xlDelimited` to break the text based upon a delimiter value. Use `xlFixedWidth` if the text is a fixed width.

Use the `TextQualifier` constants of `xlTextQualifierDoubleQuote`, `xlTextQualifierNone`, or `xlTextQualifierSingleQuote` to indicate the text qualifier character.

The delimiter is a character that indicates a separation between strings, such as a comma or space. Specify a value of `True` for the `ConsecutiveDelimiter` parameter to have consecutive delimiters treated as one. For the `Tab`, `Semicolon`, `Comma`, `Space`, and `Other` parameters, specify a value of `True` for the delimiter you use in the selected range. If you specify `Other` as the delimiter, you must type a value for the `OtherChar` parameter indicating the delimiter character.

The `FileInfo` parameter contains information for parsing individual columns in the range with the first element being the column number and the second one of the `XlColumnDataType` constants discussed in Appendix A.

Specify the character used to separate decimals as the `DecimalSeparator` parameter and the thousands separator as the `ThousandsSeparator` parameter value.

## Convert a Column of Text into Multiple Columns

① Create a new subroutine.

② Type **Dim RangeVar As Range**, replacing `RangeVar` with the name of the range variable.

③ Type **Set RangeVar = Columns(1)**, replacing `Columns(1)` with the range containing values to separate.

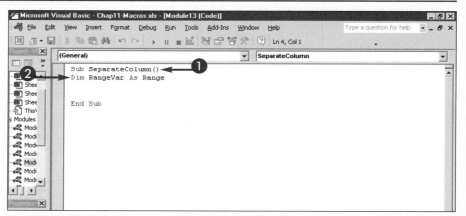

④ Type **RangeVar.TextToColumns**.

⑤ Type **Destination :=Range("B1")**, replacing `Range("B1")` with the location to place the cells.

⑥ Type **DataType:=xlDelimited**.

⑦ Type **Comma:=True**.

⑧ Switch to Excel and run the macro.

● Excel breaks the contents of the specified column into two separate columns.

```
Sub SeparateColumn()
Dim RangeVar As Range

Set RangeVar = Columns(1)

RangeVar.TextToColumns Destination:=Range("B1"), DataType:=xlDelimited, Comma:=True

End Sub
```

## Extra

Excel provides the `Parse` method that you can use to separate data values in one column into multiple columns. The method works well when you have string data that is all the same length, such as phone numbers. With the `Parse` method, you specify how the strings in each cell should break and Excel applies that format to each cell.

There are two optional parameters for the Parse method. The first parameter, `ParseLine`, is a string containing left and right brackets indicating where the cells should split. For example, [xxxx] [xxxx] breaks each string so that the first four characters are placed in the first column and the second four characters are placed in the second column. Any characters outside those characters are ignored and not moved to a new column. If the string is `"Alphabetical"`, with this `ParseLine` parameter, Excel places the first four characters `Alph` in the first column and the second four characters, `abet` in the second column. The remaining characters in the string, `ical`, are ignored because they are not specified as part of the `ParseLine` value.

The second parameter, `Destination`, specifies the range where the parsed data is placed. If you specify a range of more than one cell, Excel uses the upper-left corner of the range as the first cell.

# Find the Intersection of Two Ranges

Y ou can use the `Intersect` method to determine where multiple ranges intersect on a worksheet. A multiple area range contains more than one block of cells that may or may not be connected. You use the `Intersect` method to create a `Range` object containing the cells that are common between two ranges. For example, if you have the ranges A1 through C5 and C1 through E5, the `Intersect` method returns the range C1:C5 because those are the cells that are common to both ranges. If there are no cells in common between the specified ranges, the `Intersect` method returns an empty range.

When you use the `Intersect` method, you can assign any number of parameter values, as long as you specify at least two different ranges. Each parameter value must specify a range of cells. You can specify the ranges you assign to the

`Intersect` method using any option that returns a valid `Range` object, such as the `Range` property or the Cells property. See the sections "Using the Range Property" and "Using the Cells Property" for more information on the `Range` and `Cells` properties.

Because you must declare the variable to which you assign the multi-area range as a `Range` object, you need to use the `Set` statement as part of the assignment statement. You must use the `Set` statement whenever you assign an object to a variable. See Chapter 4 for more information on assigning objects. Keep in mind, however, that when you assign an intersecting range to a range object variable, only the cells within the intersection of the range are assigned to the variable, creating a new range that represents the intersection of the original ranges.

## Find the Intersection of Two Ranges

① Create a new subroutine.

② Type **Dim Range1 As Range**, replacing Range1 with the name of the first range.

③ Type **Dim Range2 as Range**, replacing Range2 with the name of the second range.

④ Type **Dim NewRange As Range**, replacing NewRange with the name of the combined range.

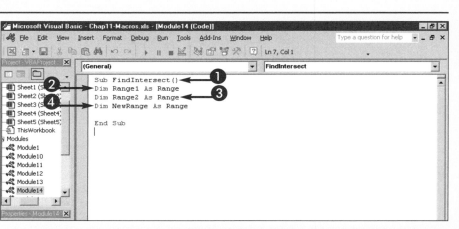

⑤ Type **Set Range1 = Range("A1:C13")**, replacing Range("A1:C13") with a reference to the first range.

⑥ Type **Set Range2 = Range("B5:D15")**, replacing Range("B5:D15") with a reference to the second range.

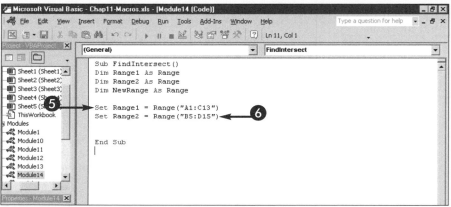

**7** Type **Set NewRange = Intersect(Range1, Range2)**.

**8** Type additional VBA code to work with the new combined range of cells.

**9** Switch to Excel and run the macro.

● The macro finds the cells that intersect both ranges.

```
Sub FindIntersect()
Dim Range1 As Range
Dim Range2 As Range
Dim NewRange As Range

Set Range1 = Range("A1:C13")
Set Range2 = Range("B5:D15")

Set NewRange = Intersect(Range1, Range2)

NewRange.Clear

End Sub
```

---

## Extra

You can use one of the different `Clear` methods to clear the contents of a cell or range of cells within your worksheet. The `Clear` method clears the entire contents, including cell values, formatting, and formulas, from the specified cells. You specify this method using the following syntax:

**Example:**
```
RangeVar.Clear
```

Whatever cells that the RangeVar references are cleared of all contents. You can use the `ClearFormats` method to clear all formatting from the specified range. All cell values and formulas remain in the cells. When you use this method, the contents of the specified range display using default formatting options. You indicate this method using the following syntax:

**Example:**
```
RangeVar.ClearFormats
```

Finally, you can clear the cell values and formulas from a range of cells using the `ClearContents` method. This method clears everything with the exception of the formatting that you applied to the cells. After using this method, you can add new values to any cells in the range and Excel applies the original formatting. The syntax for this method is similar to the other ones:

**Example:**
```
RangeVar.ClearContents
```

# Cut and Paste Ranges of Cells

Some of the most commonly used commands with any Microsoft Windows application are the Cut, Copy, and Paste commands. In fact, people use these commands so frequently that most applications have toolbar buttons for accessing them. You can also cut and paste values within a worksheet directly using VBA and the Cut method associated with the Range object.

The Cut method provides the ability to cut the values from a specific range and paste them in either the Windows Clipboard or a specific destination. The Cut method has one optional parameter, Destination, that you can use if you want to specify where you want to paste the cut values. If you do not specify a Destination parameter value, the cut range of values paste into the Windows Clipboard. If you use the Destination parameter, you must specify another Range object as the location for the values to paste. The following code illustrates the use of

the Cut method to paste the range in cells A1:A5:

```
CutRange.Cut Destination:=Range("A1:A5").
```

Keep in mind that you must make the range specified for CutRange variable and the destination range the same size, or Excel returns an error. If you do not know the size of the cut range of cells, you should specify a single cell as the destination range, for example: `CutRange.Cut Destination:=Range("A1")`.

If you specify only one cell, Excel makes it the initial cell and pastes the values in cells starting at that location. In other words, if pasting the contents requires cells A1:B4, Excel automatically uses those cells.

Keep in mind, however, that when you use the Cut method, the contents are removed from the specified cells and pasted into the new cells. The original cells appear as empty on the worksheet.

## Cut and Paste Ranges of Cells

① Create a new subroutine.

**Note:** See Chapter 3 for information on creating subroutines.

② Type **Dim CutRange As Range**, replacing CutRange with the variable containing the range to cut.

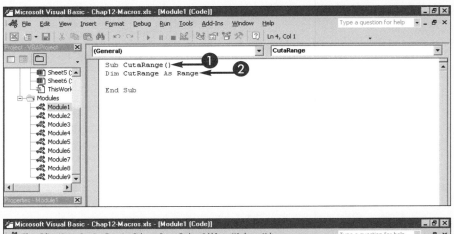

③ Type **Set CutRange = Range("B1:C5")**, replacing Range("B1:C5") with the range to cut.

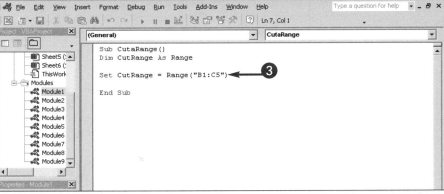

④ Type **CutRange.Cut Destination:=Range("A1")**, replacing `Range("A1")` with the range where the cut cell values should be pasted.

⑤ Type additional VBA code for working with pasted values.

⑥ Switch to Excel and run the macro.

● The specified range of cells is cut and pasted in the new location.

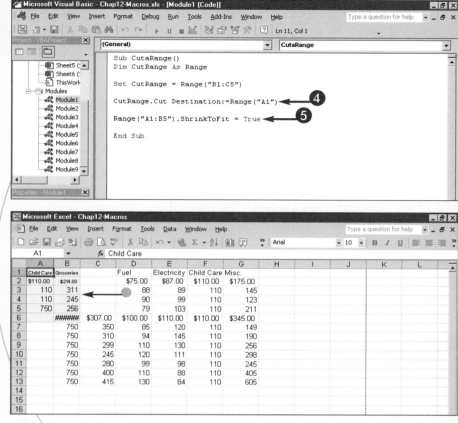

## Extra

When you paste values into cells, the cells are not always properly sized to hold the new values. If the values that you paste in the new cells are numeric and the cells are not wide enough for the entire number, Excel displays number signs, ####, indicating the cell is not properly sized. Excel provides some formatting options you can use with the `Range` object to resize cells so that values fit appropriately.

To ensure that the values pasted in the cells display properly, you can use the `ShrinkToFit` property. When you use this property, the font size of the text in a cell reduces to ensure that the entire contents of the cell display when you view the worksheet. You set the `ShrinkToFit` property by assigning a value of `True`, as shown in this code:

**Example:**
```
CurrentRange.ShrinkToFit=True
```

The other property that you can use is the `WrapText` property. Assigning a value of `True` to this property causes text to wrap within the cell so that it all displays on the worksheet.

**Example:**
```
CurrentRange.WrapText=True
```

You can also use the `AutoFit` method to resize the rows or columns in a range to allow the contents of all cells to display. To use the `AutoFit` method you type the following:

**Example:**
```
CurrentRange.Columns.AutoFit
```

# Copy and Paste Ranges of Cells

You can copy and paste cell ranges within a worksheet using the Copy method. The Copy method is essentially the same as the Copy and Paste commands within Excel, except that in Excel you are required to use two commands; that is, you first copy the desired range and move to the appropriate location, and then select the Paste command.

The Copy method associated with the Range object provides the ability to copy the values from a specific range and paste the values either in the Windows Clipboard or a specific destination. The Copy method has one optional parameter, Destination, that you can use if you want to specify where the copied values should be pasted. If you do not specify a Destination parameter value, the copied range of values is pasted in the Windows Clipboard. If you use the Destination parameter, you must specify another Range object as the location for the values to be pasted. The

following code illustrates the use of the Copy method to paste the range in cells A1:A5: CopyRange.Copy Destination:=Range("A1:A5").

Keep in mind that the range specified from the CutRange variable and the destination range must be the same size, or Excel returns an error.

If you do not know the size of the copied range of cells, you can specify a single cell as the destination range: CopyRange.Copy Destination:=Range("A1").

If you specify only one cell, Excel uses the specified cell as the initial cell and pastes the values in cells starting at that location. In other words, if pasting the contents requires cells A1:B4, Excel automatically uses those cells.

When you use the Copy method, the contents remain in the original cells, and a copy of those values is pasted in the new cells.

## Copy and Paste a Range of Cells

① Create a new subroutine.

**Note:** See Chapter 3 for information on creating subroutines.

② Type **Dim CopyRange As Range**, replacing CopyRange with the variable containing the range to copy.

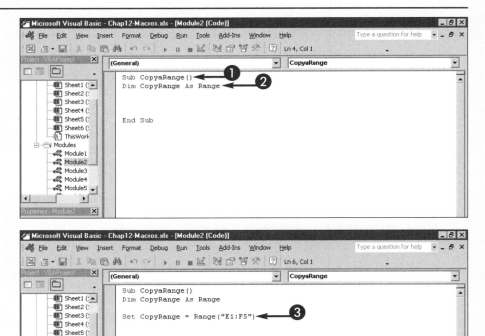

③ Type **Set CopyRange = Range("E1:F5")**, replacing Range("E1:F5") with the range to copy.

④ Type **CopyRange.Copy Destination:=Range("A1:B5")**, replacing Range("A1:B5") with the range where the copied cell values should be pasted.

⑤ Type additional VBA code for working with pasted values.

⑥ Switch to Excel and run the macro.

● The specified range of cells is copied and pasted in the new location.

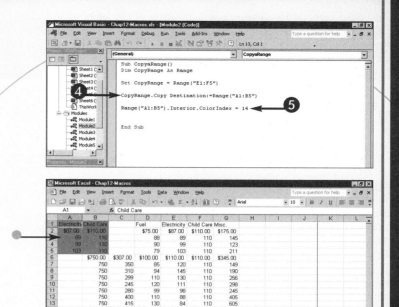

## Apply It

You can customize the background color of a cell by using the `ColorIndex` property with the `Interior` object. The `Interior` object is a child-object of the `Range` object. You set the cell background color by assigning a color index value to the `ColorIndex` property. For example, the index value of 5 makes the cells associated with the range display with a blue background.

`Columns(1).Interior.ColorIndex = 5`

You can assign an index value of 1 to 56 to the `ColorIndex` parameter, although there are only 16 different colors available, as outlined in the table.

| INDEX | COLOR |
|-------|-------|
| 1 | Black |
| 2 | White |
| 3 | Red |
| 4 | Green |
| 5 | Blue |
| 6 | Yellow |
| 7 | Fuchsia |
| 8 | Light Blue |
| 9 | Brown |
| 10 | Forest Green |
| 11 | Navy Blue |
| 12 | Yellow-Brown |
| 13 | Maroon |
| 14 | Blue-Green |
| 15 | Light Gray |
| 16 | Gray |

# Custom Paste Values in Cells

Yo can customize how values paste into a worksheet from the Windows Clipboard by using the `PasteSpecial` method. You can use the `PasteSpecial` method with values that have been added to the Windows Clipboard using the `Cut` or `Copy` methods, or even values placed there directly from Excel. With the PasteSpecial method, you can customize how the cell contents are pasted into the new range by only pasting the cell formats or even by adding the cell values to the contents of the cells from where you are pasting. The `PasteSpecial` method is essentially the same as using Edit→PasteSpecial in Excel.

Typically when you use the `Cut` or `Copy` method, you indicate where to place the cell values and Excel places the values in that location instead of in the clipboard. If you plan to use the `PasteSpecial` method with a `Cut` or `Copy` method, you should not use the `Destination` parameter with either method.

The `PasteSpecial` method has four different optional parameters: `Paste`, `Operation`, `SkipBlanks`, and `Transpose`.

The `Paste` parameter indicates how you want to paste the information into the new range. By default, Excel uses the `xlPasteAll` constant value for this parameter, which pastes the entire contents of the copied or cut cells into the new range.

The `Operation` parameter enables you to perform a mathematical operation, such as adding the current value of a cell to the pasted value. The default constant value used by Excel is `xlPasteSpecialOperationNone`, which does not perform any mathematical operations.

Set the `SkipBlanks` parameter to `True` to ignore blank cells in the clipboard and avoid having them pasted into the new cells. If selected, existing values remain in cells that would have received blank values.

If you want to transpose the data values from rows to columns or vice versa, specify a value of `True` for the `Transpose` parameter.

## Custom Paste Values in Cells

① Create a new subroutine.

**Note:** See Chapter 3 for information on creating subroutines.

② Type **For N = 2 To 6**, replacing 2 and 6 with the numbers corresponding to the columns to add.

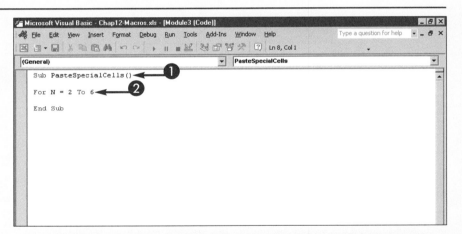

③ Type **Range(Cells(3,N), Cells(16,N)).Copy**, replacing `Cells(3,N),Cells(16,N)` with the range to copy.

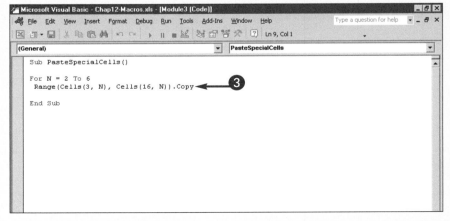

④ Type **Range(Cells(3, N + 1), Cells(16, N + 1)).PasteSpecial**, replacing `Cells(3, N + 1), Cells(16, N + 1)` with the range where the copied cell values should be pasted.

⑤ Type **Operation:=xlPasteSpecialOperationAdd**.

⑥ Type **Next**.

⑦ Switch to Excel and run the macro.

The specified range of cells is copied and added to the new range of cells.

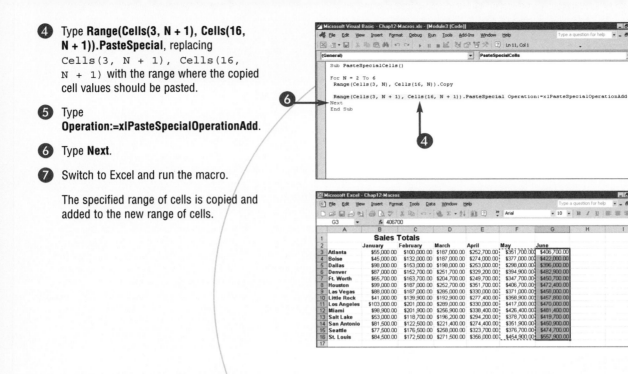

The `Paste` parameter requires one of the `XlPasteType` constant values that are described in the following table.

| XLPASTETYPE CONSTANT | DESCRIPTION |
|---|---|
| xlPasteAll | Default value. Pastes the entire contents of the cells. |
| xlPasteAllExcept Borders | Pastes everything but border settings. |
| xlPasteColumnWidths | Only sets the column widths to match. |
| xlPasteComments | Only pastes the cell comments. |
| xlPasteFormats | Only sets the cell formatting options. |
| xlPasteFormulas | Only pastes the formulas. |
| xlPasteFormulasAnd NumberFormats | Pastes the formulas and number formats. |
| xlPasteValidation | Sets the cell validation. |
| xlPasteValues | Only pastes the cell values. |
| xlPasteValuesAnd NumberFormats | Pastes the cell values and number formats. |

The `Operation` parameter requires one of the following:

`xlPasteSpecialOperation` constant values: `xlPasteSpecialOperationAdd`, `xlPasteSpecialOperationDivide`, `xlPasteSpecialOperationMultiply`, `xlPasteSpecialOperationNone`, **or** `xlPasteSpecialOperationSubtract`.

# Add Comments to a Cell

You can add comments to any cell in a worksheet using the AddComment method with the Range object. Comments are great methods for adding extra information about the value in a cell, such as how it was calculated, who provided the information, and so on. Using the AddComment method is basically the same as clicking Insert→Comment within Excel. The biggest difference is that by default when you create a comment in Excel, the name of the person creating the comment is always added to the top of the comment. When you create a comment using the AddComment method, only the text you provide is added to the comment.

When you add a comment to a cell, Excel typically places a small red triangle in the upper-right corner of the cell to indicate that the cell contains a comment. You can view the comment in the cell by dragging the cursor across the cell.

To add a comment to a cell, you need to specify the range of the cell to contain the comment, the AddComment method,

and the comment to add to the cell, for example:
```
Cells(3,3).AddComment "Sample Comment Text".
```

You can only place a comment in one cell at a time using the AddComment method. If you want to add the same comment to multiple cells, you can use a looping statement, such as a For Next loop to cycle through the range of cells to receive the comment.

If you attempt to add a comment to a cell that already contains a comment, Excel returns an error message. To avoid potential errors, you can use the ClearComments method to clear any existing comments so that comments can be added to the specified cell. When you use this method, if the specified cell does not contain any comments, the ClearComments method is ignored. You use the method as shown in this example: Cells(3,3).ClearComments.

## Add Comments to a Cell

① Create a new subroutine.

**Note:** See Chapter 3 for information on creating subroutines.

② Type **Dim SalesLocal As String**, replacing SalesLocal with the name of the string variable.

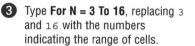

③ Type **For N = 3 To 16**, replacing 3 and 16 with the numbers indicating the range of cells.

④ Type **SalesLocal = Cells(N,1).Text**, replacing Cells(N,1) with the range containing the text string for the comment.

⑤ Type **Cells(N,2).ClearComments**, replacing Cells(N,2) with the reference to the cell to clear.

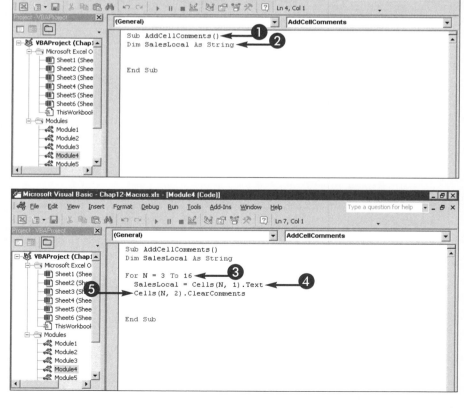

**6** Type **Cells(N,2).AddComment**, replacing `Cells(N,2)` with the reference to the cell to receive comments.

**7** Type **("Cell Comment" & SalesLocal).**

**8** Type **Next**.

**9** Switch to Excel and run the macro.

● The comments are added to the range of cells. The comment displays when you drag your cursor across the cell.

```
Sub AddCellComments()
Dim SalesLocal As String

For N = 3 To 16
  SalesLocal = Cells(N, 1).Text
  Cells(N, 2).ClearComments
  Cells(N, 2).AddComment ("January Total Sales for " & SalesLocal)
Next

End Sub
```

Excel worksheet: Chap12-Macros

| | A | B | C | D | E | F | G | H | I |
|---|---|---|---|---|---|---|---|---|---|
| 1 | | **Sales Totals** | | | | | | | |
| 2 | | January | February | March | April | May | June | | |
| 3 | Atlanta | $55,000.00 | January Total Sales for Atlanta | $252,700.00 | $351,700.00 | $406,700.00 | | |
| 4 | Boise | $45,000.00 | | | $274,000.00 | $377,000.00 | $422,000.00 | | |
| 5 | Dallas | $98,000.00 | | | $253,000.00 | $298,000.00 | $396,000.00 | | |
| 6 | Denver | $87,000.00 | | | $329,200.00 | $394,900.00 | $482,900.00 | | |
| 7 | Ft. Worth | $65,700.00 | $163,700.00 | $204,700.00 | $249,700.00 | $347,700.00 | $450,700.00 | | |
| 8 | Houston | $99,000.00 | $187,000.00 | $252,700.00 | $351,700.00 | $406,700.00 | $472,400.00 | | |
| 9 | Las Vegas | $88,000.00 | $187,000.00 | $285,000.00 | $330,000.00 | $371,000.00 | $458,000.00 | | |
| 10 | Little Rock | $41,000.00 | $139,900.00 | $192,900.00 | $277,400.00 | $358,900.00 | $457,800.00 | | |
| 11 | Los Angeles | $103,000.00 | $201,000.00 | $289,000.00 | $330,000.00 | $417,000.00 | $470,000.00 | | |
| 12 | Miami | $98,900.00 | $201,900.00 | $256,900.00 | $338,400.00 | $426,400.00 | $481,400.00 | | |
| 13 | Salt Lake | $53,000.00 | $118,700.00 | $196,200.00 | $294,200.00 | $378,700.00 | $419,700.00 | | |
| 14 | San Antonio | $81,500.00 | $122,500.00 | $221,400.00 | $274,400.00 | $351,900.00 | $450,900.00 | | |
| 15 | Seattle | $77,500.00 | $176,500.00 | $258,000.00 | $323,700.00 | $376,700.00 | $474,700.00 | | |
| 16 | St. Louis | $84,500.00 | $172,500.00 | $271,500.00 | $356,000.00 | $454,900.00 | $557,900.00 | | |
| 17 | | | | | | | | | |

## Extra

When you add a comment to a cell, Excel creates a `Comment` object for that cell. The `Comment` object is actually part of the `Comments` collection, which contains all comments within a particular range of cells. You can reference particular comments in a worksheet using the `Comments` collection and an index value. For example, to access the second comment in a worksheet you would type the following:

**Example:**
```
SecondComment=ActiveSheet.Comments(2).Text
```

You can also use the properties of the `Comment` object to customize you comments. If you want comments to automatically display on the worksheet, you need to set the `Visible` property as shown below.

**Example:**
```
Cells(1,1).Comment.Visible = True
```

This code makes the comment in cell A1 display all the time on the worksheet.

You may want to only delete comments that were created by a particular author. The `Comment` object provides an `Author` property that you can use to return the author of a comment for a cell. Remember, Excel adds the author when comments are created. To delete the comments created by a particular individual, you type something similar to the following:

**Example:**
```
CountComments = ActiveSheet.Comments.Count
For N = 1 To CountComments
    If Comment(N).Author = "John" Then
        Comment(N).Delete
    End If
Next
```

# Automatically Fill a Range of Cells

**W**hen you want to add a series of values to a range of cells, such as consecutive dates, you can use the AutoFill method to have Excel automatically perform the task for you.

When you perform an autofill, Excel uses the values in the source range to determine the type of values to add to cells in the destination. For example, if the source range is A1 and A2 and the cells contain the values Jan and Feb respectively, Excel fills the cells in the source range with the months of the year starting with Mar.

With the AutoFill method there are two parameters available for use. The first parameter, Destination, is required. This parameter must contain a Range object indicating which cells to fill. The Destination range value also needs to include the source range. For example, if the source range is A1 and A2, these cells must be included in the destination range, as shown: Range("A1:A2").AutoFill Destination:=Range("A1:A12").

This code uses the values in cells A1 and A2 to determine the pattern for adding values to the cells in the destination. If the cells are numeric, Excel finds a numeric pattern and uses that for the destination range.

If you want to specify the pattern for adding values to the destination, you need to include the Type parameter. The Type parameter accepts one of the XlAutoFillType constants indicating the type of fill. The default value xlFillDefault instructs Excel to determine a pattern based upon the source cell values. If your cells contain date values, you can use xlFillDays, xlFillWeekdays, xlFillMonths, or xlFillYears to have the cells increment by the appropriate month value. For example, if your source cell contains the value 1/15/2001 and you select a Fill value of xlFillMonths, the source cells increment by one month.

## Automatically Fill a Range of Cells

① Create a new subroutine.

**Note:** See Chapter 3 for information on creating subroutines.

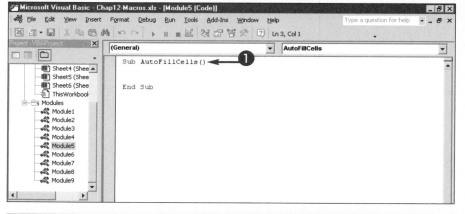

② Type **Range("A1:A2").AutoFill**, replacing Range("A1:A2") with the range containing source cells.

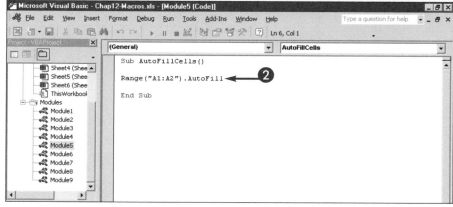

③ Type **Destination:= Range("A1:A10")**, replacing `Range("A1:A10")` with the range of cells to fill.

④ Type **Type:=xlFillMonths**, replacing `xlFillMonths` with the constant specifying the type of fill.

⑤ Switch to Excel and run the macro.

The specified cells are automatically filled.

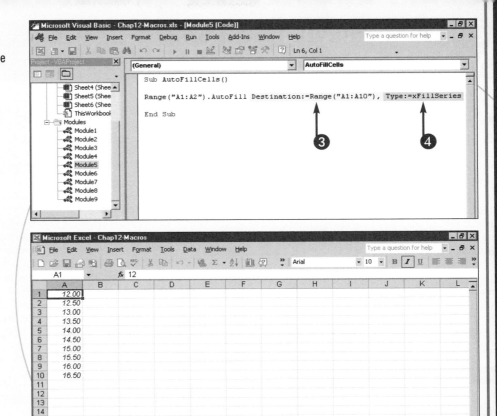

## Apply It

The `XlAutoFillType` constant values specify how Excel fills the range of cells for the `Destination` parameter. The following table describes the results of each of the `xlAutoFillType` constant values.

| CONSTANT | DESCRIPTION |
| --- | --- |
| xlFillDays | Increments the values by days. If only one date is specified, increments one day. If multiple dates are specified for the source, uses those dates to determine increment value. |
| xlFillFormats | Applies the formats of the source cells to the destination cells. |
| xlFillSeries | Creates a series based upon contents of source range. |
| xlFillWeekdays | Increments based on weekdays omitting dates that fall on Saturday or Sunday. |
| xlGrowthTrend | Fills cells based on a growth trend. |
| xlFillCopy | Copies formatting of source, and increments based on source values. |
| xlFillDefault | Default value. Excel determines fill type based upon values in source cells. |
| xlFillMonths | Increments the month portion of the date. |
| xlFillValues | Increments values based upon values in source cells. |
| xlFillYears | Increments the year portion of the date. |
| xlLinearTrend | Fills cells based on a linear trend. |

# Copy a Range to Multiple Sheets

You can copy a range of cells and place it in the same location on multiple sheets with the `FillAcrossSheets` method. When you use this method, Excel copies the specified cells to each worksheet you specify. You can copy everything in the range of cells, just the values in the cells, or only the formatting.

When you use this method, you call it by indicating the range of worksheets where Excel should copy the cells followed by the `FillAcrossSheets` method. The range of worksheets must exist within the current workbook. Also, you must specify all of the worksheets at once, such as the `Worksheets` collection object to copy to all worksheets in the workbook. If you specify individual sheets within the workbook, the worksheet containing the range must be part of the range. The method includes two different parameters, `Range` and `Fill`, as illustrated in the following line of code:

`Worksheets.FillAcrossSheets(Range, Fill).`

The first parameter, `Range`, is required. The `Range` parameter must specify the range of cells to copy to the other worksheets. You can specify the range of cells using any valid range statement. See Chapter 11 for more information on specifying ranges.

The second parameter, `Fill`, is optional. You can use this parameter to indicate how the range should copy. The `Fill` parameter accepts any one of the three `XlFillWith` constant values. If you do not specify a `Fill` parameter value, Excel uses the default value of `xlFillWithAll`, which instructs Excel to copy the entire contents of the range of cells, including the formatting. If you only want to copy the cell values, use the `xlFillWithContents` constant value. This constant value instructs Excel to copy everything but the cell formatting. On the other hand, if you only want to copy the formatting of the range of cells, specify the constant value of `xlFillWithFormats`. When you do this, Excel ignores the entire contents of the cell and only copies and applies the formatting.

## Copy a Range to Multiple Sheets

① Create a new subroutine.

**Note:** See Chapter 3 for information on creating subroutines.

② Type **Dim WS As Variant**, replacing WS with the variable to contain the worksheet range.

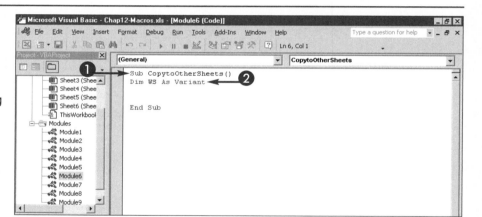

③ Type **WS = Array("Sheet1", "Sheet3", "Sheet5")**, replacing `"Sheet1"`, `"Sheet3"`, `"Sheet5"` with the worksheets to receive the cell values.

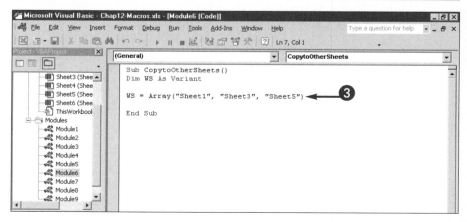

④ Type **Worksheets(WS).FillAcrossSheets**.

⑤ Type **Worksheets("Sheet").Range ("A1:G1")**, replacing `Worksheets ("Sheet").Range("A1:G1")` with the range containing the values to copy.

⑥ Type **Type:=xlFillWithContents**, replacing `xlFillWithContents` with the constant value indicating how to copy values.

⑦ Switch to Excel and run the macro.

● The cell values are copied to each worksheet in the specified range.

```
Sub CopytoOtherSheets()
Dim WS As Variant

WS = Array("Sheet1", "Sheet3", "Sheet5")
Sheets(WS).FillAcrossSheets _
    Worksheets("Sheet1").Range("A23:C25"), Type:=xlFillWithContents

End Sub
```

## Apply It

You can fill a range of cells in a specific direction within a worksheet using one of the `Fill` methods. For example, you may want to fill across a worksheet with the first value in the left corner of the range. VBA offers four `Range` object methods for filling in a specific direction: `FillUp`, `FillDown`, `FillRight`, and `FillLeft`.

You can use the `FillUp` method to fill a range of cells with the value specified in the last cell of the range. For example, if you have the range A1:A10 and apply the `FillUp` method, as illlustrated, the value in cell A10 copies and pastes in cells A1:A9.

**Example:**
```
Range("A1:A10").FillUp
```

The `FillDown` method works just opposite of the `FillUp` method. This method takes the value in the top of the range and copies it to all other cells.

You can use the `FillRight` method to fill across rows. If you use this method with the range A1:G1, Excel takes the value in cell E1 and pastes it into cells B1 through G1. The `FillLeft` method works the opposite of the `FillRight` method. This method takes the value in the last cell on the right and copies it to all cells in the remaining portion of the range.

# Place Borders around a Range of Cells

Y ou can use borders around cells on your worksheet to make specific information stand out. For example, when a worksheet contains a row of cells that totals the values in the other cells of the worksheet, the total row is typically highlighted in some fashion to make it more noticeable. One common method is to place a border around those cells.

You can add borders to a range of cells using the BorderAround method. When you apply a border to a range of cells, the border outlines the entire range of cells, not each individual cell. When you use this method, it provides different optional parameters that enable you to set the Color, LineStyle, and Weight properties for the Borders collection object associated with the range of cells.

Use the LineStyle parameter to specify the line style for the border around a range. You can specify any one of the XlLineStyle constant values. Excel uses the default value of xlContinuous to draw a continuous line around the range of cells, if you do not specify a LineStyle parameter value.

You can use the Weight parameter to specify the width of the line to border the range of cells. You can specify any one of the XlBorderWeight constant values. If you do not specify a Weight parameter value, Excel uses a default value of xlThin, which draws a thin line around the range of cells.

Use the ColorIndex parameter to specify the border color as an index value to the current color palette specified as a value between 1 and 64 or as one of the XlColorIndex constant values. Specify xlColorIndexAutomatic to use the automatic default line color. You can specify a value of xlColorIndexNone to not use the current color palette.

If you want to specify an RGB color value for the border, use the Color parameter and assign it an RGB color with the RGB function. The RGB color value ensures that you have the same color, regardless of the loaded color palette. With the RGB function, you need to specify three values from 0 to 255 indicating the red, green, and blue component values.

## Place Borders around a Range of Cells

① Create a new subroutine.

**Note:** See Chapter 3 for information on creating subroutines.

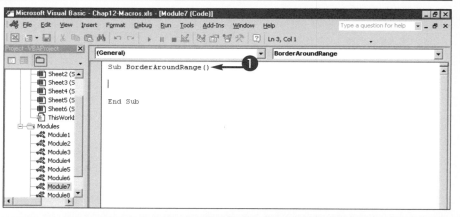

② Type **Range("A2:G2").
BorderAround**, replacing
Range("A2:G2") with the
cells where the border should
be placed.

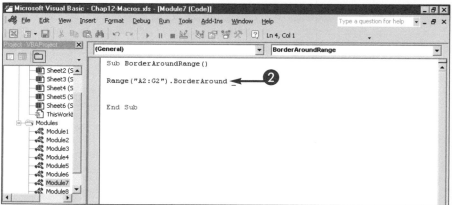

**3** Type **LineStyle:=xlDouble**, replacing `xlDouble` with the `XlLineStyle` constant for the desired line style.

**4** Type **Color:=RGB(250, 120, 220)**, replacing `250, 120, 220` with the Red, Green, and Blue values for the desired line color.

**5** Type **Weight:=xlThick**, replacing `xlThick` with the appropriate `XlBorderWeight` constant.

**6** Switch to Excel and run the macro.

● Excel draws a border around the specified cells.

## Apply It

You use the `XlLineStyle` constant values, outlined in the table, to specify the type of line to draw as the border for the range of cells.

You use the `XlBorderWeight` constant values, `xlHairline`, `xlMedium`, `xlThick`, and `xlThin`, to specify the width of the line used to draw the border for the range of cells. The type of line drawn is based upon the `XlLineStyle` parameter value.

| CONSTANT | DESCRIPTION |
|---|---|
| xlContinuous | Default value. Draws a continuous line around the range of cells. |
| xlDash | Draws a dashed line around the range of cells. |
| xlDashDot | Draws a broken line using the pattern dash and then dot. |
| xlDashDotDot | Draws a broken line using the pattern dash, dash, and dot. |
| xlDot | Draws a dotted line around the range of cells. |
| xlDouble | Draws a double continuous line around the range of cells. |
| xlLineStyleNone | Does not modify the line style. |
| xlSlantDashDot | Draws a broken line in a dash dot pattern using a slanted line. |

# Find Specific Cell Values

You can use the `Find` method to search for specific values within a range of cells. This method works essentially the same as the Edit→Find command in Excel. The `Find` method has several different parameters of which only the `What` parameter is required. You must specify the string for which you want to search as the value of the `What` parameter.

If you want to start searching from a specific cell, use the `After` parameter to reference the cell before where you want to start searching. If omitted, Excel starts the search with the top left cell in the range.

For the `LookIn` parameter, specify one of the `XlFindLookIn` constants to indicate what part of the cell to search. Type `xlValues` to look at cell values, `xlComments` to search attached comments, or `xlFormulas` to look at formulas.

You specify a value of `xlWhole` for the `LookAt` parameter to require Excel to match the entire contents of a cell. You specify `xlPart` if Excel should match a cell that contains a search string as part of the cell value.

Specify the appropriate `XlSearchOrder` constant to indicate whether to search by rows or columns. `xlByRows` searches by rows, and `xlByColumns` searches by columns.

You use the `SearchDirection` parameter to indicate the direction to search. A value of `xlNext` finds the next matching value in the worksheet. A value of `xlPrevious` finds the previous match.

Type a value of **True** for the `MatchCase` parameter if Excel should only match occurrences with the same case, all uppercase, all lowercase, and so on. If you are using double-byte language support, type a value of **True** for the `MatchByte` parameter to only match double-byte characters with double-byte characters.

Using the `SearchFormat` parameter is a little more complex. If you assign this parameter a value of `True`, you need to specify the format for the `Application.FindFormat` object.

## Find Specific Cell Values

① Create a new subroutine.

**Note:** See Chapter 3 for information on creating subroutines.

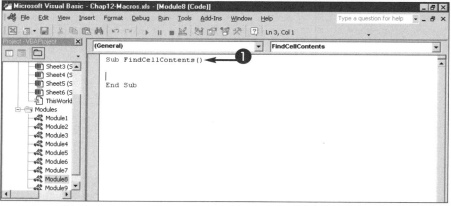

② Type **Range("A1:G16").Find**, replacing `Range("A1:G16")` with the range of cells to search.

③ Type **What:="Boise"**, replacing `Boise` with the string you want to search for.

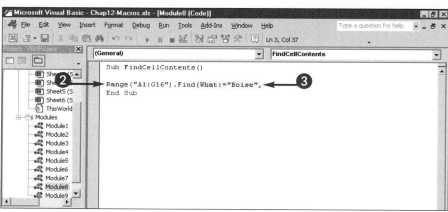

④ Type **LookAt:=xlWhole**, replacing `xlWhole` with the constant indicating the part of the string to match.

⑤ Type **LookIn:=xlValues**, replacing `xlValues` with the `XlFindLookIn` constant value indicating the part of the cell to search.

⑥ Type **SearchOrder:=xlByColumns**.

⑦ Type **.Activate** to activate the cell.

⑧ Switch to Excel and run the macro.

● The first cell containing the search text is activated.

---

### Apply It

Excel remembers the values specified for the `LookIn`, `LookAt`, `SearchOrder`, and `MatchByte` parameters. If you run a search again without these parameter values, Excel uses the settings from the previous `Find` or `Replace` method. These values are also modified if you run a `Find` or `Replace` from within Excel. To avoid running searches that have unexpected values set, you should set these values each time you run the method.

You can continue a search and find the next match using the `FindNext` method. In order to use this method you must specify an `After` parameter indicating the cell from which to start the next search. All other parameter values are used from the previous `Find` method. You use the `FindNext` method as illustrated:

**Example:**
```
SearchRange.FindNext(After)
```

Instead of finding the next occurrence of a string, you can find a previous occurrence using the `FindPrevious` method. This method searches backward from the specified location and finds a previous occurrence of a string. The `FindPrevious` requires one parameter, `Before`, which indicates the cell where the search should begin. You use the `FindPrevious` method as illustrated:

**Example:**
```
SearchRange.FindPrevious
(Before)
```

# Find and Replace Values in Cells

Y ou can use the `Replace` method to search for and replace specific values within a specific range of cells. This method works essentially the same as the Edit→Replace command in Excel.

The `Replace` method has several different parameters, with only two of them being required. You must specify the string for which you want to search as the value of the `What` parameter. You must also specify a replacement string as the value of the `Replacement` parameter. All remaining parameters are optional.

You specify a value of `xlWhole` for the `LookAt` parameter to have Excel require that the `What` value match the entire contents of a cell before replacement. Specify `xlPart` if Excel should replace a cell that contains search string as part of the cell value.

Specify the appropriate `XlSearchOrder` constant to indicate whether to search by rows or columns. The constant `xlByRows` searches by rows and the constant `xlByColumns` searches by columns.

Type a value of **True** for the `MatchCase` parameter if Excel should only match occurrences with the same case, all uppercase, all lowercase, and so on. If you are using double-byte language support, type a value of **True** for the `MatchByte` parameter to only match double-byte characters with double-byte characters.

Using the `SearchFormat` and `ReplaceFormat` parameters is a little more complex. If either of these parameters has a value of `True`, you must specify the format. For the `SearchFormat` parameter, you specify the format properties for the `Application.FindFormat` object. With the `ReplaceFormat` parameter you specify the `Application.ReplaceFormat` properties. For example, to replace the text with a bold font, you can specify the following code above your `Replace` method:
`Application.ReplaceFormat.Font.FontStyle = "Bold"`.

## Find and Replace Values in Cells

① Create a new subroutine.

**Note:** See Chapter 3 for information on creating subroutines.

② Type **Application.ReplaceFormat. Font.FontStyle = "Bold Italic"**, replacing "`Bold Italic`" with the font style to use for the replacement text.

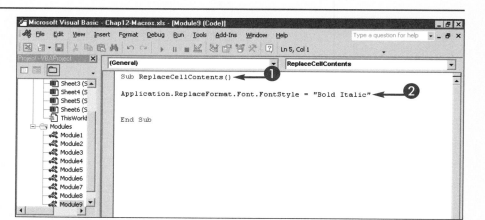

③ Type **Range("A1:G16").Replace**, replacing `Range("A1:G16")` with the range to search.

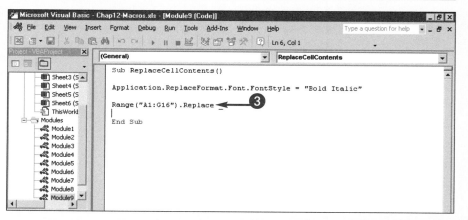

④ Type **What:="Seattle"**, replacing "Seattle" with the string to find.

⑤ Type **Replacement:="San Francisco"**, replacing "San Francisco" with the replacement string.

⑥ Type **ReplaceFormat:=True**.

⑦ Switch to Excel and run the macro.

● The specified text is replaced and reformatted as specified.

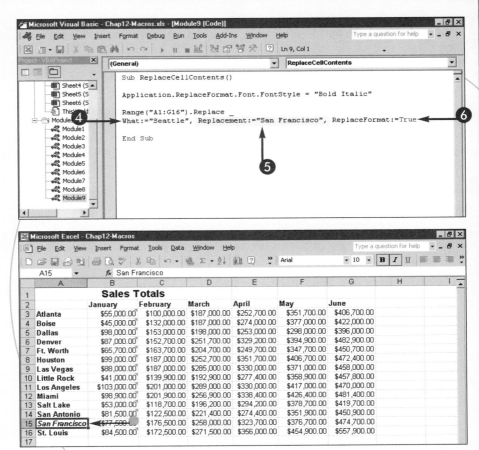

---

## Extra

When you specify a value of True for the SearchFormat parameter and the ReplaceFormat parameter, Excel looks for the search and replacement format settings. If you want to use formatting as part of the search criteria, you need to specify the format settings for the FindFormat property of the Application object. Whereas, with the ReplaceFormat parameter, you need to specify the replacement format settings using the ReplaceFormat property. Typically these settings are specified at the top of the procedure, before the code that sets the associated parameter. You use these properties to set the Font object properties for searching and replacing text. Typically you will use the With statement to set the property values. For example, to set replacement text properties you would type code similar to the following:

**Example:**
```
With Application.ReplaceFormat.Font
        .Name = "Arial"
        .FontStyle = "Bold"
        .Size = 12
End With
```

225

# UserForm Basics

Y ou can use dialog boxes to request specific information from users by providing them an interface with your VBA code. Every Microsoft Windows application utilizes dialog boxes to gather information from the user, and Excel is no exception. As an

example, you frequently interact with the Open dialog box in Excel to select a file to open. VBA provides two standard dialog boxes: MsgBox and InputBox. See Chapter 7 for more information on working with these functions.

## Parts of the Visual Basic Editor Toolbox

The Visual Basic Editor provides the option of creating custom dialog boxes that you can use with your Excel macros. These custom dialog boxes are referred to as UserForms

within the Visual Basic Editor. When you create a UserForm, you design it using the various controls available on the Toolbox.

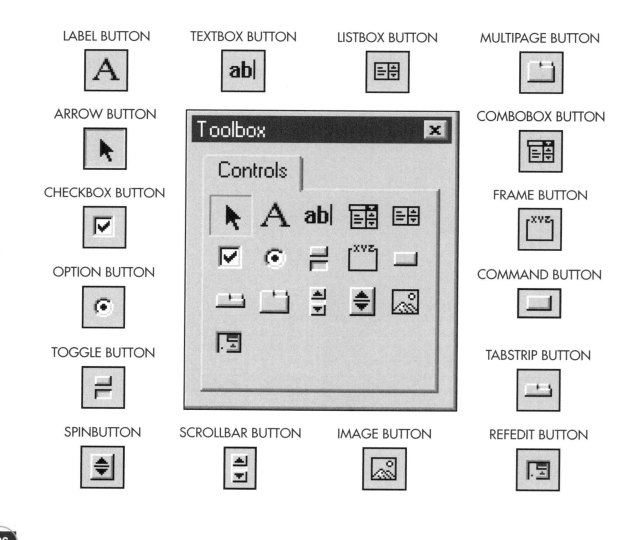

LABEL BUTTON

TEXTBOX BUTTON

LISTBOX BUTTON

MULTIPAGE BUTTON

ARROW BUTTON

COMBOBOX BUTTON

CHECKBOX BUTTON

FRAME BUTTON

OPTION BUTTON

COMMAND BUTTON

TOGGLE BUTTON

TABSTRIP BUTTON

SPINBUTTON

SCROLLBAR BUTTON

IMAGE BUTTON

REFEDIT BUTTON

## Visual Basic Editor Toolbox

The Visual Basic Editor Toolbox only displays when you select a UserForm in the Visual Basic Editor. The toolbox contains all of the controls that you can add to your custom UserForm. See the section "Create a Custom Dialog Box" for more information about adding Toolbox controls.

The Toolbox contains several different standard controls that you can add to a userform. You can also create custom controls and add them to the Toolbox. See the section "Create Custom UserForm Controls" for more information on adding custom controls.

### Label

For adding text to a UserForm. Not designed to interact with the UserForm; you add labels for informational purposes only.

### TextBox

Enables the user to type text.

### ComboBox

Enables a user to either click an item from the list or type the appropriate value.

### ListBox

For presenting a list of items from which a user can select a desired item.

### CheckBox

Enables the user to select or unselect options. Typically a CheckBox control returns a value of `True` if it is selected and `False` if it is not selected.

### OptionButton

Enables the user to select from a list of items. You have two controls in a group so that when you select one control, the other controls are unselected.

### ToggleButton

Enables you to create a button that looks either pressed or unpressed, with the pressed state returning a value of `True`, and the unpressed state returning a `False` value.

### Frame

For display purposes. Acts as a container for grouping controls.

### TabStrip

Enables you to create a multipage area for a section of your UserForm.

### CommandButton

The user clicks this to perform a specific option. When you create a CommandButton control, you specify the text that displays on the button as part of the control properties.

### MultiPage

To create tabbed dialog boxes, which enable the user to switch between pages of options on the dialog box.

By default, when you add the MultiPage control to your UserForm, it only creates two pages. You can add additional pages by right-clicking one of the Page tabs and selecting the New Page option.

### ScrollBar

Enables the user to scroll through information not on the screen, or to indicate a position on a scale, such as for providing a rating level.

### SpinButton

Enables a user to specify a value by clicking one of the arrow buttons to increment or decrement the value. Use with either a TextBox control or a Label control that displays the current value of the SpinButton control.

### Image

Use the Image control to add a graphic to the UserForm. Excel stores the graphic within the worksheet, so if you distribute the worksheet, Excel includes the graphic. You can assign the graphic any of the following file formats: .bmp, .cur, .gif, .ico, .jpg, .wmf.

### RefEdit

Consisting of a text field and a button, this enables the user to select a range of cells from a worksheet. When the user clicks a button, the corresponding dialog box minimizes so the user can drag the cursor across the worksheet to select the desired range of cells.

# Working with CommandBars

By using toolbars and shortcut menus, you can provide quick access to commonly used commands. Excel has more than 50 different built-in toolbars and about 60 different shortcut menus, all of which are part of the CommandBars collection. This collection also contains any new custom toolbars and menus you create. Due to their central location, you can easily make modifications to existing menus and toolbars, or add new ones as needed.

## Understanding the CommandBars Collection

The CommandBars collection is part of the Application object, the main object that contains all Excel-related objects.

Each individual toolbar or menu is a separate CommandBar object. You can reference these objects either by an index value or by the object name. For example, the code CommandBars("Standard") references the Standard toolbar. See Appendix A for a list of the built-in toolbars and shortcut menus in Excel.

Excel determines which type of command bar a particular object contains by the value of the Type property. Excel has three types of command bar objects, as described in the following table.

| TYPE | INTEGER | CONSTANT |
| --- | --- | --- |
| Toolbar | 0 | msoBarTypeNormal |
| Menu Bar | 1 | msoBarTypeMenuBar |
| ShortCut Menu | 2 | msoBarTypePopUp |

## Existing Menus and Toolbars

You can modify menus and toolbars either manually from Excel or you can create subroutines to modify these CommandBar objects. In Excel, you make modifications to toolbars and menus via the Customize command on the Tools menu. From the Customize menu you can add and remove both menu and toolbar options. See Chapter 1 for more information about adding macro references to toolbars and menus.

You can also write a procedure that modifies a particular menu or toolbar by adding or removing options. Each option on a toolbar or menu is a CommandBarControl object associated with the corresponding CommandBar object. You reference the CommandBarControls collection using the Controls property. You add a new option to a toolbar or menu using the Add method.

When you call the Add method with the Controls object, you can apply the optional parameters of the method to specify the type of control to add. The following table describes each of the parameters you can call with the Add method to create a new control. After you add the control, you reference the CommandBarControl properties to set the specific properties for the individual control. See the sections "Add Controls to a Toolbar" and "Add Items to a Menu" for more information on adding options to toolbars and menus.

## Existing Menus and Toolbars *(continued)*

| PARAMETER | DESCRIPTION |
|-----------|-------------|
| Type | An msoControlType constant value indicating the type of control to add. The five constant values include: msoControlButton for a standard button, msoControlEdit for an edit box, msoControlComboBox for a combo box, msoControlDropdown for a drop-down list, and msoControlPopup for another pop-up list of controls or a menu pop-up. |
| Id | An integer value specifying the built-in control to add to the command bar. If you omit this parameter, or specify a value of 1, Excel adds a blank control. |
| Parameter | Built-in controls use this parameter to pass information to Excel for running the command. |
| Before | An integer value specifying the position for the new control. You place the control before the specify control position. If you omit this parameter, Excel adds the control at the end of the command bar. |
| Temporary | Contains a Boolean value indicating whether the control is temporary. If the value of this parameter is True, the control is removed when Excel closes. |

## New Menus and Toolbars

You can create new menus and toolbars as a means of customizing Excel. To create a new menu or toolbar from a procedure, you must add a new CommandBar object to the CommandBars collection. You accomplish this with the Add method associated with the CommandBars collection with the code: CommandBars.Add.

When you utilize the Add method, Excel creates a new blank CommandBar. You can also use any of the optional parameters associated with the Add method to specify the settings for the command bar as you create it. The following table describes each of the four parameters that you can call with the Add method. See the sections "Create a Custom Toolbar" and "Create a Custom Menu" for more information on creating toolbars and menus.

| PARAMETER | DESCRIPTION |
|-----------|-------------|
| Name | Indicates the assigned name of the new command bar. If you omit this parameter, Excel assigns a default name of Custom 1 to the command bar. The number Excel associates with the name increments as you add more command bars. |
| Position | Determines the position and type of the command bar. You can specify any one of the MsoBarPosition constant values. Use msoBarLeft, msoBarTop, msoBarRight, or msoBarBottom to dock the toolbar at a specific location on the screen. Use msoBarFloating to create a floating toolbar or msoBarPopup to create a shortcut menu. |
| MenuBar | Contains a Boolean value, which indicates whether to replace the currently active menu bar with the new command bar. Typically the default value of False works best for this parameter. Specify a value of True to replace the active menu bar. |
| Temporary | Contains a Boolean value, which indicates whether the command bar is temporary. If the value of this parameter is True, Excel removes the toolbar when Excel closes. |

# Create a Custom Dialog Box

Y ou can create custom dialog boxes that you can use with any of your macros. Dialog boxes add a graphical user interface, which enables the user to execute tasks such as clicking buttons to indicate a desired selection, or typing appropriate values. When you use VBA to create macros, you also gain most Visual Basic features, including the ability to create custom dialog boxes. VBA refers to these custom dialog boxes as *Forms* or *UserForms*.

You create a custom dialog box within the Visual Basic Editor via the UserForm option. When you do this, the Visual Basic Editor creates a new UserForm called UserForm1 within the Forms folder on the Project window. See Chapter 2 for more information about the Projects window. Keep in mind, the Forms folder only displays if you have created UserForms for the current project.

You can change the name of a UserForm to make it easier to identify when you look at the UserForms listed in the Project window. To change the name of the UserForm, you need to change its Name property within the Properties window.

After you create the UserForm, you can design it using the various Toolbox controls, which only display when you select the UserForm window. You add controls to the UserForm by dragging them from the Toolbox to the appropriate location on the UserForm. For example, if you want to request a text value from the user, you drag the TextBox control onto the UserForm. After you add a control, you can resize it as needed. The Visual Basic Editor applies default values for each of the control properties. You can change the assigned values to the properties for the control within the Properties window. Keep in mind that you need to select the control on the UserForm before you can set the properties.

## Create a Custom Dialog Box

① In the Projects window, select the project where you want to add the new UserForm.

② Click Insert→UserForm.

The Visual Basic Editor creates a blank UserForm with a default name of UserForm1.

③ Type a new name for the UserForm in the Name field of the Properties window.

④ Click the UserForm.

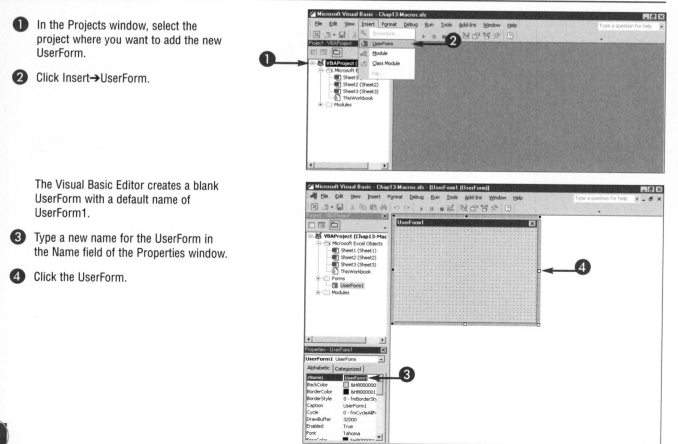

The Toolbox appears.

**5** Click a control in the Toolbox.

**6** Drag the control to the UserForm.

**7** In the Properties window, type a control name in the Name field.

Continue adding controls as desired.

**8** Click Run Sub/UserForm (▶).

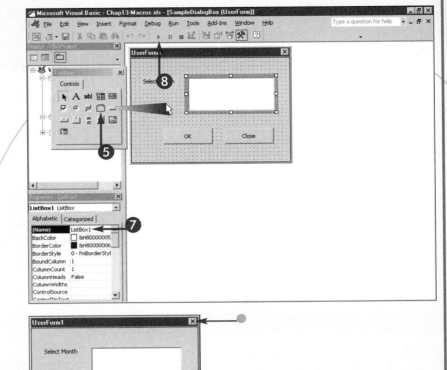

Excel displays the new dialog box.

● To return to the Visual Basic Editor, you can click the Close button (☒) on the dialog box.

## Extra

You can specify several properties for each control that you add to a UserForm. Although each control type has its own unique properties, most of the properties are common between all controls. You change the value of each control by either typing a new value or clicking ▼ and clicking a value from the drop-down list. The following table describes some of the common control properties.

| CONTROL PROPERTIES | DESCRIPTION |
| --- | --- |
| (Name) | Indicates the name of the control. |
| BackColor | Indicates the background color of the control. |
| Caption | Indicates the text that displays on the control, such as the button text. |
| Font | The font that displays all values on the control. |
| Height | The height of the control in pixels. |
| Text | The default text value of the control. |
| TextAlign | Indicates the way you align the text on the control. |
| Width | Indicates the width, in pixels, of the control. |

# Call a Custom Dialog Box from a Procedure

You can call and display any custom dialog boxes that are part of the same project as your procedure. You use custom dialog boxes to gather user input. For example, you can use the dialog box to request the values you need from the user to perform the appropriate calculations within a worksheet.

To display a custom dialog box, you use the Show method of the UserForm object. The Show method instructs Excel to display the specified UserForm. The Show method has only one optional parameter, as shown in the following code: UserForm1.Show modal.

The modal parameter determines whether the specified UserForm displays as a modal or modeless dialog box within Excel. The default value of vbModal makes the dialog box modal, which means that you must either close

or hide the dialog box before selecting any other options within Excel. When Excel opens a modal dialog box, all control is passed to that dialog box and you can only select options on the dialog box. A value of vbModeless means that although the dialog box remains open until a user closes it, a user can perform other program options.

You can close a dialog box in Excel via the Close button in the upper-right corner of the dialog box. You can also close it within your macro when you use the Unload method. Typically, all dialog boxes can contain a Close or Cancel button, which enables a user to close the dialog box. You must use the Click event for these CommandButton controls to create a procedure that calls the Unload method. See "Capture Input from a Custom Dialog Box" for more information about specifying code to run when a user clicks a button.

## Call a Custom Dialog Box from a Procedure

① Create a UserForm within the appropriate project.

**Note:** See the section "Create a Custom Dialog Box" for information on creating UserForms.

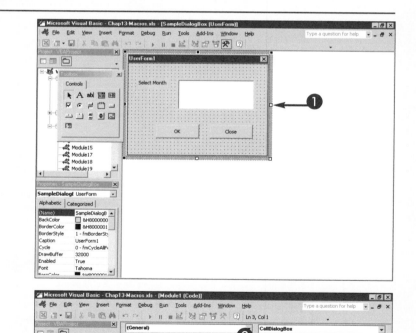

② Create a new subroutine.

**Note:** See Chapter 3 for information on creating subroutines.

③ Type **UserForm1.Show vbModal**, replacing `UserForm1` with the name of the UserForm and `vbModal` with `vbModeless` to make the dialog box modeless.

④ Switch to Excel and run the macro.

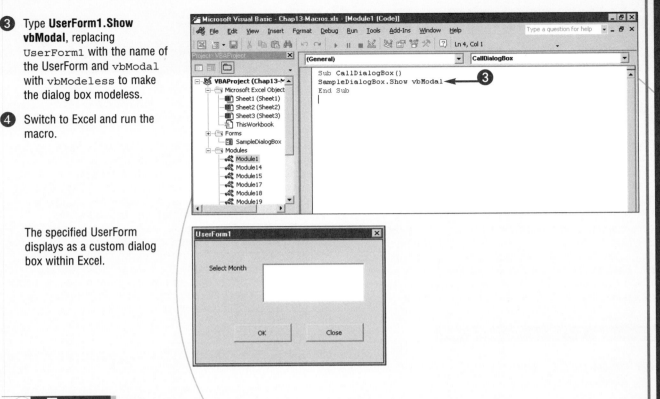

The specified UserForm displays as a custom dialog box within Excel.

---

## Extra

You can use the `Unload` statement to remove the UserForm from memory. When you call the statement, all controls on the UserForm are reset to the default values. Therefore, you cannot access the options specified by the user after the UserForm unloads from memory. To ensure that you can access the necessary values, you can either store the values in global variables or hide the UserForm until your procedure terminates. You either unload a UserForm by specifying the `Unload` statement followed by the name of the UserForm to unload, or with the shorter codes listed below.

**THIS CODE:**

```
Unload UserForm1
```

⬇

**IS EQUIVALENT TO:**

```
Unload Me
```

You can hide a UserForm so that it is no longer visible when called by a macro. To hide a UserForm, you can use the `Hide` method, which still allows you to access the form from your procedure.

**TYPE THIS:**

```
UserForm1.Hide
```

⬇

**RESULT:**

Excel hides the form.

Keep in mind that after hiding a form Excel may appear to freeze as your code continues to access the UserForm. This condition clears as soon as the code that accesses the UserForm finishes processing.

# Capture Input from a Custom Dialog Box

You typically use dialog boxes in Excel to gather input from the user. The input you capture from a user can be anything from determining which button was pressed to actual values typed by a user. You can capture the user input from the dialog box so you can return the appropriate responses by using the UserForm events. For example, when the user clicks an OK CommandButton control, you use a `CommandButton_Click` subroutine to indicate what steps to perform.

Excel considers every user interaction that occurs on a dialog box, such as scrolling through a list of items, selecting an OK button, or typing text in a text box, as an event. Each UserForm control has several different events that you can capture. The most common event that occurs is the `Click` event. This event occurs each time a user clicks a

control. To make code interact with the UserForm, you need to create procedures that execute when specific events occur.

Each UserForm you create has two elements: the graphical layout window and a code window. The graphical layout window is the location where you add controls that display on the dialog box. See the section "Create a Custom Dialog Box" for more information on designing custom dialog boxes. Each UserForm also has a code window that contains all UserForm-specific code and that you use to create the event procedures for each control. You can create event code for a specific control on the code window by double-clicking the control. By default, the Visual Basic Editor creates a `Click` event for the control when you click it. If a `Click` event already exists, the Visual Basic Editor simply displays the code window.

## Capture Input from a Custom Dialog Box

① Create a UserForm within the appropriate project.

**Note:** See the section "Create a Custom Dialog Box" for information on creating UserForms.

② On the Toolbox, click the ListBox control icon ($\boxed{\div}$).

③ Drag $\boxed{\div}$ to the UserForm.

④ Click the CommandButton control icon ($\boxed{\Box}$).

⑤ Drag $\boxed{\Box}$ to the UserForm.

⑥ In the Properties window, type **"OK"** as the Caption property value for the CommandButton Control.

The text on the CommandButton changes to reflect the value of the caption property.

⑦ Double-click the CommandButton object.

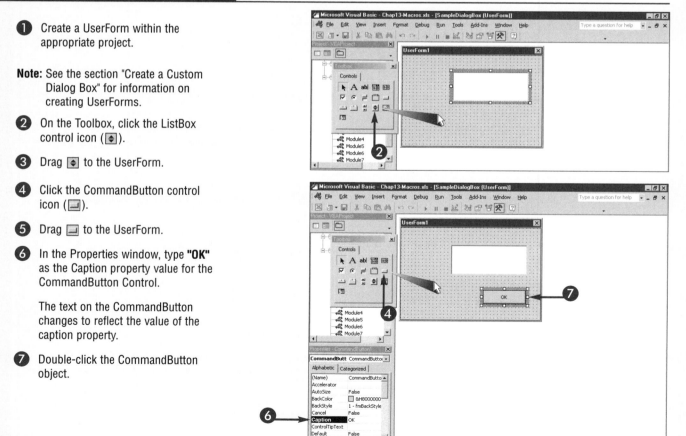

The code window for the UserForm displays.

- Excel creates a subroutine called `CommandButton1_Click()` on the code window.

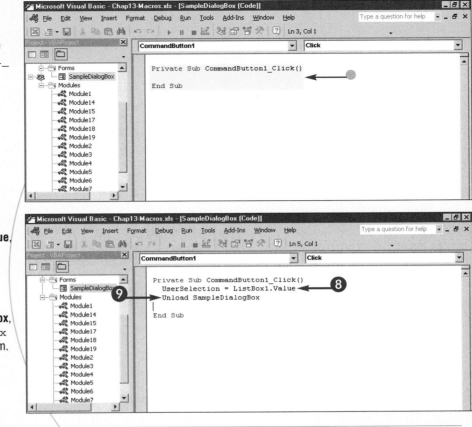

⑧ Type **UserSelection:=ListBox1.Value**, replacing `UserSelection` with the name of the global variable used to capture user input.

⑨ Type **Unload SampleDialogBox**, replacing `SampleDialogBox` with the name of the UserForm.

## Extra

The `Click` event occurs when the user clicks a control or a value in a control with the mouse button. For most controls you can write a procedure to handle the `Click` event, the most commonly captured event for dialog boxes, by simply placing the event name after the control name. All event-handling procedures require that you place an underscore character between the control name and the event name.

**Example:**
```
Sub CommandButton1_Click()
```

If you need to capture the `Click` event to determine the page or tab selected with a `MultiPage` or `TabStrip` control, the procedure also includes an index parameter value that specifies the index to the page or tab.

**Example:**
```
Sub MultiPage1_Click(1)
```

With the `MultiPage` and `TabStrip` controls, you need to create a separate procedure to handle the selection of each page or tab by using the corresponding index value.

Besides actually clicking a control with the mouse, a `Click` event also occurs when you press Enter and a control has focus, when you press the accelerator key that corresponds to the control, or when you press Spacebar and a CommandButton has focus.

continued →

You create code to monitor events caused by controls to determine when specific code should execute. Each control has its own specific events that you can capture, and the Visual Basic Editor keeps track of those for you. You can quickly create an event procedure on the code window by selecting the appropriate control name in the Object list box and then selecting the corresponding event from the Procedure list box. When you select an event, the Visual Basic Editor creates a procedure with the name of the control followed by the event name.

All control values on a UserForm are only active as long as you have the dialog box open. If you close the dialog box prior to saving user input values, you lose the user input.

To avoid any potential problems with lost data, consider saving user responses to global variables that can pass into other procedures. For example, you typically call a UserForm from another procedure to capture user responses and then pass the values back to the main procedure.

You must declare public variables at the top of your module, before any procedure code, using the `Public` statement. Doing so enables you to declare variables that all procedures within a project can access. See Chapter 3 for more information on declaring variables.

You can also use the `With` statement to shorten the code required to set properties for an object. See Chapter 4 for more information on using the `With` statement.

## Capture Input from a Custom Dialog Box *(continued)*

⑩ Create a new module.

**Note:** See Chapter 2 for information on creating modules.

⑪ Type **Public UserSelection As String**, replacing `UserSelection` with the name of the global variable.

⑫ Create a new subroutine.

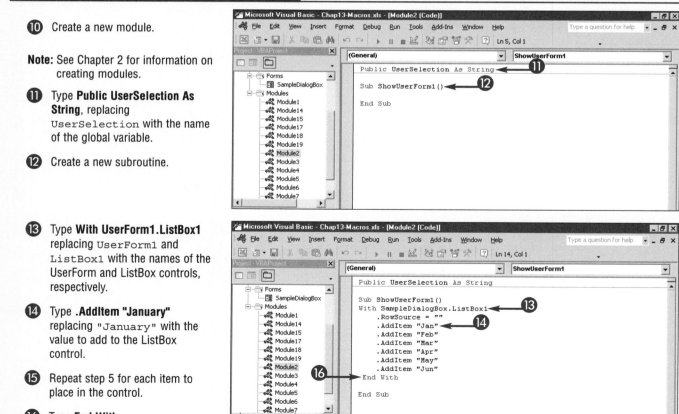

⑬ Type **With UserForm1.ListBox1** replacing `UserForm1` and `ListBox1` with the names of the UserForm and ListBox controls, respectively.

⑭ Type **.AddItem "January"** replacing `"January"` with the value to add to the ListBox control.

⑮ Repeat step 5 for each item to place in the control.

⑯ Type **End With**.

⑰ Type **SampleDialogBox**, replacing SampleDialogBox with the name of the UserForm.

⑱ Type additional VBA code to process the user selection value returned by the global variable.

⑲ Switch to Excel and run the macro.

**Note:** See Chapter 1 to run a macro.

The dialog box displays the list of values specified by the subroutine.

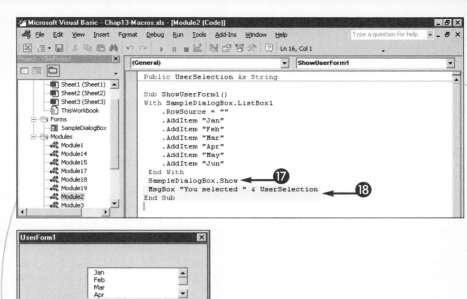

## Apply It

You capture control events to determine when to execute specific code. The following list identifies the most common events that occur with the various controls placed on UserForms. Not all events are available for each control. On the code window, check the Procedure list box to see the events associated with the selected control.

| CONTROL EVENTS | OCCURRENCE |
|---|---|
| BeforeDragOver | User is drag-and-dropping data onto a control. |
| BeforeUpdate | Before data on a control is changed. |
| Change | When the Value property of the control changes. |
| Click | When the user clicks the control with the mouse button. |
| DblClick | When the user clicks twice with the mouse on the control. |
| Enter | Before a control receives focus. |
| KeyDown | When the user presses a key. |
| MouseDown | When the user presses the mouse button. |

# Validate Input from a Dialog Box

You must validate the values specified for controls on a dialog box before passing the values back to your procedure. When you validate the data values, you do so for two major reasons. First, you ensure that the user specifies a value for a control. If the user forgets to select a control value, you can remind them immediately. Second, and probably most importantly, you ensure that errors do not occur in your code because the wrong type of data passes to a procedure.

You can create code that checks the user input for any event that occurs on the UserForm. The easiest place to do so is prior to closing the dialog box. For example, if you have a CommandButton control, such as an OK button, that passes the values to global variables and closes the dialog box, you may consider this the ideal place to validate your data. When you place the validation code in that routine, you need to use a conditional statement, such as an `If Then`

statement, to check the properties of each control. This ensures that they have the appropriate values. For example, if you want to make sure that the user typed a string in the Name text field on the dialog box, you can add the following `If Then` statement to your procedure: `If TextBox1.Text = " " Then`.

This `If Then` statement checks the `Text` property for the specified TextBox control and ensures that it contains a value. If the property is empty (there is nothing in it), your VBA code can call the `MsgBox` function to display a message indicating that a value must be specified.

Besides checking for values, you can also use the VBA validation functions to verify that the control contains the appropriate data type. For example, the statement `If Not IsNumeric(TextBox1.Value)` Then ensures that the user typed a number in a TextBox control.

---

### Validate Input from a Dialog Box

① On the UserForm, double-click the control that you want to validate the data values.

Typically an OK command button is a good location for validating data values.

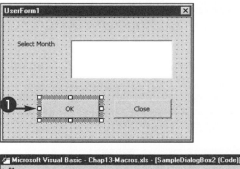

● The code window opens with the cursor at the beginning of the `Click` procedure for the selected control.

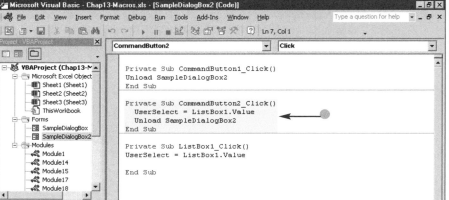

② Type **If ListBox1.ListIndex = -1 Then**, replacing `ListBox1.ListIndex = -1` with the control and property value to check.

③ Type **MsgBox "Select a value"** replacing `"Select a value"` with the text for the `MsgBox`.

④ Type **Exit Sub**.

⑤ Type **End If**.

⑥ Switch to Excel and run the macro.

- The Message Box displays if a value is not selected for the control.

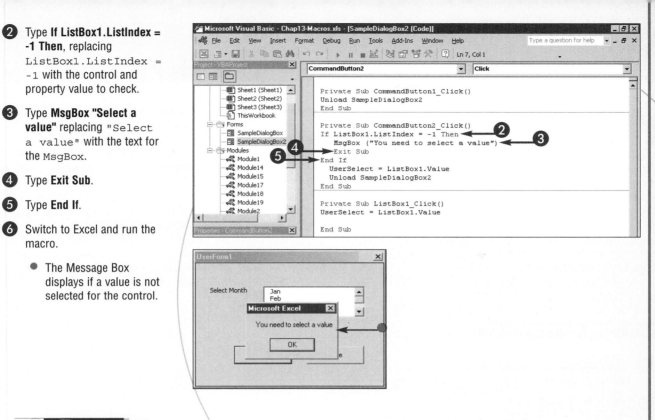

## Extra

You can use the UserForm events to launch validation code, as shown in the following code that captures the QueryClose event to ensure a value was selected for a ListBox control prior to the dialog box closing.

**Example:**
```
Private Sub UserForm_QueryClose(Cancel As
Integer, CloseMode As Integer)
If Not IsNumeric(TextBox1.Value) Then
      MsgBox "Must be a number"
      Cancel = 1
 End If
```

The QueryClose event has two arguments, Cancel and CloseMode. The Cancel argument accepts an integer value. If the value of the argument is anything other than zero, the QueryClose event stops and the associated dialog box remains open. The CloseMode argument contains a constant value indicating the cause of the QueryClose event, as shown in the following table.

| CONSTANT | VALUE | DESCRIPTION |
|----------|-------|-------------|
| vbFormControlMenu | 0 | User selected the Close button on the dialog box. |
| vbFormCode | 1 | The code initiated an Unload statement. |
| vbAppWindows | 2 | The Windows operating session is ending. |
| vbAppTaskManager | 3 | The Windows Task Manager is closing Excel. |

# Create Custom UserForm Controls

Y ou can customize the Toolbox window to suit your needs. The Toolbox that displays when you select a UserForm within the Visual Basic Editor contains all of the standard controls you can add to the UserForm. These controls display on a single tabbed page called Controls. You can change the icon that a control uses as well as the tip text that displays when you drag your cursor across the icon. You can also create new controls to add to the Toolbox.

Making modifications to existing Toolbox controls is fairly straightforward. To modify an existing control, you access the Customize Control dialog box, which enables you to change the text and load a new icon.

You create new controls by customizing and combining the existing controls on the Toolbox. For example, if you always add an OK button to all of your UserForms, you can create

a custom button and set the appropriate properties such as the Caption, Width, Height, and Default. After you create the button, you place it on the Toolbox and the Visual Basic Editor adds it as a new control. After you add your new button to the Toolbox, you can select the Customize Control option and change its name and icon.

Alternately, you can create new controls by combining multiple controls. For example, you can create a new control that consists of both an OK and a Cancel button.

To keep your custom controls separate from the existing controls on the Toolbox, consider adding a new page to the Toolbox for your controls. You create a new page on the Toolbox using the New Page option.

## Create Custom UserForm Controls

① On the ToolBox, click the control you want to customize.

② Drag it to the UserForm.

③ On the Properties window, type the control name in the (Name) field.

④ Type the text for the control in the Caption field.

⑤ On the ToolBox, right-click the Controls tab.

A menu displays the options available for the pages in the Toolbox.

⑥ Click New Page.

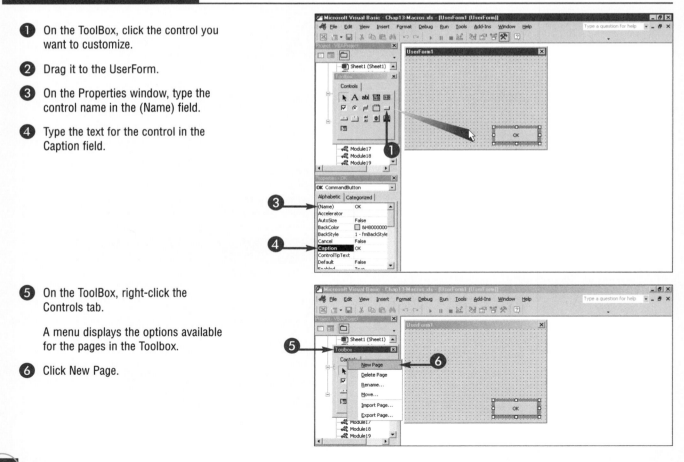

The Visual Basic Editor adds a new page to the ToolBox.

⑦ Click the control on the UserForm.

Drag the control to the ToolBox.

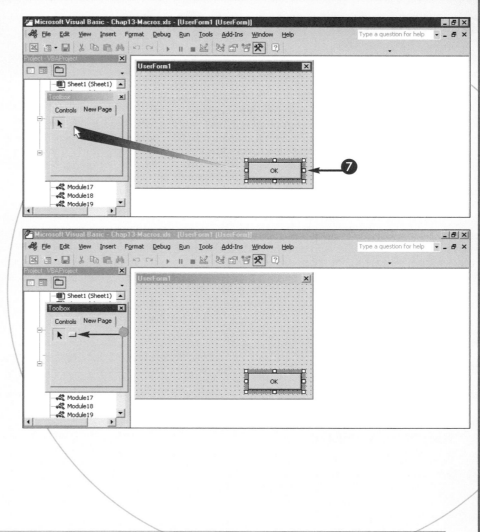

● The new control appears on the new page of the ToolBox.

You can customize the name of the new control by right-clicking the control icon and clicking the control's Customizing option.

## Apply It

When you create your new page on the Toolbox, the Visual Basic Editor adds it as the second page on the Toolbox. To change the order of the pages, you can right-click the page tab and click the Move option on the menu. Selecting this option displays the Move dialog box. To change the order of pages, click the desired page to select it, and click ▲ or ▼ to indicate the direction you want to move the page.

Creating a separate page on the Toolbox to store your custom controls enables you to export the page for loading on another machine. To export the page of custom controls, right-click the page tab and click the Export Page option. In the Export Page dialog box, specify the name and location for the page file. The Visual Basics Editor assigns the page file an extension of .Pag indicating that it is a Toolbox page file.

You import a page file into the Toolbox by right-clicking the tab menu and clicking the Import Page option. In the Import Page dialog box, specify the name and location of the page file to import.

# Create a
# UserForm Template

I f you find that you are consistently creating the same type UserForm for displaying custom dialog boxes with your macros, you can create a UserForm template file to save time and effort. When you create UserForms, the Visual Basic Editor attaches them to the project where you create them. Each time you create a new project you need to re-create the UserForm or copy it from another project using the Project window. See Chapter 2 for more information on working with the Project window.

When you create a UserForm template, you design a basic UserForm and save it to a file. You can then add the form to any other project you create. You can save a UserForm to a file via the Export File command on the File menu. This displays the Export File dialog box where you specify the name and location for saving the form file. You may

consider creating a folder that you can use for saving any common Excel project files.

When you create a UserForm for use as a template, consider keeping it fairly generic so that you can customize it for each new project. For example, if you frequently create a UserForm with a TextBox control for gathering user input and two CommandButton controls, OK and Cancel, you can create a generic version with the three controls. However, if you do not place the Label control for the text box on the template version, you can import the form and customize it for the type of data you want to gather from the user.

You add a UserForm template to a project by using the Import option. When you import a UserForm into your project, the Visual Basic Editor creates a new UserForm and assigns it the next sequential name.

## Create a UserForm Template

### CREATE A NEW FORM

①  Create a new UserForm.

**Note:** See the section "Create a Custom Dialog Box" for more information on creating UserForms.

②  Click File→Export File

The Export File dialog box displays.

③  Click ▣ and click the location where you want to save the UserForm in the Save in list box.

④  Type the form file name in the File Name field.

⑤  Click Save.

## IMPORT A USERFORM TEMPLATE

 In the Project window, click the project where you want to add the UserForm.

② Click File→Import File.

The Import File dialog box displays.

③ Click the file containing the UserForm.

④ Click Open.

The Visual Basic Editor adds the selected UserForm to the current project.

### Extra

You can specify the order that Excel uses to move between controls on the UserForm by setting the controls' tab order on the UserForm. The tab order indicates the order in which the Visual Basic Editor selects the controls when a user presses the Tab key. By default, the tab order is the order in which you added the control to the UserForm.

Each control has two properties that deal with the tab order. The first property, `TabStop`, determines whether focus stops on the control when the user presses the Tab key. If you set the property to `False` for the control, tabbing through controls on the dialog box skips over the control.

The other property, `TabIndex`, specifies a value between 0 and the number of controls indicating the tab order for the control.

You can set the tab order for the entire list of the controls on the form via the Tab Order dialog box. This dialog box displays when you right-click the UserForm and click the Tab Order option. You can change the order of the controls by clicking a control and then clicking ▲ or ▼.

# Create a Custom Toolbar

Y ou can design a VBA procedure to create new toolbars within Excel where you can place links to the custom macros you create. You create a new toolbar by adding a new `CommandBar` object to the `CommandBars` object collection. Excel comes with approximately 30 different built-in toolbars, to which you can add controls. By creating new toolbars to house your custom toolbar options, you do not affect the layout of the standard toolbars.

You can create a new toolbar by using the `Add` method associated with the `CommandBars` collection. Although the `Add` method has four different parameters, they are all optional. You should specify a name for the new toolbar using the `Name` parameter. Also, indicate the location where you want to place the toolbar in the window using the `Position` parameter values. If you want the CommandBar you create to replace the current menu bar, specify a value

of `True` for the `MenuBar` parameter. If you only want the toolbar to display after running the associated procedure, set the value of the `Temporary` parameter to `True`. If you create a temporary toolbar, it is deleted when you close Excel. To launch the toolbar again, you need to rerun the associated procedure. See the section "Working with CommandBars" for more information about the `Add` method properties.

Adding a new toolbar with the `Add` method creates a new blank toolbar that is not visible in Excel. To make it visible, you set the `Visible` property associated with the toolbar to `True`. In fact, you can use this property at any time to switch between having a visible and invisible toolbar.

After you create the toolbar, you need to use the various properties associated with the `CommandBar` object to customize the location, protection, size, and visibility.

## Create a Custom Toolbar

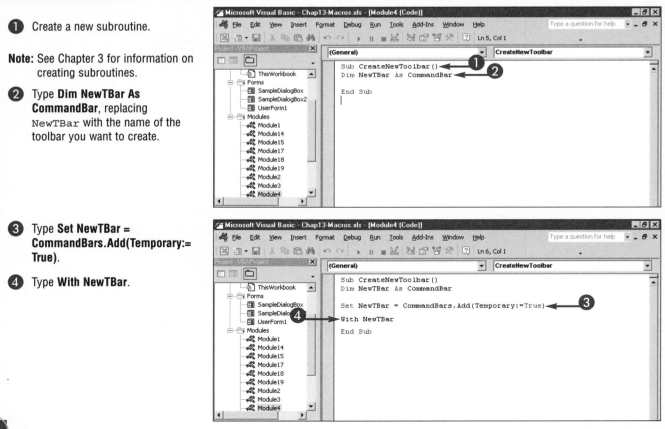

① Create a new subroutine.

**Note:** See Chapter 3 for information on creating subroutines.

② Type **Dim NewTBar As CommandBar**, replacing `NewTBar` with the name of the toolbar you want to create.

③ Type **Set NewTBar = CommandBars.Add(Temporary:= True)**.

④ Type **With NewTBar**.

Type **.Name = "MyToolbar"** replacing **"MyToolbar"** with the name of the new toolbar.

⑥ Type **.Position = msoBarFloating** replacing **msoBarFloating** with the **MsoControlType** constant value.

⑦ Type **.Visible = True**.

⑧ Type **End With**.

**Note:** See Chapter 4 for more information on using the **End With** statement with objects.

⑨ Switch to Excel and run the macro.

Excel creates the new toolbar and displays it on the window.

## Extra

If you attempt to create a custom toolbar with the same name as an existing toolbar, Excel returns an error message. To avoid these errors, you can add code to your procedure that checks for the existence of a CommandBar object with the same Name parameter as your new one. The following code checks to see if a toolbar named "MyToolbar" exists.

**Example:**
```
For Each CB In CommandBars
    If CB.Name = "MyToolbar" Then
        TBFound = "True"
    End If
Next
```

This code uses the For Each Next statement to cycle through each CommandBar object in the CommandBars collection to determine if any of the existing CommandBar objects have a Name property value of "MyToolbar". If Excel encounters a match, the TBFound variable is set to a value of True. If you see that the value of the TBFound variable is False, you can add the new toolbar. See Chapter 6 for more information on working with For Each Next statements.

# Add Controls to a Toolbar

You can add controls to a toolbar that correspond to VBA macro code or any other Excel commands that you want to execute when selecting that toolbar control. You can add controls to any toolbar available within Excel. You can add existing Excel controls to the toolbar, or you can add new controls. When you add a new control to a toolbar, you can specify the icon image to represent the control along with the tool tip text, which displays when you drag the cursor across the control. You add a new control by specifying the toolbar where you want to add the control followed by the `Add` method.

When you reference specific `CommandBar` objects within the `CommandBars` collection, you need to use the `Controls` property to return the collection of objects. When you use the `Add` method without any parameters, Excel places a

blank control on the toolbar. See the section "Working with CommandBars" for more information about the parameters available with the `Add` method. If you add an existing control to the toolbar, you can specify the ID of the control using the `Id` parameter.

When you add a control to a toolbar, you use the properties associated with the CommandBarControl Object to customize your control. If you did not assign an existing Excel command to the control, you need to indicate the action to perform when a user selects the control. You do this by specifying the name of the VBA procedure to run using the `OnAction` property.

To make the toolbar control easy to recognize, you must assign it a button image using the `FaceID` property. You can specify an image value between 0 and 3499.

## Add Controls to a Toolbar

① Create a new subroutine.

② Type **Dim CBar As CommandBar**, replacing CBar with the toolbar variable.

③ Type **Dim NewControl As CommandBarControl**, replacing NewControl with the toolbar button variable.

④ Type **Set CBar = CommandBars("MyToolbar")** replacing "MyToolbar" with the name of the toolbar.

⑤ Type **Set NewControl = CBar.Controls.Add(Type:=msoControlButton)**.

⑥ Type **With NewControl**.

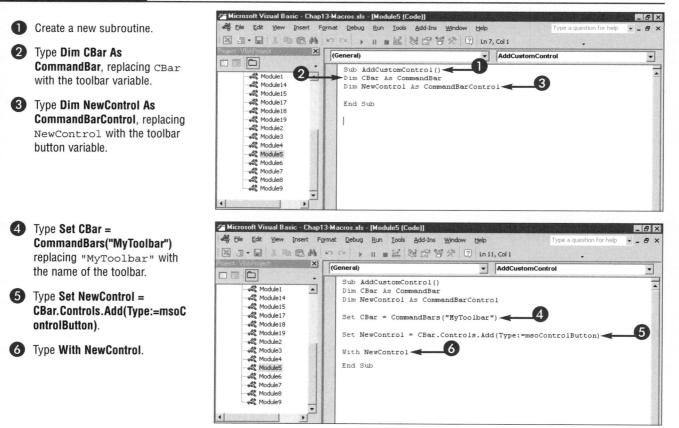

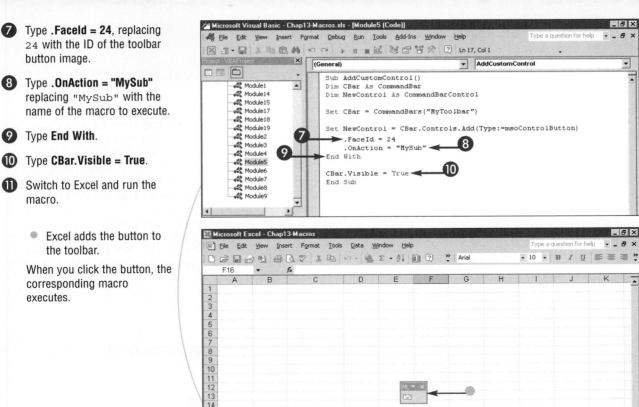

**7** Type **.FaceId = 24**, replacing 24 with the ID of the toolbar button image.

**8** Type **.OnAction = "MySub"** replacing "MySub" with the name of the macro to execute.

**9** Type **End With**.

**10** Type **CBar.Visible = True**.

**11** Switch to Excel and run the macro.

● Excel adds the button to the toolbar.

When you click the button, the corresponding macro executes.

## Apply It

When you add an existing control to a toolbar, you need to know the ID of the control to add it. You specify the control ID as the value for the `ID` property. Unfortunately, Microsoft does not provide a list of the controls within Excel. The fastest method for determining control IDs is to create a procedure that determines the IDs of the controls used on each command bar.

**TYPE THIS:**

```
Sub GetControlID()
Dim RowId As Integer
Dim CB As CommandBar
Dim CBC As CommandBarControl
RowId = 1
For Each CB In CommandBars
    Cells(RowId, 1) = CB.Name
    For Each CBC In CommandBars(CB.Name).Controls
        Cells(RowId, 2) = CBC.ID
        Cells(RowId, 3) = CBC.Caption
        RowId = RowId + 1
    Next
 Next
End Sub
```

**RESULT:**

The subroutine looks at each command bar in the `CommandBars` object and returns the name of the command bar along with a list of the control names and IDs on that particular command bar.

# Create a
# Custom Menu

Excel enables you to add custom menus to house links to VBA macros or other commonly used Excel commands. You can design a VBA procedure to create new menus that display within Excel. Typically you place most menus on the active menu bar. The active menu bar in Excel is the first object in the CommandBars collection. All menus you add become CommandBarControls on the active menu bar.

You can create a new Excel menu with the Add method associated with the CommandBarControls collection. Although the Add method has five different parameters — Type, Id, Parameter, Before, and Temporary — they are all optional. When creating a new menu, you only need to use the Type and Before parameters. You must specify a value of msoControlPopup for the Type parameter to

create a new menu. You use the Before parameter to indicate where on the menu bar to place the new menu. You do this by specifying the index value of the menu in front of which you want to place the new menu.

After you create the menu, you can set several different properties for the menu. The most commonly set property is the Caption property. The Caption property contains the display value for the menu on the menu bar. If you look at Excel menus, you see that most of them have a shortcut key that displays the menu when you click Alt and the key simultaneously. Excel identifies the shortcut key on a menu by underlining the appropriate character in the menu name. You can specify the shortcut key as part of the Caption property value by placing the & in front of the appropriate character.

## Create a Custom Menu

① Create a new subroutine.

② Type **Dim NewMenu As CommandBarControl**, replacing NewMenu with the variable for the new menu.

③ Type **Dim ExcelMenu As CommandBarControl** replacing ExcelMenu with the variable used to cycle through the menus.

④ Type **Dim Count As Integer** replacing Count with the variable that counts menus.

⑤ Type **For Each ExcelMenu In CommandBars(1).Controls**.

⑥ Type **Count = Count + 1**.

⑦ Type **Next**.

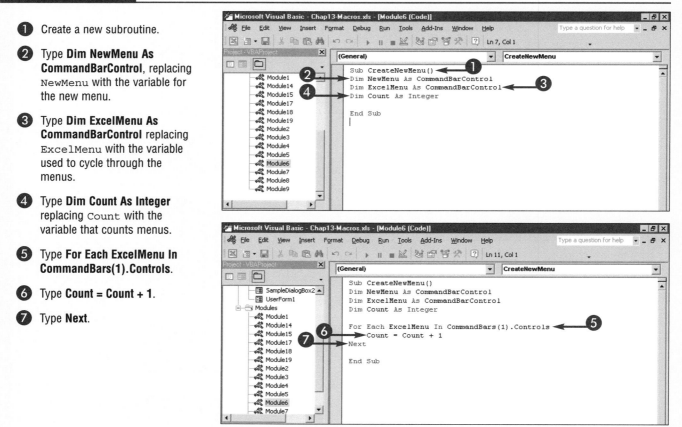

**8** Type **Set NewMenu = CommandBars(1).Controls. Add _**.

**9** Type **Type:=msoControlPopup**.

**10** Type **before:=CommandBars(1). Controls(Count).Index**.

**11** Type **NewMenu.Caption = "&Macros"** replacing "&Macros" with the name for the menu.

**12** Switch to Excel and run the macro.

● Excel creates the new menu.

```vba
Sub CreateNewMenu()
Dim NewMenu As CommandBarControl
Dim ExcelMenu As CommandBarControl
Dim Count As Integer

For Each ExcelMenu In CommandBars(1).Controls
    Count = Count + 1
Next

Set NewMenu = CommandBars(1).Controls.Add
(Type:=msoControlPopup, before:=CommandBars(1).Controls(Count).Index)

NewMenu.Caption = "&Macros"

End Sub
```

## Extra

When adding new menus to the active menu bar using the Before parameter, you need to specify an index value of an existing menu. If you do not specify a value for the Before parameter, Excel adds the new menu to the end of the active menu bar. The sample code for this section uses the For Each looping statement to count the number of menus on the active menu bar and then places the new menu before the last menu.

Another way to specify an index value involves using the FindControl method to locate the desired menu and then using the index value to specify where to place the new menu. With this method, you specify the ID setting for the menu. The example locates the Insert menu, which has an ID of 30005. The table lists the Excel built-in menus ID values.

| MENU | ID |
|------|------|
| File | 30002 |
| Edit | 30003 |
| View | 30004 |
| Insert | 30005 |
| Format | 30006 |
| Tools | 30007 |
| Data | 30011 |
| Chart | 30022 |
| Window | 30009 |
| Help | 30010 |

**Example:**
```vba
MenuIndex =
CommandBars(1).FindControl(id:=30005).Index
```

# Add Items to a Menu

You can place macros and other Excel commands that you use frequently on menus. You can place additional menu items to both existing and custom menus by adding a new `CommandButtonControl` object. Because the menu to which you add the menu item is also a `CommandButtonControl` object, the difference between the two controls is the value of the `Type` parameter. The menu has a Type parameter value of `msoControlPopup`, and the menu item has a value of `msoControlButton`. See the section "Create a Custom Menu" for more information on creating menus.

You create a menu item using the `Add` method associated with the `CommandBarControls` collection. When you call the `Add` method, the only parameter you need to use is the `Type` parameter with a value of `msoControlButton`.

You can set several different properties with the menu item. The main properties you need to set are the `Caption` and the `OnAction` properties. The `Caption` property contains

the display value for the menu item. You can also set the shortcut key that executes the menu item when you press the Alt key and the shortcut key simultaneously. Excel identifies the shortcut key on a menu by underlining the appropriate character in the menu item name. You can specify the shortcut key as part of the `Caption` property value by placing the `&` in front of the appropriate character.

The `OnAction` property specifies the macro to execute when a user clicks a menu item. To specify a macro, place the macro name in quotes. Remember that if you do not have the workbook containing the macro open when you click the menu item, Excel cannot find the specified macro. To avoid this situation, consider placing the macro in the Personal Macro Workbook. See Chapter 1 for more information on the Personal Macro Workbook.

## Add Items to a Menu

① Create a new subroutine.

② Type **Dim UseMenu As CommandBarControl**, replacing `UseMenu` with the menu variable.

③ Type **Dim NewMenuItem As CommandBarControl** replacing `NewMenuItem` with the menu item variable.

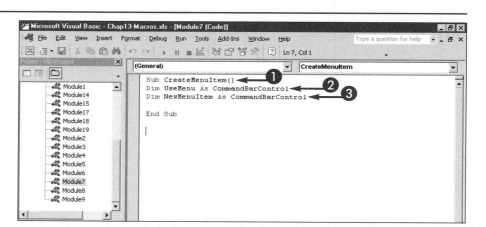

④ Type **Set UseMenu = CommandBars(1).Controls ("Macros")**, replacing `"Macros"` with the name of the menu.

⑤ Type **Set NewMenuItem = UseMenu.Controls.Add(Type:= msoControlButton)**.

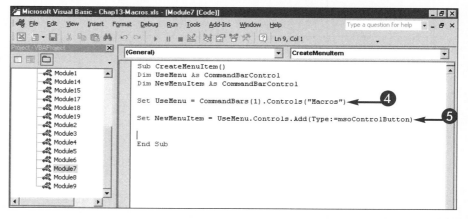

⑥ Type **With NewMenuItem**.

⑦ Type **.Caption = "Message &Box"**, replacing `"Message &Box"` with the caption for the menu item.

⑧ Type **.OnAction = "MySub"**, replacing `"MySub"` with the name of the macro to execute.

⑨ Type **End With**.

⑩ Switch to Excel and run the macro.

● Excel adds the menu item to the specified menu.

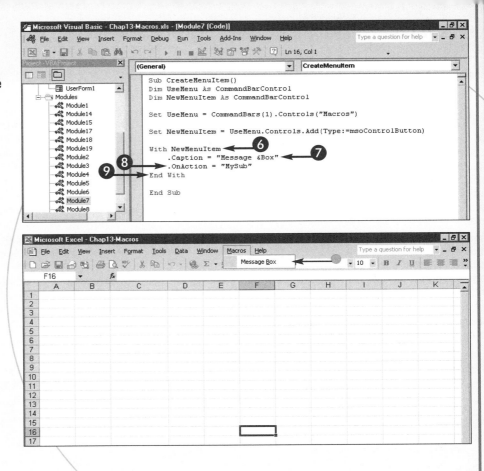

## Apply It

You can create submenus on a menu to organize commands. For example, you can create a Macro menu to group common macros together. You create submenus by adding a new `CommandBarControl` object with the type `msoControlPopup` to the main menu. You can then add new menu items to the submenu using code similar to that dealing with the `SubMenuItem` object.

### TYPE THIS:

```
Sub CreateSubMenu()
Dim MainMenu As CommandBarControl
Dim SubMenu As CommandBarControl
Dim SubMenuItem As CommandBarControl
Set MainMenu = CommandBars(1).Controls("Macros")
Set SubMenu = MainMenu.Controls.Add(Type:=msoControlPopup)
SubMenu.Caption = "&Budget"
Set SubMenuItem = SubMenu.Controls.Add(Type:=msoControlButton)
With SubMenuItem
          .Caption = "Sum Expenses"
          .OnAction = "SumExp"
End With
End Sub
```

### RESULT:

The code determines the menu where you want to place the submenu and assigns it to a `CommandBarControl` object. Next, the subroutine creates the submenu and sets the value of the `Caption` property.

251

# Create a Shortcut Menu

You can create a shortcut menu that displays when a user performs a specific action that contains commands related to VBA macro and Excel commands. A *shortcut menu* is a pop-up menu that displays when you right-click a particular location within Excel. You can create new shortcut menus or modify existing Excel shortcut menus, and you perform all shortcut menu creation and modification within the Visual Basic Editor.

A shortcut menu is similar to a toolbar in that both are actually CommandBar objects, but each has different controls. Typically a toolbar only contains icons whereas a shortcut menu can contain a combination of text descriptions and icons.

You can create a new shortcut menu by using the Add method associated with the CommandBars collection. Although the Add method has four different parameters — Name,

Position, MenuBar, and Temporary — they are all optional. You specify a name for the new shortcut menu using the Name parameter. You assign a value of msoBarPopup to the Position parameter to create a pop-up menu. If you only want the toolbar to display after running the associated procedure, use the Temporary parameter.

See the section "Working with CommandBars" for more information about the Add method properties.

After creating the shortcut menu, you need to add menu items. To do this, you create a menu item by using the Add method associated with the CommandBarControls collection. With the Add method, you use the Type parameter with a value of msoControlButton.

See the section "Add Items to a Menu" for more information about adding items to a menu and setting the menu item properties.

## Create a Shortcut Menu

① Create a new subroutine.

② Type **Dim SC As CommandBar**, replacing SC with the menu variable.

③ Type **Dim SItem1 As CommandBarControl**, replacing SItem1 with the first menu item variable.

④ Type **Dim SItem2 As CommandBarControl** replacing SItem2 with the second menu item variable.

⑤ Type **Set SC = CommandBars.Add(Name:="Test Bar", Position:=msoBarPopup)**, replacing "TestBar" with the name for the shortcut menu.

⑥ Type **Set SItem1 = SC.Controls.Add(Type:= msoControlButton)**.

⑦ Type **With SItem1**.

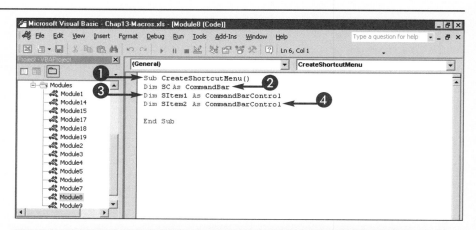

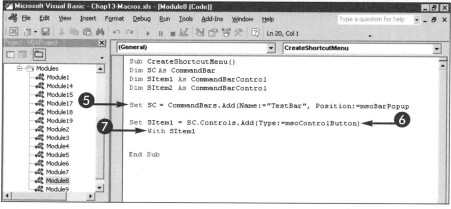

8 Type **.Caption = "Bold Range"** replacing "Bold Range" with the menu item caption.

9 Type **.OnAction = "BoldRange"** replacing "BoldRange" with the name of the macro to launch.

10 Type **End With**.

Repeat steps 6 to10 for each menu item.

11 Switch to Excel and run the macro.

● The shortcut menu displays for the appropriate event.

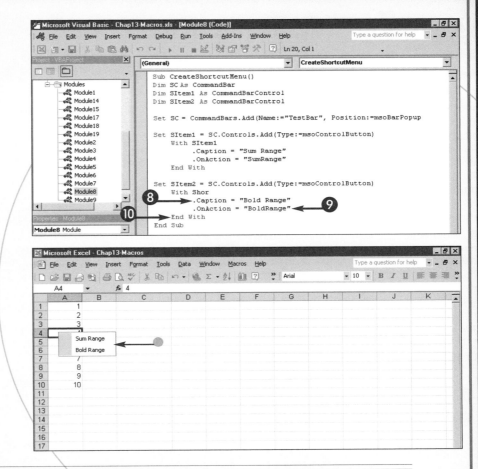

## Apply It

After you create the shortcut menu, you need to specify the code that tells Excel when to display it. Typically Excel displays shortcut menus when a particular event takes place, such as right-clicking a cell in a worksheet. Although you can use any of the Excel events to trigger the display of a shortcut menu, Excel requires you to place the code either in the `ThisWorkbook Object` code module or in a specific worksheet module. See Chapter 15 for more information on working with Excel events.

The code launches the shortcut menu if you click a cell in the range of A1:A10.

**TYPE THIS:**

```
Private Sub Worksheet_BeforeRightClick(ByVal Target As Range, Cancel As Boolean)

    If Not Intersect(Target, Range("a1:a10")) Is Nothing Then
            CommandBars("Shortcut").ShowPopup
    End If
End Sub
```

**RESULT:**

The subroutine uses the `Intersect` method to determine if the clicked cell is part of the target range of A1:A10. If you click a cell in the target range, the TestBar shortcut menu displays.

# Delete Custom Toolbars and Shortcut Menus

You can delete any of the custom toolbar or shortcut menus you no longer need to keep them current. Because all toolbars and shortcut menus are `CommandBar` objects, to delete one, you need to remove the associated object. Excel does not allow you to delete the built-in `CommandBar` objects. When you delete a custom `CommandBar` object, you can no longer access it within Excel. If you want to use the toolbar or shortcut menu again, you need to run the corresponding macro to re-create it.

One of the most important reasons for deleting a `CommandBar` object is to allow you to reload it. You generally reload when you make changes to the `CommandBar` object and want to reflect these changes in the currently loaded `CommandBar` object. Excel does not allow you to load a `CommandBar` object with the same name as an existing object. Therefore, if you decide to modify a menu or toolbar, you need to delete the existing version to load the new one.

You remove a custom `CommandBar` object using the `Delete` method associated with the object. To use this method, you simply indicate the `CommandBar` object to delete followed by the `Delete` method. For example, to delete a toolbar named TestBar, you would type **CommandBar("TestBar").Delete**.

Excel returns an error if you attempt to remove a built-in toolbar or menu. You can make sure a menu or toolbar is custom by looking at the value of the `BuiltIn` property for the CommandBar control. If the `BuiltIn` property has a value of `True`, the associated CommandBar control is one of the standard ones that comes with Excel, and you cannot delete it.

You can create a procedure that removes all of the custom toolbars and shortcut menus you have created by checking the value of the `BuiltIn` property. All custom menus and toolbars have a `BuiltIn` property value of `False`.

## Delete Custom Toolbars and Shortcut Menus

**①** Create a new subroutine.

**②** Type **Dim CBar As CommandBar**, replacing CBar with the command bar variable.

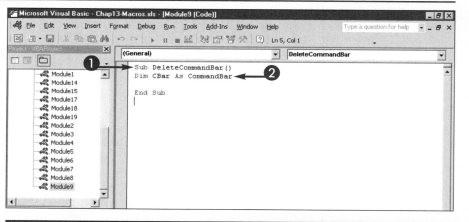

**③** Type **For Each CBar in CommandBars**.

**④** Type **If CBar.BuiltIn = False Then**.

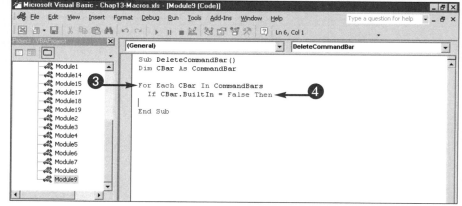

**⑤** Type **CBar.Delete**.

**⑥** Type **End If**.

**⑦** Type **Next**.

**⑧** Switch to Excel and run the macro.

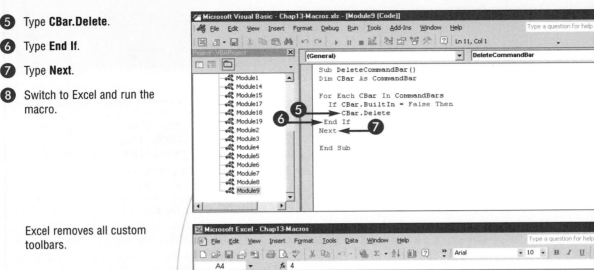

Excel removes all custom toolbars.

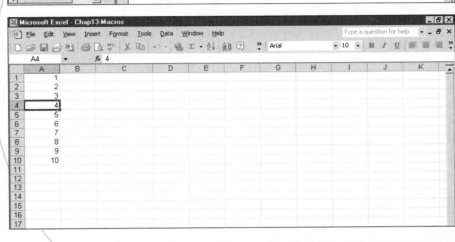

## Extra

You can also modify toolbars and menus from within Excel by clicking Tools→Customize. To prevent a user from modifying a menu or toolbar within Excel, you can set the msoBarProtection constant value for the Protection property. The example shows code that protects a toolbar so that a user cannot add or remove buttons. You can specify the constant values using the table.

**Example:**
```
CommandBars("MacroToolbar").Protection =
msoBarNoCustomize
```

| CONSTANT | DESCRIPTION |
|----------|-------------|
| msoBarNoChangeDock | Cannot change docking of command bar. |
| msoBarNoChange Visible | Cannot change Visible property. |
| msoBarNoCustomize | Cannot add or remove buttons. |
| msoBarNoHorizontal Dock | Cannot dock on left or right side of window. |
| msoBarNoMove | Cannot move command bar object. |
| msoBarNoProtection | Removes all protection. |
| msoBarNoResize | Cannot resize command bar object. |
| msoBarNoVerticalDock | Cannot dock on top or bottom of window. |

# Chart Basics

You can use Excel charts to create a graphical representation of data within a workbook and to illustrate specific relationships between the selected data values. Excel provides several different types of charts, and you can customize the attributes of each chart type for your data.

Excel maintains all charts as `Chart` objects within the Excel Object Model. Although seemingly straight forward, you may find working with the `Chart` object initially overwhelming both due to the number of other objects it contains, and because your interaction with it largely depends on the type of chart or worksheet you have.

## Chart Sheets

*Chart sheets* are actually separate sheets within the Workbook. As you add chart sheets to a workbook, a separate page tab displays at the bottom of the Excel window, similar to the Sheet tabs. By default, Excel names each chart sheet Chart1, Chart2, and so on. But, just like a worksheet, you can change the name of the Chart Sheet.

Excel stores all chart sheets as `Chart` objects, which are children of the corresponding `Workbook` object. Each `Chart` object has several different child objects that represent the

various elements of the chart. For example, the `ChartTitle` object represents the title for the chart. You can change the text displayed, font used, font characteristics (bold, italics, and so on), border, and color of the chart title by using the different properties, methods, and child objects associated with the `ChartTitle` object.

## Embedded Charts

When you place a chart on a worksheet you create an *embedded* chart. By having the chart embedded on the worksheet you can easily view the chart and worksheet data simultaneously. Also, by using embedded charts, you can place multiple charts on one worksheet. Because the embedded chart resides on a worksheet, you must access that particular worksheet to modify a chart. Remember, each sheet in a workbook is a separate object, such as a `Worksheet` object or `Chart` object. However, because an embedded chart resides entirely within a particular worksheet, the chart becomes a

child to a `Worksheet` object. Actually the `Worksheet` object contains a `ChartObject` collection object, which contains all `Chart` objects within the single worksheet.

Although at first glance an embedded chart appears more complex because of the extra objects involved, when you access the chart object on the Worksheet, it contains the same child objects, properties, and methods as a Chart sheet. For example, you use the `Legend` object to make modifications to the legend for the embedded chart.

## Chart Object Children Objects

The complexity of the `Chart` object stems from the fact that it contains so many child objects, which represent the different components that make up the chart. Each of these objects has its own properties and methods necessary for making

modifications to the object, and some even have their own child objects. The following table describes each of the child objects for the `Chart` object.

## Chart Object Children Objects *(continued)*

| OBJECT | DESCRIPTION |
|--------|-------------|
| Axes Collection | Collection of the Axis objects including `AxisTitle`, `Border`, `Gridlines`, and `TickLabels` objects. |
| ChartArea | Chart area including the `Border`, `Font`, and `Interior` objects. |
| ChartGroups Collection | Collection of `ChartGroup` objects representing each group of data on the chart. |
| ChartObjects Collection | Collection of the `Chart` objects on the sheet. |
| ChartTitle | Represents the chart title. Includes `Border`, `Characters`, `Font`, and `Interior` objects. |
| Corners | Represents the corners of a 3-D chart. |
| DataTable | Represents the chart data table. Includes a `Border` object. |
| Floor | Represents the floor of a 3-D chart. Includes `Border` and `Interior` objects. |
| Hyperlinks Collection | Contains one `Hyperlink` object for each hyperlink in the range of data. |
| Legend | Represents the legend of the chart. Includes `Font`, `Border`, `Interior`, and `LegendEntries` objects. |
| OLEObjects Collection | Collection of `OLEObjects` in the sheet. Includes `Border` and `Interior` objects. |
| PageSetup | Contains the page setup information including margin settings, paper size, and so on. |
| SeriesCollection Collection | Contains `Series` objects representing the data in the chart. Includes `Border`, `Points`, and `Interior` objects. |
| Shapes Collection | Collection of the shapes within the chart. |
| Tab | Represents a tab on a chart. |
| Walls | Represents the walls of a 3-D chart. Includes `Border` and `Interior` objects. |

## Chart Types

If you look at the Chart Type dialog box within Excel, you can see that Excel offers an enormous number of different charts. Although Excel has 14 standard types of charts, each chart type has at least two different sub-types that you can select. Excel provides additional customized charts on the Custom Types page. You select the chart type by specifying an `xlChartType` constant value for the `ChartType` property. The actual list of available chart types is rather extensive because it includes all of the chart sub-types. See Appendix A for the available `xlChartType` constant values.

# Create a Chart Sheet

You can use VBA to add a new chart sheet to your workbook. When you create a chart, VBA creates a new `Chart` object, which contains all the chart options that correspond to the chart. Each `Chart` object contains several objects that represent the settings for the chart. For example, the `ChartTitle` object contains the chart title as well as its font and border properties, and other associated attributes. See the section "Chart Basics" for more information concerning the various child objects for the `Chart` object.

Because you have the option of either creating a new chart sheet or embedding a chart in a worksheet, you may find the creation of a `Chart` object a little confusing. When creating a new chart sheet, you use the `Chart` object directly, whereas with an embedded chart, you use a `ChartObjects` object. See the section "Embed a Chart within a Worksheet" for more information on creating embedded charts.

To create a separate chart sheet, you use the `Add` method with the `Charts` object. With this method, you can use three different parameter values to specify the location of the chart sheet and the number of sheets to add. You use the `Before` parameter to specify the sheet before which you want to place the new chart sheet. For example, to place the new chart sheet at the beginning of the workbook, you type a value of **Sheets(1)**. You use the `After` parameter to indicate the sheet after which you want to place the new sheet. If you want to create multiple chart sheets, you can use the `Count` parameter to indicate the number of sheets to add.

When you create the new chart, you use the various properties, methods, and a child object of the Chart object to specify the type of chart, chart title, fonts used, and so on.

## Create a Chart Sheet

① Create a new subroutine.

**Note:** See Chapter 3 for information on creating subroutines.

② Type **Dim NewChart As Chart**, replacing `NewChart` with the name of the chart variable.

③ Type **Set NewChart = ThisWorkbook.Charts.Add()**.

④ Type **NewChart.Name = "New Chart Sheet"**, replacing `"New Chart Sheet"` with the name for the chart.

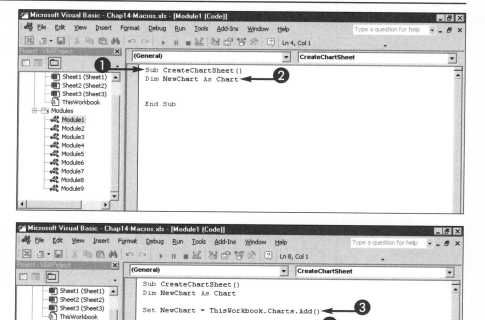

**5** Type **NewChart.ChartType = xlColumnClustered**, replacing xlColumnClustered with the new chart type.

**Note:** See Appendix A for the xlChartType constant values.

**6** Type **NewChart.SetSourceData Source:=Worksheets("Sheet1"). Range("A1:A5")** replacing Worksheets("Sheet1"). Range("A1:A5") with the range of values for the chart.

**7** Switch to Excel and run the macro.

**Note:** See Chapter 1 for more on running a macro.

Excel creates a new chart sheet with the specified range of data graphed.

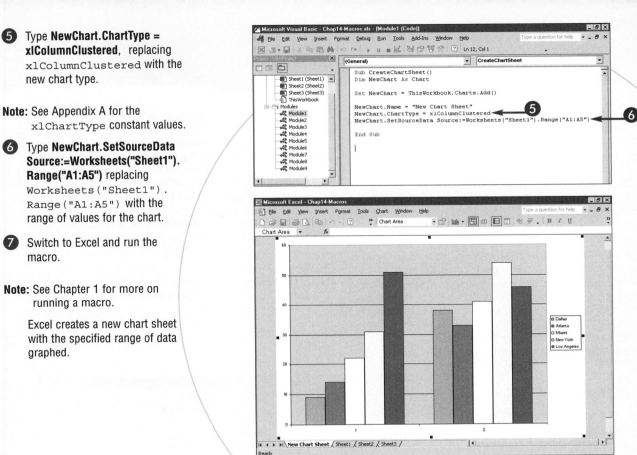

---

## Apply It

With any chart, you must specify the chart's range of data. No matter what other information you specify for a chart you create, if you omit the data source information, your chart appears blank. You use the SetSourceData method to specify the data source for your chart. The SetSourceData method has two different parameters, as illustrated in the following code:

```
NewChart.SetSourceData(Source, Range)
```

You must use the Source parameter to specify the actual data range for the chart. The Source parameter can reference any valid data range. See Chapter 11 for more on defining a range of values. Remember when working with a chart sheet that you also need to indicate the name of the worksheet containing the data as part of the range reference. For example, the following code references the range of cells contained in Sheet1 in the same workbook.

**Example:**
```
NewChart.SetSourceData(Source:=Worksheets("Sheet1").Range("A1:B15")
```

With the SetSourceData method, you can use the PlotBy parameter, which requires that you specify one of the xlRowCol constant values to instruct Excel how to plot the data in the specified range. A value of xlColumns instructs Excel to plot the data by columns. Use the value xlRows to have Excel plot the values by rows.

# Embed a Chart within a Worksheet

You can use VBA to embed a new chart to a worksheet in the existing workbook. When you embed a chart, Excel creates a new `Chart` object, which contains all the options that correspond to the chart. Each `Chart` object contains several objects that represent the settings for the chart, such as the `ChartTitle` object, which contains the chart title, its font and border properties, and other associated attributes. See the section "Chart Basics" for more information about the various child objects for the `Chart` object.

When you embed a chart on a worksheet, the corresponding `Chart` object that Excel creates becomes an actual part of the `Worksheet` object. Because you can place multiple embedded charts on one worksheet, the `Worksheet` object consists of a `ChartObjects` collection object that contains all `Chart` objects on the worksheet. Because of this, when you add and remove embedded charts, Excel requires you to use the `ChartObjects` collection object.

To add a chart to an existing worksheet, you must use the `Add` method with the `ChartObjects` object. The `Add` method has four optional parameter values, which help you indicate the location and size of the chart in points: `Left`, `Top`, `Width`, and `Height`. You use the `Left` parameter to specify the location of the chart in relation to the left edge of column A. You use the `Top` parameter to specify the location of the chart in relation to the top edge of row A. You use the `Width` parameter to indicate the initial width, and the `Height` parameter to specify the initial height of the chart object.

You specify the type of chart that Excel creates using the `ChartType` property. With this property you specify the chart type using one of the `XlChartType` constant values. For example, to create a line chart, you use the constant `xlLine`. See Appendix A for the `XlChartType` constants.

## Embed a Chart within a Worksheet

 Create a new subroutine.

 Type **Dim EChart As ChartObject**, replacing `EChart` with the name of the embedded chart variable.

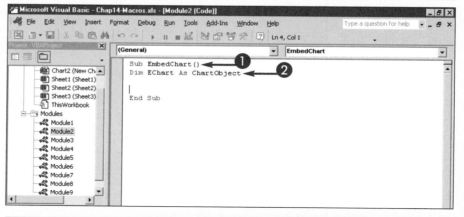

③ Type **Set EChart = Sheets("Sheet1").ChartObjects. Add()**, replacing `Sheets("Sheet1")` with the name of the worksheet to contain the chart.

④ Within the `Add` method parentheses, type **Left:=50, Top:=30, Width:=400, Height:=400**, replacing the numbers with the points measurement values.

⑤ Type **EChart.Chart.SetSourceData Source:=Range("A1:D5")**, replacing `Range("A1:D5")` with the range reference.

⑥ Type **EChart.Chart.ChartType = xl3Dcolumn**, replacing `xl3DColumn` with the xlChartType constant for the chart to create.

**Note:** See Appendix A for the `xlChartType` constant values.

⑦ Switch to Excel and run the macro.

Excel embeds the new chart into the worksheet.

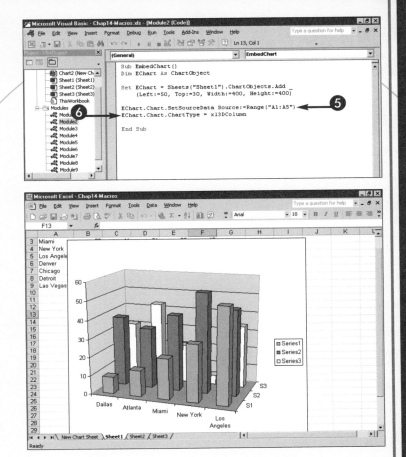

---

## Extra

The only real difference between embedded charts and chart sheets is the fact that the Chart object for an embedded chart is part of the `ChartObject` collection for the worksheet, whereas the `Chart` object for a chart sheet is part of the `Workbook` object. Other than that, if you compare the code that creates an embedded chart to the code that adds a new chart sheet, you may notice that specifying chart properties and methods requires reference to the `Chart` object. This is due to the fact that when you create a new chart sheet you create a new `Chart` object, but when you create an embedded chart you add a `Chart` object to the `ChartObjects` collection for a worksheet and, therefore, the `Chart` object becomes a child of the `ChartObjects` collection object. To set the chart type of an embedded chart, you specify the following:

**Example:**
```
Worksheets("Sheet1").ChartObject(1).Chart.ChartType = xlColumnStacked
```

This code sets the chart type of the first chart object in the worksheet named Sheet1 to a stacked column chart. If you compare that code to the code required for changing the chart type of a chart sheet, you see the similarities.

**Example:**
```
Sheets("Chart1").ChartType = xlColumnStacked
```

**W**hen you create a new chart within Excel, the Chart Wizard appears to step you through the process and requires that you specify numerous properties such as the chart location and the chart data values. With VBA, you can use the ChartWizard method to quickly format a chart without the need to set each individual property.

You use the ChartWizard method with a specific Chart object. This method includes eleven different optional parameters, which you can only use with this method and which enable you to set properties for the chart: Source, Gallery, Format, PlotBy, CategoryLabels, SeriesLabels, HasLegend, Title, CategoryTitle, ValueTitle, and ExtraTitle. You must set any additional properties individually.

You use the Source parameter to specify or modify any valid range of data that creates the chart. Keep in mind that when you work with a chart sheet, you must specify the name of the worksheet containing the data. See Chapter 11 for more information on defining cell ranges.

You use the Gallery parameter to specify one of the xlChartType constant values to indicate the desired chart type. Specify a value of 1 to 10 for the Format parameter to use one of the built-in formats for the selected chart type.

You use an xlRowCol constant value of xlRows or xlColumns for the PlotBy parameter, which determines whether the data series is in rows or columns within the specified range. You stipulate an integer value for the CategoryLabels and SeriesLabels parameters to indicate the number of category and series labels, respectively. You state a value of True for HasLegend parameter if you want a chart legend.

You enter the chart title as the value of the Title parameter, and use the CategoryTitle and ValueTitle parameters to stipulate category and value axis titles. For a 3-D chart, specify a series axis title for the ExtraTitle parameter.

## Apply Chart Wizard Settings to a Chart

① Create a new subroutine.

② Type **Dim SelectChart  As Chart**, replacing SelectChart with the chart variable.

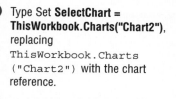

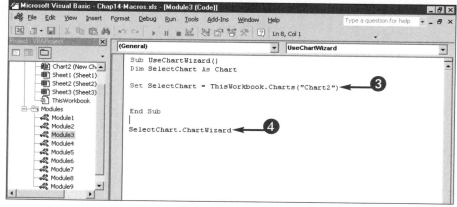

③ Type Set **SelectChart = ThisWorkbook.Charts("Chart2")**, replacing ThisWorkbook.Charts ("Chart2") with the chart reference.

④ Type **SelectChart.ChartWizard**.

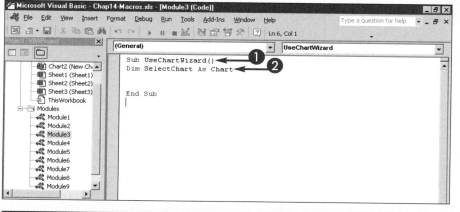

⑤ Type **Gallery:=xl3Dline**, replacing `xl3DLine` with the appropriate `XlChartType` constant.

⑥ Type **Format:=2**, replacing `2` with a value between `1` and `10` indicating the built-in format.

⑦ Type **CategoryLabels:=True**.

⑧ Type any additional ChartWizard parameter values.

⑨ Switch to Excel and run the macro.

Excel modifies the selected chart using the specified values.

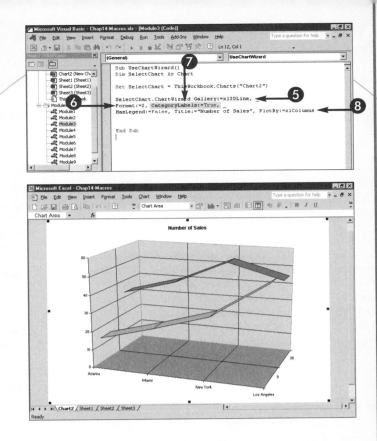

## Extra

When you use the `Gallery` parameter with the `ChartWizard` method, you need to specify an `xlChartType` constant value for the chart. Although the actual `xlChartType` constant values available are rather extensive, as outlined in Appendix A, you use only the subset of constant values with the `Gallery` parameter:

| CONSTANT | DESCRIPTION |
|---|---|
| xlArea | Plots individual values and colors in an area to emphasize data series. |
| xlBar | Displays data in horizontal columns to illustrate data relationships. |
| xlColumn | Displays data in vertical columns to illustrate data relationships. |
| xlLine | Plots individual data values on a continuous line to illustrate data trends. |
| xlPie | Displays each data in relationship to the entire whole. |
| xlRadar | Plots each data series on a separate axis. |
| xlXYScatter | Plots multiple data sources across uneven time frames. |
| xlCombination | Creates a combination chart. |
| xl3DLine | Plots data on a continuous line with a 3-D representation. |
| xl3DPie | Displays data relationships in relation to the entire pie with a 3-D representation. |
| xl3DSurface | Plots data values to create a 3-D topographical-looking chart. |
| xlDoughnut | Displays data values as a relationship to the entire circle. |

# Add a New Data Series to a Chart

After you create a chart, you can redefine the range of data Excel uses to display values on the chart by adding a new data series. A *data series* consists of a group of data values, which Excel displays on the chart. For example, if you have a bar chart showing the monthly sales in Dallas for each month of the year, you can add another data series that contains the sales in Miami for the year.

To define a new data series to add to the existing range of data, you create a new `Series` object and add it to the `SeriesCollection` collection object with the `Add` method. The `SeriesCollection` collection object represents all data series Excel plots on a specific chart, with each data series representing a new `Series` object.

To add a new data series to the chart, you use the `Add` method. When you use the `Add` method with a `SeriesCollection` object, you can use five different

parameters: `Source`, `Rowcol`, `SeriesLabels`, `CategoryLabels`, and `Replace`. You must specify a `Source` parameter to indicate the data series to add to the chart. Remember, you only need to specify the range for the new data series; if the range you specify includes the existing range, Excel duplicates those values on the chart.

Use the `Rowcol` parameter to indicate whether the new values are in rows or columns by specifying a constant of `xlColumns` or `xlRows`. Setting the `SeriesLabels` and `CategoryLabels` parameters indicates that the first row or column contains the corresponding labels. If you specify a value of `True` for the `CategoryLabels` parameter and the `Replace` parameter, Excel replaces the current category labels with the labels from the new range.

## Add a New Data Series to a Chart

① Create a new subroutine.

② Type **Dim UseChart As Chart**, replacing `UseChart` with the Chart variable.

③ Type **Set UseChart = ThisWorkbook.Charts(1)**, replacing `ThisWorkbook.Charts(1)` with the chart reference.

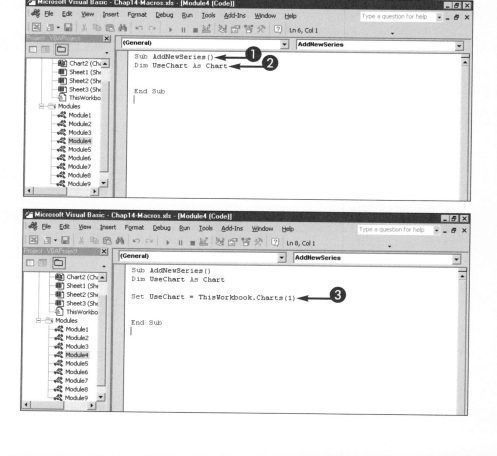

④ Type
**UseChart.SeriesCollection.Add Source:=Worksheets("Sheet1"). Range("D1:D7")**, replacing `Worksheets("Sheet1"). Range("D1:D7")` with the range to add to the chart.

⑤ Switch to Excel and run the macro.

Excel adds the specified data series to the chart.

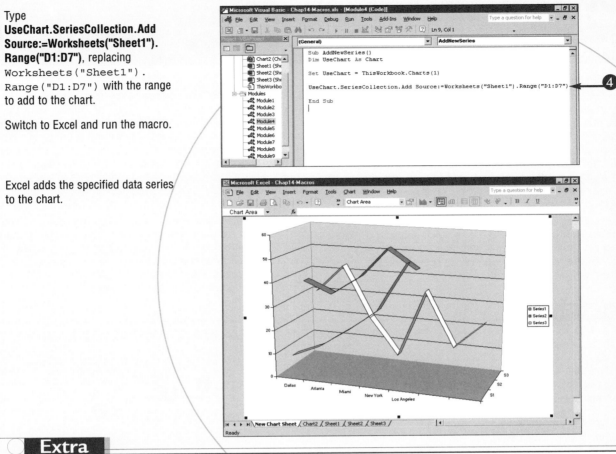

## Extra

After you specify the range of data for a chart, you can extend the values used of a particular data series. When you extend a data series, you add additional data values to the end of a particular data series. You can extend an existing data series collection using the `Extend` method with the `SeriesCollection` object. The `Extend` method provides three different parameters for extending the data series. The `Source` parameter indicates the source of the data values to add to the existing data series. You can use the `Rowcol` parameter to stipulate whether the new values are in rows or columns. You specify the value for this parameter with either the `xlRow` or `xlColumn` parameter. If the new range contains category labels in the first row, specify `True` for the `CategoryLabels` parameter. The following code illustrates how to extend a data series:

**Example:**
```
SelectChart2.SeriesCollection.Extend
Source:=Worksheets("Sheet1").Range("A10:D13")
```

You can remove a series for a chart using the `Delete` method. To remove a data series from a chart, you need to use the index value of the series you want to remove, as illustrated in the following code, which removes the second data series:

**Example:**
```
SelectChart2.SeriesCollection(2).Delete
```

# Format Chart Text

s with all elements of a chart, you can customize the text that displays on the chart by changing the font attributes. When Excel adds text to a chart either as the chart title, axis labels, or even data labels, it applies default formatting to the specified text. For example, typically the text for a chart title is formatted using the default font, normally Arial, and bold with a font size of 12 point. You can customize the text of the ChartTitle object, and all other objects on the chart, using the Font object.

The Font object enables you to set the font attributes for all text values. You use the properties associated with the Font object to set the font attributes you want to modify. By setting the font attributes, you ensure that the appearance of the text on the chart is uniform.

Excel enables you to format the text that displays on the chart. When you use the Font object properties with the ChartTitle object, you modify the look of the chart title. To change the text that Excel displays as the legend text, use the Font object properties with the Legend object. You can set the font attributes for the entire chart using the Font object with the ChartArea object. For example, if you want to change the font for the entire chart, you apply the Font object properties to the ChartArea object.

When you work with the ChartArea object, you can set the font settings for the entire chart and then use the individual objects to customize various portions of the chart. The following objects enable you to set the Font object: ChartTitle, DataTable, Legend, Characters, AxisTitle, DataLabel, and TickLabels.

## Format Chart Text

**1** Create a new subroutine.

**2** Type **Dim SelectChart As Chart**, replacing SelectChart with the name of the chart variable.

**3** Type **Set SelectChart = ThisWorkbook.Charts(1)**, replacing ThisWorkbook.Charts(1) with the chart to format.

**4** Type **With SelectChart**.

**Note:** See Chapter 4 for more information on using the With statement.

**5** Type **.ChartArea.Font.Name = "Tahoma"**, replacing "Tahoma" with the name of the font to use for the chart.

**6** Type **.ChartArea.Font.Color = RGB(0,0,255)**, replacing (0,0,255) with the RGB color values.

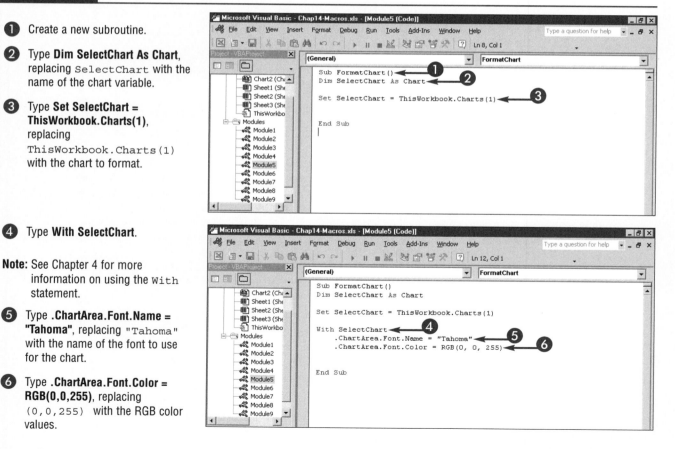

7 Type **With .ChartTitle.Font**.

8 Type **.Size = "14"**, replacing `"14"` with the font size for the chart title.

9 Specify additional `Font` property values.

10 Type **End With**.

11 Type **End With**.

12 Switch to Excel and run the macro.

Excel applies the specified text formatting to the chart.

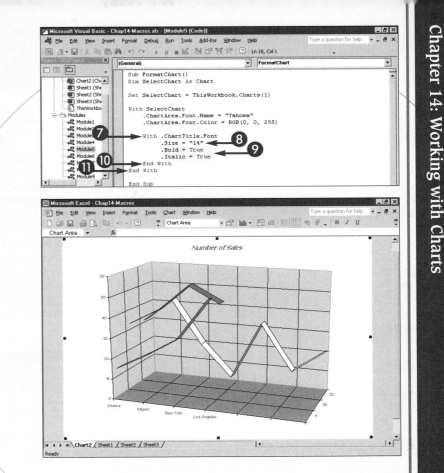

## Apply It

You may not always want to apply the same font settings to the entire chart object. For example, you may want to underline the first character in the chart title. To format specific characters with the text of an object, the `AxisTitle`, `ChartTitle`, and `DataLabel` objects enable you to use the `Characters` object. When you utilize this object, you specify the character within the text string where formatting should start as well as the number of characters to format. For example, to format the first character in the chart title that you want to underline, you type code similar to the sample coding. Notice that the `Characters` object includes two parameter values. The first parameter value, in example 1, indicates the character in the text string where Excel first applies the formatting. The second parameter value indicates the number of characters to which Excel applies formatting.

**TYPE THIS:**

```
ThisWorkbook.Charts(1).ChartTitle.
Characters(1,2).Font.Underline = True
```

→

**RESULT:**

Excel underlines the first and second characters in the chart title, but all remaining characters maintain their original font settings. If you already set the `BOLD` property of the `ChartTitle` object, the first two characters are not bold and underlined.

# Create Charts with Multiple Chart Types

Y ou can create charts that apply different chart types to each data series. For example, you may want to create a column chart to display one series of data and then add another series that plots the data as a continuous line on the chart. These types of chart features enable you to create more complex-looking charts. By using multiple chart types, you create a chart that appears as a combination of various types of charts.

To set the chart type for a data series, you need to specify the SeriesCollection object that represents the data series that you want to modify. The SeriesCollection collection object contains each of the data series in the range of data on the chart as an individual SeriesCollection object. You reference an individual object using the corresponding index value, which Excel numbers from 1 to

the number of data series in the range of data for the chart. For example, to reference the second data series, you can specify SeriesCollection(2).

To set the chart type for a data series, you need to modify the ChartType property for the specific SeriesCollection object. When you initially create your chart, you can either use this method to set the chart type for each individual data series or you can set the chart type for the entire chart, and then modify the ChartType property for the individual data series that you want to change.

When you utilize the ChartType property, you need to assign it one of the xlChartType constant values that represent the chart type you want to use for the data series. See Appendix A for a list of the xlChartType constant values that you can assign to the ChartType property.

## Create Charts with Multiple Chart Types

 Create a new subroutine.

 Type **Dim NewChart As Chart**, replacing NewChart with the chart variable.

 Type **Set NewChart = ThisWorkbooks.Charts.Add()**.

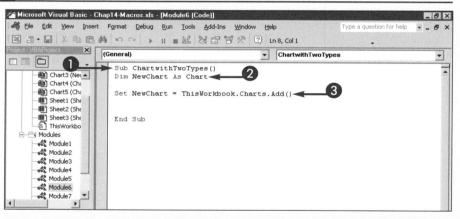

 Type **NewChart.SetSourceData Source:=Workbooks("Sheet1"). Range("A1:D9")**, replacing Workbooks("Sheet1"). Range("A1:D9") with the range of data for the chart.

 Type **NewChart.ChartType = xlColumnClustered**, replacing xlColumnClustered with the chart type constant.

 Type **NewChart.PlotBy = xlColumns**.

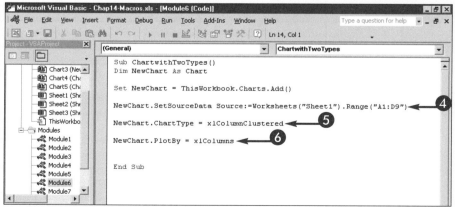

**7** Type **NewChart.SeresCollection(2).ChartType = xlLine**, replacing 2 with the series reference and `xlLine` with the desired chart type.

**8** Switch to Excel and run the macro.

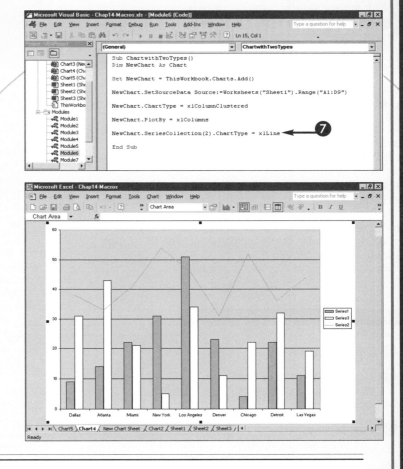

Excel creates a new chart using the first chart type value for the entire chart and modifying the chart type for the referenced data series.

## Extra

You can use a different chart type for each data series. Excel keeps track of the different series chart types and groups the common types together as `ChartGroup` objects. Each `ChartGroup` object contains one or more data series with the same chart type. Excel stores all `ChartGroup` objects within the `ChartGroups` collection object, which you can access via the `ChartGroup` property.

Because of these series groupings, the `ChartGroups` object provides methods for returning the collection of the `ChartGroup` objects that correspond to the particular type. For example, if you want to access the line chart type `ChartGroup` objects, you use the `LineGroups` method. The example illustrates how to count the number of column chart types in a chart. You can use the methods in the table with the `ChartGroup` objects.

**Example:**
```
DataSeriesCount =
ThisWorkbook.Charts(1).ColumnGroups.Count
```

| METHOD | DESCRIPTION |
|---|---|
| `AreaGroups` | Determines the number of series with an area data type. |
| `BarGroups` | Determines the number of series with a bar chart data type. |
| `ColumnGroups` | Determines the number of series with a column chart data type. |
| `DoughnutGroups` | Determines the number of series with a doughnut chart data type. |
| `LineGroups` | Determines the number of series with a line chart data type. |
| `PieGroups` | Determines the number of series with a pie chart data type. |

# Determine Variations in a Series of Data

You can use up and down bars on a line chart to illustrate the variations in different data series shown on a line chart. By assigning up and down bars to a line chart, you can compare the first data series to the last data series to easily view where the values ascend or descend. You place up and down bars on your chart using the HasUpDownBars property.

Part of the DownBars object, down bars connect the points on the first data series with the lower values in the final series. Conversely, up bars, part of the UpBars object, connect the points on the first data series with the higher values in the final series.

You can customize the look of the UpBars and DownBars objects with the Border and Interior object properties. The Interior object determines how the interior of each bar appears, for example, whether the bar has a solid color or a pattern. The Border object controls the border drawn around each bar. You customize each of these objects with the corresponding properties. If you add up and down bars to your chart, you want to customize the color of each bar type so that you can easily distinguish the difference between the up bars and the down bars. You customize the color of the bar types using the Color property of the Interior object.

When you use the Color property, you specify the color you want to apply with the RGB function. This function accepts three values in the range of 0 to 255, indicating the amount of red, green, and blue in the color. The color values range from black at 0, 0, 0 and white at 255, 255, 255.

## Determine Variations in a Series of Data

① Create a new subroutine.

② Type **Dim NewChart As Chart**, replacing NewChart with the chart variable.

③ Type **Set NewChart = ThisWorkbook.Charts.Add().**

④ Type **NewChart.ChartType = xlLine**.

⑤ Type **NewChart.SetSourceData Source:=Worksheets("Sheet1"). Range("A1:C5")** replacing Worksheets("Sheet1"). Range("A1:C5") with the data range.

⑥ Type **With NewChart.LineGroups(1)**.

⑦ Type **.HasUpDownBars = True**.

8. Type **UpBars.Interior.Color = RGB(255,255,0)**, replacing (255,255,0) with the color reference.

9. Type **DownBars.Interior.Color = RGB(0,0,255)**, replacing (0,0,255) with the color reference.

10. Type additional properties for the up and down bars.

11. Type **End With**.

12. Switch to Excel and run the macro.

    Excel creates the line chart using up and down bars to indicate differences in point values.

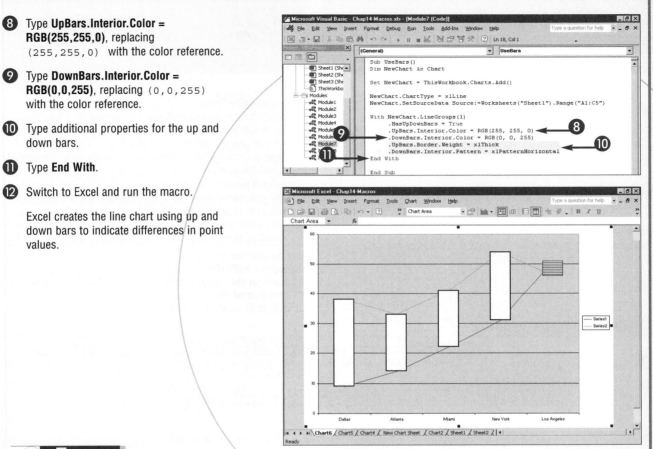

You can use `Border` and `Interior` objects with several of the `Chart` object child objects to customize the border and interior settings. Each object has multiple properties to customize it as shown in the following table:

| PROPERTY | OBJECT | DESCRIPTION |
|---|---|---|
| Color | Border Interior | Uses the RGB function to select the color by specifying a value between 0 and 255 for each color element: red, green, and blue. |
| ColorIndex | Border Interior | An index value between 1 and 56 indicating the desired palette color. |
| LineStyle | Border | An xlLineStyle constant from Appendix A specifying the style of the border line. |
| Parent | Border | Indicates the parent object. |
| Weight | Border | An xlBorderWeight constant from Appendix A specifying the line weight of the border. |
| InvertIfNegative | Interior | A value of True inverts the interior pattern for negative values. |
| Pattern | Interior | An xlPattern constant from Appendix A indicating the pattern for the interior. |
| PatternColor | Interior | Uses the RGB function to select the pattern color by specifying a value between 0 and 255 for each color element: red, green, and blue. |
| PatternColorIndex | Interior | An index value between 1 and 56 indicating the desired palette color for the pattern. |

# Add a Data Table to the Chart

Y ou can add data tables to any chart you create. You use data tables to provide a list of the values you see on the corresponding chart. Because the data values that Excel plots on a chart can come from different ranges of data, data tables work well for showing the actual data values from the chart in a concise table.

Excel stores the data table associated with a chart in the DataTable object. The HasDataTable property, associated with the Chart object, specifies whether a data table actually displays for the selected chart. This property only accepts Boolean values of either True or False. To display a data table for a chart, you need to set this property to True.

After you set the HasDataTable property, you can customize the data table using the properties associated with the DataTable object. Just like the other objects associated with

the Chart object, the DataTable object has its own list of associated properties and methods. For example, you can customize the font settings and border settings for the data table. You can specify the font for the data table using the Font property. With the Font property, you use the properties associated with the Font object to specify the actual font properties of the text. For example, DataTable.Font.Name = "Arial" specifies that the data table uses the Arial font. See the section "Format Chart Text" for more information on working with the Font object on a chart.

You select and unselect the display of borders for the data table using the HasBorderHorizontal, HasBorderOutline, and HasBorderVertical properties. By default, Excel displays borders on a data table. The Border object contains the entire borders for the data table. You can customize the border using the associated properties.

## Add a Data Table to the Chart

① Create a new subroutine.

② **Type SelectChart As Chart** replacing SelectChart with the chart variable.

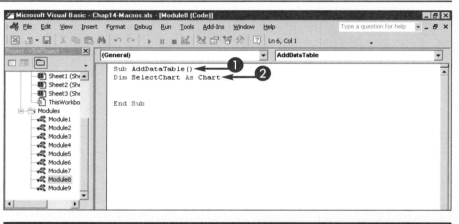

③ Type **Set SelectChart = ThisWorkbook.Charts(1)**, replacing ThisWorkbook.Charts(1) with the chart to modify.

④ Type **SelectChart.HasDataTable = True**.

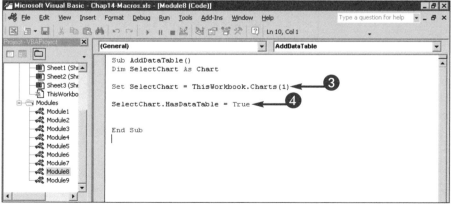

⑤ Type **SelectChart.DataTable.Font.Name = "Tahoma"**, replacing `"Tahoma"` with the font name.

⑥ Type **SelectChart.DataTable.Border.Color = RGB(0,0,255)**, replacing `(0,0,255)` with the border color.

Type any additional chart or data-table-related statements.

⑦ Switch to Excel and run the macro.

● Excel displays the chart with the data table at the bottom.

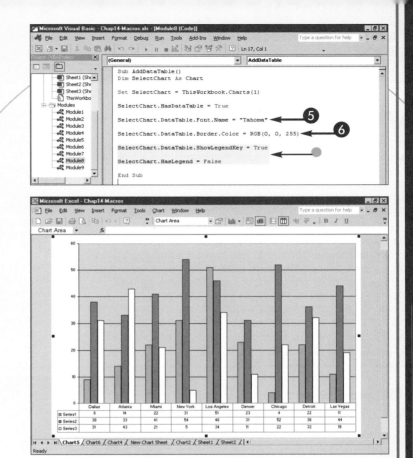

## Extra

When you add a data table to a chart, you have the option of combining the chart legend with the data table. By doing so, you can create a more readable chart because you can quickly see which chart series has the specified data values.

To create a data table containing the chart legend, you need to set the `ShowLegendKey` property to `True` for the `DataTable` object. By default, Excel sets this value to `True`, but it is a good idea to specify this value to ensure its proper setting. Use the following code to set the value of the `ShowLegendKey` property.

**Example:**
```
ThisWorkbook.Charts(1). DataTable.
ShowLegendKey = True
```

If you display the legend as part of the data table, you typically do not want the legend to display separately on your chart. To hide the legend, you can set the `HasLegend` property for the `Chart` object to `False`, as illustrated with the following code:

**Example:**
```
ThisWorkbook.Charts(1).HasLegend =
False
```

273

# Customize the Chart Axis

Y ou customize each axis on your chart with the Axis object properties and methods. Most charts that you create have a default of two different axes, the category axis and the values axis. For example, if you look at a standard column chart, the category axis runs horizontally across the bottom of the chart while the values axis runs vertically on the left side of the chart. When dealing with 3-D charts, there is a third series axis.

Each chart axis is a separate Axis object. The Axes collection object contains all Axis objects for the chart. You can use the Axes method to access an individual chart Axis object. When you use the Axes method, specify a value for the Type parameter indicating the axis that you want to remove. Specify one of the XlAxisType constants to indicate the axis type for this parameter. You can specify xlValue for the value axis, xlCategory for the category axis, or xlSeriesAxis for the third axis on the 3-D chart.

You can customize each axis using the AxisTitle, Border, Gridlines, DisplayUnitLabel, and TickLabels child objects. Each of these objects has additional child objects and corresponding properties and methods. The AxisTitle object represents the title that Excel adds to the corresponding axis. You can specify the text that displays for the axis title with the Caption property. You can customize the appearance of the axis title by calling the Font object properties. See the section "Format Chart Text" for more information on working with the Font object on a chart.

You set the HasTitle property to True to specify that the axis has a title. You can also customize the other objects in a similar fashion. For example, the Border object represents the axis border along the chart. You can use the Color property to change the color of that axis.

## Customize the Chart Axis

 Create a new subroutine.

 Type **Dim SelectChart As Chart**, replacing SelectChart with the chart variable.

 Type **Set SelectChart = ThisWorkbook.Charts(1)**, replacing ThisWorkbook.Charts(1) with the chart reference.

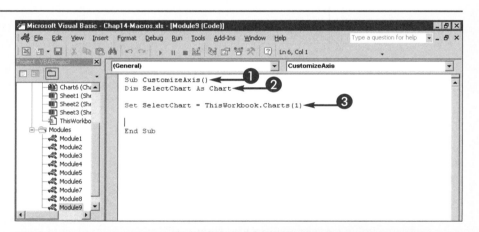

 Type **With SelectChart.Axes(xlValue)**, replacing xlValue with the axis constant value.

 Type **.HasTitle = True**.

 Type **.AxisTitle.Text = "Value Axis"**, replacing "Value Axis" with the axis title.

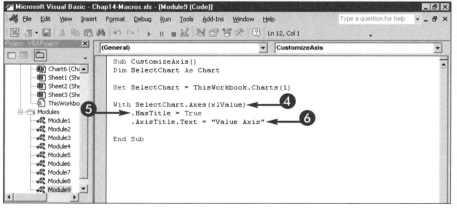

**7** Type **.HasMajorGridlines = True**.

**8** Type **.MajorGridlines.Border.Color = RGB(0,0,255)** replacing (0,0,255) with the color reference.

**9** Type **.MajorGridlines.Border.LineStyle = xlDash**, replacing xlDash with the xlLineStyle constant value.

**Note:** See Appendix A for the xlLineStyle values.

**10** Type **End With**.

**11** Switch to Excel and run the macro.

Excel updates the specified axis.

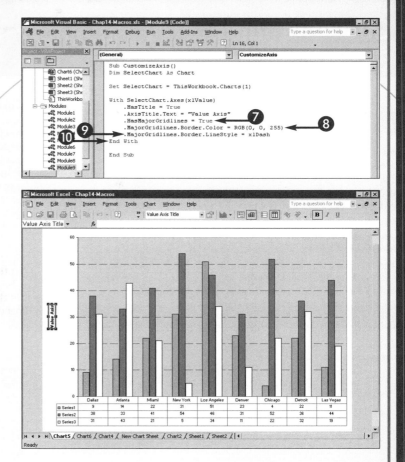

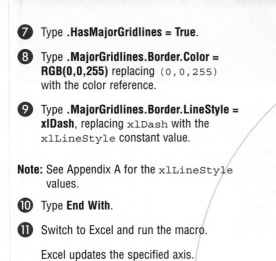

## Extra

You can add gridlines on a chart so that a user can determine a value at a specific point. Gridlines run either horizontally or vertically from the corresponding axis and extend the tick marks. You can use the Gridlines object to customize the gridline settings for a particular axis by adding both major and minor gridlines. A major gridline appears at each label on the axis and minor gridlines appear at even intervals between the major gridlines. The following code illustrates how to use the HasMajorGridlines property to turn on the gridlines and how to customize the appearance of the gridlines with the MajorGridlines property. Notice that the code customizes the appearance of the gridlines for the specified axis by utilizing the Border object. You can use the following properties with the Border object: Color, ColorIndex, LineStyle, Parent, and Weight.

**Example:**
```
With Charts(1).Axes(.xlValue)
        .HasMajorGridlines = True
        .MajorGridlines.Border.Color = RGB(0,255,0)
        .MajorGridlines.Border.LineStyle = xlDot
        .MajorGridlines.Border.Weight = xlThin
End With
```

275

# Understanding Excel Events

**A**n *event* occurs within Excel whenever you perform any type of action. For example, if you click a particular cell, a Click event occurs. You can use these events to trigger the execution of particular procedures by creating event-handling procedures. *Event-handling* procedures are exactly what the name describes, procedures that execute when a particular event occurs.

You can monitor five different types of events within Excel: workbook, worksheet, chart, UserForm, and application events. To trap or capture an event with an event-handling procedure, you must place the procedure code in the correct type of module. For example, you must place all workbook-related events in the ThisWorkbook object code module.

## Workbook Events

Excel associates workbook level events with the corresponding workbook where they reside. You need to place the procedures within the ThisWorkbook object module. You create these procedures by naming them Workbook_event name. The following table lists each of the available workbook events.

| EVENT | DESCRIPTION |
|---|---|
| Activate | Excel activates the workbook. |
| AddinInstall | An add-in installs a workbook. |
| AddinUninstall | An add-in uninstalls a workbook. |
| BeforeClose | A workbook closes. See the section "Run a Procedure before Closing a Workbook." |
| BeforePrint | Excel prints a portion of a workbook. |
| BeforeSave | Excel saves a workbook. See the section "Run a Procedure before Saving a Workbook." |
| Deactivate | Excel deactivates a workbook. |
| NewSheet | Excel adds a new sheet to a workbook. |
| Open | Excel opens a workbook. See the section "Run a Procedure as a Workbook Opens." |
| PivotTableCloseConnection | Occurs after a Pivot table report closes the data source connection. |
| PivotTableOpenConnection | Occurs after a Pivot table report opens the data source connection. |
| SheetActivate | Excel activates a sheet in the workbook. |
| SheetBeforeDoubleClick | Occurs before a user double-clicks a sheet. |
| SheetBeforeRightClick | Occurs before a user clicks with the right mouse button. |
| SheetCalculate | Excel calculates a sheet. |
| SheetDeactivate | Excel deactivates a sheet. |
| SheetFollowHyperlink | A user clicks a hyperlink on a sheet. |
| SheetPivotTableUpdate | Excel updates a sheet of a Pivot table report. |
| SheetSelectionChange | The selection changes on a workbook. |
| WindowActivate | Excel activates a workbook window. |
| WindowDeactivate | Excel deactivates a workbook window. |
| WindowResize | Excel resizes a workbook window. |

## Worksheet Events

Excel associates worksheet-level events with the currently selected worksheet. You need to place event-handling procedures related to a worksheet in the code module for the worksheet object. The following table lists each of the available worksheet events.

| EVENT | DESCRIPTION |
|---|---|
| Activate | Excel activates the worksheet. |
| BeforeDoubleClick | Occurs before the user double-clicks the worksheet with the mouse. |
| BeforeRightClick | Occurs before the user clicks the worksheet with the right mouse button. |
| Calculate | Excel calculates the worksheet. |
| Change | Occurs when a user or external link modifies cells on the worksheet. See the section "Monitor a Range of Cells for Changes." |
| Deactivate | Excel deactivates the worksheet. |
| FollowHyperlink | User selects a Hyperlink on the worksheet. |
| PivotTableUpdate | Occurs after a Pivot table report is updated on the worksheet. |
| SelectionChange | Selection changes on the worksheet. |

## Chart Events

Excel associates Chart level events with the currently selected chart sheet. You need to place event-handling procedures related to a chart in the code module for the chart object. The following table lists the available chart events for which you can create event-handling procedures.

| EVENT | DESCRIPTION |
|---|---|
| Activate | Excel activates the chart sheet. |
| BeforeDoubleClick | Occurs before the user double-clicks the chart sheet with the mouse. |
| BeforeRightClick | Occurs before the user clicks the chart sheet with the right mouse button. See the section "Run a Procedure When Right-Clicking a Chart." |
| Calculate | Occurs after Excel plots the chart. |
| Deactivate | Excel deactivates the chart sheet. |
| DragOver | The user drags a range of cells over a chart. |
| DragPlot | The user drags and drops a range of cells onto the chart. |
| MouseDown | The user presses a mouse button over the chart. |
| MouseMove | The position of a mouse changes over a chart. |
| MouseUp | The user releases a mouse over the chart. |
| Resize | The user resizes the chart. |
| Select | The user selects a chart element. |
| SeriesChange | Occurs when the user changes the value of a chart data point. |

continued ➔

## UserForm Events

Excel associates UserForm events not only with the form but also with each of the controls that exist on the form. You need to place event-handling procedures related to a UserForm in the code module for the UserForm object. The following table lists the available UserForm events.

| EVENT | DESCRIPTION |
|---|---|
| Activate | Excel activates the UserForm. |
| AddControl | Excel adds a run-time control to the UserForm. |
| BeforeDragOver | The user performs a drag-and-drop operation. |
| BeforeDropOrPaste | The user releases the mouse button to paste the data from the drag-and-drop operation. |
| Click | The user clicks the mouse on a UserForm object. See Chapter 14 for information on capturing the Click event. |
| DblClick | The user double-clicks the mouse on a UserForm object. |
| Deactivate | The user deactivates the UserForm. |
| Error | Excel detects a UserForm control error. |
| KeyDown | The user presses a key. |
| KeyPress | The user presses an ANSI key. An ANSI key produces a visible character. |
| KeyUp | The user releases a key. |
| MouseDown | The user presses a mouse button. |
| MouseMove | The user moves a mouse on the UserForm. |
| MouseUp | The user releases the mouse button. |
| QueryClose | Excel closes the UserForm. |
| RemoveControl | Excel removes a control from the UserForm at run-time. |
| Scroll | The user repositions a Scroll box on a control. |
| Terminate | Excel terminates the UserForm. |
| Zoom | The user zooms the UserForm. |

## Application Events

Application events include all events that the `Application` object recognizes. To access an application event you create a class module to contain your application event-handling procedure code. See the section "Run a Procedure When Excel

Creates a Workbook" for more information on placing event-handling code in a class module.

The following table provides a list of the application-level events that occur within Excel.

| EVENT TYPE | DESCRIPTION |
|---|---|
| `Application` | An event that occurs for the application, in this case Excel. For example, Excel triggers the `NewWorkbook` event when it creates a new workbook. |
| `NewWorkbook` | Occurs when Excel creates a new workbook. See the section "Run a Procedure When Excel Creates a Workbook" |
| `SheetActivate` | Excel activates any sheet in any workbook. |
| `SheetBeforeDoubleClick` | Event occurs before the user double-clicks any sheet with the mouse. |
| `SheectBeforeRightClick` | Event occurs before the user clicks any sheet with the right mouse button. |
| `SheetCalculate` | Excel calculates any worksheet. |
| `SheetChange` | Cells on a worksheet change either due to a user or an external link. |
| `SheetFollowHyperlink` | A user clicks a hyperlink on a sheet. |
| `SheetPivotTableUpdate` | Excel updates a sheet of a Pivot table report. |
| `SheetSelectionChange` | The selection changes on any worksheet. |
| `WindowActivate` | Excel activates a worksheet window. |
| `WindowDeactivate` | Excel deactivates a worksheet window. |
| `WindowResize` | The user resizes a worksheet window. |
| `WorkbookActivate` | The user activates a workbook. |
| `WorkbookAddInInstall` | An add-in installs a workbook. |
| `WorkbookAddInUninstall` | An add-in uninstalls a workbook. |
| `WorkbookBeforePrint` | Excel prints an open workbook. |
| `WorkbookBeforeSave` | Excel saves an open workbook. |
| `WorkbookDeactivate` | Excel deactivates a workbook. |
| `WorkbookNewSheet` | Excel adds a new sheet to an open workbook. |
| `WorkbookOpen` | Excel opens a workbook. |
| `WorkbookPivotTableCloseConnection` | Occurs after a Pivot table report closes the data source connection. |
| `WorkbookPivotTableOpenConnection` | Occurs after a Pivot table report opens the data source connection. |

# Run a Procedure as a Workbook Opens

You can create a procedure that runs automatically each time a particular workbook opens. Because this type of procedure only executes once as the workbook opens, it works well for launching custom menus and toolbars, opening other workbooks, determining if specific conditions are met, or displaying welcome messages. The procedure executes when the workbook opens by catching the Open event that the opening workbook triggers.

To create a procedure that executes when a workbook opens, you create a new procedure and add it to the ThisWorkbook object code module for the particular workbook. In fact, all event-handling procedures that you create for monitoring workbook events must reside within the ThisWorkbook object to have Excel execute them automatically. To create a procedure that executes when a workbook opens, you name the procedure Workbook_Open.

Although the procedure resides in the ThisWorkbook object code module, it can access other procedures within the same workbook. Therefore, you can create a Workbook_Open procedure that calls procedures located in other modules.

If you have a procedure that you want to execute whenever Excel opens, you must place the procedure within the ThisWorkbook object for the Personal Macro Workbook, Personal.xls. Because the Personal Macro Workbook always loads as a hidden workbook in Excel, any procedures within this workbook appear to execute as Excel opens. Keep in mind, however, that Excel associates the Personal Macro Workbook with an individual user.

Remember, you can keep a Workbook_Open procedure from executing for a particular workbook by holding down the Shift key as the workbook opens. Because workbooks typically open rather quickly, you need to make sure you press and hold the Shift key as soon as you select the workbook.

## Run a Procedure as a Workbook Opens

① On the Projects window, locate the workbook where you want to add the Workbook_Open subroutine.

② Double-click the ThisWorkbook object node under the workbook.

The code module opens for the ThisWorkbook object.

③ In the Object box, click ▾ and then click the Workbook option.

- The Visual Basic Editor creates a new `Private` subroutine named `Workbook_Open`.

④ Type the VBA code to run when the workbook opens.

⑤ Click the Save button (🖫) to save the workbook including the new subroutine.

⑥ Close Excel.

⑦ Open the workbook in Excel.

The `Workbook_Open` procedure executes the specified VBA code as the workbook opens.

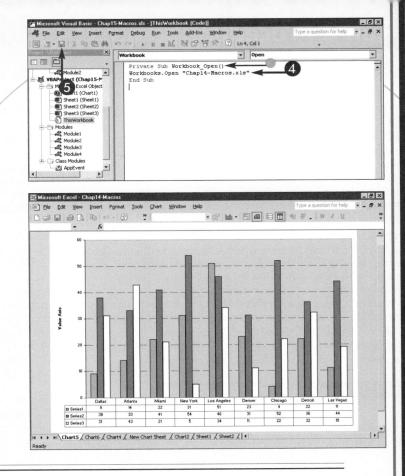

You can use the `Open` method of the `Workbooks` collection object to specify a workbook that Excel should open whenever the current workbook opens. For example, if your workbook relies on data values within another workbook, you can open that workbook whenever the current workbook opens. See Chapter 9 for more information on using the `Open` method to specify the workbook to open.

You can use the Object drop-down list on the Code window to quickly create your `Workbook_Open` subroutine. The Object drop-down list contains the available objects for which you can create subroutines within the current code module. For example, if you access the `ThisWorkbook` code module, the only available object is `Workbook`.

When you select the `Workbook` object from the Objects drop-down list, the Visual Basic Editor automatically creates a private subroutine called `Workbook_Open`. This is because the default event for the `Workbook` object is the `Open` event. If you view the Procedure drop-down list, you see all the available events for the `Workbook` object. If you select another event from the list, the Visual Basic Editor creates a new subroutine for that event.

# Run a Procedure before Closing a Workbook

Y ou can create a procedure that runs automatically before a particular workbook closes in Excel. Because this type of procedure only executes once as the workbook closes, it works well for removing custom menus and toolbars loaded when the workbook opened, closing other workbooks, recalculating, or even automatically saving the workbook. The procedure executes when the workbook closes by catching the BeforeClose event that the closing workbook triggers.

To produce a procedure that executes when a workbook closes, you create a new procedure and add it to the ThisWorkbook object code module for the particular workbook. In fact, all event-handling procedures that you create for monitoring workbook events must reside within the ThisWorkbook object in order for Excel to execute them automatically. To create a procedure that executes when a workbook closes, you name the procedure Workbook_BeforeClose.

Although the procedure resides in the ThisWorkbook object code module, it can access other procedures within the

same workbook. Therefore, you can create a Workbook_BeforeClose procedure that calls procedures located in another module.

If you have a procedure that you want Excel to execute whenever an application closes, you must place the procedure within the ThisWorkbook object for the Personal Macro Workbook, Personal.xls. Because the Personal Macro Workbook always loads as a hidden workbook in Excel, and typically only closes when you close Excel, any procedures within this workbook appear to execute as Excel closes. Keep in mind that Excel associates the Personal Macro Workbook with an individual user.

The BeforeClose event has one parameter, Cancel, that Excel passes to the procedure when the event is triggered. You can change what Excel does after the BeforeClose event completes by changing the value of the Cancel parameter. If the Cancel parameter has a value of False, which is the default, the workbook closes as normal. If you set the value of the Cancel parameter to True, Excel does not close the workbook and cancels the closing process.

## Run a Procedure before Closing a Workbook

 On the Projects window, locate the workbook where you want to add the Workbook_BeforeClose subroutine.

② Double-click the ThisWorkbook object node under the workbook.

The code module opens for the ThisWorkbook object.

③ In the Object box, click ▾ and then click the Workbook option.

④ In the Procedure box, click ▾ and then the BeforeClose option.

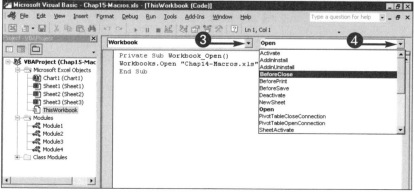

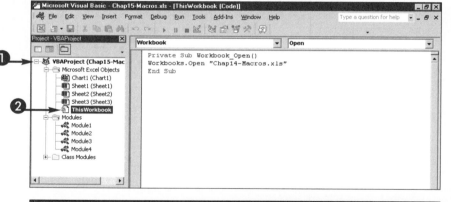

- The Visual Basic Editor creates a new Private subroutine named `Workbook_BeforeClose`.

**5** Type the VBA code to run before the workbook closes.

**6** Close the workbook.

```
Microsoft Visual Basic - Chap15-Macros.xls - [ThisWorkbook (Code)]
```

```
Workbook                              BeforeClose

Private Sub Workbook_BeforeClose(Cancel As Boolean)
Dim UserResponse As String

UserResponse = MsgBox("Do you want to close workbook " & Me.Name, vbQ
    If UserResponse = vbNo Then
        Cancel = True
    End If
    If UserResponse = vbYes Then
        Me.Save
    End If
End Sub

Private Sub Workbook_Open()
Workbooks.Open "Chap14-Macros.xls"
End Sub
```

The `Workbook_BeforeClose` procedure executes the specified VBA code as the workbook before closing the workbook.

| | A | B | C | D | E | F |
|---|---|---|---|---|---|---|
| 1 | Miami | 24 | 41 | 21 | 25 | 18 |
| 2 | New York | 31 | 54 | 5 | 17 | 24 |
| 3 | Los Angeles | 51 | 46 | 34 | 21 | 10 |
| 4 | Denver | 23 | 31 | 11 | 31 | 21 |
| 5 | Chicago | 4 | 52 | 22 | 22 | 21 |
| 6 | Detroit | 22 | 36 | 32 | 13 | 16 |
| 7 | Las Vegas | 11 | 44 | 19 | 9 | 8 |

Microsoft Excel

Do you want to close workbook Chap15-Macros.xls

Yes    No

## Extra

You can use the `Me` operator to work in a code module for a specific Excel object. When you use the `Me` operator, it references the object related to the code module. For example, if you create code in the `ThisWorkbook` object module, all code in the module correlates to the actual workbook object. When you use the `Me` operator, you reference the workbook object. Therefore, when you add the code `Me.Close` to a code module, Excel closes the corresponding workbook.

The code `Me.Close` is equivalent to using the `ThisWorkbook` object reference.

Keep in mind that with the `ThisWorkbook` object code module, you can use either the `Me` object or the `ThisWorkbook` object to reference the current workbook, a condition not true in a standard code module. If you create a code module that you do not associate with an object, you cannot use the `Me` operator to reference an object without generating an error.

You can also use the `Me` operator when working with `UserForm` code modules. In doing so, the `Me` operator references the corresponding `UserForm` and not the controls that you have added to the `UserForm`.

# Run a Procedure before Saving a Workbook

You can create a procedure that runs automatically before Excel saves a particular workbook. By creating this type of procedure, you can customize the method you use to save the workbook. For example, you may always want to display the Save As dialog box whenever the user selects the Save or SaveAs option in Excel. This procedure executes whenever you select the Save or the SaveAs options within Excel for the corresponding workbook.

To create a procedure that executes before saving a workbook, you create a new procedure using the `BeforeSave` event and add it to the `ThisWorkbook` object code module for the particular workbook. In fact, all event-handling procedures that you create for monitoring workbook events must reside within the `ThisWorkbook` object to have Excel execute them automatically. To create a procedure that executes before Excel saves the workbook, you name the procedure `Workbook_BeforeSave`.

Although the procedure resides in the `ThisWorkbook` object code module, it can access other procedures within the same workbook. Therefore, you can create a `Workbook_BeforeSave` procedure that calls procedures located in another code module within the same workbook.

The `BeforeSave` event has two parameters that Excel passes to your procedure when the event triggers. The `SaveUI` parameter indicates whether the `Save As` dialog box displays during the `Save` command. Set the value of the `SaveUI` parameter to `True` to always display the Save As dialog box. If the `Cancel` parameter has a value of `False`, Excel saves the workbook. If you set the value of the `Cancel` parameter to `True`, Excel does not save the workbook. Within the `Workbook_BeforeSave` procedure you can change the value of the `Cancel` parameter to specify whether the workbook actually saves.

## Run a Procedure before Saving a Workbook

① On the Projects window, locate the workbook where you want to add the `Workbook_BeforeSave` subroutine.

② Double-click the `ThisWorkbook` object node under the workbook.

The code module opens for the `ThisWorkbook` object.

③ In the Object box, click ▼ and then the Workbook option.

④ In the Procedure box, click ▼ and then the BeforeSave option.

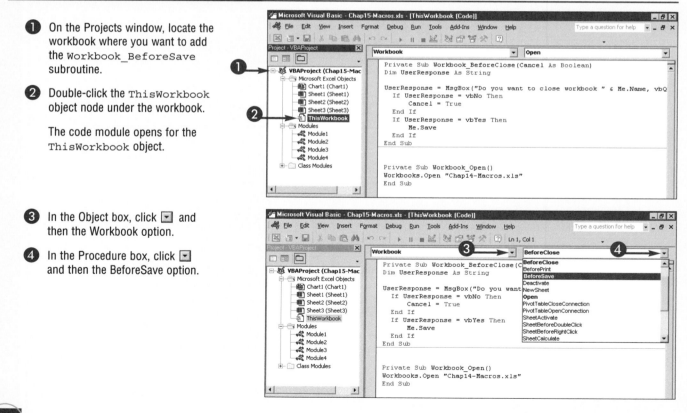

284

- The Visual Basic Editor creates a new Private subroutine named `Workbook_BeforeSave`.

**5** Type the VBA code to run before Excel saves the workbook.

**6** Switch to Excel.

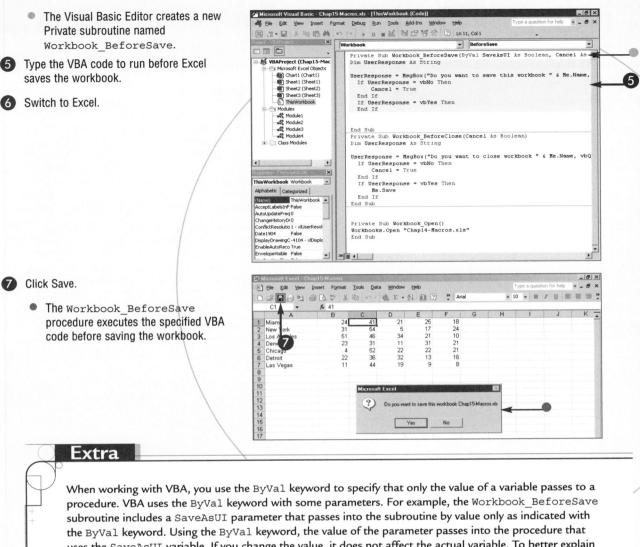

**7** Click Save.

- The `Workbook_BeforeSave` procedure executes the specified VBA code before saving the workbook.

---

## Extra

When working with VBA, you use the `ByVal` keyword to specify that only the value of a variable passes to a procedure. VBA uses the `ByVal` keyword with some parameters. For example, the `Workbook_BeforeSave` subroutine includes a `SaveAsUI` parameter that passes into the subroutine by value only as indicated with the `ByVal` keyword. Using the `ByVal` keyword, the value of the parameter passes into the procedure that uses the `SaveAsUI` variable. If you change the value, it does not affect the actual variable. To better explain this, consider the following example, where the message box displays a value of 10 because the value of `TestVal` passes in the `Test2` subroutine by value. In other words, instead of using the variable `TestVal`, the `Test2` subroutine uses a copy of the original `TestVal` variable. Any changes you make within the `Test2` subroutine do not pass back to the original subroutine, `Test1`.

**Example:**
```
Sub Test1()
    Dim TestVal As Integer
    TestVal = 12
    Call Test2(TestVal)
    MsgBox TestVal
End Sub

Sub Test2(ByVal TestVal)
    TestVal = TestVal +1
End Sub
```

# Run a Procedure When Excel Creates a Workbook

You can use the `NewWorkbook` application event to create a procedure that executes whenever Excel opens a new workbook. When you use an application event, you capture the events that the application — in this case, Excel — creates. The `NewWorkbook` event triggers whenever Excel creates a new workbook. Because the event comes from the application and not an individual object such as a workbook, or chart, you may find the process a little more complex than capturing other object events.

When working with application events, you first create a class module. Excel only makes code within a code module available to other modules within the same project or workbook. Because you create a procedure dealing with an application event, you want all open projects to access the code; therefore, you need to use a class module.

Because you must activate the event-handling code for an application object, you need to place the code module you create in a commonly used workbook. Because Excel does not recognize your application event code until the workbook containing the code opens, consider adding the code to the `Personal.xls` workbook. Because that workbook opens whenever you run Excel, the application event code activates as the workbook opens. See Chapter 1 for more information about the Personal Macro workbook.

Within the class module you define an event custom object using the `WithEvents` keyword. The `WithEvents` keyword instructs Excel to notify you whenever the `Application` object triggers a `NewWorkbook` event. You use the `Public` statement because you want all open projects to access this object variable. See Chapter 5 for more information on using the `Public` keyword.

## Run a Procedure When Excel Creates a Workbook

① On the Project window, click to highlight a workbook you open frequently.

You must open this workbook to activate the event code.

② Click Insert→Class Module.

Excel creates a blank class module.

③ Type a name for the code module in the (Name) field on the Properties window.

④ Type **Public WithEvents AppEvent As Application**, replacing `AppEvent` with the name of the application event object.

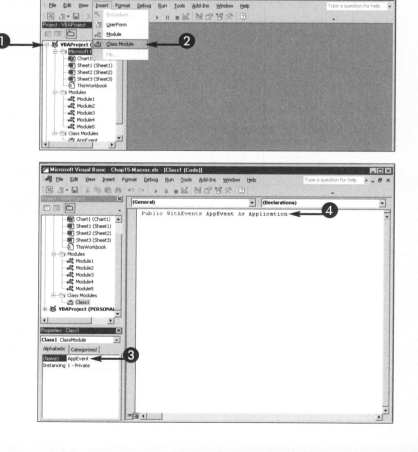

- The class module name changes to the name you specify in step 3.

**5** In the Object list, click ⏷ and then the option you named in step 3.

- Excel creates a `Private AppEvent_NewWorkbook` subroutine where `AppEvent` is the name of the application object you created in step 4.

**6** Type the VBA code to execute when a new workbook opens.

**7** In the Projects window, double-click the `ThisWorkbook` object for the open workbook.

## Extra

When you specify the public `Application` object using the `WithEvents` keyword, the Visual Basic Editor creates a new object and adds it to the Object drop-down list. When you select this object, the Procedure box contains a list of all corresponding application events. To create a new event procedure, you select the object from the Object drop-down list and the appropriate event from the Procedure drop-down list. When you do this, the Visual Basic Editor creates the new subroutine with the appropriate arguments. For example, if your object is `AppEvent` and you select the `WindowActivate` event, the Editor adds the following code to the class module:

**Example:**
```
Private Sub AppEvent_WindowActivate(ByVal Wb As Workbook, ByVal Wn As Window)

End Sub
```

You can use the Object Browser to find out more about a particular event by pressing F2. Type the event you want to know about and click the Search icon (🔍). The Object Browser displays a list of the matching items. Excel indicates the Events with a small lightning bolt icon (⚡). If you click an event, the event syntax displays at the bottom of the Object Browser window.

continued →

Y ou use the NewWorkbook event to determine when Excel has created a new workbook. The NewWorkbook event has one parameter value that passes into the subroutine. The Wb parameter contains the newly created workbook. You can access any of the methods and properties of the new workbook to customize the created workbook. For example, you can use the Name property to return the name of the new workbook. See Chapter 9 for more information on working with the Workbook object.

Creating the NewWorkbook subroutine in the class module simply defines the code to run for the event, but does not activate the code. To activate the subroutine, add code to a Workbook_Open procedure that activates the Application

event procedure. Because the Application event code is meant to work with all events generated by the application, you want to add the class module and the activation code to a workbook you open frequently, such as the Personal Macro workbook.

To activate the class module code, the module containing the activation procedure must contain a Dim statement, which declares an object of the type defined in the class module. You must place the Dim statement at the top of the code module. For example, Dim NewAppEvent As New AppEvent creates a new object variable of the type created in the class module. Within a procedure, you add a Set statement, which actually activates the event. To make the Set statement execute automatically, you place the Set statement within the Workbook_Open procedure.

## Run a Procedure When Excel Creates a Workbook (continued)

The code module opens for the ThisWorkbook object.

⑧ Type **Dim Test As New AppEvent** at the top of the code module, replacing Test with the local object created in step 4 and AppEvent with the object module created in step 3.

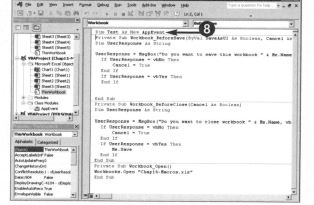

⑨ In the Workbook_Open subroutine, type **Set Test.AppEvent = Excel.Application**, replacing Test with the variable in step 7 and AppEvent with the variable created in step 3.

**Note:** If the Workbook_Open subroutine does not exist, see the section "Run a Procedure as a Workbook Opens" for information on creating one.

⑩ Close and reopen Excel.

⑪ Open the workbook containing the `Workbook_Open` subroutine referenced in step 8.

⑫ Click New.

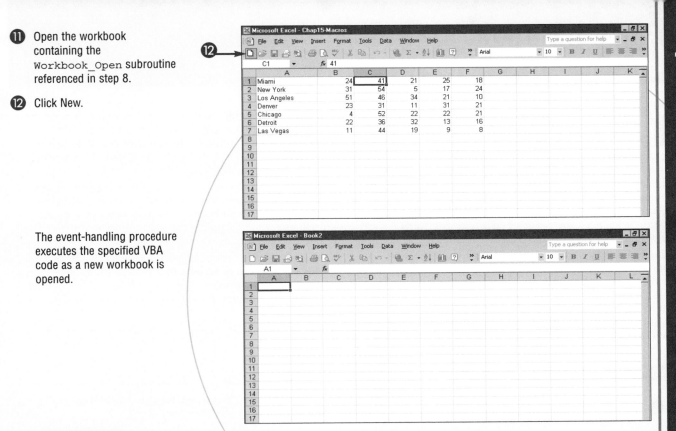

The event-handling procedure executes the specified VBA code as a new workbook is opened.

## Apply It

When you open the workbook containing the code that activates the application event, the code continues to execute each time you trigger the event. You may find circumstances where you need to deactivate an event so that it no longer triggers. To do so, you can create a separate subroutine that you can call from within Excel at any point to cancel an event. Essentially, you set the property of the application object to Nothing, as shown in the code:

**TYPE THIS:**

```
Sub CancelEvent()

Set OpenAppEvent.AppEvent = Nothing

End Sub
```

**RESULT:**

The code cancels the event for the current session of Excel. The next time you execute Excel, the event is activated again.

Keep in mind that you must use the same object and property references that you used to create the application object. It is a good idea to create this type of subroutine to enable you to disable an event-handling procedure at any time. Another method you can use is to set the EnableEvents property to false for the Application object, as shown in this code:

**TYPE THIS:**

```
Sub CancelEvents()

Applcation.EnableEvents = False

End Sub
```

**RESULT:**

This code disables all event-handling procedures for the current session of Excel. The next time you execute Excel, the event-handling procedures are reactivated.

# Monitor a Range of Cells for Changes

You can create a procedure that watches a particular cell or ranges of cells until a change occurs. To monitor a range of cells, you capture the Change event that triggers for the Worksheet object. Excel triggers this event when the user or an external link changes the values within the selected worksheet. When Excel triggers the event, it sends your event-handling function a Range object containing the cells that changed. You design your procedure to check the range of cells and determine if they are within the range of cells you are monitoring.

Because the event you monitor relates to an individual worksheet, you place the event-handling procedure within the object module code that corresponds to the appropriate worksheet. For example, to monitor the changes to Sheet1, you place the code in the code module for Sheet1. To capture the Change event, you must name the procedure you create Worksheet_Change.

The Change event has one parameter, Target, whose value Excel passes when it triggers the Change event. The Target parameter receives the range of cells that were altered. This value passes to your procedure by value so that you receive a copy of the range of cells.

Although the Worksheet_Change procedure resides in a sheet object code module, it can access other procedures within the same workbook. Therefore, you can create a Worksheet_Change procedure that calls procedures located in another module.

Keep in mind, Excel only triggers this event when cell values change due to modifications made by the user or an external link. It does not trigger if a formula or procedure performs a calculation that changes the value, or if you add an object.

## Monitor a Range of Cells for Changes

① On the Projects window, locate the worksheet where you want to add the Worksheet_Change subroutine.

② Double-click the sheet object code that corresponds to the appropriate worksheet.

The code module opens for the selected sheet object.

③ In the Object box, click ▾ and then the Worksheet option.

④ In the Procedure box, click ▾ and then the Change option.

- The Visual Basic Editor creates a new Private subroutine named `Worksheet_Change`.

⑤ Type the VBA code to run when the workbook opens.

**Note:** See Chapter 11 for information on using the `Intersect` method to compare ranges.

⑥ Switch to Excel and click a cell.

The `Worksheet_Change` procedure executes the specified VBA code to determine if the selected cell is within the specified range.

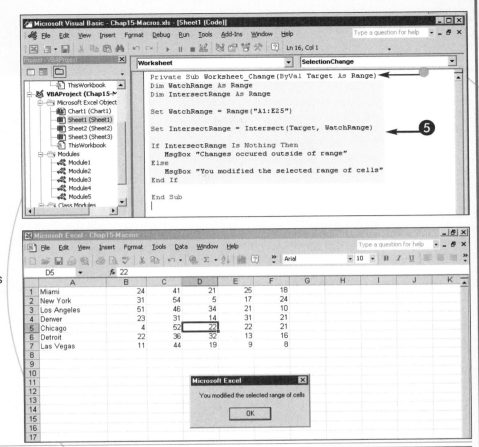

## Extra

Because Excel only triggers the `Change` event when a user or external link changes the values of cells, you may find instances where you expect Excel to trigger a change event, and it does not. The following table compares incidents where Excel triggers a `Change` event versus times it does not.

| TRIGGER CHANGE EVENT | DOES NOT TRIGGER CHANGE EVENT |
| --- | --- |
| Type value in a cell | Calculate new value for formula |
| Edit➜Clear Formats | Change cell formatting |
| Edit➜Fill | Data➜Form |
| Press Delete | Data➜Sort |
| Edit➜Delete | Change from a procedure (macro) |
| Tools➜Spelling | Insert➜Comment |
| Edit➜Replace | Insert➜Picture |
| | Insert➜Diagram |

You can use the `Calculate` event to determine when cell values change due to recalculating a worksheet. You create an event-handling procedure for this event in the same fashion as the `Change` event. The only real difference is that the `Calculate` event does not have any parameter values. The following code shows how to initiate a `Calculate` procedure:

**Example:**
```
Private Sub Worksheet_Calculate()

End Sub
```

# Execute a Procedure at a Specific Time

You can create a procedure that executes at a specific time by capturing the OnTime event. For example, you can set a reminder message that pops up at a specific time while editing a workbook.

Unlike most other events, the OnTime event is not associated with a specific object. You, therefore, must access this event using the OnTime method that is associated with the Application object.

There are four different parameters you use with the OnTime method, with only the first two being required: EarliestTime, Procedure, LatestTime, and Schedule. You use the EarliestTime parameter to specify the time when the procedure executes. You express the time using the Excel time-numbering system. You must use the Procedure parameter to indicate the name of the procedure to execute at the specified time. Remember to enclose the procedure name in quotes.

Use the optional LatestTime parameter to indicate the latest time when the procedure can run. If the procedure has not run by the time specified by this parameter, it does not run. The other optional parameter, Schedule, has a default value of True to schedule the OnTime procedure to run again at the specified time or False to clear a previously set procedure.

Because the OnTime event is not associated with a specific object, you can place your procedure containing the method for accessing the event in any code module. Of course, if you must place the OnTime method procedure in a standard code window, you need to run the corresponding macro before the OnTime event code activates. You can also consider placing the OnTime method within the Workbook_Open procedure so that it loads the event code as the workbook opens. See the section "Run a Procedure as a Workbook Opens" for more information.

## Execute a Procedure at a Specific Time

① In the Projects window, double-click the ThisWorkbook object.

The code module opens for the ThisWorkbook object.

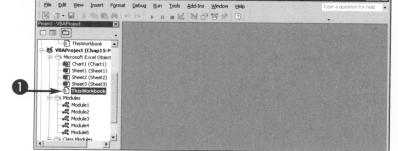

② In the Workbook_Open procedure, type **Application.OnTime Now + Timevalue("00:01:00"), "ShowWelcome"**, replacing Now + TimeValue("00:01:00") with a valid time expression and "ShowWelcome" with the procedure to run.

**Note:** See the section "Run a Procedure as a Workbook Opens" for information on the Workbook_Open procedure.

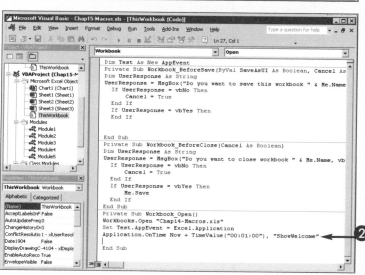

③ Create a new subroutine with the same name as the procedure specified in step 2.

**Note:** See Chapter 3 for information on creating subroutines.

④ Type the VBA code to run when the subroutine executes.

⑤ Close Excel.

⑥ Open the workbook in Excel.

The `Workbook_Open` subroutine activates the `OnTime` method and the specified procedure executes at the appropriate time.

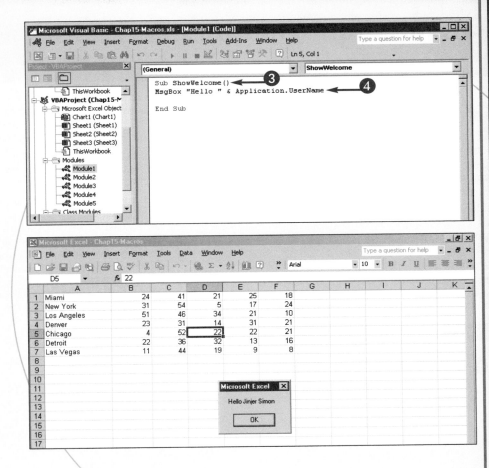

## Extra

The `EarliestTime` and `LatestTime` parameters expect time values based on Excel's time numbering system, which stores all times as decimal values ranging from 0.0 to 0.99999999. For example, Excel stores 12:00 noon as `0.5` and 6:00 PM as `0.75`. Because dealing with fractional times becomes a little mind-boggling, VBA provides the `TimeValue` function, which you can use to convert a standard time into the decimal equivalent required by the two parameters. To use this function, you simply place the time you want to convert within quotes. For example, `TimeValue("5:45 PM")` converts 5:45 PM to the appropriate decimal value.

You can use any valid time string with the `TimeValue` function.

Another useful VBA time function is the `Now` function, which returns the current date and time. When you use the `Now` function in combination with a `TimeValue` function, you can specify a time within a specific amount of time from the current time. For example, to have an event take place in 30 minutes, you express the time as follows:

**Example:**
```
Now + TimeValue("00:30:00")
```

Notice that you use the addition sign (+) to join the numeric values returned by the two functions.

# Execute a Procedure When You Press Keys

Y ou can create a procedure that executes when you press a specific key or combination of keys. For example, you can change the built key combination of Ctrl+S for saving a workbook to display your own custom pop-up dialog box. To do this, you capture the OnKey event. If you specify a key combination that Excel already uses, your new definition overrides the Excel combination.

Unlike most other events, the OnKey event is not associated with a specific object. For this reason, you access this event by using the OnKey method that is associated with the Application object.

The OnKey method has two different parameters. You use the Key parameter to specify the key combination, which you express as a string consisting of the combined keys you capture. You represent standard keys, such as a and 5,

by simply typing the character for the key. You specify non-standard keys, such as Delete and Insert, by placing the key name in brackets, such as {DELETE} or {INSERT}.

You must use the Procedure parameter to indicate the name of the procedure to execute at the specified time. Remember to enclose the procedure name in quotes.

Because the OnKey event is not associated with a specific object, you can place your procedure containing the method for accessing the event in any code module. Keep in mind that if you place the OnKey method procedure in a standard code window, you need to run the corresponding macro before the OnKey event code activates. You can place the OnKey method within the Workbook_Open procedure so that it loads as the workbook opens. See a section "Run a Procedure as a Workbook Opens" for more information.

## Execute a Procedure When You Press Keys

① In the Projects window, double-click the ThisWorkbook object node.

The code module opens for the ThisWorkbook object.

② In the Workbook_Open procedure, type **Application.OnKey "^s," "CustomSave"**, replacing "^s" with a valid key combination string and "CustomSave" with the procedure to run.

**Note:** See the section "Run a Procedure as a Workbook Opens" for information on the Workbook_Open procedure.

③ Create a new subroutine with the same name as the procedure specified in step 2.

**Note:** See Chapter 3 for information on creating subroutines.

④ Type the VBA code to run when the subroutine executes.

⑤ Close Excel.

⑥ Open the workbook in Excel.

⑦ Press the custom key combination.

● The `Workbook_Open` subroutine activates the `OnKey` method and the specified procedure executes when you press the key combination.

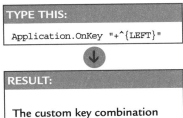

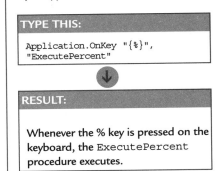

## Apply It

When specifying keys that do not display a character, such as Delete or Down Arrow, you stipulate the name of the key within braces, such as {Delete} or {Down}. For some specific keys, Excel provides special characters to represent the key when you combine them with other characters:

| CHARACTER | REPRESENTS |
|-----------|------------|
| + | SHIFT |
| ^ | CTRL |
| % | ALT |
| ~ | ENTER |

If you want to assign a particular key combination back to its original meaning in Excel, you omit the `Procedure` parameter:

**TYPE THIS:**

```
Application.OnKey "+^{LEFT}"
```

**RESULT:**

The custom key combination assignment is removed and Excel executes the default command for that key combination, if one exists.

To use one of these special characters in your key combination, enclose the character in braces. For example, to specify a procedure to execute when you press the percent sign, you type the following code.

**TYPE THIS:**

```
Application.OnKey "{%}",
"ExecutePercent"
```

**RESULT:**

Whenever the % key is pressed on the keyboard, the `ExecutePercent` procedure executes.

# Run a Procedure When Right-Clicking a Chart

You can create a procedure that runs automatically each time a user right-clicks on a particular chart with the mouse. To create this type of procedure, you need to capture the BeforeRightClick event associated with the appropriate Chart object.

To create a procedure that executes when a user right-clicks a chart, you create a new procedure and add it to the object code module for the particular chart. In fact, all event-handling procedures that you create for monitoring chart events must reside within the appropriate chart object code module to have Excel execute them automatically. To create a procedure that executes when right-clicking a chart, you name the procedure Chart_BeforeRightClick.

Although the procedure resides in a chart object code module, it can access other procedures within the same workbook. Therefore, you can create a

Chart_BeforeRightClick procedure that calls procedures located in another module. The procedures you create only execute for the chart in whose code module you place them. If you want to have the procedure execute for multiple charts, you copy the procedure to each module.

The BeforeRightClick event has one parameter, Cancel, that passes to the event when it triggers. If the Cancel parameter has the default value of False, the right-click event procedure performs after your procedure executes. If you set the value of the Cancel parameter to True, Excel does not perform the default procedure.

Keep in mind, Excel does not perform the BeforeRightClick event if the mouse pointer is over a shape, a toolbar, or a menu bar. See Chapter 14 for more information about working with charts.

## Run a Procedure When Right-Clicking a Chart

① On the Projects window, double-click the chart object node for the chart where you want to place the Chart_BeforeRightClick subroutine.

The code module opens for the chart object.

② In the Object box, click ▾ and then the Chart option.

③ In the Procedure box, click ▾ and then the BeforeRightClick option.

The Visual Basic Editor creates a new Private subroutine named `Chart_BeforeRightClick`.

④ Type the VBA code to run when the user right-clicks the chart.

⑤ Switch to Excel.

⑥ Right-click the chart.

The `Chart_BeforeRightClick` procedure executes the specified VBA code.

## Apply It

Instead of capturing a right-mouse click on the entire chart, you may want to capture a double-click on an individual chart element. For example, you can execute a procedure when the user double-clicks the Chart Area by typing the following code:

### TYPE THIS:

```
Private Sub Chart_BeforeDoubleClick(ByVal
ElementID As Long, ByVal Arg1 As Long,
ByVal
Arg2 As Long, Cancel As Boolean)
        If ElementID = xlChartArea Then
            Call ShowChartData
        End If
End Sub
```

### RESULT:

This code checks the value of the `ElementID` parameter to determine what element of the chart was selected.

You can use the following constants to represent the chart element you want to capture.

```
xlAxis, xlAxisTitle, xlChartArea,
xlChartTitle, xlCorners,
xlDataLabel, xlDisplayUnitLabel,
xlDownBars, xlDropLines,
xlErrorBars, xlFloor,
xlHiLoLines, xlLegend,
xlLegendEntry, xlMajorGridlines,
xlMinorGridlines, xlNothing,
xlPivotChartDropZone,
xlPivotChartFieldButton,
xlPlotArea, xlRadarAxisLabels,
xlSeries, xlSeriesLines, xlShape,
xlTrendline, xlUpBars, xlWalls
```

# VBA and Excel Object Model Quick Reference

## VBA Statements Quick Reference

**Legend:**

Plain courier text = required      [] = optional      | = or

*Italics* = user-defined      . . . = list of items

### File and Folder Handling

| STATEMENT | DESCRIPTION |
|---|---|
| ChDir *path* | Changes to the specified folder location. |
| ChDrive *drive* | Changes to the specified drive. |
| Close [*filenumber*] | Closes a file opened using the Open statement. |
| FileCopy *source, destination* | Copies a file from the source to the specified destination. |
| Kill *pathname* | Deletes files from a disk. Use wildcards * for multiple characters and ? for single characters. |
| Lock [#]*filenumber*[, *recordrange*] | Locks all or a portion of an open file to prevent access by other processes. |
| Open *pathname* For *mode* [Access *access*] [lock] As [#]*filenumber* [Len=*reclength*] | Opens the specified file to allow input/output operations. |
| MkDir *path* | Creates a new directory or folder. |
| Print #*filenumber*[, *outputlist*] | Writes display-formatted data sequentially to a file. |
| Put [#]*filenumber*, [*recnumber*,] *varname* | Writes data contained in a variable to a disk file. |
| Reset | Closes all files opened using the Open statement. |
| RmDir *path* | Removes the specified folder. |
| SetAttr *pathname, attributes* | Sets the attribute information for the specified file. |
| Unlock [#]*filenumber*[, *recordrange*] | Unlocks a file to allow access by other processes. |
| Width #*filenumber, width* | Assigns the output line width for a file opened using the Open statement. |
| Write #*filenumber*[, *outputlist*] | Writes data to a sequential text file. |

### Interaction

| STATEMENT | DESCRIPTION |
|---|---|
| AppActivate *title*[, *wait*] | Activates an application window. |
| DeleteSetting *appname, section*[, *key*] | Deletes a section or key setting from an application's entry in the Windows Registry. |
| SaveSetting *appname, section, key, setting* | Saves an application entry in the application's entry in the Windows Registry. |
| SendKeys *string*[, *wait*] | Sends one or more keystrokes to the active window as if they were typed on the keyboard. |

## Program Flow

| STATEMENT | DESCRIPTION |
|---|---|
| `[Public | Private] Declare Sub` *name* `Lib` *"libname"* `[Alias` *"aliasname"*`] [([`*arglist*`])]` | Declares a reference to an external DLL library function. |
| `Do [{While | Until}` *condition*`]`<br>  `[`*statements*`]`<br>`Loop` | Repeats a block of statements while or until a condition is true. The condition is checked at the beginning of the loop. |
| `Do`<br>  `[`*statements*`]`<br>`Loop [{While | Until}` *condition*`]` | Repeats a block of statements while or until a condition is true. Because the condition is checked at the end of the loop, the block of statements always executes at least once. |
| `Exit Do | For | Function | Property | Sub` | Exits the specified `Do Loop`, `For Next`, `Function`, `Sub`, or `Property` code. |
| `For Each` *element* `In` *group*<br>`[`*statements*`]`<br>`Next [`*element*`]` | Repeats a block of statements for each element in an array or collection. |
| `For` *counter* `=` *start* `To` *end* `[Step` *step*`]`<br>  `[`*statements*`]`<br>`Next [`*counter*`]` | Repeats a section of code the specified number of times. |
| `[Public | Private | Friend] [Static] Function` *name*<br>`[(`*arglist*`)] [As` *type*`]`<br>`[`*statements*`]`<br>`[`*name* `=` *expression*`]`<br>`End Function` | Defines a procedure that returns a value. |
| `If` *condition* `Then`<br>`[`*statements*`]`<br><br>`[ElseIf` *condition-n* `Then`<br>`[`*elseifstatements*`] . . .`<br><br>`[Else`<br>`[`*elsestatements*`]]`<br><br>`End If` | Conditionally executes a block of statements based upon the value of an expression. |
| `[Public | Private | Friend] [Static] Property Get` *name*<br>  `[(`*arglist*`)] [As` *type*`]`<br>`[`*statements*`]`<br>`[`*name* `=` *expression*`]`<br>`End Property` | Declares the name and arguments procedure. |
| `[Public | Private | Friend] [Static] Property Let` *name*<br>  `([`*arglist*`,]` *value*`)`<br>`[`*statements*`]`<br>`End Property` | Declares the name and arguments of a procedure that assigns a value to a property. |
| `[Public | Private | Friend] [Static] Property Set` *name*<br>  `([`*arglist*`,]` *reference*`)`<br>`[`*statements*`]`<br>`End Property` | Declares the name and arguments of a procedure that sets a reference to an object. |

*continued*

continued →

## VBA Statements Quick Reference *(continued)*

### Program Flow (continued)

| STATEMENT | DESCRIPTION |
|---|---|
| `Select Case` *testexpression*<br>`[Case` *expressionlist-n*<br>  *[statements-n]]* . . .<br>`[Case Else`<br>  *[elsestatements]]*<br>`End Select` | Executes one block out of a series of statement blocks depending upon the value of an expression. |
| `[Private \| Public \| Friend][Static] Sub` *name* `[(arglist)]`<br>*[statements]*<br>`End Sub` | Declares the name, arguments, and code that form a Sub procedure. |
| `While` *condition*<br>  *[statements]*<br>`Wend` | Executes a block of statements as long as the specified condition is true. |
| `With` *object*<br>  *[statements]*<br>`End With` | Executes a block of statements on a single object or on a user-defined data type. |

### Variable Declaration

| STATEMENT | DESCRIPTION |
|---|---|
| `[Public \| Private] Const` *constname* `[As` *type*`] =` *expression* | Declares a constant value. |
| `Dim [WithEvents]` *varname*`[([`*subscripts*`])] [As [New]` *type*`]` | Declares variables and allocates the appropriate storage space. |
| `Friend [WithEvents]` *varname*`[([`*subscripts*`])] [As [New]` *type*`]` | Declares a procedure or variable to only have scope in the project where it is defined. |
| `Option Compare {Binary \| Text \| Database}` | Specifies the default comparison method to use when comparing strings. |
| `Option Explicit` | Forces declaration of all variables within the module. |
| `Option Private` | Indicates that all code within the entire module is `Private`. This option is used by default. You can overwrite the effects of this option by declaring a specific procedure `Public`. |
| `Private [WithEvents]` *varname*`[([`*subscripts*`])] [As [New]` *type*`]` | Declares variables and procedures to only have scope within the current module. |
| `Public [WithEvents]` *varname*`[([`*subscripts*`])] [As [New]` *type*`]` | Declares variables and procedures to have scope within the entire project. |

### Variable Declaration (continued)

| STATEMENT | DESCRIPTION |
|---|---|
| ReDim [Preserve] *varname*(*subscripts*) [As *type*] | Changes the dimensions of a dynamic array. |
| [Private \| Public] Type *varname*<br>*elementname* [([*subscripts*])] As *type*<br>[*elementname* [([*subscripts*])] As *type*]<br>. . . | Defines a custom data type. |
| End Type | |

# VBA Function Quick Reference

### Legend:

Plain courier text = required     [] = optional     | = or

*Italics* = user-defined     . . . = list of items

### Array Functions

| FUNCTION | DESCRIPTION | RETURNS |
|---|---|---|
| Array(*arg1*,*arg2*, *arg3*, . . .) | Creates a variant array containing the specified elements. | Variant |
| LBound(*arrayname*[, *dimension*]) | Returns the smallest subscript for the specified array. | Long |
| UBound(*arrayname*[, *dimension*]) | Returns the largest subscript for the specified array. | Long |

### Data Type Conversion Functions

| FUNCTION | DESCRIPTION | RETURNS |
|---|---|---|
| Asc(*string*) | Returns the character code of the first letter in a string. | Integer |
| CBool(*expression*) | Converts an expression to Boolean data type (True or False). | Boolean |
| CByte(*expression*) | Converts an expression to Byte data type. | Byte |
| CCur(*expression*) | Converts an expression to Currency data type. | Currency |
| CDate(*expression*) | Converts an expression to a Date data type. | Date |
| CDbl(*expression*) | Converts an expression to Double data type. | Double |
| CDec(*expression*) | Converts an expression to a decimal value. | Variant (*Decimal*) |
| Chr(*charactercode*) | Converts the character code to the corresponding character. Chr(9) returns a tab, Chr(34) returns quotation marks, etc. | Variant |
| CInt(*expression*) | Converts an expression to an Integer data type; rounding any fractional parts. | Integer |

*continued*

continued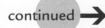

## VBA Function Quick Reference *(continued)*

### Data Type Conversion Functions (continued)

| FUNCTION | DESCRIPTION | RETURNS |
|---|---|---|
| CLng(*expression*) | Converts an expression to the Long data type. | Long |
| CSng(*expression*) | Converts an expression to the Single data type. | Single |
| CStr(*expression*) | Returns a string containing the specified expression. | String |
| CVar(*expression*) | Converts any data type to a Variant data type. All numeric values are treated as Double data types and string expressions are treated as String data types. | Variant |
| Format(*expression*[, *format*[, *firstdayofweek*[, *firstweekofyear*]]]) | Formats the expression using either predefined or user-defined formats. | Variant |
| FormatCurrency(*Expression*[, *NumDigitsAfterDecimal* [, *IncludeLeadingDigit* [,*UseParensForNegativeNumbers* [, *GroupDigits*]]]]) | Formats the expression as a currency value using the system-defined currency symbol. | Currency |
| FormatDateTime(*Date*[, *NamedFormat*]) | Formats an expression as a date and time. | Date |
| FormatNumber(*Expression* [, *NumDigitsAfterDecimal* [, *IncludeLeadingDigit* [, *UseParensForNegativeNumbers* [, *GroupDigits*]]]]) | Formats the expression as a number. | Mixed |
| FormatPercent(*Expression* [,*NumDigitsAfterDecimal* [,*IncludeLeadingDigit* [,*UseParensForNegativeNumbers* [,*GroupDigits*]]]]) | Returns the expression formatted as a percentage with a trailing % character. | String |
| Hex(*number*) | Converts a number to a hexadecimal value. Rounds numbers to nearest whole number before converting. | String |
| Oct(*number*) | Converts a number to an octal value. Rounds numbers to nearest whole number before converting. | Variant (*String*) |
| Str(*number*) | Converts a number to a string using the Variant. data type | Variant (*String*) |
| Val(*string*) | Returns the numeric portion of a string formatted as a number of the appropriate data type. | Mixed |

# VBA Function Quick Reference *(continued)*

## Date and Time Functions

| FUNCTION | DESCRIPTION | RETURNS |
|---|---|---|
| Date | Returns the current system date. | Date |
| DateAdd(*interval, number, date*) | Returns a date that is the specified interval of time from the original date. | Date |
| DateDiff(*interval, date1, date2[, firstdayofweek[, firstweekofyear]]*) | Determines the time interval between two dates. | Long |
| DatePart(*interval, date[, firstdayofweek[, firstweekofyear]]*) | Returns the specified part of a date. | Integer |
| DateSerial(*year, month, day*) | Converts the specified date to a serial number. | Date |
| DateValue(*date*) | Converts a string to a date. | Date |
| Day(*date*) | Returns a whole number between 1 and 31 representing the day of the month. | Integer |
| Hour(*time*) | Returns a whole number between 0 and 23 representing the hour of the day. | Integer |
| Minute(*time*) | Returns a whole number between 0 and 59 representing the minute of the hour. | Integer |
| Month(*date*) | Returns a whole number between 1 and 12 representing the month of the year. | Integer |
| Now | Returns the current system date and time. | Date |
| Second(*time*) | Returns a whole number between 0 and 59 representing the second of the minute. | Integer |
| Time | Returns the current system time. | Date |
| Timer | Indicates the number of seconds that have elapsed since midnight | Single |
| TimeSerial(*hour, minute, second*) | Creates a time using the specified hour, minute, and second values. | Date |
| TimeValue(*time*) | Converts a time to the serial number used to store time. | Date |
| WeekDay(*date, [firstdayofweek]*) | Returns a whole number representing the first day of the week. | Integer |
| Year(*date*) | Returns a whole number representing the year portion of a date. | Integer |

continued →

## VBA Function Quick Reference *(continued)*

### File and Folder Handling Functions

| FUNCTION | DESCRIPTION | RETURNS |
|---|---|---|
| CurDir(*drive*) | Returns the current path. | String |
| Dir[(*pathname*[, *attributes*])] | Returns the name of the file, directory, or folder that matches the specified pattern. | String |
| EOF(*filenumber*) | Returns -1 when the end of a file has been reached. | Integer |
| FileAttr(*filenumber, returntype*) | Indicates the file mode used for files opened with the Open statement. | Long |
| FileDateTime(*pathname*) | Indicates the date and time when a file was last modified. | Date |
| FileLen(*pathname*) | Indicates the length of a file in bytes. | Long |
| FreeFile(*rangenumber*) | Returns the next file number available for use by the Open statement. | Integer |
| GetAttr(*pathname*) | Returns a whole number representing the attributes of a file, directory, or folder. | Integer |
| Input(*number*, [#]*filenumber*) | Returns a string containing the indicated number of characters from the specified file. | String |
| Loc(*filenumber*) | Indicates the current read/write position in an open file. | Long |
| LOF(*filenumber*) | Returns the size in bytes of a file opened using the Long Open statement. | Long |
| Seek(*filenumber*) | Specifies the current read/write position with a file opened with the Open statement. | Long |

### Financial Functions

| FUNCTION | DESCRIPTION | RETURNS |
|---|---|---|
| DDB(*cost, salvage, life, period*[, *factor*]) | Specifies the depreciation value for an asset during a specific time frame. | Double |
| FV(*rate, nper, pmt*[, *pv*[, *type*]]) | Determines the future value of an annuity based on periodic fixed payments. | Double |
| IPmt(*rate, per, nper, pv*[, *fv*[, *type*]]) | Determines the interest payment on an annuity for a specific period of time. | Double |
| IRR(*values()*, [, *guess*]) | Determines the internal rate of returns for a series of cash flows. | Double |
| MIRR(*values(), finance_rate, reinvest_rate*) | Returns the modified interest rate of returns for a series of periodic cash flows. | Double |

# VBA Function Quick Reference *(continued)*

## Financial Functions (continued)

| FUNCTION | DESCRIPTION | RETURNS |
|---|---|---|
| NPer(*rate, pmt, pv*[, *fv*[, *type*]]) | Returns the number of periods for an annuity. | Double |
| NPV(*rate, values()*) | Returns the net present value of an investment. | Double |
| Pmt(*rate, nper, pv*[, *fv*[, *type*]]) | Returns the payment amount for an annuity based on fixed payments. | Double |
| PPmt(*rate, per, nper, pv*[, *fv*[, *type*]]) | Returns the principal payment amount for an annuity. | Double |
| PV(*rate, nper, pmt*[, *fv*[, *type*]]) | Returns the present value of an annuity. | Double |
| Rate(*nper, pmt, pv*[, *fv*[, *type*[, *guess*]]]) | Returns the interest rate per period for an annuity. | Double |
| SLN(*cost, salvage, life*) | Determines the straight-line depreciation of an asset for a single period. | Double |
| SYD(*cost, salvage, life, period*) | Determines the sum-of-years' digits depreciation of an asset for a specified period. | Double |

## Information Functions

| FUNCTION | DESCRIPTION | RETURNS |
|---|---|---|
| CVErr(*errornumber*) | Returns a user-defined error number. | Variant |
| Error[(*errornumber*)] | Returns the error message for the specified error number. | String |
| IsArray(*varname*) | Indicates whether a variable contains an array. | Boolean |
| IsDate(*expression*) | Indicates whether an expression contains a date. | Boolean |
| IsEmpty(*expression*) | Indicates whether a variable has been initialized. | Boolean |
| IsError(*expression*) | Indicates whether an expression is an error value. | Boolean |
| IsMissing(*argname*) | Indicates whether an optional argument was passed to a procedure. | Boolean |
| IsNull(*expression*) | Indicates whether an expression contains no valid data. | Boolean |
| IsNumeric(*expression*) | Indicates whether an expression is a number. | Boolean |
| IsObject(*identifier*) | Indicates whether a variable references an object. | Boolean |
| TypeName(*varname*) | Specifies the variable type. | String |
| VarType(*varname*) | Specifies the subtype of a variable. | Integer |

continued →

## VBA Function Quick Reference *(continued)*

### Interaction Functions

| FUNCTION | DESCRIPTION | RETURNS |
|---|---|---|
| Choose(*index, choice-1,* [*choice-2, ...*]) | Selects and returns a value from a list of arguments. | Mixed |
| DoEvents() | Yields execution so the operating system can process other events. | Integer |
| Iif(*expr, truepart, falsepart*) | Evaluates the expression and returns either the truepart or falsepart parameter value. | Mixed |
| InputBox(*prompt*[, *title*] [, *default*] [, *xpos*] [, *ypos*] [, *helpfile, context*]) | Displays a dialog box prompting the user for input. | String |
| GetAllSettings(*appname, section*) | Returns a list of key settings and their values from the Windows Registry. | Variant |
| GetObject([*pathname*][, *class*]) | Returns a reference to an object provided by an ActiveX Component. | Variant |
| GetSetting(*appname, section, key*[, *default*]) | Returns a key setting value from an application's entry in the Windows registry. | Variant |
| MsgBox(*prompt*[, *buttons*] [, *title*] [, *helpfile, context*]) | Displays a message box and returns a value representing the button pressed by the user. | Integer |
| Partition(*number, start, stop, interval*) | Indicates where a number occurs within a series of ranges. | String |
| QBColor(*color*) | Returns the RGB color code for the specified color. | Long |
| Switch(*expr-1, value-1*[, *expr-2, value-2 ...*]) | Evaluates a list of expressions and returns a value associated with the first True expression. | Variant |
| RGB(*red, green, blue*) | Returns a number representing the RGB color value. | Long |

### Mathematical Functions

| FUNCTION | DESCRIPTION | RETURNS |
|---|---|---|
| Abs(*number*) | Returns the absolute value of a number. | Mixed |
| Atn(*number*) | Returns the arctangent of a number. | Double |
| Cos(*number*) | Returns the cosine of an angle. | Double |

## Mathematical Functions (Continued)

| FUNCTION | DESCRIPTION | RETURNS |
| --- | --- | --- |
| Exp(*number*) | Returns the base of the natural logarithms raised to a power. | Double |
| Fix(*number*) | Returns the integer portion of a number. With negative values, returns first negative value greater than or equal to number. | Integer |
| Int(*number*) | Returns the integer portion of a number. With negative values, returns the first negative number less than or equal to the number. | Integer |
| Log(*number*) | Returns the natural logarithm of a number. | Double |
| Round(*expression* [, *numdecimalplaces*]) | Rounds a number to the specified number of decimal places. | Mixed |
| Rnd[(*number*)] | Returns a random number between 0 and 1. | Single |
| Sgn(*number*) | Returns 1 for a number greater than 0, 0 for a value of 0, and -1 number less than zero. | Integer |
| Sin(*number*) | Specifies the sine of an angle. | Double |
| Sqr(*number*) | Specifies the square root of a number. | Double |
| Tan(*number*) | Specifies the tangent of an angle. | Double |

## String Manipulation Functions

| FUNCTION | DESCRIPTION | RETURNS |
| --- | --- | --- |
| nStr([*start,* ]*string1,* string2[, *compare*]) | Specifies the position of one string within another string. | Long |
| InStrRev(*stringcheck, stringmatch*[, *start*[, *compare*]]) | Specifies the position of one string within another starting at the end of the string. | Long |
| LCase(*string*) | Converts a string to lowercase. | String |
| Left(*string, length*) | Returns the specified number of characters from the left side of a string. | String |
| Len(*string* \| *varname*) | Determines the number of characters in a string. | Long |
| LTrim(*string*) | Trims spaces from the left side of a string. | String |
| Mid(*string, start*[, *length*]) | Returns the specified number of characters from the center of a string. | String |
| Right(*string, length*) | Returns the specified number of characters from the right side of a string. | String |
| RTrim(*string*) | Trims spaces from the right side of a string. | String |
| Space(*number*) | Creates a string with the specified number of spaces. | String |

*continued*

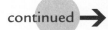
continued

## VBA Function Quick Reference *(continued)*

### String Manipulation Functions (continued)

| FUNCTION | DESCRIPTION | RETURNS |
|---|---|---|
| Spc(*n*) | Positions output when printing to a file. | String |
| Str(*number*) | Returns a string representation of a number. | String |
| StrComp(*string1, string2[, compare]*) | Returns a value indicating the result of a string comparison. | Integer |
| StrConv(*string, conversion, LCID*) | Converts a string to the specified format. | String |
| String(*number, character*) | Creates a string by repeating a character the specified number of times. | String |
| Tab[(*n*)] | Positions output when printing to a file. | String |
| Trim(*string*) | Trims spaces from left and right of a string. | String |
| UCase(*string*) | Converts a string to uppercase. | String |

## VBA Function Constants and Characters

### vbMsgBoxStyle Constants (MsgBox Function)

| CONSTANT | VALUE | DESCRIPTION |
|---|---|---|
| vbAbortRetryIgnore | 2 | Displays Abort, Retry, and Ignore buttons. |
| vbApplicationModal | 0 | Creates application modal message box. |
| vbCritical | 16 | Displays Critical Message icon. |
| vbDefaultButton1 | 0 | Makes first button default. |
| vbDefaultButton2 | 256 | Makes second button default. |
| vbDefaultButton3 | 512 | Makes third button default. |
| vbDefaultButton4 | 768 | Makes fourth button default. |
| vbExclamation | 48 | Displays Warning Message icon. |
| vbInformation | 64 | Displays Information Message icon. |
| vbMsgBoxHelpButton | 16384 | Adds a Help button. |

# VBA Function Constants and Characters *(continued)*

## vbMsgBoxStyle Constants (MsgBox Function) (continued)

| CONSTANT | VALUE | DESCRIPTION |
|---|---|---|
| vbMsgBoxRight | 524288 | Right aligns text in the box. |
| vbMsgBoxRtlReading | 1048576 | Used only with Hebrew and Arabic systems for right-to-left reading. |
| vbMsgBoxSetForeground | 65536 | Makes message box the foreground window. |
| vbOKCancel | 1 | Displays OK and Cancel buttons. |
| vbOKOnly | 0 | Displays only the OK button. |
| vbQuestion | 32 | Displays Warning Query icon. |
| vbRetryCancel | 5 | Displays Retry and Cancel buttons. |
| vbSystemModal | 4096 | Creates a system modal message box. |
| vbYesNo | 4 | Displays Yes and No buttons. |
| vbYesNoCancel | 3 | Displays Yes, No, and Cancel buttons. |

## vbDayOfWeek Constants

| CONSTANT | VALUE | DESCRIPTION |
|---|---|---|
| vbUseSystemDayofWeek | 0 | Uses the system defined first day of week. |
| vbSunday | 1 | Sunday (default). |
| vbMonday | 2 | Monday. |
| vbTuesday | 3 | Tuesday. |
| vbWednesday | 4 | Wednesday. |
| vbThursday | 5 | Thursday. |
| vbFriday | 6 | Friday. |
| vbSaturday | 7 | Saturday. |

## vbFirstWeekOfYear Constants

| CONSTANT | VALUE | DESCRIPTION |
|---|---|---|
| vbUseSystem | 0 | Uses system defined first week of year. |
| vbFirstJan1 | 1 | Starts with week in which January 1 occurs (default). |
| vbFirstFourDays | 2 | Starts with the first week that has at least four days in the new year. |
| vbFirstFullWeek | 3 | Starts with first full week of the year. |

continued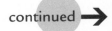

## VBA Function Constants and Characters *(continued)*

### Format Function Characters

| DATE/TIME CHARACTERS | DISPLAYS |
|---|---|
| d | Day with no leading zero. |
| ddd | Three-letter abbreviation of day (Sun. – Sat.). |
| dddd | Full day name (Sunday). |
| ddddd | Complete date using short date format. |
| dddddd | Complete date using long date format. |
| w | Day of week as number (1 for Sunday). |
| ww | Week of year as number. |
| m | Month with no leading zero. |
| mmm | Three letter abbreviation of month (Jan.-Dec.). |
| mmmm | Complete month name. |
| q | Quarter of year. |
| y | Day of year as number. |
| yy | Year as 2-digit number. |
| yyyy | Year as 4-digit number. |
| h | Hour with no leading zero. |
| n | Minutes with no leading zero. |
| s | Seconds with no leading zero. |
| ttttt | Complete time using system time format. |
| c | Date as ddddd and time as ttttt. |

### Format Function Predefined Formats

| FORMAT | DESCRIPTION |
|---|---|
| General Date | Uses general date format. |
| Long Date | Uses system-defined long date, such as Tuesday, August 7, 2001. |
| Medium Date | Uses the medium date format, such as 07-Aug-01. |
| Short Date | Uses system-defined short date, such as 8/7/2001. |
| Long Time | Uses system-defined long time, such as 5:45:30 P.M. |
| Medium Time | Uses the medium time format, such as 05:45 P.M. |

# VBA Function Constants and Characters *(continued)*

## Format Function Predefined Formats (continued)

| FORMAT | DESCRIPTION |
|---|---|
| Short Time | Uses the short time format, such as 17:45. |
| General Number | Uses the general number format. |
| Currency | Places the appropriate currency symbol in front of the number. |
| Fixed | Uses a fixed decimal format. |
| Standard | Uses standard formatting. |
| Percent | Converts the expression to a percentage. |
| Scientific | Displays the expression using scientific notation. |
| Yes/No | Converts the expression to a Yes or No value. |
| True/False | Converts the expression to a True or False value. |
| On/Off | Converts the expression to an On or Off value. |

# Excel Object Model Constants

## XlColumnDataType Constants

| CONSTANT | VALUE | DESCRIPTION |
|---|---|---|
| xlDMYFormat | 4 | DMY format date. |
| xlDYMFormat | 7 | DYM format date. |
| xlEMDFormat | 10 | EMD format date. |
| xlGeneralFormat | 1 | General format. |
| xlMDYFormat | 3 | MDY format date. |
| xlMYDFormat | 6 | MYD format date. |
| xlSkipColumn | 9 | Skip Column. |
| xlTextFormat | 2 | Text format. |
| xlYDMFormat | 8 | YDM format date. |
| xlYMDFormat | 5 | YMD format date. |

## XlFileFormat Constants

| CONSTANT | VALUE | DESCRIPTION |
|---|---|---|
| xlAddIn | 18 | Excel add-in. |
| xlCSV | 6 | Comma-separated values format. |
| xlCSVMac | 22 | Macintosh comma-separated values format. |

*continued*

continued →

## Excel Object Model Constants *(continued)*

### XlFileFormat Constants (continued)

| CONSTANT | VALUE | DESCRIPTION |
|---|---|---|
| xlCSVMSDOS | 24 | MSDOS comma-separated values format. |
| xlCSVWindows | 23 | MS Windows comma-separated values format. |
| xlCurrentPlatformText | -4158 | Text file based on current operating system. |
| xlDBF2 | 7 | DBase II format. |
| xlDBF3 | 8 | DBase III format. |
| xlDBF4 | 11 | DBase IV format. |
| xlDIF | 9 | Data interchange format. |
| xlExcel2 | 16 | Excel 2.0 format. |
| xlExcel2FarEast | 27 | Excel 2.0 format – Far East version. |
| xlExcel3 | 29 | Excel 3.0 format. |
| xlExcel4 | 33 | Excel 4.0 format. |
| xlExcel4Workbook | 35 | Excel 4.0 workbook format. |
| xlExcel5 | 39 | Excel 5.0 format. |
| xlExcel7 | 39 | Excel 97 format. |
| xlExcel9795 | 43 | Excel 95 – 97 format. |
| xlHtml | 44 | HTML format. |
| xlIntlAddIn | 26 | Excel international Add-in. |
| xlIntlMacro | 25 | Excel international macro. |
| xlSYLK | 2 | Symbolic link format. |
| xlTemplate | 17 | Template file format. |
| xlTextMac | 19 | Macintosh text file format. |
| xlTextMSDOS | 21 | MSDOS text file format. |
| xlTextPrinter | 36 | Text file created for a printer (.prn). |
| xlTextWindows | 20 | MS Window text file format. |
| xlUnicodeText | 42 | Unicode text file format. |
| xlWebArchive | 45 | Web archive format (.mht). |
| xlWK1 | 5 | Lotus 2.x format. |
| xlWK1ALL | 31 | Lotus 2.x .all format. |

## XlFileFormat Constants (continued)

| CONSTANT | VALUE | DESCRIPTION |
|---|---|---|
| xlWK1FMT | 30 | Lotus 2.x .fmt format. |
| xlWK3 | 15 | Lotus 3.x format. |
| xlWK3FM3 | 32 | Lotus 3.x and Lotus 1-2-3 for Windows format. |
| xlWK4 | 38 | Lotus 4.0 format. |
| xlWKS | 4 | MS Works file format. |
| xlWorkbookNormal | -4143 | Excel workbook format. |
| xlWorks2FarEast | 28 | MS Works file – Far East format. |
| xlWQ1 | 34 | Quattro Pro for MSDOS format. |
| xlXMLSpreadsheet | 46 | XML format. |

## MsoFileType Constants

| CONSTANT | VALUE | DESCRIPTION |
|---|---|---|
| msoFileTypeAllFiles | 1 | All file types. |
| msoFileTypeBinders | 6 | Microsoft Office Binder file. |
| msoFileTypeCalendarItem | 11 | Microsoft Outlook Calendar item. |
| msoFileTypeContactItem | 12 | Microsoft Outlook Contact item. |
| msoFileTypeDatabases | 7 | Database files. |
| msoFileTypeDataConnectionFiles | 17 | Database connection files. |
| msoFileTypeDesignerFiles | 22 | Designer files. |
| msoFileTypeDocumentImagingFiles | 20 | Document imaging files. |
| msoFileTypeExcelWorkbooks | 4 | Microsoft Excel Workbooks. |
| msoFileTypeJournalItem | 14 | Journal items. |
| msoFileTypeMailItem | 10 | Microsoft Outlook Mail message. |
| msoFileTypeNoteItem | 13 | Microsoft Outlook Note item. |
| msoFileTypeOfficeFiles | 2 | All Microsoft Office file types. |
| msoFileTypeOutlookItems | 9 | Microsoft Outlook files. |
| msoFileTypePhotoDrawFiles | 16 | Microsoft PhotoDraw files. |
| msoFileTypePowerPointPresentations | 5 | Microsoft PowerPoint files. |
| msoFileTypeProjectFiles | 19 | Microsoft Project files. |
| msoFileTypePublisherFiles | 18 | Microsoft Publisher files. |
| msoFileTypeTaskItem | 15 | Microsoft Outlook Task item. |
| msoFileTypeTemplates | 8 | Template files. |

*continued*

continued

## Excel Object Model Constants *(continued)*

### MsoFileType Constants (continued)

| CONSTANT | VALUE | DESCRIPTION |
|---|---|---|
| msoFileTypeVisioFiles | 21 | Visio files. |
| msoFileTypeWebPages | 23 | Web pages including .htm, .asp, and .mht files. |
| msoFileTypeWordDocuments | 3 | Microsoft Word documents. |

### XlChartType Constants

| CONSTANT | VALUE | CHART TYPE |
|---|---|---|
| xl3DArea | -4098 | 3D Area. |
| xl3DAreaStacked | 78 | 3D Stacked Area. |
| xl3DAreaStacked100 | 79 | 100% Stacked Area. |
| xl3DBarClustered | 60 | 3D Clustered Bar. |
| xl3DBarStacked | 61 | 3D Stacked Bar. |
| xl3DBarStacked100 | 62 | 3D 100% Stacked Bar. |
| xl3DColumn | -4100 | 3D Column. |
| xl3DColumnClustered | 54 | 3D Clustered Column. |
| xl3DColumnStacked | 55 | 3D Stacked Column. |
| xl3DColumnStacked100 | 56 | 3D 100% Stacked Column. |
| xl3DLine | -4101 | 3D Line. |
| xl3DPie | -4102 | 3D Pie. |
| xl3DPieExploded | 70 | Exploded 3D Pie. |
| xlArea | 1 | Area. |
| xlAreaStacked | 76 | Stacked Area. |
| xlAreaStacked100 | 77 | 100% Stacked Area. |
| xlBarClustered | 57 | Clustered Bar. |
| xlBarOfPie | 71 | Bar of Pie. |
| xlBarStacked | 58 | Stacked Bar. |
| xlBarStacked100 | 59 | 100% Stacked Bar. |
| xlBubble | 15 | Bubble. |
| xlBubble3DEffec | 87 | Bubble with 3D effects. |

## XlChartType Constants (continued)

| CONSTANT | VALUE | CHART TYPE |
|---|---|---|
| xlColumnClustered | 51 | Clustered Column. |
| xlColumnStacked | 52 | Stacked Column. |
| xlColumnStacked100 | 53 | 100% Stacked Column. |
| xlConeBarClustered | 102 | Clustered Cone Bar. |
| xlConeBarStacked | 103 | Stacked Cone Bar. |
| xlConeBarStacked100 | 104 | 100% Stacked Cone Bar. |
| xlConeCol | 105 | 3D Cone Column. |
| xlConeColClustered | 99 | Clustered Cone Column. |
| xlConeColStacked | 100 | Stacked Cone Column. |
| xlConeColStacked100 | 101 | 100% Stacked Cone Column. |
| xlCylinderBarClustered | 95 | Clustered Cylinder Bar. |
| xlCylinderBarStacked | 96 | Stacked Cylinder Bar. |
| xlCylinderBarStacked100 | 97 | 100% Stacked Cylinder Bar. |
| xlCylinderCol | 98 | 3D Cylinder Column. |
| xlCylinderColClustered | 92 | Clustered Cone Column. |
| xlCylinderColStacked | 93 | Stacked Cone Column. |
| xlCylinderColStacked100 | 94 | 100% Stacked Cylinder Column. |
| xlDoughnut | -4120 | Doughnut. |
| xlDoughnutExploded | 80 | Exploded Doughnut. |
| xlLine | 4 | Line. |
| xlLineMarkers | 65 | Line with Markers. |
| xlLineMarkersStacked | 66 | Stacked Line with Markers. |
| xlLineMarkersStacked100 | 67 | 100% Stacked Line with Markers. |
| xlLineStacked | 63 | Stacked Line. |
| xlLineStacked100 | 64 | 100% Stacked Line. |
| xlPie | 5 | Pie. |
| xlPieExploded | 69 | Exploded Pie. |
| xlPieOfPie | 68 | Pie of Pie. |
| xlPyramidBarClustered | 109 | Clustered Pyramid Bar. |
| xlPyramidBarStacked | 110 | Stacked Pyramid Bar. |
| xlPyramidBarStacked100 | 111 | 100% Stacked Pyramid Bar. |
| xlPyramidCol | 112 | 3D Pyramid Column. |
| xlPyramidColClustered | 106 | Clustered Pyramid Column. |

*continued*

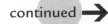

continued ➜

## Excel Object Model Constants *(continued)*

### XlChartType Constants (continued)

| CONSTANT | VALUE | CHART TYPE |
|---|---|---|
| xlPyramidColStacked | 107 | Stacked Pyramid Column. |
| xlPyramidColStacked100 | 108 | 100% Stacked Pyramid Column. |
| xlRadar | -4151 | Radar. |
| xlRadarFilled | 82 | Filled Radar. |
| xlRadarMarkers | 81 | Radar with Data Markers. |
| xlStockHLC | 88 | High-Low-Close. |
| xlStockOHLC | 89 | Open-High-Low-Close. |
| xlStockVHLC | 90 | Volume-High-Low-Close. |
| xlStockVOHLC | 91 | Volume-Open-High-Low-Close. |
| xlSurface | 83 | 3D Surface. |
| xlSurfaceTopView | 85 | Top View Surface. |
| xlSurfaceTopViewWireframe | 86 | Top View wireframe Surface. |
| xlSurfaceWireframe | 84 | 3D Surface wireframe. |
| xlXYScatter | -4169 | Scatter. |
| xlXYScatterLines | 74 | Scatter with Lines. |
| xlXYScatterLinesNoMarkers | 75 | Scatter with Lines and No Data Markers. |
| xlXYScatterSmooth | 72 | Scatter with Smoothed Lines. |
| xlXYScatterSmoothNoMarkers | 73 | Scatter with Smoothed Lines and No Data Markers. |

### XlLineStyle Constants

| CONSTANT | VALUE | DESCRIPTION |
|---|---|---|
| xlContinuous | 1 | Continuous solid line. |
| xlDash | -4155 | Dashed line. |
| xlDashDot | 4 | Line with the pattern dash dot. |
| xlDashDotDot | 5 | Line with the pattern dash dot dot. |
| xlDot | -4118 | Dotted line. |
| xlDouble | -4119 | Double solid line. |
| xlSlantDashDot | 13 | Slanted line with the pattern dash dot. |
| xlineStyleNone | -4142 | No line. |

# Excel Object Model Constants *(continued)*

## XIBorderWeight Constants

| CONSTANT | VALUE | DESCRIPTION |
|---|---|---|
| xlHairline | 1 | Creates a very thin line. |
| xlMedium | -4138 | Creates a medium width line. |
| xlThick | 4 | Creates a thick line. |
| xlThin | 2 | Creates a thin line. |

## XIPattern Constants

| CONSTANT | VALUE | DESCRIPTION |
|---|---|---|
| xlPatternAutomatic | -4105 | System default. |
| xlPatternChecker | 9 | Checkered pattern. |
| xlPatternCrissCross | 16 | Criss-cross pattern. |
| xlPatternDown | -4121 | Downward pattern. |
| xlPatternGray16 | 17 | 16% gray pattern. |
| xlPatternGray25 | -4124 | 25% gray pattern. |
| xlPatternGray50 | -4125 | 50% gray pattern. |
| xlPatternGray75 | -4126 | 75% gray pattern. |
| xlPatternGray8 | 18 | 8% gray pattern. |
| xlPatternGrid | 15 | Grid pattern. |
| xlPatternHorizontal | -4128 | Horizontal pattern. |
| xlPatternLightHorizontal | 11 | Light horizontal pattern. |
| xlPatternLightVertical | 12 | Light vertical pattern. |
| xlPatternLightDown | 13 | Light downward pattern. |
| xlPatternLightUp | 14 | Light upward pattern. |
| xlPatternNone | -4142 | No pattern. |
| xlPatternSemiGray75 | 10 | 75% semi-gray pattern. |
| xlPatternSolid | 1 | Solid color, no pattern. |
| xlPatternUp | -4162 | Upward pattern. |
| xlPatternVertical | -4166 | Vertical pattern. |

continued →

## Excel Built-in Menus and Toolbars *(continued)*

### Excel CommandBars

| CONSTANT | NAME | TYPE |
|---|---|---|
| 1 | Worksheet Menu Bar | Menu Bar |
| 2 | Chart Menu Bar | Menu Bar |
| 3 | Standard | Toolbar |
| 4 | Formatting | Toolbar |
| 5 | PivotTable | Toolbar |
| 6 | Chart | Toolbar |
| 7 | Reviewing | Toolbar |
| 8 | Forms | Toolbar |
| 9 | Stop Recording | Toolbar |
| 10 | External Data | Toolbar |
| 11 | Formula Auditing | Toolbar |
| 12 | Full Screen | Toolbar |
| 13 | Circular Reference | Toolbar |
| 14 | Visual Basic | Toolbar |
| 15 | Web | Toolbar |
| 16 | Control Toolbox | Toolbar |
| 17 | Exit Design Mode | Toolbar |
| 18 | Refresh | Toolbar |
| 19 | Watch Window | Toolbar |
| 20 | PivotTable Field List | Toolbar |
| 21 | Borders | Toolbar |
| 22 | Protection | Toolbar |
| 23 | Text To Speech | Toolbar |
| 24 | Drawing | Toolbar |
| 25 | Query and Pivot | Shortcut Menu |
| 26 | PivotChart Menu | Shortcut Menu |
| 27 | Workbook tabs | Shortcut Menu |
| 28 | Cell | Shortcut Menu |

## Excel CommandBars (continued)

| CONSTANT | NAME | TYPE |
|---|---|---|
| 29 | Column | Shortcut Menu |
| 30 | Row | Shortcut Menu |
| 31 | Cell | Shortcut Menu |
| 32 | Column | Shortcut Menu |
| 33 | Row | Shortcut Menu |
| 34 | Ply | Shortcut Menu |
| 35 | XLM Cell | Shortcut Menu |
| 36 | Document | Shortcut Menu |
| 37 | Desktop | Shortcut Menu |
| 38 | Nondefault Drag and Drop | Shortcut Menu |
| 39 | AutoFill | Shortcut Menu |
| 40 | Button | Shortcut Menu |
| 41 | Dialog | Shortcut Menu |
| 42 | Series | Shortcut Menu |
| 43 | Plot Area | Shortcut Menu |
| 44 | Floor and Walls | Shortcut Menu |
| 45 | Trendline | Shortcut Menu |
| 46 | Chart | Shortcut Menu |
| 47 | Format Data Series | Shortcut Menu |
| 48 | Format Axis | Shortcut Menu |
| 49 | Format Legend Entry | Shortcut Menu |
| 50 | Formula Bar | Shortcut Menu |
| 51 | PivotTable Context Menu | Shortcut Menu |
| 52 | Query | Shortcut Menu |
| 53 | Query Layout | Shortcut Menu |
| 54 | AutoCalculate | Shortcut Menu |
| 55 | Object/Plot | Shortcut Menu |
| 56 | Title Bar (Charting) | Shortcut Menu |
| 57 | Layout | Shortcut Menu |
| 58 | Pivot Chart Popup | Shortcut Menu |
| 59 | Phonetic Information | Shortcut Menu |
| 60 | Auto Sum | Shortcut Menu |
| 61 | Paste Special Dropdown | Shortcut Menu |

*continued*

continued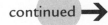

## Excel Built-in Menus and Toolbars (continued)

### Excel CommandBars (continued)

| CONSTANT | NAME | TYPE |
|---|---|---|
| 62 | Find Format | Shortcut Menu |
| 63 | Replace Format | Shortcut Menu |
| 64 | WordArt | Toolbar |
| 65 | Picture | Toolbar |
| 66 | Shadow Settings | Toolbar |
| 67 | 3-D Settings | Toolbar |
| 68 | Drawing Canvas | Toolbar |
| 69 | Organization Chart | Toolbar |
| 70 | Diagram | Toolbar |
| 71 | Borders | Toolbar |
| 72 | Borders | Toolbar |
| 73 | Draw Border | Toolbar |
| 74 | Chart Type | Toolbar |
| 75 | Pattern | Toolbar |
| 76 | Font Color | Toolbar |
| 77 | Fill Color | Toolbar |
| 78 | Line Color | Toolbar |
| 79 | Order | Toolbar |
| 80 | Nudge | Toolbar |
| 81 | Align or Distribute | Toolbar |
| 82 | Rotate or Flip | Toolbar |
| 83 | Lines | Toolbar |
| 84 | Connectors | Toolbar |
| 85 | AutoShapes | Toolbar |
| 86 | Callouts | Toolbar |
| 87 | Flowchart | Toolbar |
| 88 | Block Arrows | Toolbar |

# Excel Built-in Menus and Toolbars *(continued)*

## Excel CommandBars (continued)

| CONSTANT | NAME | TYPE |
|---|---|---|
| 89 | Stars & Banners | Toolbar |
| 90 | Basic Shapes | Toolbar |
| 91 | Insert Shape | Toolbar |
| 92 | Shapes | Shortcut Menu |
| 93 | Inactive Chart | Shortcut Menu |
| 94 | Excel Control | Shortcut Menu |
| 95 | Curve | Shortcut Menu |
| 96 | Curve Node | Shortcut Menu |
| 97 | Curve Segment | Shortcut Menu |
| 98 | Pictures Context Menu | Shortcut Menu |
| 99 | OLE Object | Shortcut Menu |
| 100 | ActiveX Control | Shortcut Menu |
| 101 | WordArt Context Menu | Shortcut Menu |
| 102 | Rotate Mode | Shortcut Menu |
| 103 | Connector | Shortcut Menu |
| 104 | Script Anchor Popup | Shortcut Menu |
| 105 | Canvas Popup | Shortcut Menu |
| 106 | Organization Chart Popup | Shortcut Menu |
| 107 | Diagram | Shortcut Menu |
| 108 | Layout | Shortcut Menu |
| 109 | Select | Shortcut Menu |
| 110 | Task Pane | Toolbar |
| 111 | Add Command | Shortcut Menu |
| 112 | Built-in Menus | Shortcut Menu |
| 113 | System | Shortcut Menu |
| 114 | Clipboard | Toolbar |
| 115 | Envelope | Toolbar |
| 116 | Online Meeting | Toolbar |

# What Is on the CD-ROM

The CD-ROM included in this book contains many useful files and programs. Before installing any of the programs on the disc, make sure that a newer version of the program is not already installed on your computer. For information on installing different versions of the same program, contact the program's manufacturer. For the latest and greatest information, please refer to the ReadMe file located at the root of the CD-ROM.

## System Requirements

To use the contents of the CD-ROM, your computer must be equipped with the following hardware and software:

- A PC with a Pentium III or faster processor
- Microsoft Windows 95, 98, 2000, NT 4.0, or Windows XP
- Microsoft Excel 2000 or 2002
- At least 128MB of total RAM installed on your computer
- A double-speed (8x) or faster CD-ROM drive
- A monitor capable of displaying at least 256 colors or grayscale
- A network card

## Author's Source Code

These files contain all the sample code from the book. You can browse these files directly from the CD-ROM, or you can copy them to your hard drive and use them as the basis for your own projects. To find the files on the CD-ROM, open the D:\Samples folder. To copy the files to your hard drive, just run the installation program D:\Samples.EXE. The files will be placed on your hard drive at C:\ProgramFiles\ExcelProgVB. You will need Microsoft Excel installed on the machine to run the sample macros.

## Acrobat Version

The CD-ROM contains an e-version of this book that you can view and search using Adobe Acrobat Reader. You cannot print the pages or copy text from the Acrobat files. An evaluation version of Adobe Acrobat Reader is also included on the disc.

## Installing and Using the Software

For your convenience, the software titles appearing on the CD-ROM are listed alphabetically.

### Acrobat Reader

*Freeware.* Acrobat Reader lets you view the online version of this book. For more information on using Adobe Acrobat Reader, see the section "Using the E-Version of This Book." From Adobe Systems, www.adobe.com.

### Barcode Add-in for Office

*Demo.* Barcode Add-in from IDAutomation.com Inc. provides the ability to print the following types of barcodes from Excel: Code 39, UPC, EAN, UCC-128, Code 128, POSTNET, PLANET, Codabar, Booklan, interleaved 2 of 5, no-interleaved 2 of 5, and Code11. You can find more information at www.idautomation.com/activex/.com.

### Code Crafter 2000

*30-day trial.* Code Crafter 2000 from Code Craft Corporation provides a collection of utility functions that can be used to create and maintain VBA code. You can find more information at www.codecrafter.com.

### MsgBuilder

*Freeware.* MsgBuilder from TraderCat Ltd. is a development tool that enables you to create properly formatted VBA `MsgBox` statements and functions. You can find more information at www.tradercat.com.

### VBAcodePrint Add-In

*Shareware.* VBAcodePrint from StarPrint2000 provides the ability to print VBA source code using user-defined colors and fonts. You can customize page margins, line spacing, print quality, paper orientation, scaling, and more. You can find more information at www. jn-software.com.

### VBCode Cutter

*Shareware.* VBCode Cutter from Progressive Data Solutions is a VBA code Library & Development tool that enables you to store VBA code snippets that you can drag and drop into a module. You can find more information at www.pdsolutions.com.au.

## Troubleshooting

We tried our best to compile programs that work on most computers with the minimum system requirements. Your computer, however, may differ, and some programs may not work properly for some reason.

The two most likely problems are that you do not have enough memory (RAM) for the programs you want to use, or you have other programs running that are affecting the installation or running of a program. If you receive error messages like `Not enough memory` or `Setup cannot continue`, try one or more of these methods and then try using the software again:

- Turn off any antivirus software.
- Close all running programs.
- In Windows, close the CD-ROM interface and run demos or installations directly from Windows Explorer.
- Have your local computer store add more RAM to your computer.

If you still have trouble installing the items from the CD-ROM, please call the Wiley Customer Service phone number: 800-762-2974 (outside the U.S.: 317-572-3994). You can also contact Customer Service by e-mail at techsupdum@wiley.com.

# Using the E-Version
## of This Book

You can view *Excel Programming: Your visual blueprint for creating interactive spreadsheets* on your screen using the CD-ROM included at the back of this book. The CD-ROM allows you to search the contents of each chapter of the book for a specific word or phrase. The CD-ROM also provides a convenient way of keeping the book handy while traveling.

You must install Adobe Acrobat Reader on your computer before you can view the book on the CD-ROM. This

program is provided on the disc. Acrobat Reader allows you to view Portable Document Format (PDF) files, which can display books and magazines on your screen exactly as they appear in printed form.

To view the contents of the book using Acrobat Reader, display the contents of the disc. Double-click the PDFs folder to display the contents of the folder. In the window that appears, double-click the icon for the chapter of the book you want to review.

---

### Using the E-Version of This Book

#### FLIP THROUGH PAGES

① Click one of these options to flip through the pages of a section.

First page ⏮

Previous page ◀

Next page ▶

Last page ⏭

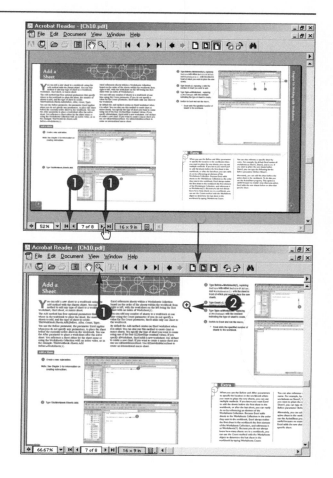

#### ZOOM IN

① Click 🔍 to magnify an area of the page.

② Click the area of the page you want to magnify.

● Click one of these options to display the page at 100% magnification (🔲) or to fit the entire page inside the window (🔲).

## FIND TEXT

**1** Click 🔍 to search for text in the section.

The Find dialog box appears.

**2** Type the text you want to find.

**3** Click Find to start the search.

● The first instance of the text is highlighted.

### Extra

To install Acrobat Reader, insert the CD-ROM into a drive. In the screen that appears, click Software. Click Acrobat Reader and then click Install at the bottom of the screen. Then follow the instructions on your screen to install the program.

You can make searching the book more convenient by copying the PDF files to your computer. To do this, display the contents of the CD-ROM and then copy the PDFs folder from the CD-ROM to your hard drive. This allows you to easily access the contents of the book at any time.

Acrobat Reader is a popular and useful program. There are many files available on the Web that are designed to be viewed using Acrobat Reader. Look for files with the .pdf extension. For more information about Acrobat Reader, visit the www.adobe.com/products/acrobat/readermain.html. Web site.

**(c)** This limited warranty gives you specific legal rights, and you may have other rights that vary from jurisdiction to jurisdiction.

6.  **Remedies.**

    **(a)** WPI's entire liability and your exclusive remedy for defects in materials and workmanship shall be limited to replacement of the Software Media, which may be returned to WPI with a copy of your receipt at the following address: Software Media Fulfillment Department, Attn.: Excel Programming: Your visual blueprint for creating interactive spreadsheets, Wiley Publishing, Inc., 10475 Crosspoint Blvd., Indianapolis, IN 46256, or call 1-800-762-2974. Please allow four to six weeks for delivery. This Limited Warranty is void if failure of the Software Media has resulted from accident, abuse, or misapplication. Any replacement Software Media will be warranted for the remainder of the original warranty period or thirty (30) days, whichever is longer.

    **(b)** In no event shall WPI or the author be liable for any damages whatsoever (including without limitation damages for loss of business profits, business interruption, loss of business information, or any other pecuniary loss) arising from the use of or inability to use the Book or the Software, even if WPI has been advised of the possibility of such damages.

**(c)** Because some jurisdictions do not allow the exclusion or limitation of liability for consequential or incidental damages, the above limitation or exclusion may not apply to you.

7.  **U.S. Government Restricted Rights.** Use, duplication, or disclosure of the Software for or on behalf of the United States of America, its agencies and/or instrumentalities "U.S. Government" is subject to restrictions as stated in paragraph (c)(1)(ii) of the Rights in Technical Data and Computer Software clause of DFARS 252.227-7013, or subparagraphs (c) (1) and (2) of the Commercial Computer Software - Restricted Rights clause at FAR 52.227-19, and in similar clauses in the NASA FAR supplement, as applicable.

8.  **General.** This Agreement constitutes the entire understanding of the parties and revokes and supersedes all prior agreements, oral or written, between them and may not be modified or amended except in a writing signed by both parties hereto that specifically refers to this Agreement. This Agreement shall take precedence over any other documents that may be in conflict herewith. If any one or more provisions contained in this Agreement are held by any court or tribunal to be invalid, illegal, or otherwise unenforceable, each and every other provision shall remain in full force and effect.

# INDEX

## Symbols

' (single quote) before comment lines in VBA code, 43
' (apostrophe), 60, 61
- (subtraction) operator, 48, 56
&
    before shortcut key characters in menu options, 17, 248, 249, 250
    specify the data type for a variable, 55
& (concatenation) operator, 48, 62, 110, 111
!, data type for a variable, 55
#, data type for a variable, 55
####, 209
$, data type for a variable, 55
$ (String type declaration symbol), 122, 123
% (ALT) character, 295
%, data type for a variable, 55
* (asterisk) wildcard, 156, 158
* (multiplication) operator, 48, 56
/ (division) operator, 48, 56
? (question mark symbol) wildcard, 156, 158
@, data type for a variable, 55
\ (integer division) operator, 48, 56
^ (CTRL) character, 295
^ (exponential) operator, 48, 56
_ (underscore) character in event-handling procedures, 235
~ (ENTER) character, 295
+ (addition) operator, 48, 56, 62
+ (SHIFT) character, 295
<Out of context> value, 132
= (equals sign) operator, 72

## A

absolute references for macros, 4
Access databases, 145
AccessMode parameter, 147
Acrobat Reader, 322, 325
Activate method, 151, 183
active menu bar, 248
active workbook, 3
ActiveCell property, 64
ActivePrinter parameter, 178
ActiveSheet property, 69, 155, 161
ActiveWorkbook property, 146, 152
Add method
    to add controls, 246
    with the ChartObjects collection, 229, 244–245
    with the ChartObjects object, 260
    with the Charts object, 258
    with a Controls object, 228
    create new menus, 248
    with a SeriesCollection object, 264
    with the Sheets object, 160
    of the Workbooks collection, 154

Add Watch dialog box, 132, 133
AddComment method, 214–215
addition (+) operator, 56, 62
AddToMRU parameter, 140, 147
After parameter
    with the Add method, 160, 161
    with the Copy method, 166
    with Find, 222, 223
    with the Move method, 164
AllowEdit property, 191
alphabetical order, sort worksheets in, 180–181
Alt key, menu option shortcuts, 17
Alt+F11 shortcut key, 23, 25
Always trust macros from this source option, 41
And operator, 49
ANSI character code, 126
apostrophe ('), 60, 61
application events, 279, 286, 287
Application object, 64
Area Collection, 187
area ranges, 186–187
AreaGroups method, 269
arguments, 74
arithmetic operators, 48, 56
"Array already dimensioned" error message, 88
Array function, 86, 87
array functions, 301
array is fixed or temporarily locked error, 139
arrays, 47
    check if a specified value is, 79
    convert lists to, 86–87
    declare, 82–85
    redimension, 88–89
    specify the size of, 82, 83
    user-defined data types in, 90–91
As statement, 68
Assign Macro dialog box, 15, 17, 35
asterisk (*) wildcard, 156, 158
Author property, 215
Auto Data Tips option, 29
Auto Indent option, 29
Auto List Member option, 29
Auto Quick Info option, 29
Auto Syntax Check option, 29, 128
AutoFill method, 216–217
AutoFit method, 209
available macros, 6
Axes collection object, 274
Axes method, 274

## B

BackColor control property, 231
background color for cells, 211

328

# INDEX

# INDEX

# INDEX

numeric characters in the Format function, 121
numeric data types, 45
numeric expressions, 120–121
numeric values, 57, 79

# O

Object Browser, 64, 66–67, 287
object collections. *See* collections
object comparison, 72
Object data type, 45
"Object doesn't support this property or method" error message, 108
object libraries, 66
Object list box, 20, 287
object methods, 74–75
Object Model, 64. *See also* Excel Object Model
object variables, 68–69, 72–73
objects, 21, 64, 65, 70–71, 72, 79
Office object library, 66
Offset property, 188–189
On Error Resume Next statement, 129, 136–137, 138
OnAction property, 246, 247, 250
one-dimensional array, 47
OnKey event, 294–295
OnTime event, 292–293
Open dialog box, 6, 77, 144–145
Open event, 280
Open method, 140–141, 281
Open property, 144
open workbooks, 150–151
OpenConflictDocument parameter, 141
Open_DialogBox() macro, 77
OpenText method, 142–143
Operation parameter with PasteSpecial, 212
operators, 48–49
Option Base 1 statement, 83
Option Compare statement, 126, 127
Option Explicit statement, 54
optional arguments, call procedures with, 75
OptionButton control, 226, 227
Options dialog box, 28–29
Or operator, 49
Origin parameter, 141, 143

# P

.Pag extension, 241
PageSetup object, 179
parameters, 51
Parent property, 171

parentheses, effect on precedence order, 48
Parse method, 205
Password parameter
    with the Open method, 140
    with the Protect method, 174
    with the Save As method, 147, 172, 173
    with the Unprotect method, 175
Password property, 155
password protected projects, 26–27
password protection of worksheets, 174–175
passwords, case-sensitivity of, 174, 176
Paste button, 37, 43
Paste parameter, 212
PasteSpecial method, 212–213
Path/File access error message, 156
Path property of the Workbook object, 155
pathname argument for the Kill statement, 156
Permission Denied error, 156
personal digital signatures, 40
Personal Macro Workbook, 3, 6, 12–13
    add functions to, 53
    availability of, 14, 16
    place startup macros in, 36
    rename macros in, 34, 35
    view and modify macros in, 22
personal security certificate, create, 19
personal signature, 18
Personal.xls file, 3, 12
Personal.xls project, 34, 35
PieGroups method, 269
PlotBy parameter, 259, 262
points, 201, 202
pop-up message boxes, 110–111
pound signs, specify dates and times, 45
precedence order for arithmetic operators, 48
predefined Excel shortcut keys, override, 5
Preserve statement, 88
Preview parameter, 178
print area, specify for a worksheet, 179
Print dialog box, 77
PrintArea property, 179
PrintOut method, 178
PrintToFile parameter, 178
private functions, 52
Private keyword, 50, 52, 80, 81
private module level, 80
Private statement, 38, 39
private subroutines, 50
procedure level, 80
Procedure list box, 20
Procedure parameter, 292, 294
procedure-level arrays, 84

# INDEX

# INDEX

# INDEX